Practical Recording Techniques

Practical Recording Techniques

Bruce Bartlett
Jenny Bartlett

SAMS
PUBLISHING
A Division of Prentice Hall Computer Publishing
201 West 103rd Street, Indianapolis, IN 46290

To family, friends, and music.

© 1992 by Sams

International Standard Book Number: 0-672-30265-9
Library of Congress Catalog Card Number: 91-68191

95 94   8 7 6 5 4 3 2

Interpretation of the printing code: the rightmost number of
the first series of numbers is the year of the book's printing;
the rightmost number of the second series of numbers is the
number of the book's printing. For example, a printing code
of 92-1 shows that the first printing of the book occurred in
1992.

Printed in the United States of America

Publisher
Richard K. Swadley

Associate Publisher
Marie Butler-Knight

Managing Editor
Elizabeth Keaffaber

Acquisitions Editor
Charlie Dresser

Development Editor
Wayne Blankenbeckler

Manuscript Editor
Albright Communications, Incorporated

Copy Editor
Barry Childs-Helton

Editorial Coordinator
Charles Hutchinson

Editorial Assistants
Hilary Adams
Martha Norris

Cover Photography
David Kadlec

Illustrators
Don Clemons
Bruce Bartlett
William D. Basham
Ralph E. Lund

Designer
Michele Laseau

Indexer
John Sleeva

Production Team
Claudia Bell, Mike Britton, Keith Davenport, Mark Enochs, Brook Farling, Joelynn
Gifford, Debbie Hanna, Carrie Keesling, Phil Kitchel, Bob LaRoche, Laurie Lee, Jay
Lesandrini, David McKenna, Matthew Morrill, Cindy L. Phipps, Dennis Sheehan,
M. Louise Shinault, Ann Taylor, Corinne Walls, Mary Beth Wakefield,
Jenny Watson, Phil Worthington

*Special thanks to Kirk Butler and John Lazott for
ensuring the technical accuracy of this book.*

CONTENTS

5 Hum Prevention   *79*

6 Microphones   *105*

7 Basic Microphone Techniques   *129*

PREFACE

Recording is a highly skilled craft combining art and science. It requires technical knowledge as well as musical understanding and critical listening ability. By learning these skills, you can capture a musical performance and reproduce it with quality sound for the enjoyment and inspiration of others. Your recordings will become carefully tailored creations—a legacy that can bring pleasure to many people for years to come.

Practical Recording Techniques is a hands-on, practical guide for beginning and intermediate recording engineers, producers, musicians—anyone who wants to make better recordings by understanding recording equipment and techniques. With this information you can work in a home studio, a small professional studio, or an on-location recording session.

This book guides the beginner through the basics, showing how to make quality recordings with the new breed of inexpensive home-studio equipment. But it also offers up-to-date information on the latest recording technology, such as:

- Digital tape recording

- Hard-disk recording

- Keyboard and digital workstations

- SMPTE

- MIDI

First, you receive an overview of the recording-and-reproduction chain. Next, you learn how to equip a home studio, from low-budget to advanced.

The basics of sound and signals are explained so that you know what the impact is when you adjust the controls on a piece of recording equipment. Studio setup is covered next, including suggestions for improving your acoustics, choosing monitor speakers, and preventing hum.

Each piece of recording equipment is explained in detail, as well as the control-room techniques you use during actual sessions. A large chapter is devoted to the recent technology of MIDI-studio recording methods. Two sections on remote recording cover techniques for both popular and classical music.

A special chapter explains how to judge recordings and improve them. The engineer must know not only how to use the equipment, but also how to tell good sound from bad. The last chapter answers the question, "Why do you record?"

Finally, four appendixes explain the decibel, SMPTE time code, room modes, and where to look for further education.

Practical Recording Techniques covers many topics not covered in similar texts:

- Choosing and operating cassette recorder-mixers

- Hum prevention

- Latest monitoring methods

- Microphone selection and placement

- The digital audio tape recorder (DAT)

- Documenting the recording session

- Audio-for-video techniques

- Recording the spoken word

- On-location recording

- Troubleshooting bad sound

- Recognizing good sound

Compiled from my experience as a professional recording engineer, this book provides you with tips and shortcuts for making great-sounding tapes, whether in a professional studio, on location, or at home.

ACKNOWLEDGMENTS

Thank you to Larry and Elaine Zide of *Modern Recording & Music* and *db* magazine for giving me permission to draw from my "Recording Techniques" series and new book, *Your MIDI Recording Studio*.

Thank you to Crown International for allowing me the time to work on this book. For my education, thank you to The College of Wooster, Crown International, Shure Brothers Inc., Astatic Corporation, and all the studios I've worked for.

My deepest thanks to Jenny Bartlett for her many helpful suggestions as a layperson consultant and editor. She made sure this book could be understood by beginners.

A note of appreciation goes to the Pat Metheny Group and Samuel "Adagio for Strings" Barber, among many others, whose compositions inspired the chapter, "Music: Why You Record."

Finally, to the musicians I've recorded and played with, a special thanks for teaching me indirectly about recording.

Bruce Bartlett

Trademark Acknowledgments

All terms mentioned in this book that are known to be trademarks or service marks are listed below. In addition, terms suspected of being trademarks or service marks have been appropriately capitalized. Sams cannot attest to the accuracy of this information. Use of a term in this book should not be regarded as affecting the validity of any trademark or service mark.

Amiga is a trademark of Commodore Business Systems.

Aphex Aural Exciter is a registered trademark of Aphex Systems, Ltd.

Atari is a registered trademark of Atari Corp.

Auricle is a trademark of Auricle Control Systems.

Clicktracks, AudioTrax, and Master Tracks Pro are trademarks of Passport Designs, Inc.

Cue and Studio Vision are trademarks of Opcode Systems.

THE RECORDING-REPRODUCTION CHAIN

Making a quality recording gives you a real sense of pride and achievement. With your skills, you can help artists realize their visions in sound. You can capture a musical performance on tape with exciting realism, or enhance the music with creative effects.

Making a good recording involves more than plugging a microphone into a tape deck and hitting the record button. Let's face it: modern recording equipment and techniques are sophisticated. Before you can achieve a quality recording, you must understand the equipment, learn the techniques, and know the jargon.

This book separates the multitude of equipment and procedures into easily understandable parts. It lists the equipment you need, tells what it does, and suggests how to use it effectively. After studying this book and practicing with actual recording equipment, you'll make great-sounding tapes that you can be proud of.

Overview

Musical sound starts with musicians and their instruments, goes through a series of changes and manipulations, and ends with the musical experience in the ears and mind of the listener. The series of events and equipment that are involved in sound recording and playback is called the *recording-reproduction chain*. This chapter takes a broad view of the parts of the chain; later chapters describe each part in detail.

The Parts of the Chain

The following list examines the parts of the chain for three different recording setups, from simple to complex:

Live stereo recording

Recording directly into a tape recorder with a stereo microphone or two microphones

Live mixed recording

Recording with several mics into a mixer, which is connected to a tape recorder

Multitrack recording

Recording with several mics into a mixer, which is connected to a multitrack tape recorder; each track or path on tape contains the sound of a different instrument, and the multiple tape tracks are mixed after the recording session

Live Stereo Recording

Live stereo recording is often used for recording classical music performed by an orchestra, symphonic band, pipe organ, quartet, or soloist. The microphones pick up the overall sound of the instruments plus the concert hall acoustics. Figure 1.1 is a diagram of the elements in this chain.

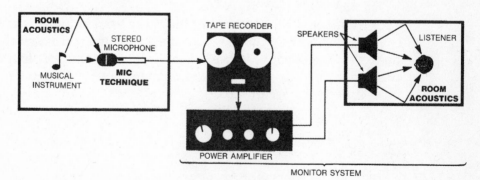

Figure 1.1 The recording-reproduction chain using a stereo microphone and a tape recorder.

Musical Instruments

A musical instrument is a tool to convert musical ideas and feelings into sound. Playing technique and instrument quality affect the sound the instrument produces. Sound waves travel in all directions from the instrument, and a different tone quality is heard at different positions around the instrument.

The loudness of that sound is measured in *decibels (db)* with 1 db as the smallest change in loudness that the human ear can hear.

Room Acoustics

The musical instruments radiate sound waves, which travel through the air and bounce or reflect off the walls, ceiling, and floor of a room. These reflections add a desirable sense of ambience or space in a concert hall. In a pop-music recording studio, however, uncontrolled reflections can muddy and obscure the music you are recording.

Microphones

The sound waves from the instruments, and from the room surfaces, travel to the microphone. This device converts the sound waves into a corresponding electrical signal. At various stages in the chain, the strength or level of this signal is measured in decibels.

Microphone Technique

Select the microphone and place it carefully to achieve the desired sound quality. The microphone's characteristics and its placement affect the recorded tone quality (bass-midrange-treble), the amount of room acoustics that are picked up, and stereo effects. Good mic technique is crucial in making a quality recording.

The Tape Recorder

The electrical signal from the microphone or instrument goes into a tape recorder—cassette deck, open-reel deck, or digital audio tape (DAT). The electrical signal is converted into a magnetic signal that is stored on magnetic tape. A tape recorder acts like a time machine, storing the music in magnetic form for playback at a later date.

As the tape moves during recording, magnetic signals are stored on tape along a *track*—a path on tape containing a recorded signal. One or more tracks can be recorded side by side on a single tape. For example, a 2-track tape machine can record two tracks on tape, such as the two different audio signals required for stereo recording.

During playback, the magnetic signals on tape are converted back into electrical signals. Noise-reduction devices such as Dolby or dbx often are built into the recorder to reduce tape hiss, which is a rushing sound like wind in the trees.

The Monitor System

To hear the signal you're recording, you need a monitor system: a stereo power amplifier and headphones or loudspeakers. The sound from the system allows you to judge how well your recording techniques are working.

Because the electrical signal from the recorder is too weak to drive loudspeakers directly, you need a stereo power amplifier. This strengthens or amplifies the recorder's output signal enough to drive the speakers. Headphones need only a very small power amplifier.

Loudspeakers or headphones convert the electrical signal from the power amplifier into sound. This sound resembles that produced by the original instruments. In addition, the listening room acoustics affect the sound reaching the ears of the listener—the end of the chain.

Live Mixed Recording

Live mixed recording is a more complex way to record, which is illustrated by the block diagram in Figure 1.2. It includes all the elements mentioned before, but with more components. A microphone is placed close to each instrument or singer. All the microphones plug into a *mixer*, which blends or mixes all the microphone signals into one composite signal, stereo or mono. You record this signal with a tape recorder while monitoring with headphones or speakers. Electronic and electric instruments can be recorded direct into your mixer without a microphone. More on this later.

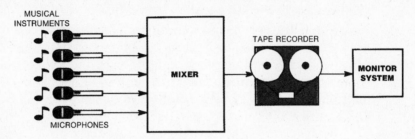

Figure 1.2 The recording-reproduction chain using multiple microphones and a mixer.

Because each microphone is close to its sound source, the mic picks up very little room acoustics. This results in a close, clear sound that's generally desirable in recording pop music or narration. To further enhance clarity, you might add some sound-absorbent material on the floor, walls, and ceiling.

The microphone signals feed into a mixer, which combines them into a composite signal, stereo or mono. The mixer also has a volume control for each microphone. While monitoring the mixer's signal, you adjust the volume of each instrument's signal to create a pleasing loudness balance. For example, if the guitar is too quiet relative to the voice, simply turn up the volume control for the guitar microphone until it blends well with the voice. That's a lot easier than grouping the musicians around a single microphone and moving them until you hear a good balance.

Many mixers let you control other aspects of sound besides volume. You can control tone quality (bass and treble), stereo position (left, right, or center), and special effects (such as artificial reverberation, which sounds like room acoustics).

Finally, you record the output signal of the mixer with a tape recorder, and monitor the signal with the monitor system.

Multitrack Recording

One problem with the previous setup is that you have to mix while the musicians are playing. If you make a mistake while mixing—one instrument is too quiet, for instance—the musicians have to play the song again until you get the balance right.

The solution is to use a multitrack recorder, which records 4 to 48 tracks side by side on a single tape. You record the signal of each microphone independently on each separate track and then mix these recorded signals after the performance is done. You either can record a different instrument on each track or different groups of instruments on each track (see Figure 1.3).

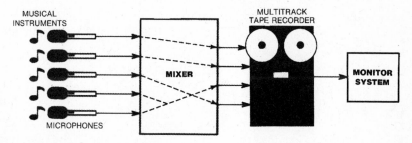

Figure 1.3 Multitrack recording.

The Mixing Console

The mixing console is a big, sophisticated mixer. It's used during multi-track recording mainly to amplify the weak microphone signals up to a level suitable for the tape recorder, and to assign each microphone signal to the desired tape track. In the previous section, "Live Stereo Recording," the 2-track tape recorder has its own mic preamplifiers, so no mixer is needed.

After the recording session, play all the tracks through the mixing console to mix or combine them with a pleasing balance. That is, mix the recorded signals from the tape tracks, rather than the live signals from the microphones.

Play back the multitrack tape of the performance several times, adjusting the balance among tracks until the mix is perfected. The final mix usually is recorded on a 2-track stereo tape recorder (cassette, open-reel, or DAT) (see Figure 1.4), and the resulting 2-track tape is the final product.

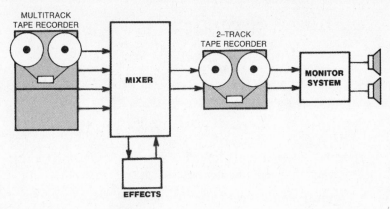

Figure 1.4 Multitrack mixdown.

For home recording studios, the multitrack recorder and mixer can be combined into a single unit called a *recorder-mixer*. It is usually a multitrack cassette recorder and mixer in a single portable chassis.

There's another benefit of multitrack recording. You can record a few instruments or vocals, then go back later and add more parts on unused tracks. This process is called *overdubbing*. If you play several instruments, you can record yourself playing each instrument one at a time. Listen to the previously recorded tracks to keep your place in the song, and play along with them.

If several musicians are overdubbing at once, you need a system that enables them to hear each other, and previously recorded material, through headphones. Many mixing consoles include a *cue mixer* built in, which is used to create a cue mix heard over headphones. The signal from the cue mixer is strengthened by a power amplifier before it goes to a multiple-connector box that the headphones plug into.

You might want to connect external devices called *signal processors* to your mixer. They produce special effects to enhance the sound quality. Some examples are reverberation (which mimics room acoustics), echo, and compression.

Every Link Is Important

To illustrate how all this equipment might be used, a block diagram of a small home-studio setup is shown in Figure 1.5. A typical layout of a larger multitrack recording studio is shown in Figure 1.6.

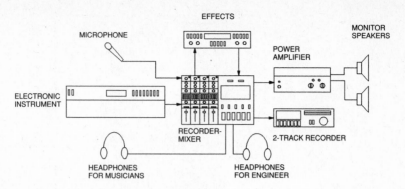

Figure 1.5 A recorder-mixer home studio.

The following list reviews all the changes the music goes through from the start of the chain to the end. Electronic instruments (a synth, for example) produce electrical signals that are recorded straight into the mixer (step 5).

1. The musical instrument converts motion into sound waves.

2. The resulting sound waves are modified by room reflections (room acoustics).

3. At the microphone, the modified sound waves are converted into electricity (the signal).

4. The sound reproduced by the microphone is affected by microphone selection and placement (microphone technique).

5. All the signals are combined and routed to individual channels in the mixer, and are modified by signal processors.

6. The mixer's electrical signal is recorded—changed into a magnetic signal for storage.

7. The magnetic signal is played back—changed into an electrical signal.

8. The electrical signal is amplified and changed back into sound waves by the monitor amplifier and loudspeakers.

9. The loudspeakers' sounds are modified by sound reflections from the listening room.

10. The sound reaches the listener's ears and is heard as music.

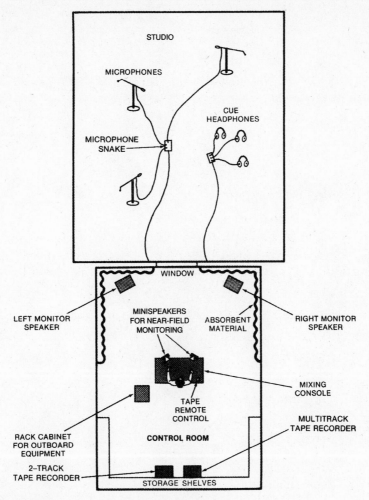

Figure 1.6 Layout of a typical recording studio.

While all this is going on, musicians might be using a cue system and headphones to listen to each other and the tape.

The end product of the recording end of the chain is the master tape. Additional links in the reproduction chain include tape copies, compact-disc manufacturing, and the listener's playback system.

Each link of the recording-reproduction chain contributes to the sound quality of the finished recording. A bad-sounding master tape can be caused by any weak link—low-quality microphones, bad mic placement, improperly set mixer controls, and so on. A good-sounding tape results when you optimize every part of the chain. This book will help you reach that goal.

EQUIPPING YOUR HOME STUDIO

It's every musician's dream. You want to set up a home recording system—one with good-quality sound, yet affordable. With today's easy-to-use sound tools, you can do just that. This chapter focuses on tape recording equipment, rather than MIDI recording equipment (synths, samplers, sequencers, and drum machines), but MIDI users should find the information useful, too, because a MIDI home studio requires most of the equipment mentioned here.

Basic Equipment

What equipment do you need in a multitrack home studio?

- A multitrack cassette recorder-mixer or a separate mixer and multitrack recorder (cassette or open-reel)

- A 2-track recorder to record the final mix (cassette deck, open-reel deck, or DAT recorder)

- Microphones and mic stands

- A monitoring system (two speakers and a power amplifier, or headphones)

- Effects (reverb, delay, compression, etc.)
- Cables
- Rack and patch bay (optional)
- Miscellaneous equipment

Recorder-Mixer

A recorder-mixer is a small, portable unit combining a mixer with a multitrack cassette recorder (see Figure 2.1). Some recorder-mixers use a multitrack open-reel recorder; some use a video cassette recorder. You plug microphones and electric musical instruments into the mixer, which amplifies their signals and routes them to tape tracks. The 4-track cassette recorder can record up to 4 tracks, each with a different instrument on it. After recording the tracks, you mix or combine them to 2-channel stereo, and record the mix on a separate 2-track recorder. The recording made on that machine is the final product.

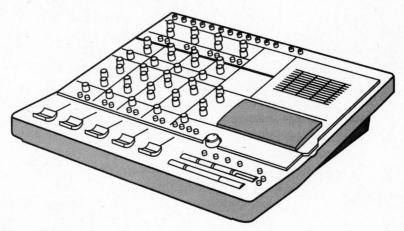

Figure 2.1 A recorder-mixer.

Recorder-mixers currently on the market include units made by Fostex, Tascam, AMR, Yamaha, Vestax, Akai, and Sansui. Their prices range from $339 to $3,300 suggested retail.

As the price increases, you get cleaner, crisper sound, more inputs, more features, and more tracks. The sections that follow cover the features briefly; a detailed explanation is given in Chapter 11.

Overdubbing

All recorder-mixers have the overdubbing feature. While listening to tracks already recorded, you play along with them and record a new part on an unused track. For example, suppose you've already recorded bass and drums and you want to add guitar. You listen to a headphone mix of the bass track, drum track, and your guitar signal. While the bass and drum tracks play, you play your guitar along with them and record the guitar on an unused track.

Simultaneous Recording on All Tracks

Simultaneous recording is useful especially for recording a live performance. When you record in a studio, you often can record 1 or 2 tracks at a time, but when you record a live performance, you need to record all the tracks at once. Not all recorder-mixers let you do this.

Punch-In/Out

Use the punch-in and punch-out functions to correct mistakes. As the tape is playing, punch into record mode just before the mistake, play a new correct part that is recorded, and punch out of record mode when you're finished. Most recorder-mixers accept a footswitch so you can punch in with your foot while playing your instrument.

Bouncing Tracks

When you bounce (or *ping-pong*) tracks, you mix two or three tracks together and record the result on an unused track. Then you can erase the original tracks, freeing them for recording more instruments. This way you can record up to nine tracks with a 4-track machine. All recorder-mixers permit bouncing.

Tape Speed

Tape speed is the rate at which tape moves past the record/playback head. In cassette recorders, two speeds are available: $1\frac{7}{8}$ inches-per-second (ips) and/or $3\frac{3}{4}$ ips. On machines running at $1\frac{7}{8}$ ips, you can play standard commercial cassettes, but recordings made at $3\frac{3}{4}$ ips sound crisper and clearer. Reel-to-reel units record at $7\frac{1}{2}$ or 15 ips.

Pitch Control

Available in all recorder-mixers, pitch control lets you adjust the tape speed up or down slightly so you can match, by ear, the pitch of recorded tracks to the pitch of new instruments to be recorded.

EQ (Equalization)

Equalization means tone control. The simplest units have no equalization; you're stuck with the sound you get from your microphones. Others have a single 3-band graphic equalizer—sliding controls that affect bass, midrange, and treble. Most inexpensive units include a bass and treble control, one set per input. Fancier recorder-mixers have *sweepable* or *semiparametric EQ*, which lets you vary continously the frequency you want to adjust. This type of EQ offers the most control over the tone quality of each instrument you're recording.

Effects Loop (Aux Loop)

The effects loop is a set of connectors (labeled "send" and "return") for hooking up an external effects unit, such as a reverb or delay device. Effects add a professional polish to your productions.

If your recorder-mixer has no effects loops, you still can record music, but without any effects. It sounds rather dead and plain. A unit with one effects loop lets you add one type of effect; a unit with two effects loops lets you add two for even more sonic interest. A stereo effects loop lets you hear effects in stereo, if your effects device is a stereo unit.

Some recorder-mixers have digital reverb built in so that you don't need to buy an external reverb unit.

Noise Reduction

A noise reduction circuit reduces the tape hiss that is inherent in magnetic tape recording. Dolby C and dbx work best; Dolby B is less effective. All help you make cleaner, less noisy recordings.

Autolocate

Autolocate stores cue-point locations in memory, and shuttles the tape to these locations. You could use this feature to move tape repeatedly between the two preset points, at the beginning and end of a punch-in, for example.

Return-to-zero is also called *zero stop* or *memory rewind*. When you enable return-to-zero, the tape rewinds to a preset point that you mark "000" on the tape counter. This feature makes it easy to practice repeatedly on a punch-in or mix.

Solenoid Switches

When you push one of your tape-motion controls, the action can be either mechanical or solenoid operated. Solenoid switching is gentler to the tape, and often includes logic, which protects the tape from rapid changes in tape motion.

XLR-Type Balanced Inputs

XLR-type microphone input connectors look like three small holes arranged in a triangle. If your mixer has such an input, you can run long mic cables without picking up hum. This type of connector is found only in high-end units. Most recorder-mixers use ¼-inch phone *jacks* (receptacles) for mic inputs, which is adequate for small studios.

Insert Jacks (Access Jacks)

Insert jack connectors let you plug in a compressor (or other signal processor) in line with an input signal. They make it easy to modify the sound of a single instrument or vocal. Only the more expensive units have this feature.

Sync Track

A sync track (usually the highest numbered track) records a synchronization tone from a MIDI sequencer. The tone synchronizes tape tracks with sequencer tracks. In this way, you can have your sequencer play synthesized bass, drums, and keyboards while your multitrack cassette deck plays vocals and acoustic instruments—all in sync.

This is a great way to get extra tracks for little cost. Plus, when you do your mixdown, all the synth tracks play "live" (from the synth outputs) rather than from tape. The result is a cleaner mix.

Any track on any multitrack recorder can record the sync tone. But a dedicated sync track has its own input connector for the sync tone, and allows noise reduction to be switched off for more reliable recording.

The sync track also is used for SMPTE (Society of Motion Picture and Television Engineers) time code (see Appendix B).

Direct Box

A direct box is a useful accessory for recorder-mixers with XLR-type mic inputs. A direct box is a small device that connects an electric instrument (guitar, bass, synth) and a mixer mic input. It lets you record electric instruments directly into your mixer without a microphone. You can buy a direct box for as little as $50.

A useful feature in a direct box is a filter, which simulates the tone quality of a guitar amplifier/speaker. (See Chapter 8 for more information.)

Most 4-track machines have ¼-inch phone jacks for inputs. In this case, simply use a short guitar cord between your instrument and mixer input.

A direct box or guitar cord picks up a very clean sound, which may be undesirable for electric guitar. If you want to pick up the distortion of the guitar amp, use a microphone instead. Or try a direct box that plugs into the external speaker jack on your guitar amp. It picks up the amp distortion, and filters it (reduces the treble) to make it sound more like a guitar speaker.

The Bottom Line

What features should you expect in different price ranges? In recorder-mixers costing under $500, you can expect

- 2 microphone inputs
- 1 effects send or none
- Dolby B or dbx noise reduction
- Pitch control

- 1⅞ ips tape speed

- Equalization: none, bass and treble, or overall graphic

You can record 1 or 2 tracks at a time, building up to 4 tracks for later mixing down to 2-track stereo. For example, you might first record a keyboard part on 1 track and then add bass, drums, and vocals—one at a time—on the remaining tracks.

In units costing between $500 and $1,000, typical features include

- 2 to 6 mic inputs

- Bass and treble EQ

- 1 or 2 effects sends

- dbx or Dolby C noise reduction

- 3¾ ips tape speed (in most models)

Some have a dedicated sync track for synchronizing the multitrack tape to MIDI instruments; some also have an autolocate feature. You can record up to 4 tracks at a time.

Recorder-mixers that cost between $1,000 and $2,500 offer

- 4 to 8 mic inputs (perhaps with XLR-type balanced inputs for less hum)

- Sweepable (semiparametric) EQ

- 1 or 2 effects sends

- dbx or Dolby C noise reduction

- 3¾ ips tape speed

Most units have a sync track; some have an autolocate feature. One model (the Sansui WS-X1) even has a built-in 2-track cassette deck for recording the final mix. All recorder-mixers permit overdubbing and bouncing tracks.

With the high end of cassette recorder-mixers, you can record up to 8 independent tracks, with each track containing the sound of one or more instruments. Recorder-mixers with 8 tracks range in price from $1,600 to $3,300. The 8-track cassette recorder is either built into a recorder-mixer (as in the Tascam 488 Portastudio and 688 Midistudio), or is a stand-alone unit that you use with a mixer.

For highest quality, consider using a separate mixer and an 8-track open-reel recorder (see Figure 2.2). You can buy the recorder for around $2,000 (including built-in noise reduction); a 16-track recorder with built-in noise reduction can be bought for less than $6,000. The sound quality of open-reel recorders is good enough to make commercial recordings.

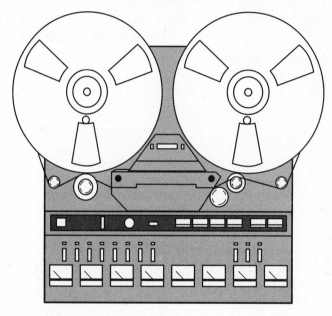

Figure 2.2 An 8-track open-reel recorder.

An 8-track machine is much more convenient to use than a 4-track machine. You can record 8 different instruments or groups of instruments without the chore of bouncing tracks. In addition, when you record a band on a 4-track unit, you often must combine several instruments on each track, so you can't readjust the level, tone, or effects of each instrument independently within a recorded track. Eight tracks are usually enough to record each instrument on its own track so that you can control the sound of each instrument individually.

Although an 8-output mixer is commonly used with an 8-track recorder, a lower-cost alternative is a 4-output mixer, such as shown in Figure 2.3. It can be used with an 8-track recorder by recording only 4 tracks at a time, or by using the direct-out jacks in the mixer. Each direct-out jack is fed an amplified signal from each input, so if your mixer has 8 inputs, you can record 8 tracks simultaneously (one instrument per track) from the direct outputs.

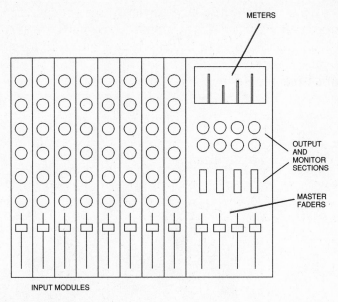

Figure 2.3 An 8-in, 4-out mixer.

2-Track Recorder

A 2-track recorder is another major component of your home studio. When you connect this recorder to the outputs of your recorder-mixer, the 2-track machine can record your final stereo mix of the tape tracks. You still have your multitrack tape, which can be remixed at a later date. Good cassette decks for stereo mastering cost about $200 and up.

You might prefer to master on a 2-track open-reel recorder (see Figure 2.4). Open-reel is the preferred master-tape format for commercial record and tape duplication. Compared to a cassette deck, the open-reel deck costs much more, but has higher sound quality and permits *editing*. Editing is the cutting and splicing of recording tape to remove unwanted noises, to change the sequence of songs, or to combine parts of two or more different takes.(See Chapter 9 for further information on the 2-track open-reel recorder.)

Highest sound quality is available by mastering to a DAT recorder (see Chapter 9). It does not permit editing unless you copy from one DAT recorder to another or use a digital audio workstation.

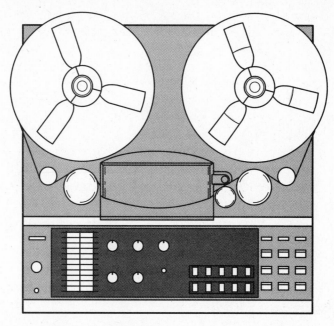

Figure 2.4 A 2-track open-reel recorder.

Microphones

Although synthesizers and direct boxes have reduced the need for microphones, you'll still want some to record vocals and acoustic instruments.

Good mics are essential for quality sound—and you get what you pay for. If you experiment with various types of microphones, you find big differences in fidelity among them. Some makers of quality mics include AKG, Audio Technica, Beyer, Countryman, Crown, Electro-Voice, Neumann, Sanken, Schoeps, Sennheiser, Shure, and Yamaha.

Two microphones costing at least $125 each are recommended. Although $125 may seem like a lot of money for a microphone, you can't skimp here and expect to get quality sound. Any distortion or weird tone quality in the microphone may be difficult or impossible to remove later. It's false economy to use a cheap mic.

You may be able to borrow some good microphones, or use the ones you use normally for P.A. Your ears should tell you if the fidelity is adequate for your purpose. Some people are happy to get any sound on tape; others settle for nothing less than professional sound quality.

How many mics and mic inputs do you need? It depends on the instruments you want to record. If you want to mic a drum set, you might need 8 mics and 8 mic inputs, mixing those to 1 or 2 tracks. On the other hand, if you use a drum machine, you might need only one good mic for vocals and acoustic instruments. You can use one microphone on several different instruments and vocals if you overdub them one at a time.

The most useful types for home recording are probably the cardioid condenser and cardioid dynamic. The cardioid pickup pattern helps reject room acoustics for a tighter sound. The condenser type is commonly used on cymbals, acoustic instruments, and studio vocals; dynamics are used typically on drums and electric amps. (For more information on microphones, see Chapter 6.)

Monitor System

The monitor system lets you hear what you're recording and mixing. You can use a pair of high-quality headphones, or a pair of loudspeakers and a power amplifier. The speakers should be accurate, high-fidelity types costing at least $100 each. Your home stereo might be good enough to serve, but skimping on a monitor system is not a smart move.

Near-field studio monitor speakers (described in Chapter 4) are suitable for home use. Also available are powered minispeakers with built-in amplifiers. Minispeakers lack deep bass but take up little room.

If your monitor speakers are in the same room as your microphones, the mics pick up the sound of the speakers. This causes feedback or a muddy sound. In this case, it's better to monitor with headphones while recording.

If you're recording only yourself, one set of headphones is enough. But if you're recording another musician, you both need headphones. Many recorder-mixers have two headphone jacks for this purpose.

If you want to overdub several people at once, you need headphones for all of them. For example, if you're overdubbing three harmony vocalists, each one needs headphones to hear previously recorded tracks to sing with.

To connect all these headphones, you could build a headphone junction box—an aluminum or plastic box containing several headphone jacks. These are wired to a cable coming from your mixer's headphone jack. Or, you could use a splitter cable, which makes two jacks out of one.

Effects

Effects such as reverberation, delay, and chorus can add sonic excitement to a recording. They are produced by signal processors (see Figure 2.5).

Figure 2.5 Signal processor.

The most essential effect is *reverberation*, a slow decay of sound such as you hear just after you shout in an empty gymnasium (HELLO-O-O-o-o-o...). Reverberation adds a sense of space; it can put your music in a concert hall, a small club, or a cathedral. This effect is usually produced by a *digital reverb unit*, available for $200 and up. One example is the Alesis Microverb III.

Another popular effect is *echo*, a repetition of a sound (HELLO-hello-hello). It's made by a *delay unit*, which also provides other effects such as chorus, doubling, and flanging. Delay units are made by Audio Digital, Lexicon, and Eventide, among others.

The *compressor* is normally used as an automatic volume control for vocals. A compressor keeps the vocal track at a more even volume, making it easier to hear throughout a mix. Home-studio units start around $125; one manufacturer of compressors is dbx.

A *multi-effects processor* combines several effects in a single box. These effects can be heard one at a time or several at once. You even can customize the sounds by pushing buttons to change the presets. Some examples are the Yamaha SPX1000, Alesis Quadraverb, and Digitech 128 Plus. (See Chapter 10 for more information on effects.)

Cables and Connectors

Once you have all this hardware, you need several types of cables to carry signals from one component to another. These are covered in detail later in this chapter.

Rack and Patch Bay

A rack is an enclosure to mount signal processors and other equipment in; a patch bay or patch panel in a rack is a group of connectors that are wired to equipment inputs and outputs.

Miscellaneous Equipment

Other equipment for your home studio includes a power outlet strip, masking tape to label inputs and cables, head-cleaning fluid and cotton swabs to clean the tape heads, splicing tape, single-edge razor blades, a grease pencil/marker for editing, and empty reels and boxes.

You also need blank tape for your recorder. Brand-name metal or chrome cassette tape is recommended for best sound quality. Use the tape suggested by the recorder manufacturer.

Four Studio Setups

Now that you know the necessary equipment, you're ready to combine it into a complete recording system. The following sections detail four different home studios, each at a different level of price and sophistication. All the prices given are suggested list; you can save money by shopping for discounts or buying used equipment.

Assume you're using your home stereo and headphones for monitoring and cassette mastering, and you borrowed some mic stands from your sound-reinforcement system. Cable costs are omitted.

Personal Studio

This low-budget setup can be used to document your ideas, to work out musical arrangements, or to play your song ideas to your band. It's good enough to make audition tapes for club owners and music publishers, but not good enough to make a demo tape to send to a record company. (Optional effects add $200 or more.) If you want to learn the basics of multitrack recording without spending a great deal, this is the way to go:

4-track recorder-mixer	$449
2 microphones ($100 each)	$200
Total	**$649**

Good-Quality 4-Track Studio

This setup is good enough to make audition tapes for club owners and music publishers, but is not quite good enough to make demos for record companies (although some would disagree).

4-track recorder-mixer	$ 840
4 microphones ($150 each)	$ 600
1 digital reverb	$ 200
Total	**$1,640**

High-Quality 4-Track Studio

This setup is good enough to make demo recordings to send to record companies. If your band has simple instrumentation, you might even be able to record commercial tapes and albums.

4-track recorder-mixer	$1,500
4 microphones ($250 each)	$1,000
4 headphones (for overdubs)	$ 160
1 multieffects processor	$ 400
Total	**$3,060**

High-Quality 8-Track Studio

This system is good enough to make commercial recordings. Add more expense for a professional monitor system.

8-track recorder-mixer	$2,450
2-track open-reel recorder or DAT	$ 800

3 microphones ($250 each) and 3 microphones ($150 each)	$1,200
Microphone snake	$ 200
4 headphones (for overdubs)	$ 160
1 multieffects processor or digital reverb	$ 400
Total	**$5,210**

You can substitute an 8-track open-reel tape recorder plus an 8-in, 4-out mixer (for a total of $3,300) for the 8-track recorder-mixer in this list. A microphone *snake* is a thick multiconductor cable wired to multiple mic connectors (see Figure 2.6).

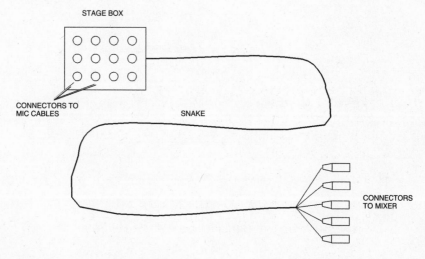

Figure 2.6 A stage box/snake.

Putting together a high-quality home recording system needn't cost much. As technology develops, better equipment is available at lower prices. That dream of owning your own studio is within reach.

Setting Up Your Studio

Once you have your equipment, you need to connect it with cables and possibly install equipment racks and acoustic treatment.

Cables and Connectors

Cables carry electrical signals from one audio component to another. They are usually made of one or two insulated conductors (wires) surrounded by a fine-wire mesh *shield* that reduces hum. Outside the shield is a plastic or rubber insulating jacket.

Cables are either *balanced* or *unbalanced*. A balanced line is a cable that uses two conductors to carry the signal, surrounded by a shield (see Figure 2.7). An unbalanced line has a single conductor surrounded by a shield (see Figure 2.8). To see how many conductors a cable has, either remove some cable insulation with a wire stripper, or open the connector and look inside.

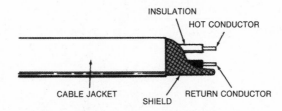

Figure 2.7 A 2-conductor shielded, balanced line.

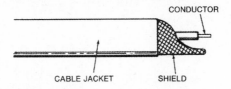

Figure 2.8 A 1-conductor shielded, unbalanced line.

Recording equipment also has balanced or unbalanced connectors. Be sure your cables match your equipment. Balanced equipment has a 3-pin (XLR-type) connector (see Figure 2.9); unbalanced equipment has a ¼-inch phone jack (see Figure 2.10) or RCA phono jack connector (see Figure 2.11).

The balanced line rejects hum better than an unbalanced line, but an unbalanced line under 10 feet long usually provides adequate hum rejection and costs less.

A cable carries one of these three signal levels or voltages:

• Mic level (about 2 millivolts, or .002 volt)

- Line level (0.316 volt for unbalanced equipment, 1.23 volts for balanced equipment)

- Speaker level (about 20 volts)

The term "0.316 volt" also is known as "–10 dbV"; the term "1.23 volts" also is known as "+4 dbm" (see Appendix A).

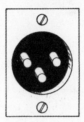

Figure 2.9 A 3-pin XLR-type connector used in balanced equipment.

Figure 2.10 A ¼-inch phone jack used in unbalanced equipment.

Figure 2.11 An RCA phono jack used in unbalanced equipment.

Connector Types

There are several types of connectors used in audio. Figure 2.12 shows a ¼-inch phone plug, used with cables for unbalanced microphones, synthesizers, and electric instruments. The tip terminal is soldered to the cable's center conductor; the sleeve terminal is soldered to the cable shield.

Figure 2.13 shows an RCA or phono plug, used to connect unbalanced line-level signals. The center pin is soldered to the cable's center conductor; the cup terminal is soldered to the cable shield.

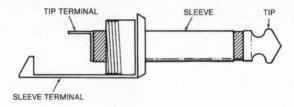

Figure 2.12 A ¼-inch phone plug.

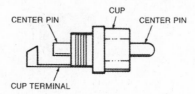

Figure 2.13 An RCA phono plug.

Figure 2.14 shows a 3-pin professional audio connector (sometimes called XLR-type), used with cables for balanced microphones and balanced recording equipment. The female connector (see Figure 2.14A) plugs into equipment outputs. The male connector (see Figure 2.14B) plugs into equipment inputs. Pin 1 is soldered to the cable shield, pin 2 is soldered to the "hot" red or white lead, and pin 3 is soldered to the remaining lead. This wiring applies to both female and male connectors.

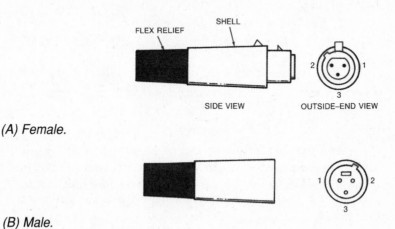

(A) Female.

(B) Male.

Figure 2.14 XLR-type connectors.

28

Figure 2.15 shows a stereo phone plug, used with stereo headphones and with some balanced line-level cables. For headphones, the tip terminal is soldered to the left-channel lead, the ring terminal is soldered to the right-channel lead, and the sleeve terminal is soldered to the common lead. For balanced line-level cables, the sleeve terminal is soldered to the shield; the tip terminal is soldered to the hot red or white lead, and the ring terminal is soldered to the remaining lead.

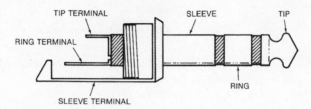

Figure 2.15 A stereo phone plug.

If you have unbalanced microphone inputs (¹/₄-inch diameter holes) on your recorder or mixer, use a balanced cable from mic to input. This reduces hum. Solder the shield and black lead to the long ground lug (sleeve terminal) on the phone plug. Solder the white or red lead to the small center lug (tip terminal) on the phone plug (see Figure 2.16).

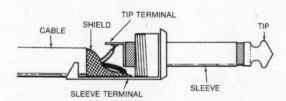

Figure 2.16 Wiring a balanced mic cable to an unbalanced ¹/₄-inch phone plug.

When connecting balanced equipment to unbalanced equipment, use the connection shown in Figure 2.17 to compensate for level differences. Balanced equipment operates at a relatively high level or voltage (called +4 dbm or +4); unbalanced equipment operates at a lower level (called –10 dbV or –10).

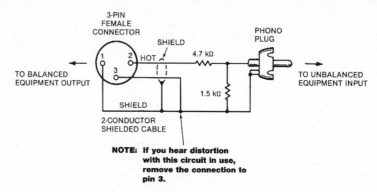

Figure 2.17 A circuit for matching a balanced +4 dbm output to an unbalanced −10 dbV input reduces the level 12 db.

Cable Types

Cables are also classified according to their function. In a studio, you use four types of cables: mic cables, guitar cords, patch cords, and speaker cables.

A mic cable is usually 2-conductor shielded—it has two wires to carry the signal—surrounded by a fine-wire cylinder or shield that reduces hum pickup. On one end of the cable is a connector that plugs into the microphone, usually a female XLR-type. On the other end is either a ¼-inch phone plug or a male XLR-type connector that plugs into your mixer.

Rather than running several mic cables to your recorder-mixer, you might consider using a snake. A snake is especially convenient if you're running long cables to recording equipment in a separate room.

A guitar cord is made of 1-conductor shielded cable with a ¼-inch phone plug on each end. Use it to record instruments direct—the electric guitar, electric bass, synthesizer, and drum machine.

Patch cords connect your recorder-mixer to external devices: an effects unit, stereo cassette deck, and power amplifier. An unbalanced patch cord is made of 1-conductor shielded cable with either a ¼-inch phone plug or an RCA phono connector on each end. A stereo patch cord is two patch cords joined together. Professional balanced equipment is interconnected with a 2-conductor shielded cable having a female XLR on one end and a male XLR on the other. Professional patch bays use balanced cables, even though they may look like unbalanced cables.

A speaker cable connects the power amp and each loudspeaker. Speaker cables are normally made of lamp cord (zip cord). To avoid wasting power, speaker cables should be as short as possible, and should be heavy gauge (between 12 and 16 gauge). Number 12 gauge is thicker than 14; 14 is thicker than 16.

Rack/Patch Panel

You might want to mount your signal processors in a *rack*, a wooden or metal enclosure with mounting holes for equipment (see Figure 2.18). You also might want to install a *patch panel* or *patch bay*—a group of connectors that are wired to equipment inputs and outputs. Using a patch panel and patch cords, you can change equipment connections easily. You also can bypass or patch around defective equipment. Note that patch bays increase the chance of hum pickup slightly because of the additional cables and connectors. Figure 2.19 shows some typical patch-panel assignments.

Acoustic Treatment

Is it necessary to build an acoustically perfect studio for recording pop-music groups? If you mike close with directional microphones, record most instruments direct, and/or overdub instruments one at a time, you can make excellent-sounding recordings in an ordinary room, such as a living room. Plus, musicans enjoy playing in rooms that are not highly damped with acoustical materials.

Under what conditions should you add some acoustic treatment to your recording room?

- Your studio is a very live environment, such as a garage or concrete-block basement.

- Your recording room is very small.

- Outside noises are excessive.

- You want the freedom to mike several feet away.

For more detailed information, see the section "Modifying Studio Acoustics" in Chapter 3.

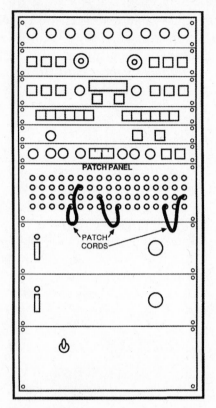

Figure 2.18 A rack and patch panel.

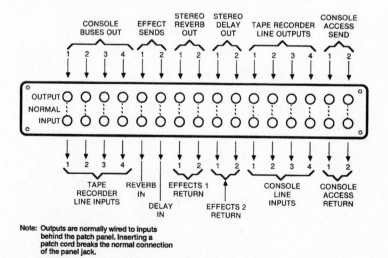

Figure 2.19 Some typical patch-panel assignments.

For budget or improvised studios, acoustic treatment is necessarily limited. Try surrounding the instrument and its microphone with thick blankets or sleeping bags hung a few feet away. For inexpensive acoustic treatment, carpet the floor and add sound-absorbing panels (see Figure 2.20). Follow these instructions to make the panels:

1. Build a 30-inch by 72-inch by 6-inch rectangular frame of perforated masonite.

2. Wearing a dust mask, remove the paper or foil cover (if necessary) from two strips of 6-inch fiberglass insulation. Place the strips side by side inside the frame.

3. Cover the frame with muslin or burlap.

4. Screw a hook into the top for hanging, or balance the panel against a wall.

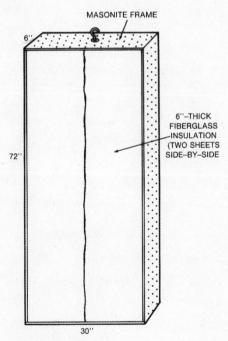

Figure 2.20 A sound-absorbing panel.

Place one of these panels behind the instrument you're recording. If necessary, add panels spaced evenly around the walls until your recordings sound reasonably dry (free of audible room reverberation), if this is the desired effect.

Equipment Connections

The instruction manuals of your equipment tell how to connect each component to the others. In general, use cables as short as possible to reduce hum, but long enough to be able to make changes.

Be sure to label all your cables on both ends according to what they plug into, for example, "Mixer ch. 1 monitor out," or "Reverb ch. 2 input." If you change connections temporarily, or the cable becomes unplugged, you know where to plug it back in.

Typically, you follow this procedure to connect equipment (see Figure 2.21):

1. Plug audio equipment and electric musical instruments into outlet strips fed from the same circuit breaker.

2. Connect mics and direct boxes to mic cables.

3. Connect mic cables either to the snake junction box, or directly into mixer mic inputs. Connect the snake connectors into mixer mic inputs.

4. Set the output volume of synthesizers and drum machines about $^3/_4$ up. Connect synthesizers and drum machines to mixer line inputs. If this causes hum, use a direct box. If you lack a direct box, and the instrument and mixer both have 3-prong power cords, try cutting or unsoldering the cable shield at the instrument end of the cable.

5. Connect mixer main outputs to a 2-track recorder.

6. Connect 2-track recorder outputs to mixer 2-track inputs (if any).

7. Connect mixer monitor outputs to power-amplifier inputs.

8. Connect power amplifier outputs to loudspeakers.

9. Connect mixer aux-send connectors to digital delay or reverb inputs.

10. Connect delay or reverb outputs to mixer aux-return or bus-in connectors.

11. If you're using a separate mixer and multitrack recorder, connect mixer bus 1 to recorder track 1 in, bus 2 to track 2, and so on. Also connect recorder track 1 out to mixer tape-track 1 in; connect track 2 out to mixer tape-track 2 in, and so on.

12. If you're using headphones for the musicians in the studio, connect the cue output to a small amplifier to drive their headphones.

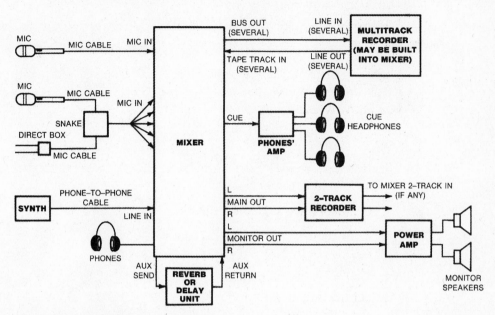

Figure 2.21 Equipment connections.

This chapter covered the equipment and connectors for a home studio. The rest of this book explains each piece of equipment and how to use it for best results.

SOUND, SIGNALS, AND STUDIO ACOUSTICS

When you make a recording, you deal with at least two types of invisible energy: sound waves and electrical signals. They carry the musician's message. If you know the properties of sound and signals, you understand what you're doing as you manipulate them in the recording process.

Sound Wave Creation

To produce sound, most musical instruments vibrate against air molecules, which pick up the vibration and pass it along as sound waves. When these vibrations strike your ears, you hear sound.

To illustrate how sound waves are created, imagine a vibrating speaker cone in a guitar amp. When the cone moves out, it pushes the adjacent air molecules closer together. This forms a *compression*. When the cone moves in, it pulls the molecules farther apart, forming a *rarefaction*. As illustrated in Figure 3.1, the compressions have a higher pressure than normal atmospheric pressure; the rarefactions have a lower pressure than normal.

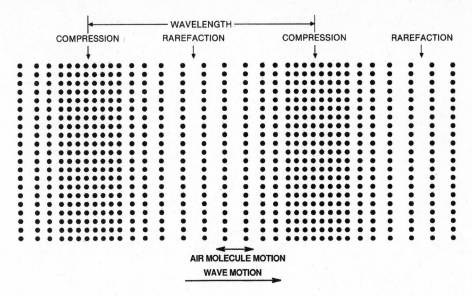

Figure 3.1 A sound wave.

These disturbances are passed from one molecule to the next in a springlike motion—each molecule vibrates back and forth to pass the wave along. The sound waves travel outward from the sound source at 1,130 feet per second, the speed of sound.

At some receiving point, such as an ear or a microphone, the air pressure varies up and down as the disturbances pass by. Figure 3.2 is a graph showing how sound pressure varies with time—the "wave" motion. The high point of the graph is called a *peak*; the low point is called a *trough*. The horizontal center line of the graph is normal atmospheric pressure.

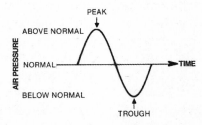

Figure 3.2 Sound pressure vs. time of one cycle of a sound wave.

Characteristics of Sound Waves

Figure 3.3 shows three waves in succession. One complete vibration from normal to high to low pressure and back to the starting point is called one *cycle*. The time it takes to complete one cycle—from the peak of one wave to the peak of the next—is called the *period* of the wave. One cycle is one period long.

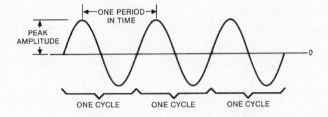

Figure 3.3 Three cycles of a wave.

Amplitude

At any point on the wave, the vertical distance of the wave from the center line is called the *amplitude* of the wave. The amplitude of the peak is called the *peak amplitude*. The more intense the vibration, the greater the pressure variations, and the greater the peak amplitude. The greater the amplitude, the louder the sound.

Frequency

The sound source (in this case, the guitar-amp loudspeaker) vibrates back and forth many times a second. The number of cycles completed in one second is called *frequency*. The faster the speaker vibrates, the higher the frequency of the sound. Frequency is measured in *hertz (Hz)*, which stands for cycles per second. One-thousand hertz is one kilohertz, abbreviated kHz.

The higher the frequency, the higher the perceived pitch of the sound. Low-frequency tones (such as 100 Hz) are low-pitched; high-frequency tones (such as 10,000 Hz or 10 kHz) are high-pitched. Doubling the frequency raises the pitch one *octave*.

Children can hear frequencies from 20 Hz to 20 kHz, and most adults with good hearing can hear up to 15 kHz or higher. Each musical instrument produces a range of frequencies—for example, 40 Hz to 5 kHz, or 500 Hz to 15 kHz.

Wavelength

When a sound wave travels through the air, the physical distance from one peak (compression) to the next is called a *wavelength* (refer to Figure 3.1). Low frequencies have long wavelengths (several feet); high frequencies have short wavelengths (a few inches or less).

Phase and Phase Shift

The *phase* of any point on the wave is its degree of progression in the cycle—the beginning, the peak, the trough, or anywhere in between. Phase is measured in degrees, with 360 degrees being one complete cycle. The beginning of a wave is 0 degrees; the peak is 90 degrees (¼-cycle), and the end is 360 degrees. Figure 3.4 shows the phase of various points on the wave.

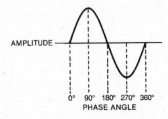

Figure 3.4 The phase of various points on a wave.

If there are two identical waves traveling together, but one is delayed with respect to the other, there is a *phase shift* between the two waves. The more delay, the more phase shift. Phase shift also is measured in degrees. Figure 3.5 shows two waves separated by 90 degrees (¼-cycle) of phase shift. The dashed wave lags the solid wave by 90 degrees.

When there is a 180-degree phase shift between two identical waves, the peak of one wave coincides with the trough of another. If these two waves are combined, they cancel out. This phenomenon is called *phase cancellation*. You often can hear it as an unnatural tone quality when two microphones picking up the same source are mixed together. You also hear it when a microphone is near a hard reflective surface so that the microphone picks up both direct and reflected sounds.

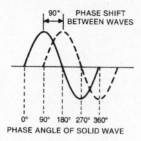

Figure 3.5 Two waves that are 90 degrees out-of-phase.

Harmonic Content

The type of wave shown in Figure 3.2 is called a *sine wave*. It is a pure tone of a single frequency, such as that produced by a tone generator. However, most musical tones have a complex waveform, which has more than one frequency component. All sounds are combinations of sine waves of different frequencies and amplitudes. Figure 3.6 shows sine waves of three frequencies combined to form a complex wave.

The lowest frequency in a complex wave is called the *fundamental frequency*. It determines the pitch of the sound. Higher frequencies in the complex wave are called *overtones* or *upper partials*. If the overtones are multiples of the fundamental frequency, they are called *harmonics*. For example, if the fundamental frequency is 200 Hz, the second harmonic is 400 Hz and the third harmonic is 600 Hz.

The harmonics and their amplitudes help determine the tone quality or *timbre* of a sound, and help to identify the sound as being from a trumpet, piano, organ, voice, etc.

Noise (such as tape hiss) contains all frequencies and has an irregular, nonperiodic waveform.

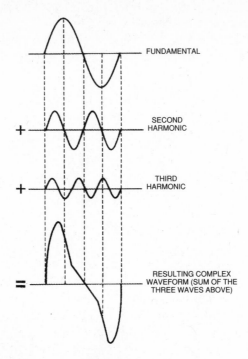

Figure 3.6 The addition of fundamental and harmonic waveforms to form a complex waveform.

Envelope

Another identifying characteristic of a sound is its *envelope*. This is the rise and fall in volume of one note. The envelope connects the peaks of successive waves that make up a note. An envelope has four sections: *attack*, *decay*, *sustain*, and *release* (see Figure 3.7). During the attack, a note rises from silence to its maximum volume. Then it decays from maximum to some midrange level. This middle level is the sustain portion. During release, the note falls from its sustain level back to silence.

Percussive sounds, such as drum hits, are so short that they have only a rapid attack and decay. Other sounds, such as organ or violin notes, have slow attacks and high-level, long sustains. Guitar plucks and cymbal crashes have quick attacks and slow releases.

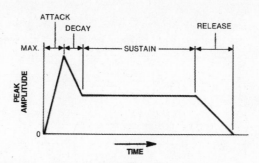

Figure 3.7 The four sections of the envelope of a note.

Signal Characteristics of Audio Devices

When a sound wave is converted to electricity by a microphone, this electricity is called the *signal*. It corresponds in frequency and amplitude to the original sound wave.

When this signal passes through an audio device, the device may alter the signal. It may change the level of particular frequencies, or add unwanted sounds that are not in the original signal.

Frequency Response

The *frequency response* of an audio device is the range of frequencies it reproduces at an equal level (within a tolerance, such as ±3 db). Frequency response is often plotted on a graph showing the signal level versus frequency (see Figure 3.8). Signal level is measured in decibels, and frequency is measured in hertz. In the illustration, the frequency response is 50 Hz to 12,000 Hz (±3 db). That means the audio device with this response passes all frequencies from 50 Hz to 12,000 Hz at a nearly equal level, and low-pitched sounds and high-pitched sounds are reproduced equally well. The response is down 3 db at 50 Hz and 12,000 Hz, and up 3 db at 5,000 Hz.

If the response is the same at all frequencies within the specified range, it forms a horizontal straight line, and so is called a *flat frequency response* (see Figure 3.9).

For high-fidelity reproduction, an audio device should have a flat frequency response over the range of frequencies that the musical instrument or voice produces. That way, fundamentals and harmonics are reproduced in the same proportion as they occurred in the original sound source. Because the ratio of fundamentals and harmonics affects the tone quality or timbre, preserving the original ratio also preserves the original tone quality.

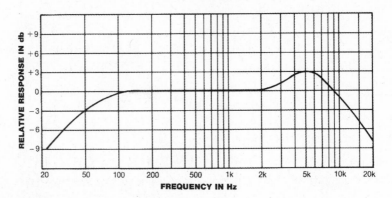

Figure 3.8 An example of a frequency response.

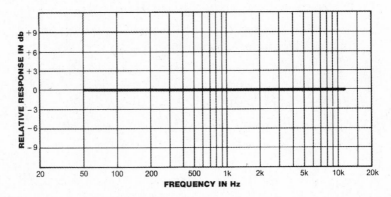

Figure 3.9 A flat frequency response.

If the frequency response decreases (rolls off) at high frequencies (as in the right side of Figure 3.8), the upper harmonics are weakened and the result is a dull sound. If the response rolls off at low frequencies (as in the left side of Figure 3.8), the fundamentals are weakened and the result is a thin sound. If either rolls off beyond the range of frequencies that an instrument produces, the roll off is inaudible.

In general, the wider the frequency response (the greater the range of frequencies that are reproduced equally), the higher the fidelity. A wide frequency response generally results in accurate reproduction. A frequency response of 200 Hz to 8,000 Hz (±3 db) is narrow (poor fidelity), a response of 80 Hz to 12,000 Hz is wider (better fidelity), and a response of 20 Hz to 20,000 Hz is widest (best fidelity).

Also, the flatter the frequency response, the greater the fidelity or accuracy. A response deviation of ±3 db is good, ±2 db is better, and ±1 db is excellent.

The frequency response of an audio device may be altered intentionally from flat for special effect. Also, a microphone sometimes may sound best with a nonflat response. In general though, a wide, flat response results in high-fidelity reproduction.

Noise

Every audio component produces noise, and this is not desirable in recordings. Noise can be made less audible by keeping the signal level relatively high. If the signal in an audio device is very low, you have to turn up the listening volume in order to hear the signal well. Turning up the volume of the signal also turns up the volume of the noise, however, so that you hear noise along with the signal. If the signal level is high to start with, you don't have to turn up the listening level so high and the noise remains in the background.

Distortion

If the signal level is too high, *distortion* occurs. It gives a gritty, grainy quality to the signal. Distortion is sometimes called *clipping* because the peaks and troughs of the waveform are clipped off so that they are flattened. To hear distortion, simply record a signal at a very high recording level (with the meters going well into the red area) and play it back.

Optimum Signal Level

You want the signal level high enough to cover up the noise, but low enough to avoid distortion. Every audio component works best at a certain optimum signal level, and this is usually indicated by a "0" on a meter or lights that show the signal level.

Figure 3.10 is a diagram showing the range of signal levels in an audio device. At the bottom is the *noise floor* of the device—the level of noise it produces even with no signal. At the top is the *distortion level*—the point at which the signal distorts. In between is a range in which the signal may vary. On the average, it should be maintained around the 0 point.

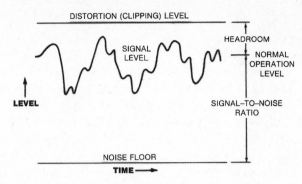

Figure 3.10 The range of signal levels in an audio device.

Signal-to-Noise Ratio

The level difference in db between the signal level and the noise floor is called the *signal-to-noise ratio (S/N)* (refer to Figure 3.10). The higher the signal-to-noise ratio, the cleaner the sound. A signal-to-noise ratio of 50 db is fair, 60 db is good, and 70 db or greater is excellent.

To illustrate signal-to-noise ratio, imagine a person yelling a message over the sound of a train. The message being yelled is the signal; the noise is the train. The louder the message, or the quieter the train, the greater the signal-to-noise ratio. The greater the signal-to-noise ratio, the clearer the message.

Headroom

The level difference in db between the normal signal level and the distortion level is called *headroom* (refer to Figure 3.10). The greater the headroom, the greater the signal level the device can handle without running into distortion. If an audio device has a lot of headroom, it can pass high-level peaks through without clipping them.

Behavior of Sound in Rooms

Because most music is recorded in rooms, you need to understand how room surfaces affect sound.

Echoes

Musical instruments vibrate against air molecules, creating sound waves that travel outward in all directions. Some of the sound travels directly to the listener (or to a microphone) and is called *direct sound*. The rest strikes the walls, ceiling, floor, and furnishings of the recording room. At those surfaces, some of the sound energy is absorbed, some is transmitted through the surface, and the rest is reflected back into the room.

Because sound waves take time to travel (about 1 foot per millisecond), the reflected sound arrives after the direct sound reaches the listener. The delayed arrival of a reflected sound causes an echo of the original sound (see Figure 3.11). In large rooms you sometimes hear single echoes; in small rooms you often hear a short, rapid succession of echoes called *flutter echoes*.

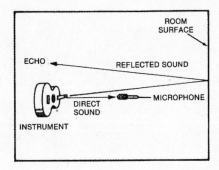

(A) Echo formation.

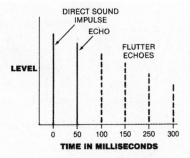

(B) Intensity vs. time of direct sound and its echoes.

Figure 3.11 Echoes.

Reverberation

Recall from Chapter 2 that sound reflects not just once but many times from all the surfaces in the room. This reverberation sustains the sound of the instrument in the room for a short time, even after each note has stopped sounding.

In physical terms, reverberation is a series of multiple echoes, decreasing in intensity with time, so closely spaced in time as to merge into a single continuous sound, eventually being completely absorbed by the inner surfaces of a room. The timing of the echoes is random, and the echoes increase in number as they decay. Figure 3.12 shows how reverberation develops in a recording room.

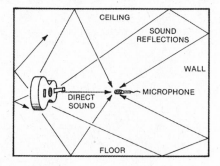

(A) Reverberation information.

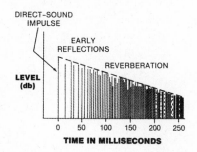

(B) Intensity vs. time of direct sound, early reflections, and reverberation.

Figure 3.12 Reverberation.

The time it takes for sound to decay to 60 db below the original steady-state sound level is called the *reverberation time* (abbreviated T_{60} or RT60). Reverberation time is typically measured at 500 Hz, and sometimes at other frequencies.

Reverberation comes to the listener from every direction because it is a pattern of multiple sound reflections off the walls, ceiling, and floor. You have the ability to localize the direction of sounds in space, so you can distinguish between the direct sound of an instrument (coming from a single location), and the reverberation (coming from everywhere else). You can ignore the reverberation and concentrate on the sound source.

A microphone does not have this ability to distinguish between the direct sound and the reverberation. In a playback of a recording, the recorded reverberation is no longer heard from all sides. Instead, it comes from the same point as the original sound (in front of the listener, between the playback speakers). As a result, the reverberation may seem much more noticeable on the tape playback than it was when heard live.

Too much reverberation in a recording gives a distant sound quality, with reduced clarity and presence. Consequently, pop-music recording generally requires a fairly nonreverberant studio, with a reverberation time of about 0.4 second or less. Classical music, however, should be recorded in "live," reverberant concert halls (RT60 about 1 to 3 seconds) because reverberation is a desirable part of the sound of classical music.

How To Make Good Recordings Without Building a Studio

Chapter 2 discusses the merits of building your own pop-music recording studio. If that is not convenient for you, or you don't want the expense or trouble of building a studio, there are other options. Because of its size, a club or auditorium where a band plays can be a suitable recording room. A large living room opening into other quiet rooms also can make a good studio. A basement studio tends to be quiet (except for the furnace) because the surrounding earth blocks outside sounds.

Reducing Recorded Reverberation and Leakage

Sound from an instrument travels to the nearest microphone, and also "leaks" into the microphones intended to pick up other instruments. This overlap of the sound of an instrument into the microphone of another instrument is called *leakage* (or *bleed* or *spill*).

It's very important to minimize leakage—to ensure that each microphone picks up only its intended instrument. Suppose the piano microphone hears a lot of drum leakage (see Figure 3.13). The recorded track of the piano contains not only the clean, tight sounds of the piano, but also the delayed, muddy drum sound. In the final mix, the overall drum sound is distant and dirty, rather than close-up and clean.

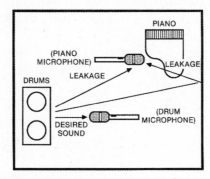

Figure 3.13 An example of leakage.

Leakage also makes it harder to mix the various instruments independently. Increase the level of the piano microphone, and the leaked drum sound also increases. Decrease the level of the drum microphones, and the drum leakage remains in the mix.

Fortunately, leakage can be minimized in several ways:

- Spread out the musicians in the studio (in moderation).

- Place microphones very close to instruments.

- Use directional microphones.

- Record direct.

- Use acoustic baffles (goboes or flats) between and around instruments.

- Overdub instruments.

- Record in a large room.

The sound of an instrument gets quieter as you move away from it. When you double the distance from a sound source in a dead room, the sound level drops 6 db. So, to decrease the loudness of the leakage, put the instruments farther apart.

There are limits to this separation. If the musicians are too far apart, they aren't able to play together in synchronization. Some closeness is needed for ensemble playing. Also, the sound level of an instrument in a room decreases with distance only up to a point and then stays constant due to the room reverberation. Great spacing between instruments may not further improve separation. In addition, if instruments are placed too far apart, the delays in the leakage are very long, making the leakage sound even more distant and muddy. You sometimes can achieve clarity by placing the instruments a short distance apart—6 to 12 feet, for instance. This shortens the delays.

As a microphone is placed closer to a sound source, the recorded level of the source gets louder, but the level of the leakage and reverberation does not. So, a microphone placed close to an instrument picks up a high ratio of wanted-to-unwanted sound. With close miking—for example, a miniature mic mounted on an acoustic guitar or on a banjo drum head— each microphone probably hears little except the instrument it's aimed at. Be cautious. Too-close miking sometimes can color the tone quality.

A microphone with a directional pickup pattern (such as cardioid, supercardioid, or bidirectional) is less sensitive to leakage approaching the microphone from the rear and/or sides, and rejects reverberation. For example, a cardioid microphone is most sensitive to the sound source it is aimed at, and attenuates sounds coming from the sides by about 6 db, and from the rear by about 20 db. Such microphones reduce leakage pickup as long as the leakage is not coming from in front of the microphone, or is not reflected into the front of the microphone.

Most directional mics boost the bass when placed close. If you roll off the excess bass at the mixer, you also reduce low-frequency leakage and reverberation.

Amplified instruments such as synthesizers and electric guitars can be recorded direct by connecting their output directly to the mixing console through a transformer or a direct box. Because the microphone is eliminated, no leakage or reverberation is picked up in the signal of an instrument fed directly to the mixer.

A *gobo* is a portable wall-like structure, usually built of several layers of wood (4 inches thick, for instance) and covered with absorbent material on one or both sides. By preventing sound from passing through it, the gobo isolates the sound of one instrument from another.

Use goboes as a last resort because they have several drawbacks:

- Goboes color the tone quality of the surrounded instrument by reflecting sound into the microphone. The direct sound and de- layed reflections cause phase interference which cancels certain frequencies.

- They dull the sound of leakage because they block only mid-to-high frequencies. Low frequencies travel around the gobo to the microphone, resulting in muddy-sounding leakage.

- They degrade the performance of cardioid microphones by preventing leakage from entering each microphone from the rear, where cancellation is greatest.

- Goboes are large and heavy, and they can block your view of the musicians.

Leakage becomes a problem whenever loud instruments and quiet instruments are recorded at the same time. The signal from a microphone used on a quiet instrument must be turned up high on the console to get sufficient level, and that makes it sensitive to leakage from loud instruments. It may be best to record all the loud instruments (electric guitars and drums) at one time and then go back and overdub the acoustic guitar, strings, piano, and vocals. Or record all the quiet instruments first and then the loud ones. Overdubbing also lets you mike farther away to pick up a more natural timbre from the instrument.

Some engineers like to overdub every instrument for perfect isolation and cleanest sound. However, this loses the emotional interaction among musicians that occurs when they all play together.

Recording in a large room allows greater physical separation between players and weakens leakage reflections due to the longer travel paths to the walls.

If you use all these leakage-reducing tricks, you may be able to make very good recordings without spending any money on room treatment. Unless your recording room is very poor acoustically, you probably can avoid the expense and trouble of building a studio.

A little leakage is not always a bad thing. *Creative leakage* is the use of some controlled leakage to achieve a "loose," "live," or "dirty" effect in the recording. The microphones are placed a little farther from the instruments than normal to pick up some leakage. In fact, creative leakage is an important technique in pop/rock recording.

Reducing Studio Noise

In most studios, you have to deal with a variety of unwanted sounds, such as appliances, air conditioning, traffic, airplanes, and noisy neighbors. The following suggestions keep these noises out of your recordings:

- In a home studio, ask your family to cooperate by being quiet while you're recording with microphones.

- Turn off appliances and telephones while recording.

- Pause for ambulances and airplanes to pass.

- Close windows.

- Close doors and seal the edges with towels.

- Remove small objects that can rattle or buzz.

Modifying Studio Acoustics

If you're able to make good recordings in an ordinary room as just described, you can skip this section. However, if your studio is small, noisy, or very live—or if you want to mike more than a foot away from the sound source—consider working on the room acoustics.

Controlling Reverberation, Flutter Echoes, and Leakage

You want to keep the reverberation time to about 0.4 second in a pop-music studio. Because reverberation is caused by sound reflections off room surfaces, any surface that is highly sound-absorbent helps to reduce reverberation, flutter echoes, and leakage.

A low-cost absorbent surface is the wide-range sound-absorbing panel discussed in Chapter 2 (see Figure 2.20). If you're recording just one musician at a time, start with one wide-range absorber placed behind the musician. That may be adequate for recording, even though the room will still be pretty live. You can add more damping or absorption, a little at a time, until your recordings sound as dead or as live as you want.

High frequencies are best absorbed by porous, fibrous materials such as fiberglass insulation, acoustic tile, foam plastic, carpeting, and curtains. Spacing these materials several inches from the wall (instead of on the wall) extends their absorption into the midbass region. Low-frequency absorbers called *bass traps* can be formed of flexible surfaces such as wood paneling or linoleum mounted over a sealed air space of several inches. Cavities such as closets or air spaces behind couches are also effective sound absorbers.

It's important to have equal sound absorption at all frequencies up to about 4,000 Hz. Suppose a room is highly absorbent at high frequencies, but not at low frequencies. The highs are absorbed quickly but the lows continue bouncing around the room. Consequently, the reverberation time is short at high frequencies and long at low frequencies. If you record in such a room, both the live and recorded sound are likely to be boomy and muddy, due to the persistence of low-frequency reverberation. Translated into material terms, if your recording room has an abundance of fibrous absorbent materials but has no bass traps, you can expect dull and muddy sound. Tacking carpet to all the walls is *not* the way to create a good-sounding studio.

You don't want the room to be completely absorbent (dead) because such an environment is stifling. In such a room, musicians may feel they are playing in a vacuum—they get no reinforcement or enhancement from sounds reflecting from nearby walls. Some reflections are beneficial, not only for the musicians' comfort, but for the sense of "air" and liveliness they add to the recorded sound. Reflections also enhance the apparent loudness, apparent transient response, and timbre of acoustic instruments.

Add absorption a little at a time until the recorded room acoustics sound good to you. The following simple acoustic treatments reduce reverberation:

- Open closet doors, and place couches and books a few inches from the walls.

- Carpet the floor.

- Hang canvas from the ceiling in deep folds.

- Hang thick curtains or blankets at least two feet from the walls, if possible.

- Attach open-cell acoustic-foam wedges (such as Sonex or Cutting Wedge) on or near the walls. The thicker the foam, the better the low-frequency absorption. Four-inch foam on the wall absorbs frequencies from about 400 Hz up.

- In a basement studio, nail acoustic tile to the ceiling joists, with fiberglass insulation in the air space between tiles and ceiling.

- For bass trapping, make some panel absorbers by nailing $\frac{1}{4}$-inch and $\frac{1}{8}$-inch plywood panels to 2-inch furring strips (battens) and placing fiberglass insulation in the air space behind the panel (see Figure 3.14). Cover about half the wall area in this manner. Alternatively, you can buy ready-made tubular bass traps.

- For wide-range absorption, attach 2-inch or 4-inch pressed fiber-glass board (Owens-Corning Type 703, 3 lb./cu. ft.) onto 2-inch by 6-inch studs, spaced 4 feet apart on the existing wall, with fiber-glass insulation in the air space. Placing the absorbent material in sections, rather than all together, promotes an even distribution, or *diffusion*, of sound in the room.

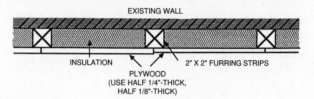

Figure 3.14 An example of bass-trap construction: a panel absorber.

Controlling Room Resonance

If you play an amplified bass guitar through a speaker in a room, and do a bass run up the scale, you hear some notes at which the room resonates, reinforcing the sound. These resonant frequencies, most noticeable below 300 Hz, are called *room modes* or *normal modes*. Resonance peaks of up to 10 db can occur. They give a "tubby" or "boomy" coloration to musical instruments and should be minimized.

Rectangular rooms have less problem with resonance than square rooms (see Appendix C). Large rooms are generally preferred for recording over small ones because the large room's resonant frequencies are lower; hence, they are more likely to be below the musical range.

A common misconception is that nonparallel walls eliminate room modes. Actually, low-frequency resonance is not significantly affected by this type of construction. A better solution is to use bass traps, which can be tuned to the resonant frequencies of the room.

Making a Quieter Studio

The following tips muffle noises from outside the studio:

- Weatherstrip doors all around, including underneath. (Leave the doors open for ventilation when not recording.)

- Replace hollow doors with solid doors.

- Block openings in the room with thick plywood and caulking.

- Put several layers of plywood and carpet on the floor above the studio, and put insulation in the air space between the studio ceiling and the floor above.

- When building a new studio, reduce noise transmission through the walls by using plastered concrete blocks, because massive walls reduce sound transmission. Nail gypsum board to 2-inch by 4-inch staggered studs on 2-inch by 6-inch footers as seen in Figure 3.15. Staggering the studs prevents sound transmission through the studs. Fill the airspace between walls with insulation.

Table 3.1 summarizes the requirements for a good pop-music studio.

Table 3.1 Requirements for a good pop-music studio.

Requirement	Result
Nonparallel or absorbent walls	No flutter echoes
Sufficient sound-absorbent surfaces on walls, ceiling, and floor	Fairly low reverberation time (about 0.4 second)
Flexible panels, cavities and fibrous materials, or fibrous materials spaced from walls and ceiling	Equal reverberation time at frequencies up to 4 kHz
A few hard reflective room surfaces	Early reflections to enhance the sound of acoustic instruments
A large or nonsquare room and bass traps	Minimized room modes
A large, sound-absorbent room	Low leakage

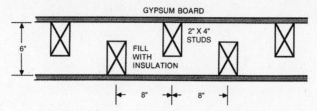

Figure 3.15 Staggered-stud construction to reduce noise transmission.

Your recording room may not need the acoustic treatments presented here—do some trial recordings to find out. If you do need some adjustments, however, the suggestions in this chapter should point you in the right direction.

MONITORING

One of the most exciting moments in recording comes when the finished mix is played over the big studio monitor speakers. The sound is so clear you can hear every detail, and so powerful you can feel the deep bass throbbing in your chest.

The monitor system is used to listen to the output signals of the console or the tape recorders. It consists of the console monitor mixer, the power amplifiers, loudspeakers, and the listening room. Each power amplifier boosts the electrical power of a console signal to a sufficient level to drive a loudspeaker; the speaker converts the electrical signal into sound, and the listening-room acoustics affect the sound from the speaker.

The monitor system is a critical link in the recording-reproduction chain because it provides the feedback that tells what you're doing to the recorded sound. Based on what you hear, you adjust the mix and judge the effectiveness of your microphone technique. The monitor system affects the settings of many controls on the console, as well as the microphone selection and placement, and all those settings affect the sound you're putting on tape.

Using inadequate monitors can result in a poor-sounding product. For example, if your monitor speakers are weak in the bass, you tend to boost the bass in the mix until it sounds right over those monitors. When that mix is played over speakers with a flatter response, it sounds too bassy. Thus, using monitors with weak bass results in bassy recordings. Similarly, using monitors with exaggerated treble results in dull recordings, and so on. In general, colorations in the monitors are inverted in the final tape. That's why it's so important to use an accurate monitor system—one with a wide, smooth frequency response. Such a system lets you hear exactly what's on the tape.

Speaker Requirements

The requirements for an accurate studio monitor are

- Wide, smooth frequency response
- Controlled dispersion
- High sensitivity
- High output capability

The on-axis frequency response of the direct sound should be within ±4 db from 40 Hz to 15 kHz to ensure accurate tonal reproduction. For a minimonitor, the low end should extend to at least 70 Hz.

A studio monitor should focus its sound on the listener and prevent radiation to the sides and rear of the speaker enclosure. This reduces reflections from nearby surfaces that can degrade the speaker's frequency response and stereo imaging. In monitoring a recording, you want to hear what's on tape rather than hear sound reflections from the room surfaces. Thus, a monitor should have *controlled dispersion*, a relatively narrow spread of sound leaving the loudspeaker.

Dispersion is measured in *coverage angle*, the angle of uniform loudness in front of the speaker. Technically, it's the angle off-axis where the speaker output is down 6 db compared to the output on-axis. The horizontal coverage angle of a monitor should be about 60 to 90 degrees—just wide enough to cover the console area evenly. Ideally, that angle should be maintained at all frequencies so that people seated anywhere behind the console hear the same tonal balance.

Sensitivity is the sound pressure level a speaker produces at 1 meter when driven with 1 watt of *pink noise*. Pink noise is random noise with equal energy per octave. This noise is either band-limited to the range of the speaker or is a $\frac{1}{3}$-octave band centered at 1 kHz. A sensitivity specification of 93 db SPL (Sound Pressure Level) is considered high (typical of studio monitors); a specification of 85 db SPL is considered low (typical of home bookshelf speakers).

High output capability is the quality of a speaker to play loudly without burning out. It's often necessary to monitor at high levels to hear quiet details in the music, and, when you record musicians who play loudly in the studio, it can be a letdown for them to hear a quiet playback. Consequently, a maximum output capability of 110 db SPL is typically required.

This formula calculates the maximum output capability of a speaker (how loud it can play):

$$db\ SPL = 10\ \log(P) + S$$

where db SPL is the sound pressure level obtainable at 1 meter, P is the continuous sine-wave power rating of the speaker, and S is the sensitivity rating in db SPL/1 watt/1 meter.

For example, if a speaker is rated at 100 watts maximum continuous power, and its sensitivity is 94 db SPL/watt/meter, its maximum output SPL (at 1 meter from the speaker) is

$$10\ \log(100) + 94 = 114\ db$$

The level at 2 meters is about 4 to 6 db less.

The following characteristics normally are not given numeric specifications, but it's important to note them:

- Good transient response

- Clarity and detail

- Low distortion

- High efficiency

Good transient response is the ability of the speaker to accurately follow the attack and decay of musical sounds. Transient response is aided by aligning the acoustic centers of the woofer and tweeter so that their signals arrive at the listener at the same time.

The listener should be able to hear small differences in the sonic character of instruments, and to sort them out in a complex musical passage.

Low distortion is necessary because it enables you to listen to the speaker for a long time without your ears hurting.

Efficiency is the ratio of sound power output to electrical power input. A high-efficiency speaker is louder than a low-efficiency speaker when both are driven by the same input power. High efficiency also means less amplifier overheating because less power is needed for the same loudness.

Near-Field Monitors

Many professional recording studios use large monitor speakers that provide excellent bass reproduction. However, they are expensive, heavy, difficult to install, and affected by the acoustics of the control room.

If you want to avoid this hassle and expense, consider using a pair of *near-field monitor speakers* (see Figure 4.1). A near-field monitor is a small, wide-range speaker, typically using a cone-shaped woofer and dome-shaped tweeter. You place a pair of them about 3 feet apart on top of the console meter bridge, or on stands about 3 feet from you.

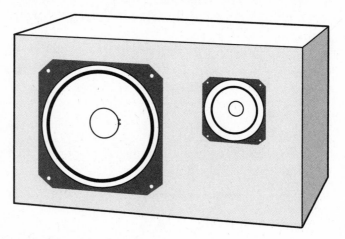

Figure 4.1 A near-field monitor speaker.

This technique, developed by audio consultant Ed Long, is called *near-field monitoring*. Because the speakers are close to your ears, you hear mainly the direct sound of the speakers and tend to ignore the room acoustics. This way, the speakers tend to sound the same in any environment, so you save the cost and time of treating your control room acoustically. Plus, near-field monitors sound very clear, need little or no equalization, and provide sharp stereo imaging.

Near-field speakers are far more popular than large wall speakers. Near-field monitors are specially designed for close listening—they have enough bass to sound full when placed far from walls. Some examples are the Digital Designs DD161a and DD261a, Peavey PRM 308S, Yamaha NS10M Studio, and Meyer HD-1. Good near-field monitors cost $200 and up.

Although most near-field monitors lack deep bass, they can be supplemented with a subwoofer to reproduce the complete audio spectrum.

Headphones

High-quality headphones are a low-cost alternative to loudspeakers for the home studio. You may find that headphones provide adequate isolation if the music you're recording is quiet.

Compared to loudspeakers, the advantages of headphones are

- Much lower cost

- No room-acoustics coloration

- Consistent tone quality in different environments

- On-location recording convenience

- Ease of hearing small changes in the mix

- Sharper transient response due to absence of room reflections

The disadvantages of headphones are

- Discomfort after long listening sessions

- Distortion of tone quality (with cheap headphones)

- Noncapability of projecting bass notes through your body

- Variance of bass response due to headphone pressure against the head

- Physical placement of sound in your head rather than out front

- Lack of room reverberation causing you to mix in an inappropriate amount of artificial reverberation

- Distortion of stereo spread (for panned signals or coincident-pair stereo recording)

Even though headphones may not sound like speakers, you can do your mixes over headphones to match commercial records heard over those same headphones. Then your mixes sound commercial over speakers.

If you're monitoring as the musicians are playing, use closed-cup headphones to block out sounds from the studio.

Large Speaker Systems and Crossovers

If you use large monitors in or near the walls, everyone in the control room (including the group you're recording) can hear the speakers loudly and clearly.

63

Most large studio monitors are designed for high efficiency, typically using a ported 15-inch woofer for the lows and a tweeter with a horn for the highs (see Figure 4.2). The horn efficiently couples the tweeter's sound to the air, the same way a megaphone does. The port resonates at low frequencies to reinforce the bass. An alternative to a port is a passive radiator, which is an electrically unconnected speaker cone.

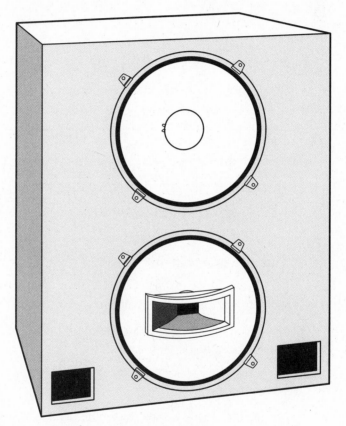

Figure 4.2 Large studio monitor loudspeaker.

A *one-way* speaker system uses a single cone speaker. An example is a minimonitor used to simulate compact stereos and car radios. A *two-way* system (the most popular) has a woofer and a tweeter. A *three-way* system uses a woofer, a midrange driver (with or without a horn), and a tweeter. A *four-way* system covers the widest range by adding a super tweeter.

A *crossover* or *dividing network* is a circuit that divides the monitor signal into two or more frequency bands. In the crossover, a *lowpass filter* sends the low frequencies to the woofer; a *highpass filter* sends the high frequencies to the tweeter and keeps out low-frequency components that could damage the tweeter. Some crossovers include a *bandpass filter* to route middle frequencies to a midrange driver.

The *crossover frequency* is the frequency above which the woofer stops working and the tweeter takes over. The lowpass filter passes frequencies below the crossover frequency; the highpass filter passes frequencies above the crossover frequency. This frequency is set below the upper limit of the woofer and above the lower limit of the tweeter—typically between 500 and 2,500 Hz. There may be an additional crossover around 5,000 Hz between a midrange driver and a tweeter.

At the crossover frequency, the crossover response slopes down 3 db. At frequencies beyond the crossover frequency, the output of the crossover network does not suddenly cut off; rather, the output slopes down by 6, 12, or 18 db per octave.

If the crossover is connected after the power amplifier, the crossover operates at high power levels and is called a *passive crossover* (see Figure 4.3). That is, it is made of passive (nonamplifying) components. Typically, a passive crossover is built into a speaker system. If the crossover precedes the power amps, it operates at line level and is called an *active crossover* or *electronic dividing network* (see Figure 4.4). It includes active (amplifying) components such as transistors.

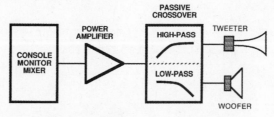

Figure 4.3 A monitor system using a passive crossover.

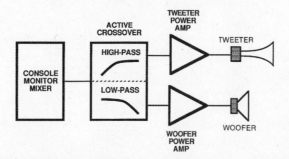

Figure 4.4 A biamped monitor system using an active crossover.

65

An active crossover is used in a *biamped* system where the woofer and tweeter are driven by separate power amplifiers. The active crossover is connected ahead of the power amps. Low-frequency signals from the crossover go to the power amp driving the woofer; high-frequency signals from the crossover go to the power amp driving the tweeter. Because tweeters are more efficient than woofers, the tweeter amp can be about 25 percent of the power of the woofer amp.

Biamping has several advantages:

- Distortion components from the woofer power amplifier do not reach the tweeter, so there is less likelihood of tweeter burnout if the amplifier clips. In addition, clipping distortion in the woofer amplifier is made less audible.

- Intermodulation distortion is reduced at high levels.

- Peak power output is greater than that of a single amplifier of equivalent power.

- Direct coupling of amplifiers to speakers improves transient response—especially at low frequencies.

- Biamping reduces the inductive and capacitive loading of the power amplifier.

- The full power of the tweeter amp is available regardless of the power required by the woofer amp.

A three-way speaker system can be triamped, or can be biamped by putting a passive crossover before the tweeter (see Figure 4.5).

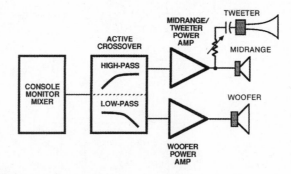

Figure 4.5 A biamped monitor system using an active crossover and a passive crossover.

The main advantage of a nonbiamped speaker is that it has been designed and tested for flat frequency response as a system, and is ready to use out of the box. There is no chance of misbalancing the driver levels, so you're more likely to get a flat response. Also, passive crossovers can be specially designed for a particular speaker system to improve its phase response and frequency response.

Placement of Large Monitor Speakers

Having a pair of quality speakers doesn't guarantee good sound reproduction; you have to install, equalize, and use them properly for best results.

The closer a loudspeaker is to the walls, ceiling, or floor, the more bass it produces. Why? If a speaker is placed in the middle of a room, it radiates low frequencies in all directions (into "full space"). If the speaker is placed against a wall, the low-frequency energy is concentrated into half the space, which boosts the lows by 3 db. Putting a speaker in a corner maximizes bass output by concentrating the low-frequency energy into one-quarter the space. The highs aren't much affected by speaker placement near a surface, because high frequencies radiate mainly out front. Check the speaker instructions for recommended placement relative to the room surfaces.

There are several ways to install large monitor speakers, each with advantages and disadvantages. One way is to put them on shelves or platforms against a wall. Unfortunately, this arrangment can degrade the frequency response. Low-frequency sounds radiating around the speaker reflect off the rear wall, are delayed, and combine with the direct sound in front of the speaker (see Figure 4.6). This results in phase cancellations or a *comb-filter effect* in the midbass region.

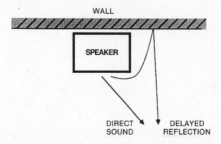

Figure 4.6 Speaker placement near a wall may cause phase cancellations due to delayed reflections combining with the direct sound.

One way to prevent rear-wall reflections is to flush-mount the monitors in the wall. They should be isolated mechanically from the wall by foam rubber, fiberglass insulation, or rubber shock mounts. This prevents sound from traveling through the wall and ceiling to the listener before the direct sound arrives through the air.

If flush-mounting is impractical, you can weaken the wall reflections by placing the speakers at least 3 feet from the rear wall and 4 feet from the side walls.

Another arrangement is the *live end-dead end (LEDE)* room treatment, invented by Don Davis and Chips Davis. The front half of the control room around the speakers is made very sound-absorbent (dead) by applying muslin-covered fiberglass insulation or absorbent acoustic foam (such as Sonex or Cutting Wedge) to the walls and ceiling. This prevents reflections from the surfaces near the speakers. The wall behind the engineer is hard and reflective (live) to provide ambience and increase loudness. This surface is broken up, rather than flat, to diffuse the sound. Reflection Phase Gratings (the RPG diffusor or the Art Diffusor) are often used for this purpose. Figure 4.7 shows this type of LEDE control room.

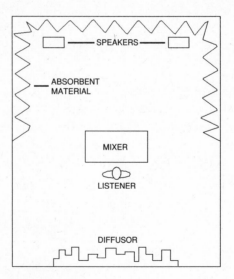

Figure 4.7 An LEDE control room.

LEDE rooms are not necessarily all absorbent in the front and reflective in the rear. The speakers can be flush-mounted in a hard-wall array that is angled to eliminate early reflections at the listener's ears (see Figure 4.8). The idea is to create a reflection-free zone at the mixing position.

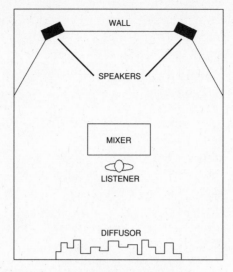

Figure 4.8 An LEDE control room with angled walls.

A certified LEDE room has to meet certain criteria, but many control rooms can be improved simply by putting thick absorbent material on the walls behind and to the sides of the speakers, or by pulling the speakers out from the walls at least 2 feet. Some of the claimed benefits of an LEDE control room are

- Mixes are easier and faster to do because you hear more of the sound from the studio and less from the control room.

- The overall sound is clearer.

- Stereo imaging and depth are improved greatly.

- Frequency response is flatter.

- Boominess and ringing are reduced, and transient response is sharpened.

- LEDE-monitored recordings hold up well on many home hi-fi speakers.

In any control room, the speakers are mounted at ear height or slightly higher so that the sound path is not obstructed by the mixing console. For best stereo imaging, align the speaker drivers vertically and mount the speakers symmetrically with respect to the side walls. Place the two speakers as far apart as you're sitting from them (about 8 feet); aim them toward you, and sit exactly between them (see Figure 4.9).

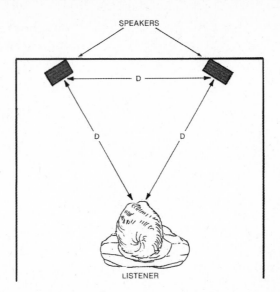

Figure 4.9 The recommended speaker/listener relationship for best stereo imaging.

Polarity and Stereo Balance

Of course, wire the speakers in the same polarity to obtain a sharp center image. For both channels, connect the amplifier positive terminal (+ or red) to the speaker positive terminal (+ or red). Polarity adjustment also is called "speaker phasing."

Also wire the speakers in correct *absolute polarity* so that their speaker cones vibrate in the same direction as the live instrument at the onset of a note. The effect of absolute polarity is a subtle increase in clarity and solidity. To determine whether a speaker is wired in correct absolute polarity, follow this procedure:

1. Place a microphone of standard polarity (pin 2 hot) inside a kick drum.

2. Have someone beat the drum while you watch the monitor-speaker woofer.

3. The woofer cone should go out (toward you) the instant the drum is struck. If the opposite occurs, reverse the speaker leads of both speakers.

To adjust the stereo balance, play a mono musical signal and assign it to channels 1 and 2 at the console. Adjust the channel 1 and 2 master faders so that the signal reads the same on the channel 1 and 2 VU meters. Then, while sitting behind the console exactly midway between the speakers, listen to the image of the sound between the speaker pair. It should be localized midway between the monitors—that is, straight ahead. If necessary, center the image by adjusting the monitor trim pots on the console, or by adjusting the left or right volume control on the power amplifier. Note that an off-center listener hears the image shifted toward one side.

Power Requirements

Check the loudspeaker rating for recommended amplifier power. A power amp of 150 watts continuous average power per channel should be sufficient for use with high-efficiency studio monitors (see Figure 4.10). Too much power is better than too little, because an underpowered system is likely to clip. The resulting distortion can damage tweeters.

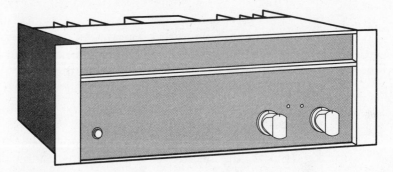

Figure 4.10 A power amplifier.

Some performance requirements for a monitor power amplifier are

- Distortion under 0.05 percent

- Capability of driving any load down to 2 ohms

- Capability of controlling or damping loudspeaker vibration (high *damping factor*)

- Long-term durability and resistance to overheating

Two valuable amplifier features are independent channel-level controls and an accurate indicator for distortion or clipping.

To avoid losing power from heating the speaker cables, put the power amps close to the speakers and use short cables with thick conductors. The low resistance of these cables allows maximum damping of the speaker by the power amplifier. Use the following list to select cable gauge based on cable length:

Cable Length	Gauge
Less than 25 feet	#16
25 to 50 feet	#14
50 to 100 feet	#12

Room Acoustics

The acoustics of the control room affect the sound of the speakers. As described in Chapter 3, sound waves leaving the speaker strike the room surfaces. At those surfaces, some frequencies are absorbed and others are reflected. At the listener's ears, the sound waves reflected from the room surfaces combine with the direct sound. Only those reflections arriving within 20 to 65 milliseconds after the direct sound blend or fuse with the direct sound to affect the perceived spectrum or tonal balance. After about 65 milliseconds, an echo is heard.

Suppose the walls are covered with carpet so that they absorb only the high frequencies. Then the walls reflect mainly the low frequencies. When you listen to a speaker playing in such a room, you hear the direct sound from the speaker plus the bassy wall reflections, giving a total sound that is bass-heavy. Now suppose the walls are made of wood paneling mounted on studs. Such a vibrating surface absorbs lows and reflects highs. The total sound you hear probably is thin and overly bright.

Clearly, the room surfaces should reflect (or absorb) all frequencies about equally to avoid coloring the sound of the speakers. Equal absorption (± 25 percent) from about 250 Hz to 4,000 Hz is usually adequate. As described in the previous chapter, you can use flexible panels to absorb lows, in combination with fibrous materials or foam to absorb highs. Or use thick fibrous material spaced from the wall and ceiling.

Room resonances or *standing waves* can cause some notes to blare out and others to disappear. These resonances should be controlled as described in Chapter 3.

Room acoustics also affect the decay-in-time of the sound coming from the speakers. When a note in a reproduced recording suddenly ends, the sound of that note continues to bounce around the room, causing echoes and reverberation that prolong the sound. This long decay of sound is not part of the recording, so the control room should be relatively dead. That is, it should have a short reverberation time. A typical living room has a reverberation time of about 0.4 second; the control room should have the same so that the engineer hears about the same amount of ambience that a home listener hears. A totally dead room is uncomfortable to listen in.

Reducing wall reflections near the monitors also improves the stereo imaging of the monitors. All the information about sound-image location is in the direct sound coming from the speakers; wall reflections can only confuse the listener as to the correct location of the sound images.

Typically, the control room is isolated acoustically from the studio so that you hear only the sound from the monitors, not the live sound from the studio musicians. In a home studio, you can achieve isolation simply by putting the control-room equipment in a room far removed from the studio, with the doors closed.

To build a control room with good isolation near the studio, you may need to use double-wall construction with staggered studs, and with fiberglass insulation between the two walls. The door between the control room and studio should be solid wood and should be weatherstripped all around—including underneath. Use a double-pane window (mounted in rubber) between the control room and studio.

Synthesizers and drum machines often are set up and monitored in the control room.

Room Equalization

When you equalize a room, you adjust the frequency response of the monitor chain to flatten the speaker/room response at the listener's position. Equalization can smooth out the frequency response of the speaker itself, but cannot remove peaks and dips narrower than $\frac{1}{3}$-octave wide. Also, equalization can compensate somewhat for the room's frequency response, which depends partly on the absorption versus frequency of its acoustic treatment. Note that equalization is not effective against standing waves because they vary with the listener's position. Neither is equalization a cure for poor room acoustics or narrow-band speakers.

Work on the room treatment and speaker placement first and then apply as little equalization as possible. If a flat-response speaker is installed in a room with equal absorption at all frequencies, little or no equalization is needed. Near-field monitors are usually not equalized.

To equalize a monitor/listening room for flat response, you need a ⅓-octave realtime analyzer (RTA), a pink noise generator (usually built into the analyzer), a laboratory-calibrated instrumentation microphone, and a ⅓-octave equalizer (preferably a graphic type). The RTA and microphone can be rented from a sound-system dealer. Set up the test equipment as follows:

1. Connect the equalizer between the console monitor output and the power-amplifier input (or the active-crossover input if the system is biamped).

2. Set the controls of the graphic equalizer to their center (flat) positions.

3. Put the microphone at the listener's position and plug it into the analyzer.

4. Feed pink noise into the equalizer input. You see a frequency-response curve on the RTA screen.

The final response curve after equalization should be flat from 40 Hz up to 5 or 8 kHz and then should gradually roll off to about –10 db at 16 kHz. You probably need to do a final touch-up by ear. Rolling off the monitor high-frequency response makes the engineer boost the high frequencies in the mix. That boost is acceptable because most home hi-fi speakers roll off at high frequencies, making the end result sound natural. A mix made on monitors tuned flat up to the highest frequencies is likely to sound dull on most home systems.

Adjust the speaker's midrange and tweeter controls to get the desired response curve. Or, if the system is biamped, adjust the volume control on the tweeter power amplifier. Finally, flatten the curve using the graphic equalizer. Pull down the highest peaks in the curve first—don't apply boost if you can help it.

If you need more than about 5 db of boost or cut at any frequency, the speaker needs to be upgraded or the room treatment needs work. Add bass traps if the curve is raised at the low end. Add fiberglass insulation, carpet, or curtains if the curve is raised at the high end. A sharp dip at a certain frequency may be due to a vibrating wall panel. Stiffen it. Some dips may be caused by sound reflections off the console; these can be detected by covering the console with a heavy blanket and looking for changes in the RTA display. Don't remove those dips with the equalizer. Instead, place the monitor speakers at a height that prevents those dips (according to Chips Davis, about 15 degrees above ear level).

Lacking an RTA, you may be able to equalize the monitor system roughly by ear if your hearing is good:

1. Place a flat-response omnidirectional microphone 1 foot from a person in the studio and record that person speaking.

2. Play the recording through the monitor system at a natural level.

3. Equalize the speaker so that it sounds like the same person speaking live in the control room near the speaker.

This demonstrates the meaning of *accuracy*; the reproduced sound is similar to the original sound. As an alternative, play prerecorded music through some top quality headphones and then through the monitor speakers. Equalize the speakers to sound the way the headphones do.

Using Monitors

The listening level during mixdown should be maintained at about 85 db SPL—a typical home listening level. The Fletcher-Munson effect says that you hear less bass in a program that is played quietly than in the same program played loudly. If you mix a program while monitoring at, say, 100 db SPL, the same program sounds weak in the bass when heard at a lower listening level—which is likely in the home. Therefore, programs meant to be heard at 85 db SPL should be mixed and monitored at that level.

Another reason to avoid extreme monitor levels is that loud, sustained sound can damage your hearing or cause temporary hearing loss at certain frequencies. If you must do a loud playback for the musicians (who are accustomed to high SPLs in the studio), protect your ears by using earplugs or by leaving the room.

You can obtain an inexpensive sound level meter from your local electronics distributor. Play a musical program at 0 VU on the console meters and adjust the monitor level to obtain an average reading of 85 db SPL on the sound level meter. Mark the monitor-level setting.

Before doing a mix, you may want to play some familiar recordings over your monitors to become accustomed to a commercial tonal balance—the balance among bass, midrange, and treble. Listen to several recordings because they vary widely.

While mixing, monitor the program alternately in stereo and mono. You want to make sure there are no out-of-phase components that cancel certain frequencies in mono. Also, beware of *center-channel buildup*—instruments or vocals that are panned to center in the stereo mix sound 3 db louder when monitored in mono than they do in stereo. That is, the balance changes in mono and the center instruments are a little too loud. You may have to compromise the stereo and mono mixes so that both sound acceptable.

Mix the tracks to sound good on your accurate monitors, but also check the mix on small inexpensive speakers to see whether anything is missing or whether the mix changes drastically. Make sure that bass instruments are recorded with enough harmonics to be audible on the smaller speakers. It's a good idea to make a cassette copy of the mix and give it to the client to audition in a car, boom box, or compact stereo.

The Cue System

Recall from Chapter 1 that the cue system is a monitor system for musicians to use as they're recording. It consists of the cue mixer in the console, a cue amplifier, wiring to headphone junction boxes, and headphones. Musicians sometimes can't hear each other adequately in the studio, due to sound baffles and the volume of their own instruments. By listening over headphones, they can hear each other in a reasonable balance. They also can listen to previously recorded tracks while overdubbing.

A suggested cue system is shown in Figure 4.11. A power amplifier connected to the cue output of the console drives several resistor-isolated headphones, which are in parallel. You may want to wire the headphones permanently to the cue lines to prevent theft.

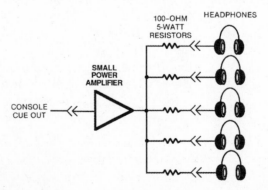

Figure 4.11 A cue system.

Make sure all headphones for a cue system are the same model so that each musician hears the same mix and level. Headphones should be

- Durable, with metal-jacket plugs

- Comfortable

- Closed-cup to avoid leakage into microphones (open-air phones may work well enough)

- Capable of providing smooth response to reduce listening fatigue

- Capable of producing high levels without burning out

Although some consoles can provide several independent cue mixes, the ideal situation is to set up individual cue mixers near each musician. Then they can set their own cue mix and listening level. The inputs of these mixers are fed from the console output buses.

Suppose a vocalist sings into a microphone and hears that mic's signal over the cue headphones. The polarity of the headphones affects the sound quality heard in the headphones. If the singer's voice and the headphones' sound are the same polarity, the headphones make a sound-wave compression at the instant a sound-wave compression hits the microphone. The voice sounds full and loud in the headphones. If the singer's voice and the headphone's sound are opposite in polarity, the voice cancels partially or has a tonal coloration in the headphones.

To ensure that the voice and headphones are the same polarity, wire a 1:1 transformer in-line with the balanced mic signal or the cue-send signal. While talking into a mic and listening to it on headphones, invert the cue signal polarity by inverting the transformer leads. The position that gives the fullest, most solid sound in the headphones is correct. If your system is unbalanced and you can't change the signal polarity, try a different brand of headphones that might be wired in different polarity.

Most of the headphones in your studio should be the same model, so that everyone hears with correct polarity. However, some people (especially vocalists) need choices of headphones so that they feel comfortable with them and perform their best.

Ultimately, what you hear from the monitors influences your recording techniques and affects the quality of your recordings. Take the time to plan and adjust the control-room acoustics. Choose and install the speakers carefully; equalize them if necessary. Monitor at proper levels and listen on several systems. You'll be rewarded with a monitor system you can trust.

5

HUM PREVENTION

You patch in a piece of audio equipment, and there it is—HUM! A low-pitched tone or buzz. What's causing it? How can you get rid of it?

This annoying sound is a tone at 60 Hz (50 Hz in Europe), and (possibly) multiples of that frequency. It can be caused by all sorts of things: audio cables picking up interference from power lines, other equipment, or lighting; noisy AC power from wall outlets; improper connections between audio equipment; or defective equipment. Hum is a persistent problem for studios.

Fortunately, hum pickup can be prevented by following good wiring practice: make secure connections to ground, use balanced lines, and prevent ground loops. All these practices are explained in this chapter, as well as other techniques to keep your audio clean and hum-free.

Grounding Definitions

To understand the information in this chapter, you need a few definitions related to grounding:

Grounding	Connecting pieces of electronic equipment to ground
Ground	A point designated as a zero-voltage reference (voltages and signals in the system are measured relative to this ground point)

Earth ground or physical ground	A connection to moist dirt, usually made through a copper ground rod or a cold-water pipe
AC mains	The 60 Hz, 120/240 V AC power wiring supplied by the power company (sometimes a type called 3-phase)
Phase	One part or one leg of a 3-phase power wiring

Providing a secure ground connection to your audio equipment is one way to reduce hum. There are several ways to do this.

The Safety Ground

If you look at a modern AC outlet, you see three holes. The U-shaped hole is the safety ground. This terminal connects by a long wire to the power company's earth ground: a copper rod driven in the earth, a skyscraper's underground steel structure, or a metal cold-water pipe.

Many electronic devices have 3-wire power cords; the round ground pin on the cord is connected to the equipment *chassis*. The chassis is a metal housing that surrounds the circuitry in a piece of audio equipment. When you plug a device's 3-prong power cord into an outlet, the chassis of the device is connected to the safety ground. If a short circuit occurs accidentally between the chassis and a hot power line, the chassis current flows to the safety ground rather than through someone touching the chassis. This prevents shocks.

Suppose you're installing a studio in a home or building with older wiring that lacks a 3-wire safety ground. If your studio setup is large, or if there are powerful broadcast transmitters nearby, you probably need to install a safety ground.

> **Caution:** If you're unfamiliar with electrical wiring practices, hire an electrician. Make sure you know what you're doing before you start fooling around inside the circuit-breaker box. Otherwise, you might be severely shocked, or be held liable if someone else is shocked. Be sure to check your local electrical code before doing any AC power wiring.

First, look inside the main circuit-breaker box of your house or building. Inside the box, near the bottom, is a heavy copper plate called the *ground bus bar*. The ground bus is a terminal, plate, or screw connection to the console chassis. All the building's ground wires (bare or with green insulation) connect to it. (In some instances, the "neutral" (white) wires also connect to this bar.) The ground bus bar is connected to earth ground, such as a metal cold-water pipe or a copper rod in the earth. Your mixing console also has a ground bus.

Run a No. 12 gauge insulated wire from the mixing console ground bus to the circuit-breaker ground bus bar. An alternative ground connection is to the metal screw that holds the cover plate to the wall outlet. Check to see whether the metal screw is actually grounded by connecting a neon circuit tester between the screw and either of the outlet sockets. If the tester glows in one of the sockets, the screw is grounded. If the tester doesn't glow in either socket, you can't use the metal screw as a ground.

An audio component other than the mixer also might have a ground terminal. If you hear hum in your system, try connecting this terminal to the safety ground.

Preventing Hum Pickup in Audio Cables

Audio cables pick up hum from oscillating electrostatic and magnetic fields radiated from power lines in the walls. Power lines act as one plate of a capacitor, and the conductors in audio cables act as the other plate.

Electrostatic Interference

An oscillating electrostatic field is set up between the power line's capacitor plate and the audio cable's capacitor plate, causing hum to be transmitted (coupled) from the power lines to the cable conductors. An electrostatic field couples best at high frequencies, and so is heard as a buzz primarily made up of the upper harmonics of 60 Hz.

The audio cable conductors can be protected from this electrostatic field by a surrounding shield. Recall from Chapter 2 that a shield is a conductive enclosure around signal-carrying conductors, used to keep out electrostatic hum fields and radio frequency interference. In audio cables, a shield usually takes the form of a foil or metal-braid cylinder around one or two conductors. The greater the shield coverage, the better it rejects hum, so use audio cable with foil shielding for permanent wiring.

Metal racks, equipment chassis, and microphone handles also are shields. If you connect a metal chassis to ground, the chassis becomes an effective shield against electrostatic hum fields. Shields must be connected to ground to be effective, because the ground provides a drain path for shield charges caused by the electrostatic fields.

Magnetic Interference

Power lines and transformers also act as electromagnets, radiating magnetic lines of force that oscillate at 60 Hz and its harmonics. These lines of force "cut" through the conductors in audio cables, causing the conductors to generate electricity at 60 Hz and its harmonics. Magnetic fields couple best at low frequencies, and so are usually heard as a low tone at 60 Hz. A magnetic hum field is directional, so you can detect it by rotating the device that is producing hum. If the hum level varies, the hum is induced magnetically.

A shield must be made of a magnetic material (such as steel) to block magnetic hum fields. This shield need not be grounded unless you also want to use it for electrostatic shielding.

There are a number of steps that you can take to avoid magnetic interference:

- Avoid using fluorescent lights in the studio.

- Install your equipment at least several inches (or feet) from the large power transformers in power amplifiers.

- Separate power cords from audio cables.

- Use AC isolation transformers or line filters in on-location work.

Fluorescent lights radiate strong magnetic hum fields. If fluorescent lights can't be removed, be sure the lighting fixtures are grounded, and replace faulty ballasts. Inside each fixture, install a noise filter (available from electronics supply houses). Also avoid silicon control rectifier (SCR) light dimmers—they put "hash" and buzzes on the AC line. Rather, use multiway incandescent bulbs to vary the studio lighting levels.

Installing your equipment inches or feet from the large power transformers is important especially for cassette decks and tape recorders. Power transformers in audio equipment also radiate magnetic hum fields.

Power cables and extension cords radiate hum fields that audio cables can pick up, so separate these two types of cables by at least 1 foot. If they must cross, do so at right angles and space them apart; this reduces the coupling between cables.

AC isolation transformers or line filters are available from electronic supply houses.

Buzzes in on-location work are often caused by interference from stage lighting circuits. Keep lighting cables and power wiring well away from audio cables. Again, if these cables must cross, cross them at right angles and space them apart.

Balanced versus Unbalanced Lines

Hum fields are rejected better by balanced lines than by unbalanced lines. Recall from Chapter 2 that a balanced line is a cable that uses two conductors to carry the signal, surrounded by a shield (see Figure 5.1). The two conductors are semi-isolated from ground. The shield does not carry the signal; it is connected to ground and keeps electrostatic fields out of the conductors. Balanced cables and equipment use 3-pin pro audio connectors (XLR-type connectors). Professional audio equipment uses balanced connectors.

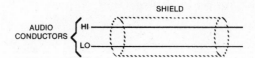

Figure 5.1 A balanced line.

In a balanced line, the two conductors pick up equal amounts of hum interference. The cable plugs into a balanced input, which is sensitive to the voltage difference between the two conductors. Because there is little or no difference in hum voltage between the two conductors, hum picked up by the cable is not amplified, or is cancelled in the process.

Twisted-pair audio cable picks up less magnetically induced hum than nontwisted-pair cable. This is because twisted conductor pairs occupy the same point in space on the average, so they are the same distance from the magnetic hum source and receive equal hum interference. This equal interference is then cancelled by the balanced input circuitry of the equipment.

An unbalanced line is a cable that uses a single conductor surrounded by a shield (see Figure 5.2). An unbalanced cable has either an RCA phono plug or a ¼-inch 2-conductor phone plug. Unbalanced equipment has RCA phono jacks, or has ¼-inch phone jacks. Home stereos and semipro recording equipment use unbalanced connectors.

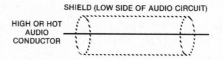

Figure 5.2 An unbalanced line.

Both the conductor and the shield carry the audio signal, so the shield isn't as effective in blocking electrostatic hum as it is in a balanced line. Also, the inner conductor and outer shield are at different impedances to ground, so they pick up different amounts of hum interference. This difference in induced hum voltage is amplified by the equipment the cable is plugged into. In spite of these drawbacks, unbalanced lines under 10 feet long, used in controlled environments, usually provide adequate hum rejection.

When connecting balanced equipment to unbalanced equipment, you may want to add a 1:1 ratio audio isolation transformer at the unbalanced input or output (see Figure 5.3). This allows most of the interconnecting cable to be balanced.

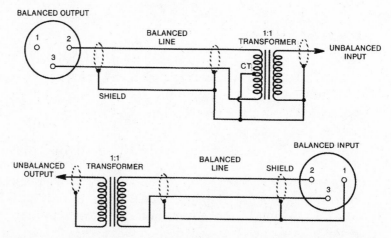

Figure 5.3 Transformer connections between balanced and unbalanced equipment.

Preventing Ground Loops

A major cause of hum is a ground loop. It is the circuit loop that is formed when equipment is connected to ground through more than one path. It occurs when two pieces of audio gear are connected to each other through a shield and also through the AC safety ground.

Figure 5.4 shows a ground loop. Two equipment chassis are connected to two separate safety grounds by their AC cords. Also, the equipment chassis are connected together by the shield of the audio cable. The shield and safety-ground wires form a ground loop. A ground loop also can be created between two cable shields connected to the same pieces of equipment.

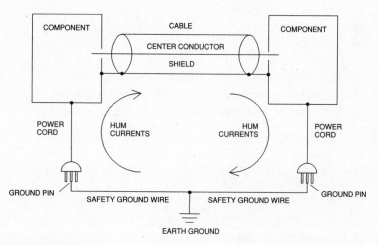

Figure 5.4 A ground loop.

How does a ground loop create hum? In two ways:

- A ground loop acts like a big coil of wire, creating an antenna that is sensitive to hum fields radiated by power wiring in the walls. The bigger the area of the loop, the more hum interference it picks up.

- If the voltage on each chassis is not the same (that is, if the chassis are not connected equally well to earth ground) a 60 Hz current flows between the two chassis, causing a hum signal.

You can get rid of ground loops in several ways:

- Make the loop area small.
- Connect all chassis to the same ground.
- Disconnect the shield at one end.
- Prevent ground loops in racks.
- Prevent accidental ground loops.

The following measures reduce the area of a ground loop, which in turn reduces hum pickup:

- If possible, keep your equipment close together and use short audio cables.
- When running send-and-return cables to a signal processor, tape these cables together.
- When running separate left-channel and right-channel cables for a stereo hookup, tape these cables together. Better yet, use a stereo cable, which combines both channel pairs in a single cable.

Connecting All Chassis to the Same Ground

If you connect all chassis to the same ground, all chassis are at the same ground voltage, so no hum current can flow between them when they are connected by cables.

Suppose you're trying to record a synthesizer by connecting it to your mixer. The synth is plugged into a wall outlet in one room, and the mixer is plugged into a wall outlet in another room. When you connect them with a guitar cord, you hear hum. What's going on?

Chances are that the outlets are fed from different circuit breakers, so the outlets are at different ground voltages. When you plug your synth and mixer into these separated outlets, and connect the equipment together with a guitar cord, the difference in ground voltages makes a 60 Hz hum current flow between the synth and mixer. That's a ground loop.

One solution is to plug all your equipment into one or more outlet strips fed from the same circuit breaker. That way, the ground voltage for all the equipment is the same. Plug the electric musical instruments and recording equipment into the same strips. Use long, thick extension cords if necessary for distant equipment, but make sure that the current requirement of the system (the sum of the equipment fuse ratings) doesn't exceed the amperage rating for that circuit.

Another solution is to use a transformer-isolated direct box between the synth and your mixer. Unlike a guitar cord, the transformer passes the signal without connecting the two chassis together.

The orientation of 2-prong AC cords makes a difference, too. For each piece of audio gear, rotate the 2-prong power cord in its outlet to find the minimum-hum position. Follow this procedure to find the best orientation for the plug:

1. Find an electrical ground such as a metal cold-water pipe, the U-shaped hole in 3-prong wall outlets, or the metal screw that holds the cover plate to the wall outlet.

2. Check to see whether the U-shaped hole or metal screw is actually grounded by connecting a neon tester between the hole or screw and the outlet sockets. If the tester glows in either of the sockets, the hole or screw is grounded. If not, use the cold water pipe ground for the procedure. If you are using the cold-water pipe as ground, be sure that part of the line is not plastic pipe, or this will not be a proper ground.

3. Unplug all the audio cables and ground leads from the component under test. Turn it on.

4. Connect the neon tester between the component's chassis and the ground (from step 1). If the tester glows, reverse the AC power plug in the outlet. The position causing no glow is correct.

5. Mark the proper polarity on all outlets and equipment plugs.

> **Caution:** If the tester glows with both orientations of the plug, the chassis is hot electrically, and the piece of equipment should be repaired before use.

If you have a small home-recording system with 2-prong power cords and short unbalanced cables, you should have no hum problems if you follow these suggestions.

Disconnecting the Shield at One End

Another way to prevent ground loops is to break the loop by disconnecting the cable shield at one end so that no hum current flows between equipment. Normally, this works only for balanced equipment with XLR-type connectors.

Wire the cable shields to prevent ground loops as follows: In each line-level balanced cable, connect the shield *at one end only* (in the female XLR connector) (see Figure 5.5). That is, solder the cable shield to pin 1 in the female connector going to the equipment output. Leave the shield unsoldered in the male connector going to the equipment input—cut it short and shrink-tube it so that it doesn't short to other contacts.

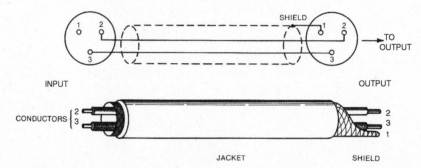

Figure 5.5 Recommended shield connections for balanced line-level cables.

This arrangement is called a *telescoping shield* because the shield, being unconnected at one end, could be squeezed together or collapsed like a telescope. The two conductors from pins 2 and 3 carry the audio signal. The shield still drains electrostatic interference to ground through its single ground connection.

If the shield were connected at both ends, hum currents might flow between the two components. That is, a ground loop might be set up between the shield and the safety ground wires, causing hum.

A microphone cable is an exception to this rule. A microphone-cable shield should be tied (connected) to pin 1 on both ends; otherwise, the microphone housing isn't grounded. Be sure to label your different types of cables accordingly.

In the cables that connect unbalanced equipment, the shield normally must be connected to ground at *both* ends because the shield carries the signal along with the center conductor. Usually this doesn't create a serious ground loop unless the components have 3-wire power cords.

However, if the two components are plugged into outlets on different circuit breakers, they may be at different ground voltages, which can cause a slight hum. Try to plug all equipment into the same outlet strip.

Suppose you have two pieces of unbalanced equipment that must be plugged into AC outlets on different breakers. If you hear hum after connecting them, use two cables instead and wire a 1:1 isolation transformer between them (see Figure 5.6). This disconnects the shield and breaks a ground loop.

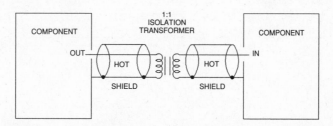

Figure 5.6 Wiring an isolation transformer between two unbalanced devices.

Another way to disconnect the shield is by using a direct box. If you get hum when you plug a synth into your mixer with a guitar cord, use a direct box instead. On the direct box, flip the ground-lift switch to the lowest hum position.

Suppose two unbalanced devices each have 3-prong power cords plugged into the same strip and they are connected by a cable. Unsolder or cut the shield at one end of that cable to break a ground loop (see Figure 5.7). The safety-ground leads, instead of the shield, serve as the signal return path.

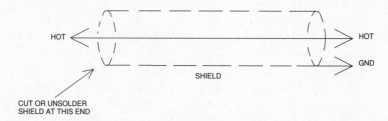

Figure 5.7 Using telescoping 1-conductor shielded cable for connecting unbalanced equipment with 3-prong power cords.

If you pick up radio frequency interference (RFI) with a telescoping shield, connect the unconnected end of the shield of each cable to pin 1 through a 0.01 uF capacitor. This works for balanced or unbalanced circuits, and is explained in more detail later in this chapter.

If you ground a microphone-connector box locally that is installed in a wall, this creates a ground loop. Do not ground the connector box except through its cable shield (see Figure 5.8).

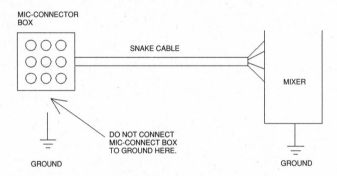

Figure 5.8 Proper grounding for a microphone-connector box.

Preventing Ground Loops in Racks

Recall from Chapter 2 that a rack is usually a grounded metal cabinet used to hold signal processors and patch panels. Audio equipment bolts onto *rack channels*, which are vertical metal strips with holes in them. Inside the rack is an AC outlet strip to power the rack equipment. Also inside the rack, near the bottom, a *rack ground* should be bonded securely to the rack. Try to put all unbalanced equipment in a single rack to shorten the interconnecting cables.

A ground loop can occur when two chassis of unbalanced equipment contact each other through a rack. To prevent this, consider putting unbalanced equipment in a wooden rack with wooden rack channels. Keep the chassis separated (insulated) from each other with electrical tape, or physically separated with a spacer. If you must use a rack with metal rails, isolate all the unbalanced rack equipment from the rack (and each other) by using electrical tape, nylon mounting bolts, and nylon washers.

A rack in a recording studio often contains a patch panel or patch bay. Ground loops between equipment can occur when you use a patch panel to connect one piece of equipment to another. The telescoping shield connections prevent such ground loops, provided that you

- Don't ground the jack sleeves at the patch bay. In addition, connect corresponding pairs of input and output jack sleeves together at the patch bay (see Figure 5.9). An example of a corresponding pair is "Tape Track 7 out" and "Mixer Tape Input 7."

or

- Don't connect anything to sleeves of patch bay jacks wired to equipment inputs. In addition, connect input cable shields to the rack ground bus (see Figure 5.10).

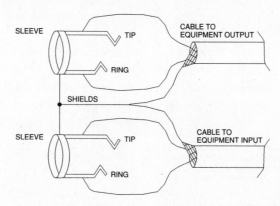

Figure 5.9 One method of wiring a patch bay to prevent ground loops.

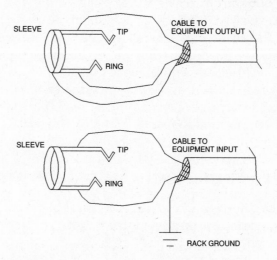

Figure 5.10 Another method of wiring a patch bay to prevent ground loops.

Preventing Accidental Ground Loops

Each audio cable should have an insulating rubber or plastic jacket to prevent ground loops. If the shield is exposed, it can contact grounded metallic surfaces at more than one point, creating a ground loop.

Inside some XLR-type cable connectors is a ground lug that contacts the metallic connector shell. If the ground lug is soldered to pin 1 (the shield's pin), the shell is connected to the shield through the ground lug and pin 1. Ground loops may occur if the shell touches a metallic surface. Also, in some equipment, the audio ground on pin 1 is isolated from the chassis. Pin 1 to ground lug defeats the isolation when an XLR is plugged in.

Do not connect the ground lug to pin 1. An exception might be in the controlled environment of a studio; if the shell is grounded through pin 1, the shell acts as a shield to reduce pickup of hum and radio frequency interference by the conductors inside the shell. However, some phantom power supplies hum if the mic cable connector shell is grounded to pin 1.

Do Not Disconnect the Safety Ground

Some people try to prevent ground loops by installing an electrical 3-to-2 adapter on each power cord. This breaks the loop by removing the safety ground. But it creates a safety hazard and is not recommended, nor is it necessary.

In an attempt to break up a ground loop, some people try to use cable shields as a safety ground and float (remove) the safety ground pins on all but one piece of equipment in a chain. However, an audio cable shield can't carry the heavy current in the event of a power short to chassis, so shocks may occur anyway. Use the other methods described earlier to prevent ground loops.

Other Hum-Reduction Techniques

Microphones and electric guitars are especially sensitive to hum pickup because they produce low-level signals. These signals need a lot of amplification, which also amplifies any hum picked up by these devices and/or their cables.

Microphone Hum

Use these tips to minimize microphone hum pickup:

- Use low-impedance microphones (150 to 600 ohms), which pick up less hum than high-impedance microphones.

- Use microphones with balanced outputs (3-pin connectors), which pick up less hum than unbalanced microphones (hot conductor plus shield).

- Use a balanced cable from the mic to the input. If you have unbalanced microphone inputs on your recorder or mixer, solder the shield and pin-3 lead to the phone plug sleeve or ground terminal; solder the pin-2 lead to the plug's hot or tip terminal.

- If the mic cable still picks up hum, unbalance the cable through a 1:1 transformer that is plugged directly into the input (refer to Figure 5.3).

- If hum pickup is severe with dynamic microphones, use dynamic microphones with humbucking coils built in. An example is the Shure Beta 58. Or change to a condenser mic.

- Use twisted-pair mic cable to reduce pickup of magnetically induced hum. The more shield coverage, the less pickup of electrostatically coupled hum. *Braided* shield generally offers the best coverage, *double-spiral wrapped* is next best, and *spiral-wrapped* is worst.

- Use star-quad cables such as those made by Canare, Mogami, or Belden.

- Routinely check the microphone cables to make sure the shield is connected at both ends.

- Check that the mic-connector set screw is securely screwed clockwise into the mic handle. This set screw is in the handle near the connector.

- For outdoor work, tape over cracks between connectors to keep out dust and rain.

Electric Guitar Hum

Electric guitars are high-impedance, unbalanced devices, which makes them especially susceptible to hum. Try the following suggestions to reduce hum associated with electric guitars:

- Replace or repair guitar cords that have broken shields. Use only high-quality cords with metal-jacket plugs.

- Flip the polarity switch (if present) on the guitar amp to the minimum-hum position.

- Flip the ground-lift switch on each direct box to the minimum-hum position.

- Have the guitarist turn up the volume of the guitar all the way, and then turn down the gain on the guitar amp.

- Have the guitarist move around or turn around (rotate) to find a spot with minimum hum pickup.

- Replace any defective tubes in the guitar amp. If the power-supply filter capacitors in the guitar amp are corroded, replace them. This replacement should be done by an authorized technician.

- Use guitars with humbucking pickups, or install modern humbuckers in older guitars.

- Use a quieter amplifier.

Reducing Radio Frequency Interference

RFI is heard as buzzing, clicks, radio programs, or "hash" in the audio signal. It's caused by CB transmitters, computers, lightning, radar, radio and TV transmitters, industrial machines, auto ignitions, stage lighting, and other sources. Many of the following techniques are the same used to reduce hum from other sources. To reduce RFI:

- Use wide copper straps or braids, rather than wires, for ground connections. This reduces the high ground resistance caused by *skin effect*—the tendency of RF signals to travel on the outside of a conductor.

- Install high-quality RFI filters in the AC power outlets. The cheap types available from local electronics shops are generally ineffective.

- Physically separate the lighting power wiring from the audio cables.

- Avoid SCR dimmers—instead, use multiwatt incandescent bulbs to vary the studio lighting levels.

- Use enclosed metal equipment racks. The metal enclosure acts as a shield.

- Avoid long ground leads and unbalanced lines that are over 10 feet long.

Also, for each unbalanced mic input, consider connecting a 0.01 uF capacitor between the hot terminal and ground (if the mixer doesn't already have such a capacitor). Then, if the shell of the mic input connector isn't grounded to the mixer chassis, connect a 0.001 uF Mylar capacitor between the shell terminal and the mixer chassis (if the mixer doesn't already have such a capacitor).

Long speaker cables can act as an RF antenna. If you suspect the cables to be the source of the RFI, bypass the RF to ground at the power-amp speaker terminals. Connect a 0.01 uF to 0.03 uF disk capacitor between one speaker lead and the amplifier chassis ground. Use one capacitor per channel. Do the same for the "ground" side of the amp's speaker terminals, if they are above chassis ground.

If RFI is still a serious problem, connect the unconnected end of the telescoping shield of each cable to pin 1 through a 0.01 uF capacitor. This bypasses the RFI to ground without connecting the audio signal to ground. Also, for balanced lines in microphone junction boxes, solder a 0.01 uF capacitor between pins 1 and 2, and between pins 1 and 3. You also could do this at the mixer at each balanced mic input.

Special Considerations for On-Location Work

In a remote recording job, you're outside the controlled environment of the studio. You need to take special precautions with power distribution, electric guitar grounding, and interconnecting multiple sound systems.

Power-Distribution System

A touring sound company should carry its own single-phase power distribution system because the building ground wiring on-location is unreliable. See Figure 5.11 for a suggested AC power distribution system.

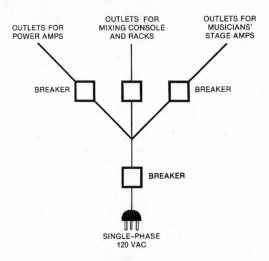

Figure 5.11 An AC power distribution system for a touring sound system.

Electric Guitar Grounding

At times, electric guitar players can receive a shock when they touch their guitar and a sound-system microphone simultaneously. This occurs when the guitar amp is plugged into an electrical outlet on stage, and the mixing console (to which the mics are grounded) is plugged into a separate outlet across the room. As stated before, these two power points may be at widely different ground voltages, so a current can flow between the grounded mic housing and the grounded guitar strings.

> **Caution:** Electric guitar shock is especially dangerous when the guitar amp and the console are on different phases of the AC mains.

It helps to power all instrument amps and audio gear from the same AC distribution outlets. That is, run a heavy extension cord from a stage outlet back to the mixing console (or vice versa). Plug all the power-cord ground pins into grounded outlets. That way, you prevent shocks and hum at the same time.

If this doesn't help, tape a foam windscreen onto each mic to insulate the guitarist from shocks. This won't help, however, if the guitarist holds the microphone.

If you're picking up the electric guitar direct, use a transformer-isolated direct box and set the ground-lift switch to the minimum-hum position.

Using a neon tester or voltmeter, measure the voltage between the electric guitar strings and the metal grille of the microphones. If there is a voltage, flip the polarity switch on the amp or reverse its AC plug in the outlet (for 2-prong plugs).

Interconnecting Multiple Sound Systems

When live concerts are recorded, three separate sound systems are commonly used: the house sound-reinforcement system, the stage-monitor system, and the recording system. These three systems share the stage-microphone signals by taking transformer-isolated, balanced feeds from a 3-way *microphone splitter* (see Figure 5.12).

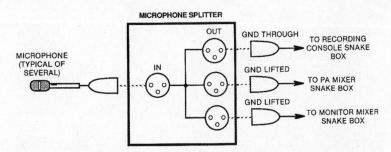

Figure 5.12 Using a microphone splitter to feed three sound systems.

To avoid ground loops between the three systems, ground the cable shields to only one mixer. At the splitter, use the ground-lift switches to disconnect the shields going to the other two mixers. Ground to the mixer that provides the least hum. You might need to power the other two mixers from outlets near the first mixer, which is providing the ground for the shields. That way, the three mixers share a common ground.

Often, a radio station or video crew takes an audio feed from a studio's mixing console. In this case, you can prevent a hum problem by using a console with transformer-isolated inputs and outputs. You also can use a 1:1 audio isolation transformer between the console and the feeds (two for stereo). Such a transformer is especially useful when interconnecting balanced and unbalanced equipment. It should have an electrostatic shield and should be able to handle +20 dbm. Mount it in a rack near the patch panel. You also can use a distribution amp with transformer isolated outputs.

If you encounter an unknown system where balanced audio cables might be grounded at both ends, use some cable ground-lift adapters to float the extra ground connection at equipment inputs (see Figure 5.13).

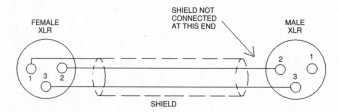

Figure 5.13 A ground-lift adapter for signal cables.

Recall from Chapter 2 that a snake box or stage box is a metal box with multiple mic connectors. If a stage box is grounded through the snake-cable shield, and the box contacts a metallic surface on stage, this condition can cause a ground loop. Don't ground stage boxes. You can also isolate the stage box from metallic surfaces—place on foam pad, wood, etc.

Special Considerations for Small Studios

If you have a small studio with fewer than 20 power cords in use, you can use the wall-outlet safety ground to ground your audio equipment. Plug your equipment into 3-wire grounded outlet strips powered by the same wall-outlet circuit breaker. If your equipment has 2-prong power cords, you probably won't have any ground-related problems if you connect the equipment as described earlier. (In particular, review the section on preventing ground loops. Also see the section on checking the ground at the wall outlet with a neon tester.)

Special Considerations for Large Studios

The following suggestions are for large professional installations using balanced audio lines. If you have a small studio, you may want to skip this section or just read it for the advice it contains.

AC Power Wiring

Hum prevention starts with properly designed power wiring. Sound-system equipment should be powered on its own circuit separate from others, such as those used for lighting or air conditioning, which can put noise spikes on the AC line.

The following are four ways to power the audio system. The first is most effective but most expensive; the last is least effective but least expensive.

- Power the audio system from its own power transformer on a telephone pole outside the studio.

- Get power from an independent breaker box.

- Have an electrician put the audio system on a different phase of the incoming AC mains than the phase(s) other equipment is connected to.

- Power the audio from its own circuit breaker.

In any case, all the audio equipment (including guitar amps in the studio or on stage) should be on the same phase of the power line to prevent hum.

It helps to use *AC isolation transformers* between the AC power outlets and the audio equipment power cords. These transformers remove RFI on the AC line generated by lightning, computers, motors, and other sources.

Telescoping Shields

In each balanced line-level cable, remove the shield from pin 1 inside the male XLR-type connector. Make sure the shield is connected to pin 1 in the female XLR connector. Then plug your recording equipment into local 3-prong grounded outlets and connect audio cables. If you don't hear any hum, you're all set. If you do, keep reading.

Establishing an Earth Ground

Even if your wall outlets have a safety ground, you can't always trust these grounds to have a low-resistance connection to earth ground. It's best to install your own earth ground by using an 8-foot copper rod or pipe (available at electrical supply stores). Drive this rod into moist earth outside the studio. You might need to use several of these, spread apart, for a good ground.

Bond No. 4 gauge, or larger, stranded insulated cable to the ground rod with a pipe clamp (available at hardware stores). In areas with RFI, use a copper strap or braid 4 to 12 inches wide and as short as possible. Run this cable (or strap) up to the console ground bus, or run it to the safety ground in the master outlet strip. The entire ground system should be very low resistance because it carries heavy currents from all the audio shields.

An alternative earth ground is a metallic cold-water pipe (copper pipe is preferable to steel). Securely bond the ground wire to the pipe with a pipe clamp. However, a ground stake is preferable to a cold-water pipe because a water pipe may have plastic sections, or can create a shock hazard for water company workers.

In less critical applications, the ground bus bar in a circuit-breaker box will do because it is connected to the power company's earth ground. However, this safety ground still may carry noise spikes and heavy currents. Again, don't do electrical wiring in the circuit-breaker box unless you know what you're doing.

Try all the earth-grounding methods and use whatever works best.

Ground Wiring

Large studios often require special wiring of the safety ground to prevent ground loops. Although studio power wiring must meet electrical code requirements, the ground wiring may be nonstandard, so confer with the electrician to make sure the work is done as described in this section and also meets code.

In most buildings, the safety ground wire is "daisy chained" or connected from one outlet to the next. This arrangement can cause hum problems because each outlet's ground terminal is at a different resistance above earth ground. Consequently, hum currents may flow between two pieces of audio equipment plugged into separate outlets.

Suppose you're installing a system in a building or home that is already wired for AC power. Install your own safety-ground wires with this procedure:

1. Using low-resistance (No. 10 gauge) stranded insulated wire, ground the chassis of each free-standing piece of equipment separately to the ground bus bar in the circuit-breaker box (or to a ground rod).

2. Connect each separate chassis of rack equipment to the rack ground bus.

3. Connect the rack ground to the ground bus bar in the circuit-breaker box (or to a ground rod).

4. *Only after performing steps 1 through 3*, install electrical 3-to-2 adapters on the 3-prong power cords to float the extra safety-ground connection.

If you're installing new power wiring, use AC outlets with isolated-ground terminals. That is, use special wall outlets that float (isolate) the ground terminal from the wall box; the wall box is grounded through the conduit. Isolated-ground outlets are available from electrical supply houses.

Typical AC outlets with modern wiring contain three wires: hot (black), neutral (white), and ground (bare or green). The ground wire goes to the U-shaped hole in the outlet. Substitute your own ground wire for the bare or green one by following this procedure:

1. Run a low-resistance (No. 10 gauge) insulated wire from each outlet's ground receptacle back to the ground bus bar in the circuit-breaker box (or to a ground rod). Try to keep the lengths of all ground leads about equal for equal resistance to earth ground. These ground wires should never short to the conduit, or you get ground loops.

2. Plug the rack equipment into the rack's AC outlet strip.

3. Plug the 3-prong AC power cord of each piece of equipment (and rack outlet strip) into an isolated-ground AC outlet.

You may want to enclose the power wiring within the walls in grounded metal conduit to prevent hum radiation from the power lines into audio circuits.

A proper grounding scheme resembles a tree (see Figure 5.14). The earth ground is the root system, the ground wires are the big branches, and the rack ground wires are the small branches. This is also called a *star* or *single-point* grounding system.

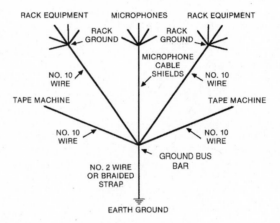

Figure 5.14 Recommended ground layout.

There's a single common ground point for the whole studio: the ground bus bar or ground rod. You connect all the equipment chassis individually to that single ground—not to each other.

Grounding provides three benefits:

- It eliminates voltage differences between equipment chassis by connecting them all solidly to earth ground. Then, when you interconnect components, there is no voltage between them to cause hum.

- It protects people from AC shorts to chassis (via the safety ground).

- It provides a drain path for the oscillating electrostatic charges built up on shields and chassis. These oscillating charges are induced by hum fields from power wiring and transformers, and by RFI fields from transmitters.

For unbalanced equipment in a small studio, these are the most important points to remember about hum prevention:

- Plug all equipment into outlet strips powered by the same breaker.
- Put unbalanced equipment in a single rack, isolated from the rack and each other.
- Use short connecting cables.
- Use balanced mic cables if possible.

For balanced equipment in a large installation:

- Put audio equipment on a separate power feed.
- Use AC isolation transformers or AC line filtering if necessary.
- Consider installing a ground rod.
- In each balanced line-level cable, connect the shield to pin 1 in the female XLR; disconnect the shield from pin 1 in the male XLR.
- If hum is still a problem, and you're installing a system in a building with *existing* power wiring, connect a separate insulated low-resistance wire from each chassis to a single ground point. Connect each chassis of rack equipment separately to rack ground, and connect the rack ground to the single ground point. Finally, put electrical 3-to-2 adapters on the power-cord plugs.
- If you're installing a recording system and *new* power wiring, use isolated-ground outlets. Connect an insulated low-resistance wire from each outlet's ground receptacle to a single ground point. Plug all the rack equipment into the same AC outlet strip in the rack. Plug all the power cords into 3-prong outlets.

By following all these tips, you should be able to connect audio equipment without introducing any hum. Good luck!

6

MICROPHONES

What microphone is best for recording a symphonic band? What's a good piano mic? Should the microphone be a condenser or dynamic, omni or cardioid?

You can answer these questions once you understand the various types of microphones and their specifications. First, it always pays to get a high-quality microphone—which costs at least $125. The microphone is a source of your recorded signal. If that signal is noisy, distorted, or tonally colored, you are stuck with those flaws through the whole recording process. Better get it right up front.

Some manufacturers of quality microphones include AKG, AMS, Astatic, Audio Technica, Beyer, Crown, Electro-Voice, Fostex, Josephson, Milab, Nakamichi, Neumann, Peavey, Schoeps, Sennheiser, Shure, Sony, Toa, and Yamaha.

Even if you operate a MIDI studio and get all your sounds from samples or synthesizers, you still might need a good microphone for sampling, or to record vocals, sax, acoustic guitar, and so on.

A microphone is a *transducer*—a device that converts one form of energy into another. Specifically, a microphone converts acoustical energy (sound) into electrical energy (the signal). Then the electrical signal is amplified and modified by your mixer. By controlling the signal, you also control the recorded sound quality.

Transducer Types

Microphones for recording can be grouped into two types depending on how they convert sound to electricity: dynamic or condenser. In a dynamic microphone, a moving conductor cuts magnetic lines of force to generate electricity. Two types of dynamic microphones are *moving-coil* and *ribbon*.

A moving-coil microphone is popularly referred to as a dynamic mic, even though it is only one member of the dynamic family (see Figure 6.1). A coil of wire attached to a diaphragm is suspended in a magnetic field. When sound waves vibrate the diaphragm, the coil vibrates in the magnetic field and generates an electrical signal similar to the incoming sound wave.

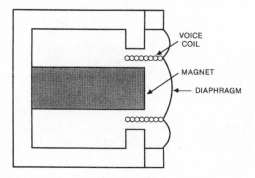

Figure 6.1 A dynamic moving-coil transducer.

In a ribbon microphone, a thin metal foil or ribbon is suspended in a magnetic field (see Figure 6.2). Sound waves vibrate the ribbon in the field and generate an electrical signal.

In a *condenser* (or *capacitor*) microphone, a conductive diaphragm and an adjacent metallic disk (backplate) are charged to form two plates of a capacitor (see Figure 6.3). Sound waves striking the diaphragm vary the spacing between the plates; this varies the capacitance and generates an electrical signal similar to the incoming sound wave.

The diaphragm and backplate can be charged either by an externally applied voltage, or by a permanently charged *electret* material in the diaphragm or on the backplate. The first type is called an *externally biased* or *air condenser* microphone; the second type is called an *electret condenser* microphone.

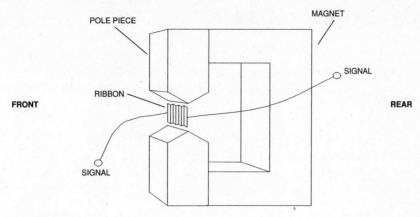

Figure 6.2 A ribbon transducer.

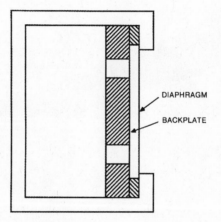

Figure 6.3 A condenser transducer.

Because of its lower diaphragm mass and higher damping, a condenser microphone responds faster than a dynamic microphone to rapidly changing sound waves (transients).

The condenser microphone (see Figures 6.4 and 6.5) generally provides a smooth, detailed sound with a very wide frequency response. With a good condenser microphone, you can hear all the "ting" of the cymbals, or the plucking of each string in a strummed guitar chord. This clear, detailed sound quality makes the condenser microphone especially suitable for miking cymbals, snare drums, acoustic instruments, and studio vocals.

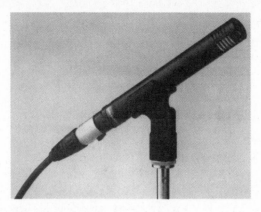

Figure 6.4 The Audio-Technica 4031 unidirectional electret condenser microphone. (Courtesy Audio-Technica U.S., Inc.)

Figure 6.5 The Shure SM-81 unidirectional electret condenser microphone. (Courtesy Shure Brothers, Inc.)

A condenser microphone requires a power supply to operate, such as a battery or external *phantom power* supply. Phantom power is 12 to 48 volts DC applied to pins 2 and 3 of the microphone connector through two equal resistors. The microphone receives phantom power and sends audio signals on the same two conductors. Many mixing consoles supply phantom powering at their mic input connectors; the microphone simply plugs into the console for its power supply.

In contrast, the moving-coil dynamic microphone works without any power supply and provides a reliable signal under a wide range of environmental conditions. A well-designed moving-coil microphone is quite rugged and can accept very loud sounds without overloading. This capability suits it for miking guitar amps and drums.

The moving-coil microphone generally has a slower transient response than the condenser type, so it can be used to soften the fine detail that the condenser picks up. A flat-response moving-coil microphone might be a good choice for woodwinds or brass if you want to take the "edge" off the sound. Moving-coil microphones generally have a rougher response than condensers or ribbons, although moving-coil units of excellent quality are available.

Ribbon microphones, while more delicate than the moving-coil variety, are often prized for their warm, smooth tone quality (see Figure 6.6). For this reason, they work well with digital recording. Ribbon mics are often used on brass instruments to mellow the tone.

Figure 6.6 The Beyer M160 hypercardioid ribbon microphone. (Courtesy Beyer Dynamic, Inc.)

Polar Pattern (Directional Pattern)

Microphones also differ in the way they respond to sounds coming from different directions. An *omnidirectional* microphone is equally sensitive to sounds arriving from all directions. A *unidirectional* microphone is most sensitive to sounds arriving from one direction—in front of the microphone—but discriminates against sounds entering the sides or rear of the microphone (see Figure 6.7). A *bidirectional* microphone is most sensitive to sounds arriving from two directions—in front of and behind the microphone—but rejects sounds entering the sides. Figure 6.8 shows various polar patterns; Figure 6.9 shows a multipattern microphone.

Figure 6.7 The Shure Model SM57 unidirectional dynamic microphone. (Courtesy Shure Brothers, Inc.)

A polar plot is not a geographical map of the reach of a microphone; a microphone does not suddenly become dead outside its polar pattern. There is no "outside." The graph plots sensitivity as distance from the origin. This is not the spatial spread of the pattern.

In most microphones, it's desirable that the polar pattern stays reasonably consistent at all frequencies. If not, you hear off-axis coloration: the mic sounds tonally different on and off axis. Uniform polar patterns at different frequencies indicate similar frequency responses at different angles of incidence.

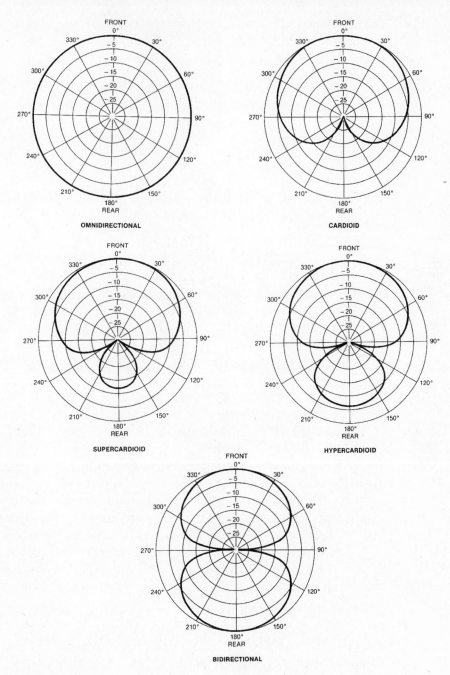

Figure 6.8 Various polar patterns, with sensitivity plotted vs. angle of sound incidence.

Figure 6.9 The AKG C-414EB/P48 multipattern dual-diaphragm condenser microphone. (Courtesy AKG Acoustics, Inc.)

The unidirectional classification can be further divided into *cardioid*, *supercardioid*, and *hypercardioid* pickup characteristics. A microphone with a cardioid pattern is sensitive to sounds arriving from a broad angle in front of the microphone. It is about 6 db less sensitive at the sides, and about 15 to 25 db less sensitive at the rear. The supercardioid pattern is 8.7 db less sensitive at the sides and has two areas of least pickup at 125 degrees away from the front. The hypercardioid pattern is 12 db less sensitive at the sides and has two areas of least pickup at 110 degrees away from the front.

To hear how a cardioid pickup pattern works, talk into a cardioid microphone from all sides while listening to its output. Your reproduced voice is loudest when you talk into the front of the microphone and softest when you talk into the rear.

Because they discriminate against sounds to the sides and rear, cardioids help to reject unwanted sounds such as room acoustics (reverberation), feedback, or leakage (off-mic sounds from other instruments). Unidirectional (cardioid) mics are the most popular choice for this reason. They provide good isolation or separation between recorded tracks.

Omnidirectional microphones have some characteristics that make them especially useful for certain applications. Use omnidirectional microphones when you need

- All-around pickup

- Pickup of room reverberation

- Low sensitivity to pop (explosive breath sounds)

- Low handling noise

- No up-close bass boost (proximity effect)

- Extended low-frequency response (in condenser microphones)

- Lower cost in general

Use unidirectional mics when you need

- Selective pickup
- Rejection of room acoustics, background noise, and leakage
- Up-close bass boost
- Better gain-before-feedback in a sound-reinforcement system
- Coincident or near-coincident stereo miking (explained in Chapter 7)

Use a cardioid pickup pattern when you need

- A broad-angle pickup of sources in front of the microphone
- Maximum rejection of sound approaching the rear of the microphone

Use a supercardioid pickup pattern when you need

- Maximum difference between front-hemisphere and rear-hemisphere pickup
- More isolation than a cardioid

Use a hypercardioid pickup pattern when you need

- Maximum side rejection in a unidirectional microphone
- Maximum isolation—maximum rejection of reverberation, leakage, feedback, and background noise

Use a bidirectional microphone when you need

- Front and rear pickup, with side sounds rejected (for across-table interviews or 2-part vocal groups, for example)
- Maximum isolation of an orchestral section miked overhead, aiming down
- Blumlein stereo miking (two bidirectional mics crossed at 90 degrees)

Note that either the condenser or moving-coil types mentioned earlier can be obtained with any kind of directional pattern (except bidirectional moving-coil). Ribbon microphones are either bidirectional or hypercardioid. Some condenser mics come with switchable polar patterns.

An omnidirectional boundary microphone (such as a Crown PZM) has a half-omni or hemispherical polar pattern. A unidirectional boundary microphone has a half-supercardioid or half-cardioid polar pattern. The boundary mounting increases the directionality of the microphone, thus reducing pickup of room acoustics. Figure 6.10 classifies microphones according to transducer type and polar pattern.

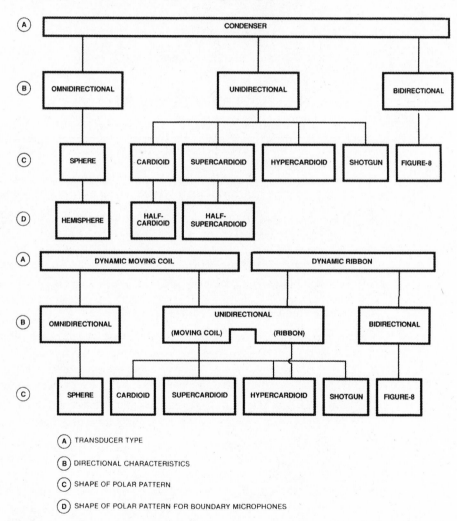

Figure 6.10 Microphone categories.

Frequency Response

As with other audio components, a microphone's frequency response is the range of frequencies that it reproduces at an equal level (within a tolerance, such as ±3 db).

The following is a list of sound sources and the frequency response of a microphone that is adequate to record the source with high fidelity. A wider-range response works too.

Most instruments	80 Hz to 15 kHz
Bass instruments	40 Hz to 9 kHz
Brass and voice	80 Hz to 12 kHz
Cymbals	300 Hz to 15 or 20 kHz
Orchestra or symphonic band	40 Hz to 15 kHz

If possible, use a microphone with a frequency response that rolls off below the lowest fundamental frequency of the instrument to be recorded. For example, the frequency of the low E string on an acoustic guitar is 82.41 Hz. A mic used on the acoustic guitar ideally should roll off below that frequency to avoid picking up low-frequency noise and room rumble. Some microphones provide a low-frequency cutoff switch for this purpose. Or, you can filter out the unneeded lows at the mixer.

A *frequency-response curve* is a graph of output level in db at various frequencies. For a microphone, the output level at 1 kHz is placed at the 0 db line on the graph, and the levels produced at other frequencies are so many db above or below that reference level.

The shape of the response curve usually indicates the tonal balance of the microphone pickup at a specified distance from the sound source. (If the distance is not specified, it's probably 2 to 3 feet.) For example, a microphone with a flat, extended response reproduces the fundamental frequencies and harmonics in the same proportion as the sound source. Thus, a flat-response mic tends to provide accurate, natural reproduction at that distance.

A microphone with a rising high end or a "presence peak" around 5 to 10 kHz emphasizes the higher harmonics (see Figure 6.11). The subjective effect is a crisp, articulate sound. This type of response is sometimes called a "tailored" or "contoured" response. It's popular for guitar amps and drums because it adds punch and emphasizes attack. Some microphones have switches to adjust the frequency response.

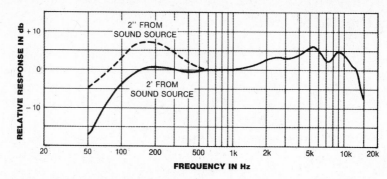

Figure 6.11 An example of the frequency response of a microphone with proximity effect and a presence peak around 5 kHz.

Most unidirectional and bidirectional microphones boost the bass when used within a few inches of a sound source. You've heard how the sound gets bassy when a vocalist sings right into the mic. This low-frequency boost related to close mic placement is called the *proximity effect*, and it's often plotted on the frequency-response graph.

In any directional mic, there are holes or screens behind the diaphragm where sound goes in. If all these holes are in the mic capsule (transducer), the mic is a single-D type. If some of the holes are in the handle, the mic is a multiple-D or variable-D type. Single-D types have the proximity effect; multiple-D or variable-D types do not.

The warmth created by the proximity effect adds a pleasing fullness to drums. In most recording situations, however, the proximity effect lends an unnatural boomy or bassy sound to the instrument or voice picked up by the mic. To minimize proximity effect, use a multiple-D or variable-D type or switch in the bass roll off on the mic (if any). Alternatively, you can roll off the excess bass with your mixer's equalizer until the sound is natural. By doing so, you also reduce low-frequency leakage picked up by the microphone.

Note that microphone placement can greatly affect the recorded tone quality. A flat-response microphone does not always guarantee high-fidelity sound, because mic placement has such a strong influence. Tonal effects of microphone placement are covered in Chapter 7.

Impedance

A microphone's impedance is its effective output resistance at 1 kHz. Any mic used for recording should be low impedance (150 to 600 ohms). Low impedance allows you to run long cables without hum pickup or high-frequency loss. Nearly all solid-state mixers are designed to accept low-impedance mics.

Normally, mixers are designed to have an input impedance at least 7 to 10 times the microphone impedance to avoid loading down the microphone. A typical mixer mic input has an impedance around 1,500 ohms.

Sensitivity

Sensitivity is a measure of the efficiency of a microphone. A high-sensitivity microphone puts out a stronger signal (higher voltage) than a low-sensitivity microphone when both are exposed to a sound source of a given loudness. A low-sensitivity mic requires more mixer gain than a high-sensitivity mic to achieve the same recording level. More gain usually results in more noise.

If you record quiet, distant instruments such as a classical guitar or chamber music, you hear more mixer noise with a low-sensitivity mic than with a high-sensitivity mic, all else being equal. With close-miked pop music, however, sensitivity matters little because the microphone signal level is well above the mixer noise floor. That is, the signal-to-noise ratio is high.

Listed below are typical sensitivity specs for the three transducer types:

Condenser: –65 db re 1 V/microbar (high sensitivity)
Moving coil: –75 db re 1 V/microbar (medium sensitivity)
Ribbon or small moving coil: –85 db re 1 V/microbar (low sensitivity)

Differences of a few db among microphones are not critical.

The louder the sound source, the higher the signal voltage the microphone produces. Very loud sources, such as kick drums or guitar amps, can cause a microphone to generate a signal strong enough to overload the mic preamp in your mixer. That's why input attenuators or *pads* are included in mixers to reduce the mic signal level from a loud source.

Maximum SPL

Another microphone specification is Maximum Sound Pressure Level (SPL), a measure of the intensity of a sound. The quietest sound you can hear, the threshold of hearing, measures 0 db SPL. Normal conversation at 1 foot measures about 70 db SPL; painfully loud sound is above 120 db SPL.

Maximum SPL is the SPL at which a microphone starts to distort, usually the SPL at which the mic produces 3% Total Harmonic Distortion (THD). Some manufacturers use 1% THD. A maximum SPL spec of 120 db is good, 135 db is very good, and 150 db is excellent.

A well-designed dynamic microphone can accept very loud sounds without overloading. Even high sound pressure levels move the diaphragm only slightly. A condenser microphone has electronics which can be overloaded by the capsule signal. If an attenuator is placed between the capsule (transducer) and electronics to prevent overload (that is, to increase maximum SPL capability), the signal-to-noise ratio (S/N) is degraded.

Self-Noise

Self-noise or *equivalent noise level* is the electrical noise a microphone produces. An A-weighted self-noise spec of 20 db SPL or less is excellent (quiet), a spec around 30 db SPL is good, and a spec around 40 db SPL is fair.

Because a dynamic microphone has no active electronics to generate noise, it has very low self-noise (hiss) compared to a condenser microphone. Therefore, self-noise for a dynamic mic usually is not specified.

Signal-to-Noise Ratio

Recall from Chapter 3 that signal-to-noise ratio is the difference between a mic's signal level and its self-noise. The higher the SPL of the sound source, the higher the S/N. For an SPL of 94 db, an S/N spec of 74 db is excellent; 64 db is good. The higher the S/N, the cleaner (more noise-free) the signal, and the greater the reach of the microphone.

Reach is the clear pickup of quiet, distant sounds due to high S/N. Reach is not specified in data sheets because any microphone can pick up a source at any distance if the source is loud enough. For example, even a cheap microphone can reach several miles if the sound source is a thunderclap.

Polarity

The polarity spec relates the polarity of the electrical output signal to the acoustic input signal. Most microphones produce a positive voltage at pin 2 with respect to pin 3 when the sound pressure pushes the diaphragm in (positive pressure).

It's important that all your microphones are of the same polarity. If you have two microphones wired in opposite polarity and combined to the same channel, low frequencies in the sound pickup are attenuated or completely canceled out. To prevent this from happening, check that all your microphones are wired identically, as follows:

1. Choose one microphone as a polarity reference. Plug it into your mixer. Talk into it from about 3 inches away and set the meter to peak around 0 VU.

2. Do the same with a second microphone and cable plugged into another input.

3. With both microphones mixed to the same channel, hold the mics together and talk into them again at a distance of 3 inches. If the meter reading is lower, the polarity of the second mic or cable is reversed with respect to the reference. In that case, remove the connector shell from the second mic's cable and reverse the connections to pins 2 and 3 (in one connector only). Use only that cable with that microphone, and mark the cable.

4. If you can remove the connector in the microphone itself, reverse the connections to pins 2 and 3 for mics that are opposite in polarity to the reference. Check a few mics before doing this to make sure the reference mic itself isn't backwards.

Special Microphone Types

The following sections describe three types of recording microphones used for special purposes: *boundary microphones*, *miniature microphones*, and *stereo microphones*.

Boundary Microphone

The boundary microphone is designed to be used on a surface such as a floor, wall, table, piano lid, baffle, or panel. One example of a boundary microphone is the Crown Pressure Zone Microphone PZM-30F (see Figure 6.12). It includes a miniature electret condenser capsule mounted face-down next to a sound-reflecting plate or boundary. Due to this construction, the microphone diaphragm receives direct and reflected sounds in phase at all frequencies, avoiding phase interference between them. Figure 6.13 is a diagram of the construction of a PZM microphone. The claimed benefits are a wide, smooth frequency response (free of phase cancellations), excellent clarity and reach, a hemispherical polar pattern, and uniform frequency response anywhere around the microphone.

Figure 6.12 The Crown PZM-30F, a boundary microphone. (Courtesy Crown International)

In the studio, a boundary microphone is typically taped to the underside of a piano lid or to the wall for pickup of room ambience. It can be used on hard baffles between instruments, or on a panel to make it directional.

Boundary microphones are also available with a unidirectional polar pattern. They have the benefits of both boundary mounting and the unidirectional pattern. Such microphones are well suited for lecterns, news desks, and stage-floor pickup of drama or musicals.

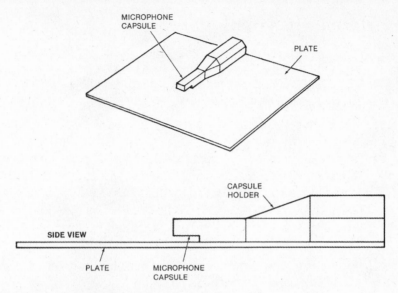

Figure 6.13 Typical PZM construction.

Miniature Condenser Microphone

Miniature condenser microphones can be attached to drum rims, flutes, horn, guitars, and so on. The sound quality is on a par with larger studio microphones and the price is relatively low. With these tiny units, you can mike a live band for recording without cluttering up the stage with boom stands (see Figure 6.14). You can mike a whole drum set with two or three of these, but you lose individual control of each drum in the mix. Still, this system is much less costly than miking each drum, and can sound quite good with some bass boost. Compared to large mics, miniature mics tend to have more noise (hiss) in distant-miking applications.

Stereo Microphone

A stereo microphone combines two directional mic capsules in a single housing for convenient stereo recording (see Figure 6.15). Simply place the mic a suitable distance and height from the sound source, and you get a stereo recording with little fuss. Because there is no spacing between the mic capsules, there also is no delay or phase shift between their signals. Stereo microphones are mono-compatible—the frequency response is the same in mono and stereo—because there are no phase cancellations if the two channels are combined.

Figure 6.14 The Crown GLM-100, a miniature condenser microphone. (Courtesy Crown International)

Figure 6.15 The AKG C422 stereo condenser microphone. (Courtesy AKG Acoustics Inc.)

Microphone Selection

Table 6.1 summarizes recording requirements and their corresponding microphone characteristics.

Table 6.1 Microphone characteristics.

Requirement	Characteristic
Natural, smooth tone quality	Flat frequency response
Bright, present tone quality	Rising frequency response
Extended lows	Omni condenser or dynamic with extended low-frequency response
Extended highs (detailed sound)	Condenser
Reduced "edge" or detail	Dynamic
Boosted bass up close	Single-D cardioid
Flat bass response up close	Omnidirectional, multiple-D cardioid, or single-D cardioid with bass roll off
Reduced pickup of leakage, feedback, and room acoustics	Unidirectional, or omni up close
Enhanced pickup of room acoustics	Omnidirectional, or unidirectional farther away
Miking close to a surface, even coverage of moving sources or large sources, inconspicuous mic	Boundary mic or miniature mic
Coincident or near-coincident stereo (see Chapter 18)	Unidirectional mics or stereo mic
Extra ruggedness	Moving coil (dynamic)
Reduced handling noise	Omni, or unidirectional with shock mount
Reduced breath popping	Omni, or unidirectional with pop filter
Distortion-free pickup of very loud sounds	Condenser with high maximum SPL spec, or dynamic
Noise-free pickup of quiet sounds	Low self-noise, high sensitivity

Suppose you want to record a grand piano playing with several other instruments. You need the microphone to reduce leakage; Table 6.1 recommends a unidirectional mic or an omni mic up close. For this particular piano, you also want a natural sound, for which the table suggests a mic with a flat frequency response. You want a detailed sound, so a condenser mic is the choice. A microphone with all these characteristics is a flat response, unidirectional condenser mic. If you're miking close to a surface (the piano lid), a boundary mic is recommended.

Now suppose you're recording an acoustic guitar on stage, and the guitarist roams around. This is a moving sound source, for which the table recommends a miniature microphone attached to the guitar. Feedback and leakage are not a problem because you're miking close, so you can use an omni mic. Thus, an omni condenser mic is a good choice for this application.

For a home studio, a suggested first choice is a cardioid condenser microphone with a flat frequency response. This type of microphone is especially good for studio vocals, cymbals and percussion, acoustic guitar, and piano. Remember that it needs a power supply to operate, such as a battery or phantom power supply.

Your second choice of microphone for a home studio is a cardioid dynamic microphone with a presence peak in the frequency response. This type is good for drums and guitar amps.

Recall that cardioid (unidirectional) is recommended over omnidirectional for a home studio because the cardioid pattern rejects the background noise and room reverb that are problems in typical home studios. Otherwise, omni mics tend to offer better performance at lower cost.

Microphone Accessories

There are many devices used with microphones to route their signals or to make them more useful, including *pop filters*, *stands* and *booms*, *shock mounts*, *cables* and *connectors*, *junction boxes* and *snakes*, and *splitters*.

Pop Filters

A much needed accessory for a vocalist's microphone is a foam pop filter or *windscreen*. When a vocalist sings a word emphasizing "p," "b," or "t" sounds, a turbulent puff of air is forced from the mouth. A microphone placed close to the mouth is hit by this air puff, resulting in a thump or little explosion called a *pop*. The windscreen reduces this problem. Some microphones have pop filters or ball-shaped grilles built in.

Pop is also reduced by placing the vocalist's mic above or to the side of the mouth, or by using an omnidirectional microphone.

Stands and Booms

Stands and booms hold the microphones and let you position them as desired. A microphone stand has a heavy metal base that supports a vertical pipe. At the top of the pipe is a rotating clutch that lets you adjust the height of a smaller telescoping pipe inside the larger one. The top of the small pipe has a standard ⅝-inch 27 thread, which screws into a microphone stand adapter.

A boom is a long horizontal pipe that attaches to the small vertical pipe. The angle and length of the boom are adjustable. The end of the boom is threaded to accept a microphone stand adapter, and the opposite end is weighted to balance the weight of the microphone.

Shock Mounts

A shock mount holds a microphone in a resilient suspension to isolate the microphone from mechanical vibrations, such as bumps to the mic stand and floor thumps.

Many microphones have an internal shock mount that isolates the microphone capsule from its housing; this reduces handling noise as well as stand thumps.

Cables and Connectors

Microphone cables carry the electrical signal from the microphone to the mixing console or tape recorder. With low-impedance microphones, you can use hundreds of feet of cable with little or no signal degradation. Some microphones have a permanently attached cable for convenience and low cost; others have a connector in the handle to accept a separate microphone cable. The second method is preferred for serious recording because if the cable breaks, you have to repair or replace only the cable, not the whole microphone.

Microphone cables are made of one or two insulated conductors surrounded by a fine-wire mesh shield to keep out electrostatic hum. If you hear a loud buzz when you plug in a microphone, check that the shield is securely soldered in place.

After acquiring a microphone, you may need to wire its 2-conductor shielded, balanced-line cable to a 3-pin audio connector:

1. Solder the shield to pin 1.

2. Solder the hot conductor to pin 2.

3. Solder the other conductor to pin 3.

The hot conductor (specified in the data sheet) produces a positive voltage at the instant that sound pressure pushes the diaphragm inward.

If the microphone output is 3-pin balanced, but your recorder or mixer mic input is an unbalanced phone jack, a different wiring is needed:

1. Solder the hot conductor to the tip terminal of the phone plug.

2. Solder both the shield and the other conductor to the long ground lug of the phone plug.

Junction Boxes and Snakes

It is messy and time-consuming to run several individual mic cables from many microphones all the way to a mixer. Recall from Chapter 2 that you can plug all the mics in the studio into a junction box or stage box with multiple connectors. The snake—a single, thick, multiconductor cable—carries the signals to the mixer. At the mixer end, the cable divides into several mic connectors that plug into the mixer.

Splitters

When recording a live band, you need to have each microphone feed its signal simultaneously to your recording mixer and the band's sound-reinforcement mixer. A microphone splitter does the job. It has one input for each microphone and two or three isolated outputs per microphone to feed each mixer.

Microphone manufacturers are happy to send you free catalogs and application notes. Your dealers may have this literature, or you can get the company addresses from them.

Remember, you can use any microphone on any instrument if it sounds good to you. Just try it and see if you like it. Quality recordings, however, always require quality microphones with a smooth, wide-range frequency response, low noise, and low distortion.

BASIC MICROPHONE TECHNIQUES

Suppose you're going to pick up a singer or musical instrument with a microphone. Which mic should you choose? Where should you place it?

Microphone selection and placement—mic technique—greatly affects the sound of a recording. Even if your tape recorder and mixer are the best available, the final result is poor unless you choose and place your microphones carefully. This chapter covers the general fundamentals of mic technique; the following chapter describes techniques for individual instruments.

Microphone Selection

Chapter 6 discusses the various types of microphones. Is there a correct microphone to use in each application? No. Every microphone sounds different; choose the microphone that gives you the sound you want. Still, there are some guidelines that apply in most situations.

Frequency Response

The frequency response of a microphone affects the reproduced tone quality. A flat-response microphone tends to sound natural; a mic with emphasized high-frequency response sounds brighter or more trebley. A microphone that rolls off below the range of the instrument minimizes pickup of room rumble; a mic that rolls off low frequencies within the range of the instrument tends to sound thin.

Most condenser microphones have an extended high-frequency response, making them suitable for cymbals or instruments requiring a detailed sound, such as acoustic guitar, strings, piano, and voice. Dynamic moving-coil microphones have a response adequate for drums, guitar amps, horns, and woodwinds.

Polar Pattern

The more room ambience that is recorded with an instrument, the more distant that instrument sounds. The more an instrument's leakage is recorded by other mics, the more distant that instrument sounds. The polar pattern of a microphone affects the amount of leakage and ambience that are picked up.

Because of its greater pickup of ambience and leakage, an omnidirectional microphone sounds more distant than a directional microphone when both are placed the same distance from an instrument. Thus, an omnidirectional microphone must be placed closer to an instrument than a directional microphone to reproduce the same sense of distance.

Quantity of Microphones

The number of microphones required varies with the recording situation. Use just two microphones (or a stereo microphone) when you want to record an overall acoustic blend of the instruments and room ambience (see Figure 7.1). Many ensembles can be recorded quite well this way. This technique is usually effective for an orchestra, symphonic band, choir, string quartet, pipe organ, small folk group, or vocal quartet.

On the other hand, pop-music groups are usually recorded with multiple microphones—one or more mics for each instrument or instrumental section. Miking every instrument lets you use your mixer to control the balance (relative loudness) among instruments by adjusting the volume control for each microphone (see Figure 7.2).

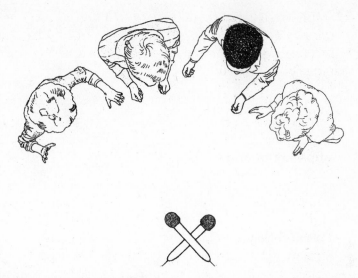

Figure 7.1 Overall miking of a musical ensemble with two distant microphones.

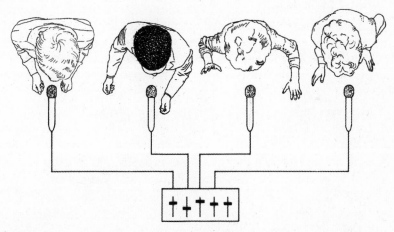

Figure 7.2 Individual miking with multiple close microphones and a mixer.

For greatest clarity in a multimic recording, use as few microphones as necessary to get a good sound. Don't use two microphones when one does the job. To achieve this, sometimes you can cover two or more sound sources with a single microphone (see Figure 7.3). A brass section of four players can be covered with just one microphone on four players, or with one microphone on every two players.

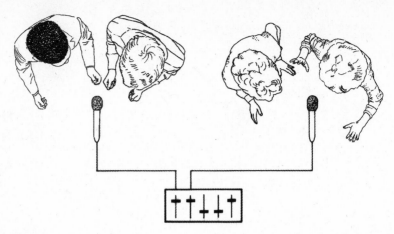

Figure 7.3 Multiple miking with several sound sources on each microphone.

The disadvantage of picking up several instruments with one microphone is that during mixdown, you can't adjust the balance among instruments recorded on the same track. For a proper blend, the instruments must be balanced acoustically in the studio while making the recording. Too-quiet instruments should be moved closer to the mic, and vice versa.

Placement of Microphones

Microphone placement affects the sense of distance of a recorded instrument. Mike close (a few inches) to achieve a tight, present sound. Mike farther away (1½ feet) for a distant, spacious sound.

The farther a microphone is from its sound source, the more the microphone picks up room acoustics, background noise, and leakage (off-mic sound) from other instruments. So, mike close to reject these unwanted sounds; mike farther away to add a live, loose, airy feel to overdubs of drums, lead guitar solos, and horns, for example.

Classical music is always recorded at a distance because concert hall reverberation is a desirable part of the sound.

Miking Distance Effects

The levels of reverberation, leakage, and background noise in a studio are pretty much the same throughout the room, at any microphone position. The closer you place a microphone to a sound source, however, the louder that source sounds at the microphone. The direct sound level increases rapidly as the mic approaches the instrument. Consequently, close mic placement picks up a high ratio of desired signal (the instrument) to undesired signal (ambience, leakage, and noise). The ear interprets this as a tight, close-up sound with *presence* (see Figure 7.4).

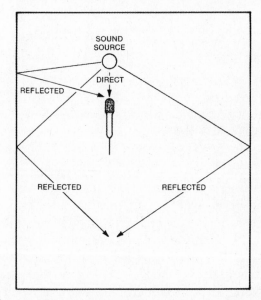

Figure 7.4 A close microphone picks up mainly direct sound, resulting in a close sound quality.

In contrast, distant miking picks up a lot of room reflections because the relative level of the direct sound decreases with distance (see Figure 7.5). To hear the effect of miking distance on the sound, record an instrument or voice at various distances from the mic.

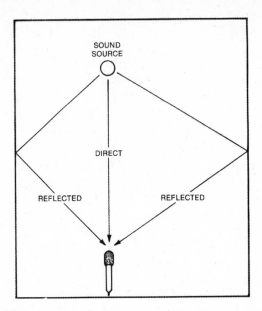

Figure 7.5 A distant microphone picks up mainly reflected sound, resulting in a distant sound quality.

If you carry distant miking to the extreme, the microphone is called an *ambience microphone*. In a studio, such a microphone is placed about 10 feet or more from an instrument to pick up more room echoes and reverberation. A popular microphone for ambience is a boundary microphone taped to the wall. Its output is mixed with the usual close-placed microphones, adding an airy or spacious feeling to the sound of the instrument being recorded. Two are often used for stereo. In live concert recording, ambience microphones placed over the audience pick up audience reaction and concert hall acoustics.

Reducing Leakage

Suppose you're close-miking several instruments simultaneously. Each microphone picks up its own instrument with a close, clear sound quality. Unfortunately, each microphone also picks up leakage from distant instruments. That nice, tight sound you hear on each mic alone may degrade into a distant, muddy sound when all the mics are heard together, due to this leakage (see Figure 7.6).

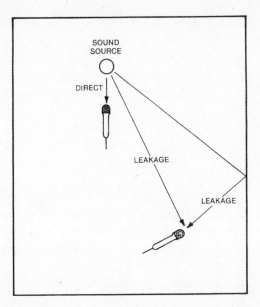

Figure 7.6 Another instrument's microphone may pick up leakage, changing the close sound quality to distant.

When you mike many instruments at once, you can reduce leakage pickup by miking each instrument very closely. Then, the sound pressure level at each microphone is high, and you can turn down the mixer gain of each microphone signal, which reduces leakage at the same time. Another way to prevent leakage is to overdub each instrument one at a time. Directional mics pick up less leakage than omnidirectional mics.

Miking Too Close

Although close miking has several benefits, you should place each microphone only as close as necessary, not as close as possible. Miking too close can make an instrument sound unnatural.

Because most instruments are designed to sound best at a distance of 1 ½ feet or more away, a flat-response microphone placed at that distance tends to pick up a natural or well-balanced timbre (tone quality). When leakage or poor room acoustics forces you to mike in close, you emphasize the part of the instrument that the microphone is near. The tone quality picked up very close may not reflect the tone quality of the entire instrument.

For example, the sound hole of an acoustic guitar strongly resonates at around 80 to 100 Hz. A microphone placed close to the sound hole hears and emphasizes this low-frequency resonance, producing a bassy, boomy recorded timbre that does not exist at a greater miking distance. To make the guitar sound more natural when miked close to the sound hole, you need to roll off the excess bass on your mixer, or use a microphone with a bass roll off in its frequency response.

In general, close miking may give a tonal imbalance, which you can correct partially with equalization or careful microphone selection and placement.

A natural tonal balance usually can be found at a miking distance equal to the size of the sound-radiating part of the instrument. If the situation allows, place the microphone as far from the instrument as the instrument is big. That way, the mic picks up all the sound-radiating parts of the instrument about equally. For example, if the body of an acoustic guitar is 18 inches long, place the mic 18 inches away for a natural tonal balance. If this sounds too distant or muddy, move in a little closer.

Tone Quality

With the microphone at a certain distance from the instrument, if you move the mic left, right, up, or down, you change the recorded tone quality. In one spot, the instrument might sound bassy; in another spot, it might sound honky, and so on. To find a good position, simply place the microphone in several different locations—and monitor the results—until you find one that sounds good to you.

Here's another way to do the same thing. To determine a good starting microphone position, try closing one ear with your finger. Listen to the instrument with the other ear and move around until you find a spot that sounds good. Put the microphone there. Then make a recording and see if it sounds the same as what you heard live. This method is *not* recommended for kick drums or screaming guitar amps!

Why does moving the mic change the tone quality? A musical instrument radiates different tone qualities in different directions, and produces different tone qualities from different parts of the instrument. Thus, you can control the recorded tone quality partly by changing the microphone position relative to the instrument. For example, Figure 7.7 shows the tonal balances picked up at various microphone positions near a guitar.

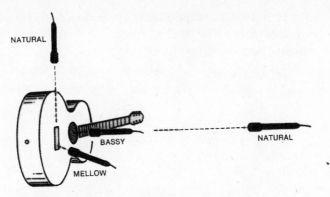

Figure 7.7 Microphone placement affects the recorded tonal balance.

Other instruments share this phenomenon. A trumpet radiates strong highs directly out of the bell, but does not project them to the sides. Thus, a recorded trumpet sounds bright when miked on-axis to the bell and sounds more natural or mellow when miked off to one side. A piano sounds fairly natural miked 1 foot over the middle strings, sounds bassy and dull miked under the soundboard, and sounds constricted miked in a sound hole.

It pays to experiment with all sorts of microphone positions until you find a sound you like. There is no one right way to place the microphones because you place them to achieve your desired tonal balance.

On-Surface Techniques

Sometimes you're forced to place a microphone near a hard reflecting surface. Applications where this might occur include recording drama or opera with the microphones near the stage floor, recording an instrument surrounded by reflective baffles, or recording a piano with the microphone close to the lid. In these situations an unnatural, filtered tone quality can result.

Recall the discussion of comb-filter effect in Chapter 4. Sound travels to the microphone via two paths: directly from the sound source, and reflected off the nearby surface. Because of its longer travel path, the reflected sound is delayed relative to the direct sound. The direct and delayed sound waves combine at the microphone, resulting in phase cancellations of various frequencies (see Figure 7.8). The series of peaks and dips in the net frequency response is the comb-filter effect. The recorded tone quality in this case can be quite colored or unnatural; it is similar to that achieved by phasing or flanging. You might prefer this as a special effect, but it reduces fidelity.

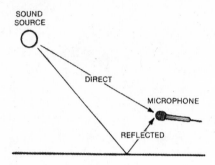

(A) Direct and reflected sound waves.

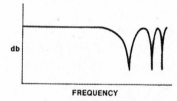

(B) Response curve.

Figure 7.8 A microphone placed near a surface picks up direct sound and delayed reflections, giving a comb-filter frequency response.

Recall from Chapter 6 that *boundary microphones* have been designed for on-surface mounting to avoid the unnatural tone quality caused by placement near a surface. They are constructed with the microphone diaphragm very close to the reflecting surface so that there is no delay in the reflected sound. Direct and reflected sounds combine in phase over the audible range of frequencies, resulting in a flat response (see Figure 7.9).

An omnidirectional boundary mic often is taped to the underside of a piano lid, to a hard-surfaced panel, or to a wall for ambience pickup. A unidirectional boundary mic commonly is used on the stage floor near the footlights, on a lectern, or on a news desk.

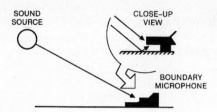

(A) Direct and reflected sound waves.

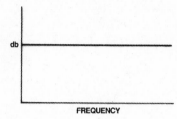

(B) Response curve.

Figure 7.9 A boundary microphone on a surface picks up direct and reflected sound waves in phase.

The Three-to-One Rule

When multiple microphones are mixed to one channel, the distance between microphones should be at least three times the mic-to-source distance. This is called the *3:1 rule* (see Figure 7.10). For example, if two microphones are each placed 1 foot from their sound sources, the microphones should be at least 3 feet apart. Following this rule prevents phase cancellations and the resulting blurred, colored sound quality.

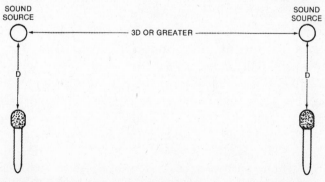

Figure 7.10 The 3:1 rule of microphone placement avoids phase interference between microphone signals.

139

Minimizing Off-Axis Coloration

Some microphones have *off-axis coloration*: a dull or colored tone quality for sources that are not directly in front of the microphone. Try to keep the sound source as on-axis as possible, especially if the source radiates strong high frequencies. For a wide-angle sound source, use a microphone that has uniform response over a wide angle. Boundary microphones and miniature microphones have almost no off-axis coloration.

Stereo Microphone Techniques

Stereo microphone techniques capture the sound of a musical ensemble as a whole, using only two or three microphones, and are frequently used to record classical-music ensembles and soloists.[1] During playback of a stereo recording, *phantom images* of the instruments are heard in various locations between the stereo speakers. These image locations—left to right, front to back—correspond to the instrument locations during the recording session.

Stereo miking is also used in the studio for background singers, piano, drum-set cymbals, vibraphone, or other large sound sources.

Goals of Stereo Miking

When you are stereo miking a large musical ensemble, one objective is *accurate localization*. When this is achieved, instruments in the center of the ensemble are accurately reproduced midway between the two playback speakers. Instruments at the sides of the ensemble are reproduced from the left or right speaker. Instruments located halfway to one side are reproduced halfway to one side, and so on.

Figure 7.11 shows three stereo localization effects. In Figure 7.11(A), various instrument positions in an orchestra are shown: left, left-center, center, right-center, right. In Figure 7.11(B), the reproduced images of these instruments are accurately localized between the stereo pair of speakers. The *stereo spread*, or stage width, extends from speaker to speaker. If the microphones are placed improperly, the effect is either the narrow stage width shown in Figure 7.11(C), or the exaggerated separation shown in Figure 7.11(D). A large ensemble should spread from speaker to speaker; a quartet can have a narrower spread.

[1]For a detailed and comprehensive explanation of stereo microphone technique, see Bartlett, *Stereo Microphone Techniques*, Boston: Focal Press, 1991.

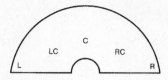

(A) Orchestra instrument locations.

(B) Images localized accurately between speakers (the listener's perception).

(C) Narrow stage width effect.

(D) Exaggerated separation effect.

Figure 7.11 Stereo localization effects (top view).

To judge these stereo localization effects, it's important to position yourself properly with respect to the monitor speakers. Sit as far from the speakers are they are spaced apart. Then the speakers appear to be 60 degrees apart, which is about the same angle an orchestra fills when viewed from the typical ideal seat in the audience (say, tenth row center). Sit exactly between the speakers (equidistant from them); otherwise, the images shift toward the side on which you're sitting and become less sharp.

Types of Stereo Microphone Techniques

There are three microphone techniques commonly used for stereo recording: the *coincident-pair (X-Y)*, the *spaced-pair (A-B)*, and the *near coincident-pair*.

Coincident-Pair

With the coincident-pair method, two directional microphones are mounted with their grilles touching and their diaphragms placed one above the other. They are also angled apart to aim approximately toward the left and right sides of the sound source or ensemble (see Figure 7.12). The greater the angle between microphones, the wider the stereo spread.

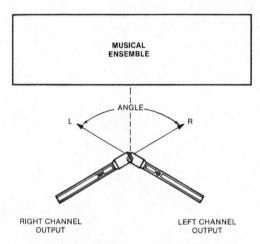

Figure 7.12 Coincident-pair technique.

The coincident-pair technique produces localized images. As described in Chapter 6 on microphones, a directional microphone is most sensitive to sounds in front of the microphone (on-axis) and progressively less sensitive to sounds arriving off-axis. That is, a directional mic produces a relatively high-level signal from the sound source it's aimed at, and produces a relatively low-level signal for all other sound sources.

Instruments in the center of the ensemble produce an identical signal from each microphone. During playback, a phantom image of the center instruments is heard midway between the stereo pair of loudspeakers because identical signals in each channel produce a centrally located image.

If an instrument is off-center to the right, it is more on-axis to the right-aiming mic than to the left-aiming mic. So the right mic produces a higher-level signal than the left mic. During playback of this recording, the right speaker plays at a higher level than the left speaker; this reproduces the image off-center to the right—where the instrument was during recording.

The coincident array codes instrument positions into level differences between channels. During playback, the brain decodes these level differences back into corresponding image locations.

Listening tests have shown that *coincident cardioid microphones* tend to reproduce the musical ensemble with a narrow stereo spread. That is, the reproduced ensemble does not spread all the way between speakers.

A coincident-pair method with excellent localization is the *Blumlein array*, which uses two bidirectional mics angled 90 degrees apart and facing the left and right sides of the ensemble.

A special form of the coincident-pair technique is the *Mid-Side (MS)* recording method (see Figure 7.13). A cardioid or omnidirectional microphone facing the middle of the orchestra is summed and differenced with a bidirectional microphone aiming to the sides. This produces left- and right-channel signals. With this technique, the stereo spread can be remote-controlled by varying the ratio of the mid signal to the side signal. This remote control is useful at live concerts, where you can't adjust the microphones physically during the concert. MS localization accuracy is excellent.

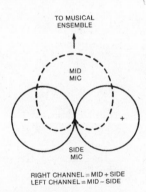

Figure 7.13 Mid-Side (MS) technique.

To make coincident recordings sound more spacious, boost the bass 4 db (+2 db at 600 Hz) in the L-R or side signal.[2]

Recall from Chapter 6 that a stereo microphone includes two coincident microphone capsules mounted in a single housing for convenience. A recording made with coincident techniques is mono-compatible, the

[2]David Griesinger, "Spaciousness and Localization in Listening Rooms and Their Effects on the Recording Technique," *Journal of the Audio Engineering Society*, 34, no. 4, (April 1986): 255-68.

frequency response is the same in mono or stereo. Because of the coincident placement, there is no time or phase difference between channels to degrade the frequency response if both channels are combined to mono. If you expect your recordings to be heard in mono (for instance, on the radio), then consider coincident methods.

Spaced-Pair

With the spaced-pair technique, two identical microphones are placed several feet apart, aiming straight ahead toward the musical ensemble (see Figure 7.14). The mics can have any polar pattern, but the omnidirectional pattern is most popular for this method. The greater the spacing between microphones, the greater the stereo spread.

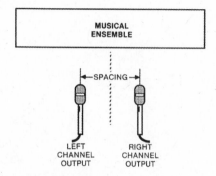

Figure 7.14 Spaced-pair technique.

Instruments in the center of the ensemble produce an identical signal from each microphone. During playback of this recording, a phantom image of the center instruments is heard midway between the stereo pair of loudspeakers.

If an instrument is off-center, it is closer to one mic than the other, so its sound reaches the closer microphone before it reaches the other one. Consequently, the microphones produce approximately an identical signal, except that one mic signal is delayed with respect to the other.

If you send an identical signal to two stereo speakers with one channel delayed, the sound image shifts off-center. With a spaced-pair recording, off-center instruments produce a delay in one mic channel, so they are reproduced off-center.

The spaced-pair array codes instrument positions into time differences between channels. During playback, the brain decodes these time differences back into corresponding image locations.

If the spacing between mics is 12 feet, for instance, instruments slightly off-center are reproduced at the left or right speaker. This could be called an exaggerated separation or ping-pong effect.

On the other hand, if the mics are less than 3 feet apart, the delays produced are inadequate to provide much stereo spread. In addition, the mics tend to favor the center of the ensemble because the mics are closest to the center instruments. You need to place the mics about 10 or 12 feet apart to record a good musical balance, but such a spacing results in exaggerated separation. One solution is to place a third microphone midway between the outer pair and mix its output to both channels. That way, the ensemble is recorded with a good balance, and the stereo spread is not exaggerated.

The spaced-pair method tends to make off-center images relatively unfocused or hard to localize because spaced microphone recordings have time differences between channels, and stereo images produced solely by time differences are unfocused. Centered instruments still are heard clearly in the center, but off-center instruments are difficult to pinpoint between speakers. This method is useful if you prefer the sonic images to be diffuse, rather than sharply focused (for a blended effect, for instance).

There's another problem with spaced microphones. Combining both mics to mono sometimes causes phase cancellations of various frequencies, which may or may not be audible.

There is an advantage with spaced miking, however. Spaced microphones are said to provide a warm sense of ambience, in which concert hall reverberation seems to surround the instruments and, sometimes, the listener.

Another advantage of the spaced-pair technique is the ability to use omnidirectional microphones. An omnidirectional condenser microphone has a more extended low-frequency response than a unidirectional condenser microphone, and tends to have less off-axis coloration.

Near Coincident-Pair

The near coincident-pair technique uses two directional microphones angled apart, with their grilles spaced a few inches apart horizontally (see Figure 7.15). Even a few inches of spacing increases the stereo spread and adds a sense of ambient warmth or "air" to the recording. The greater the angle or spacing between mics, the greater the stereo spread.

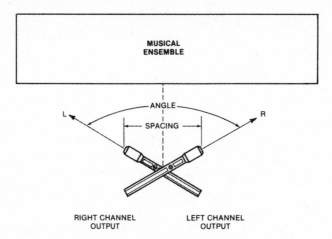

Figure 7.15 The near coincident-pair technique.

Angling directional mics produces level differences between channels; spacing mics produces time differences. The interchannel level differences and time differences combine to create the stereo effect. If the angling or spacing is too great, exaggerated separation results. If the angling or spacing is too small, the result is a narrow stereo spread.

The most common example of the near coincident method is the *ORTF* (Office de Radiodiffusion Television Francaise, or French Broadcasting Network) system, which uses two cardioid microphones angled 110 degrees apart and spaced 7 inches (17 cm) apart horizontally. This method tends to provide accurate localization. That is, instruments at the sides of the orchestra are reproduced at or very near the speakers, and instruments halfway to one side tend to be reproduced halfway to one side.

Comparing the Three Techniques

The coincident-pair technique uses two directional mics angled apart with grilles touching. The level differences between channels produce the stereo effect. With this technique,

- Images are sharp.

- Stereo spread ranges from narrow to accurate.

- Signals are mono-compatible.

The spaced-pair technique uses two mics spaced several feet apart. Time differences between channels produce the stereo effect. With this technique,

- Off-center images are diffuse.

- Stereo spread tends to be exaggerated unless a third center mic is used.

- A warm sense of ambience is created.

- Signals tend not to be mono-compatible.

The near coincident-pair technique uses two directional mics angled apart and spaced a few inches apart. Level and time differences between channels produce the stereo effect. With this technique,

- Images are sharp.

- Stereo spread tends to be accurate.

- A greater sense of "air" is created.

Mounting Hardware

With coincident and near coincident techniques, the microphones should be rigidly mounted with respect to each other so that they can be moved as a unit without disturbing their arrangment. A device for this purpose is called a *stereo microphone adapter* or *stereo bar*. It mounts two microphones on a single stand, and microphone angling and spacing are adjustable.

Microphone Requirements

The sound source dictates the requirements of the recording microphones. Most acoustic instruments produce frequencies from about 40 Hz (string bass and bass drum) to about 20,000 Hz (cymbals, castanets, triangles). A microphone with uniform response between these frequency limits does full justice to the music. The highest octave from 10 kHz to 20 kHz adds transparency, air, and realism to the recording.

You may need to roll off frequencies below 80 Hz to eliminate rumble from trucks and air-conditioning, unless you want to record organ or bass drum fundamentals.

Sound from an orchestra or band approaches each microphone from a broad range of angles. To reproduce all the instruments' timbres equally well, the microphone should have a broad, flat response at all angles of incidence within at least ±90 degrees. Stated another way, the polar pattern should be uniform with frequency. For sharp imaging, the microphone pair should be well matched in frequency response, phase response, and polar pattern.

MICROPHONE TECHNIQUES

There is no single "correct" microphone technique for any instrument because you place the mic where you hear a tonal balance and ambience pickup that you like. You can find that spot more quickly if you understand microphone characteristics and instrument sound-radiation patterns. This chapter explores various recording techniques for musical instruments and vocals. (For more detail, see Chapter 10.)

Electric Guitar

The electric guitar can be recorded in the following ways (see Figure 8.1):

- Miked, with a mic in front of the guitar amp
- Direct, with a direct box
- Both miked and direct
- Through a signal processor

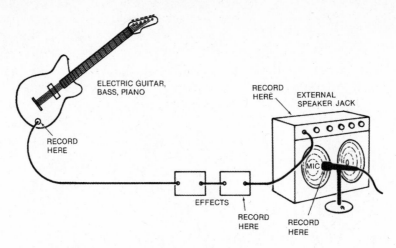

Figure 8.1 Recording an amplified-instrument system.

The style of music you're recording can suggest a good method. Miking the amp is best when you want a rough, raw sound (which includes tube distortion and speaker coloration). Rock and roll or heavy metal usually sound best with a miked amp.

Recording with a direct box, on the other hand, sounds clean and clear with extended highs and lows. It might be the best method for quiet jazz or R&B. Use whatever sounds right for the particular song you are recording.

The recorded guitar should sound full-range so that you have something to work with later in the mixdown. The highs should be bright but not too bright; the lows should be warm but not muddy. As always, first work on the sound of the instrument itself. Put on new strings if the old ones are starting to sound dull. Adjust the pickup screws (if any) for equal output from each string, and adjust the intonation and tuning.

Miking the Amp

Small practice amplifiers generally are better for recording than large, noisy stage amplifiers—unless the guitarist needs a larger sound. If you use a small amp, place it on a chair to avoid picking up sound reflections from the floor.

First, work on reducing any hum heard through the guitar amp. Set the guitar volume and treble controls up so that the guitar signal overrides hum and noise picked up by the guitar cable. Have the guitarist move around or rotate to find a spot in the room where hum disappears. Flip the polarity switch on the amp to the lowest hum position.

The most popular microphone choice for recording electric guitar is a cardioid dynamic type with a presence peak in the frequency response (a boost around 5 kHz). The cardioid pattern reduces leakage, the dynamic type withstands very loud sounds without distorting, and the presence peak adds punch. Of course, you can use any mic that sounds good to you. A flat-response condenser provides a natural sound for quieter guitar parts. If the guitar amp distorts the condenser mic, switch in its pad (if any).

For starters, mike the amp about 1 inch to 1 foot away, with the microphone aiming at the center of one of the speaker cones. Close mic placement sounds more bassy. Placement in front of the center of the speaker cone sounds bright or trebley; off-center placement sounds more mellow and reduces amplifier hiss.

You can try placing three mics side-by-side in front of the amp, with a boundary microphone on the floor. Then switch between mics while listening to the guitarist play, and choose the best-sounding microphone.

If you're overdubbing a lead guitar played through a huge stack of speakers in a reverberant room, you may want to mike the amp at a distance. A dynamic microphone placed 5 feet away can be mixed with boundary microphones on the control-room window (or one or two room mics) for ambience.

During overdubs, communications are easier if the musician is in the control room with the engineer. You still can record the guitar amp in the studio while the guitarist is playing in the control room:

1. Plug an impedance-matching transformer into the guitar. The high-Z phone plug goes into the guitar jack.

2. Plug a mic cable into the low-Z XLR side of the transformer.

3. Run the mic cable into the studio and into another impedance-matching transformer plugged into the guitar amp.

4. Mike the amp.

5. Monitor and record the microphone signal.

Recording Direct

Recording direct is also known as *direct injection* or *DI*. The electric guitar produces an electrical signal, so it can be plugged right into the mixing console—no microphone is needed. Because the mic and guitar amp are bypassed, the sound is clean and clear; it lacks the distortion and coloration of the amp. (Remember that amplifier distortion is desirable in some music.)

If you can use a short cable from guitar to mixer, and your mixer has a high-impedance unbalanced mic input (a ¼-inch phone jack), you can plug directly into the mixer. If your mixer has 3-pin balanced mic inputs, you need a *direct box* (see Figure 8.2). This converts the high-impedance unbalanced guitar signal to the low-impedance balanced signal required by the mixer.

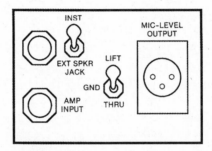

Figure 8.2 Layout of a typical direct box front panel.

Plug the electric guitar into the direct box, and plug the direct box into a microphone input. Some direct boxes let you record from the amplifier's external-speaker jack to pick up amplifier distortion. These boxes often include a lowpass filter to simulate the tone quality of the guitar-amp speaker.

The direct box should have a ground-lift switch to prevent ground loops and hum. Set it to the position where you monitor the least hum. If the guitar is connected to an amp, "lifted" usually provides the least hum; if the guitar is not connected to an amp, the opposite is true.

If you want to record the guitarist's special effects, connect the output of the effects boxes into the direct-box input, or directly into your mixer if you have ¼-inch phone jacks. Some engineers like to record a combination of direct sound and miked sound.

Studio Effects

You might want a spacious lead guitar sound. One way to get it is to send the guitar signal through a delay unit set to a few milliseconds delay. Pan the direct signal left and the delayed signal right.

You also can send the guitar signal to a harmonizer for a slight pitch change. Delay the pitch-bended signal 15 to 20 milliseconds, pan it to the right, and pan the direct signal to the left. Adjust the direct and delayed levels to spread the guitar between your monitor speakers.

Still another way to add space is to double the guitar. Have the player rerecord the same part in sync with the original part (possibly with the new part detuned just slightly). Pan the original part left and pan the doubled part right. Or "Y" the guitar cord to feed the guitar amp (recorded on the left channel) and a Leslie organ speaker (recorded on the right channel). You hear a spacious, swirling sound.

There are guitar-level signal processors (such as the Scholz Rockman, Zoom Box, Korg A-3, Art SGX2000, and Sans Amp) that add many different effects to an electric guitar, such as distortion, equalization, chorus, and compression. Plug the electric guitar straight into the processor, adjust the switches for the desired sound, and record the signal direct from the processor. You wind up with a fully produced sound with a minimum of effort.

With many direct instruments, the players have a clear idea of what their "sound" is, and give you that preprocessed direct sound. Be open to their suggestions and diplomatic about changing the sound. If they are studio players, they often have a better handle on effects, preamps, and so on, than you might as the engineer.

Electric Bass

"BWAM, dik diddy bum." Do your bass tracks sound that clear? Or are they more like "Bwuh, dip dubba duh"? If you've been bothered by muddy-sounding bass tracks, there's help. Here are some tips on recording the electric bass guitar to make it clean and easy to hear in a mix.

Put on new strings if the old ones are starting to sound dull. Adjust the pickup screws (if any) for equal output from each string. Also adjust the intonation and tuning.

The electric bass is usually recorded direct for the cleanest possible sound. A direct pickup provides deeper lows than a miked amp, but the amp gives more midrange punch. A combination of direct and miked sound provides clarity and a deep low end. The microphone can be a condenser or dynamic with a good low-frequency response, placed 1 inch to 1 foot away from the amplifier/speaker.

When combining a direct signal with a microphone signal, make sure they are in phase with each other. To do this, set them to equal levels and reverse the polarity of the direct signal or the microphone signal. The polarity that gives the most bass is correct.

Once you're satisfied with the basic pickup, have the musician play some scales to see if any notes are louder than the rest. You may be able to set a parametric equalizer to reduce the level of these notes.

The bass guitar should be fairly constant in level (a dynamic range of about 6 db) to be audible throughout a piece of music, and to avoid saturating the tape on loud peaks. To achieve this, the bass guitar signal is often run through a compressor, as described in Chapter 10. Set the compression ratio to 2:1 to 4:1, set the attack time fairly slow (8 to 20 milliseconds) to preserve the attack transient, and set the release time fairly fast ($1/4$ to $1/2$ second). If the release time is too fast, harmonic distortion occurs.

Equalization can increase the clarity of the bass guitar. It often helps to cut at 125 to 400 Hz, and/or boost at 1,500 to 2,000 Hz. (On small speakers, a boost at 300 to 500 Hz helps the bass "speak" better.) The following tips keep the bass sound clean and well defined:

- Record the bass direct.

- Use no reverb or echo on the bass, unless such an effect is desired.

- Try not to record a lot of extreme low frequencies—they aren't heard on most systems.

- Have the bass player turn down the bass amp in the studio just loud enough to play adequately. This reduces muddy-sounding bass leakage into other microphones.

- Don't even use the amp. Instead, have the musicians monitor the bass (and each other) with headphones.

- Have the bass player try new strings or a different guitar. Some guitars are much better for recording than others.

- If it suits the music, have the bass player mute the strings with the side of the hand and play with a pick for extra definition.

- Have the bass player use the treble pickup near the bridge.

If the bass part is full and sustained, it's probably best to deemphasize the pluck and let the kick drum define the rhythmic pattern. If the bass and kick drum both are rhythmic and work independently, plucks should be audible. Listen to the music first and then get a bass sound appropriate for it. A sharp, twangy timbre usually sounds wrong for a ballad; a full, round tone gets lost in a fusion piece.

To make an electric bass sound like an acoustic bass, mike the amp to pick up cabinet vibrations and use a noise gate or expander with a rapid decay, as described in Chapter 10. You might want to try a bass guitar signal processor with separate three-position switches for equalization, chorus, and sustain, as well as a high-frequency compressor and peak clipper.

Recording the Effects

Two popular effects boxes for the electric bass are the octave divider and the bass chorus. The octave box gives an extra deep, growly sound. A bass chorus gives a swirling, spacious effect.

If you want to record these effects, connect the output of the effects boxes into the direct-box input, or directly into your mixer if possible.

Synthesized Bass

Bass lines are often played on a synthesizer, partly because a synth has a wider variety of bass sounds than a bass guitar. The synth is triggered either by a piano-style keyboard, by a sequencer, or by a bass guitar plugged into a guitar-to-MIDI converter.

Record the synthesizer's audio output direct for maximum clarity. Use either a direct box into a mixer mic input, or a phone-to-phone cable.

Leslie Organ Speaker

The Leslie Organ speaker contains a rotating horn on top for highs and a woofer on the bottom for lows. A typical recording technique is to mike the top and bottom separately, a few inches to a foot away. Aim the top mic into the louvers. It's often effective to record the rotating horn in stereo, with a microphone on either side, or with microphones inside the cabinet.

Electric Keyboards

Electric pianos, synthesizers, and drum machines are usually recorded direct for maximum clarity. If the instrument output is unbalanced high impedance, use a direct box into a mixer mic input. Some inexpensive mixers and recorder-mixers have unbalanced high-impedance inputs, which can accept a keyboard signal through an ordinary cable. If the instrument output is balanced low-impedance, use a microphone cable with appropriate adapters between the instrument and mixer. For stereo keyboards, record both outputs.

If the keyboard player has several keyboards plugged into his or her own mixer, you may want to record a premixed signal from that mixer's output.

Drums

Drums are more complex and difficult to record than most other instruments. The first step is to make the drums sound good live in the studio. If the set itself sounds bad, you have a hard time making it sound good in the control room.

Goboes 4 feet tall are often placed around the set to reduce drum leakage into other mics. For more isolation, the set is placed in a *drum booth*—a small padded room with large windows. You even could record the drums in a warehouse for a huge, heavy metal sound.

One secret of creating a good drum sound lies in careful tuning. Getting a good sound on tape is much easier if you tune the set to sound right in the studio before miking it. Be sure to check with the drummer before retuning.

Old, used drum heads tend to produce a dull and muffled sound; new heads sound crisp.

Tom-Toms

You get the most pleasing tone from a tom-tom when the heads are tuned so that they are the same pitch at which the shell resonates. First, take off the heads and remove the damping mechanism—a possible source of rattles. Put the top head on and tighten the lugs by hand. Then, using a drum key, tighten opposite pairs of lugs one at a time, one full turn. Test the sound after each tightening. After all lugs are tightened in this manner, repeat the process, tightening one-half turn. Then apply heavy pressure to the head to stretch it. Continue tightening one-half turn at a time until you reach the desired pitch.

Keep the bottom head off the drum if you want best projection and the broadest range of tuning. In this case, pack the bottom lugs with felt to prevent rattles.

You may want to add the bottom head for extra control of the sound. Projection is best if the bottom head is tighter than the top head—tuned an interval of a fourth above the top head. There is a muted attack, a lot of ringing, and some note-bending. If you tune the bottom head looser than the top, the tom rings less, and has good attack.

Kick Drum

For the kick drum (bass drum), a loose head gives lots of slap and attack, and almost no tone. The opposite is true for a tight head. Tune the head to complement the style of music. A hard beater provides more attack.

Snare Drum

Tune the snare drum with the snares off. A loose batter head or top head gives a deep, fat sound. A tight batter head sounds bright and crisp. With the snare head or bottom head loose, the tone is deep, with little snare buzz; a tight snare head yields a crisp snare response. Set the snare tension just to the point where the snare wires begin to "choke" or damp the sound; then back off a little.

Sometimes a snare drum buzzes in sympathetic vibration with a bass-guitar passage or a tom-tom fill. You may be able to control the buzz by wedging a thick cotton wad between the snares and the drum stand. Experiment with the position and thickness of the wad for best results. Also, try changing the snare-head tuning.

Damping and Noise Prevention

If the tom-toms or snare drum ring excessively, tape some gauze pads or folded handkerchiefs to the edge of the heads. Put the tape on three sides of the pad so that the untaped edge is free to vibrate and dampen the head motion. Don't overdo the damping; otherwise, the drum set sounds like cardboard boxes. Depending on the song, you might want the heads to ring without any damping. To reduce excessive cymbal ringing, apply drafting tape in radial strips from bell to rim.

Oil the kick-drum pedal to prevent squeaks. Tape rattling hardware in place with drafting tape.

Miking the Drum Set

Now you're ready to mike the set. For a tight sound, place the mics very close to the edge of each drum head. For a more open, airy sound, move the mics back a few inches, use fewer mics, or mix in some room mics (such as boundary mics or omni condensers) placed several feet away. Sometimes a jazz drum set can be miked adequately with two overhead mics and one kick drum mic. Figure 8.3 shows typical microphone placements for a drum set.

Snare

Bring the mic in from the front of the set on a boom. Place it about 1 inch above the rim (or 1 inch in from the rim), angled down to aim where the drummer hits (see Figure 8.4).

You may want to aim the snare mic partly toward the hi-hat to pick up both instruments on one microphone. Be careful where you place the snare drum mic—every time the hi-hat closes, it produces a puff of air that can "pop" the snare mic. Place the mic so it is not hit by this air puff.

Either a cardioid condenser or cardioid dynamic microphone works fine—use whatever sounds best for the tune being recorded. Most mics with a cardioid pattern have proximity effect, which boosts the bass up close and adds fullness to the snare beat.

If you want to mike the snare and hi-hat separately, bring the boom in under the hi-hat, and aim the snare mic away from the hi-hat for better isolation. An alternative technique is to attach a miniature condenser mic a few inches over the snare drum rim.

Some engineers like to mike both the top and bottom heads of the snare drum as described earlier, with the microphones in opposite polarity. A mic under the snare drum gives a zippy sound; a mic over the snare drum gives a fuller sound.

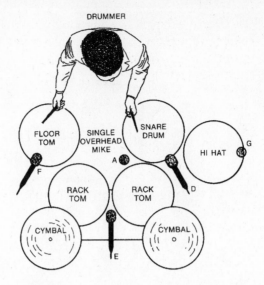

(A) Top view.

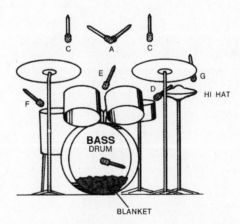

(B) Front view.

Figure 8.3 Typical microphone placements for a drum set.

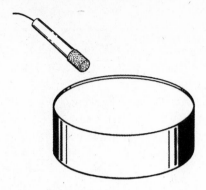

Figure 8.4 Snare drum miking.

Hi-Hat

Usually the snare mic or ambience mics pick up enough hi-hat, but if you want to mike the hi-hat separately, try a cardioid condenser microphone about 6 inches above the edge of the hi-hat, aiming at the side farthest from the drummer (see Figure 8.5). To avoid the air puff, don't mike the hi-hat off its edge. Mike it from above aiming down.

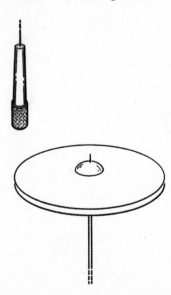

Figure 8.5 Hi-hat miking.

If the hi-hat needs more sizzle, try boosting a little at 10 or 12 kHz.

Tom-Toms

Tom-toms can be miked individually, or with one mic between each pair. One typical technique uses a cardioid dynamic or condenser mic placed 1 inch above the rim (or about 2 inches in from the rim), angled down about 45 degrees toward the drum head (see Figure 8.6). Again, the cardioid's proximity effect gives a full sound. An alternative setup is to tape mini condenser mics to the toms, peeking over the top rim of each drum. Or you might try a bidirectional microphone between two tom-toms.

Figure 8.6 Tom-tom miking.

Tom-tom mics often pick up too much leakage from the cymbals, and this is sometimes heard as a low tone. To reduce cymbal leakage and improve isolation, take the cardioid tom-tom mics and aim their "dead" rear at the cymbals. Note that a supercardioid or hypercardioid mic is sensitive partially to sounds arriving from the rear, and should be placed so that the "dead spot" aims at the cymbals.

Another way to reduce cymbal leakage is to remove the bottom heads from the toms and mike them inside a few inches from the head, off-center (see Figure 8.7). This also keeps the mics out of the drummer's way. The sound picked up inside the tom-tom has less attack and more tone than the sound picked up outside.

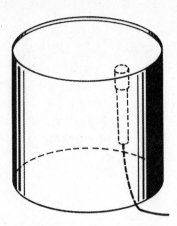

Figure 8.7 Miking a tom-tom inside.

Kick Drum

You may want to place a blanket inside the drum, pressing against the beater head to dampen the vibration and tighten the beat. The blanket shortens the decay portion of the kick drum envelope.

A microphone commonly used in the kick drum is a cardioid dynamic type with an extended low-frequency response. For starters, place it inside on a boom, a few inches from where the beater hits and slightly off-center (see Figure 8.8). Mic placement close to the beater picks up a hard beater sound, off-center placement picks up more skin tone, and placement farther away picks up a boomier shell sound. For a bigger sound, build a small tunnel with blankets and a chair and put the mic outside the kick drum.

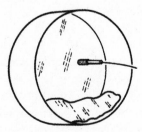

Figure 8.8 Kick drum miking.

A miniature omnidirectional condenser microphone can be hung inside near the beater for a clearly defined attack.

Cutting equalization around 300 to 600 Hz helps to remove the "cardboard box" sound, and boosting several db around 2.5 to 5 kHz adds attack, "click," or "snap."

How should the recorded kick drum sound? Thunk!—a powerful low-end thump plus the click or snap of the beater smacking the drum head.

Cymbals

Place overhead mics (cardioid condensers) 1 to 3 feet above the cymbal edges; closer miking picks up a low-frequency ring. Two mics overhead can aim straight down, or they can be angled apart for better isolation (see Figure 8.9). For mono-compatibility, mount the mic grilles together and angle the mics apart (refer to Figure 8.3A).

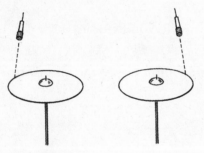

Figure 8.9 Overhead cymbal miking.

Place the cymbal mics so that they pick up all the cymbals equally. Usually not much gain is needed on the overheads because the cymbals leak into the drum mics. Recorded cymbals should sound crisp and smooth, not sizzly or harsh.

Ambience

In addition to the close drum microphones, you might want to use a distant ambience microphone when recording drum overdubs. Place the mic about 10 or 20 feet from the set to pick up room reverberation. When mixed with the close mics, it gives an open, loose, airy sound to the drums. Two are usually used for stereo. You can use omnidirectional or cardioid condenser microphones or boundary mics attached to the control-room window. Sometimes ambience mics are compressed heavily for special effect.

Boundary microphones allow some unusual opportunities for drumset miking. You can strap one on the drummer's chest to pick up the set as the drummer hears it, tape them to hard-surfaced goboes surrounding the drummer, or put them on the floor under the toms and near the kick drum.

Recording with Three Microphones

If you're limited in the number of microphones you can spare for the drums, use the setup in Figure 8.10—two miniature omnidirectional condenser mics and one kick drum mic:

1. Tape or clip one mini mic near the left rack tom and the snare drum. This mic picks up the hi-hat, snare, left rack tom, and cymbals.

2. Tape or clip another mini mic near the right rack tom and the floor toms. This mic picks up the right rack tom, floor tom, and cymbals.

3. Place the third mic in the kick drum.

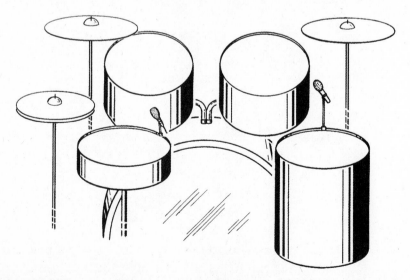

Figure 8.10 Miking a small drum set with three microphones (one in the kick drum).

Move the mics closer or farther from the toms, and ask the drummer to raise or lower the cymbals, until all the elements of the drum set are heard in a pleasing balance. With a little bass boost, you'll be surprised at the good sound and even coverage achieved with this simple setup.

Recording with Two Microphones

With some bass boost, the sound can be adequate using an even simpler method:

1. Clip a miniature omnidirectional condenser mic to the snare drum rim about 4 inches above the rim, in the center of the set, aiming at the hi-hat (see Figure 8.11).

2. Put another mic in the kick drum.

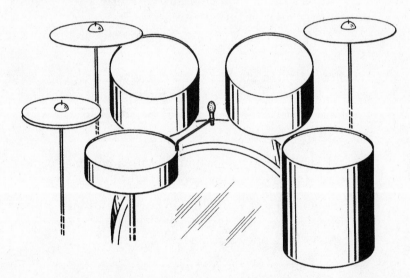

Figure 8.11 Miking a drum set with two microphones (one clipped onto the snare drum rim, the other in the kick drum).

Drum Recording Tips

After all the drum microphones are set up, ask the drummer to play. Listen for rattles and leakage by soloing each microphone. Try not to spend more than 10 or 20 minutes getting the right sound on the drums; otherwise, you waste the other musicians' time and wear out the drummer.

To keep the drum sound tight, turn off mics not in use in a particular tune, or use a noise gate on each drum mic. (See Chapter 10 for more information.)

A popular effect on the snare drum is *gated reverberation*. There's a short splash of bright-sounding reverberation, which is rapidly cut off by a noise gate or expander (described in Chapter 10). Many digital reverbs have a gated reverb setting.

Electronic drums or drum machines are recorded direct into the console for maximum clarity. If the drum machine sounds too mechanical, you can make the sound more interesting by combining real drum sounds with the machine's signal. The machine can play a steady background while the drummer does other things.

When miking drums on stage for a live recording, you don't need a forest of unsightly mic stands and booms. Instead, you can use short microphone holders that clip onto drum rims and cymbal stands, or use miniature condenser microphones.

Various equalizer settings can enhance the recorded sound of the drums:

- Boost around 200 Hz for fullness on snare drum and high toms, and around 100 Hz on floor toms. Or use a cardioid microphone up close for its bass-boosting proximity effect.

- Roll off some bass on the snare for extra clarity.

- Boost at 5 kHz (or use a mike with a presence peak) on snare and toms for attack and crispness.

- Boost at 10 kHz or higher on cymbals for brilliance and sizzle, and filter out frequencies below 500 Hz on cymbals to minimize pickup of low frequency leakage.

- Boost around 2.5 to 6 kHz on bass drum for punch, and filter out frequencies above 5 kHz on bass drum to reduce leakage from cymbals.

Drum-Set Leakage Comparisons

Miking a drum set from overhead with a single microphone provides poor isolation from other instruments. That is, if a single overhead mic is used, the drum-set pickup is relatively weak compared to the leakage. Miking from the center of the set, near the snare drum, rejects leakage and ambience much more than overhead miking. The result is a tighter sound. This near-the-snare pickup with one microphone might be a simple, inexpensive way to mike the set for demo recording or sound reinforcement.

Miking the tom-tom just over the rim reduces leakage still more (because the tom-tom is louder there), and miking it inside virtually eliminates leakage.

Other Percussion Instruments

It's a real challenge to accurately record percussion instruments. The sharp transient response of a quality condenser microphone makes it a good choice. Mike at least 1 foot away to prevent overloading the mic itself, or use a dynamic microphone with an extended high-frequency response.

Congas, bongos, and timbales (double drums) can be covered with a single microphone between the pair. A single-D moving-coil microphone with a presence peak gives a full sound with clear attack.

For xylophones and vibraphones, place two cardioid microphones $1^1/_2$ feet above the instrument, aiming down. The mics should be crossed (angled 135 degrees apart) or placed about 2 feet apart. These arrangements allow for a stereo effect and provide good coverage of the entire instrument.

Acoustic Guitar

The acoustic guitar has a delicate timbre which can be captured through careful microphone selection and placement. First, prepare the guitar for recording. Use strings designed to reduce finger squeaks, if possible. For maximum brilliance, replace old strings with new ones. Experiment with different kinds of guitars, picks, and finger picking to achieve a timbre suitable for the song.

Microphone Choice

A condenser microphone with a smooth, extended frequency response from 80 Hz up is often preferred for acoustic guitar. Such a microphone typically gives a clear, detailed quality, in which the plucking of each string is audible within a strummed chord. The reproduced sound usually has all the crispness of the live instrument.

However, the clear pickup of string noise can be distracting in some songs. You can diminish this fine detail by using a dynamic microphone, which usually has a slower *transient response* (the ability to follow sudden changes in acoustic pressure).

Miking Near the Sound Hole

If you've ever miked an acoustic guitar close to the sound hole—a popular microphone position—you've probably noticed that the recorded guitar doesn't sound much like the real thing (see Figure 8.12). The recording sounds too bassy, boomy, and thumpy because the sound hole and the air inside the guitar resonate at low frequencies (around 80 to 100 Hz). A microphone placed close to the sound hole (or in it) picks up and emphasizes this resonance, giving a bassy character to the recorded guitar.

Figure 8.12 Acoustic guitar miking close to the sound hole.

Why then is a guitar commonly miked close to the sound hole? On stage, this microphone position provides maximum loudness before feedback occurs. In the studio, it provides maximum isolation (minimum leakage pickup). The acoustic guitar, being a relatively quiet instrument, often requires such a technique.

To achieve a more natural sound in this microphone position, roll off the low frequencies on your mixer (say, –10 db or more at 100 Hz).

Contact Pickups

Best isolation—sometimes at the expense of fidelity—is achieved with a contact pickup, which attaches to the body of the guitar. For a starting point, place the pickup on or next to the bridge and adjust the position from there. Positioning a contact pickup is critical—a movement of a fraction of an inch can change the sound drastically. Each instrument has a different best location for the pickup, and every brand of pickup sounds different. Multiple pickups, or a pickup and a microphone, can be mixed.

Miniature Microphone Placement

A miniature omni condenser microphone attached to the guitar provides good fidelity. A typical mounting position is halfway between the sound hole and bridge, near the low E string (see Figure 8.13). For more isolation, tape a miniature directional mic in the sound hole and roll off the bass on your mixer.

Figure 8.13 Acoustic guitar miking with a mini mic.

Miking for a Natural Timbre

If leakage is not a problem (during an overdub, for example), a more natural sound can be achieved by miking the guitar at a distance—say 12 to 18 inches from the sound hole (see Figure 8.14). At this position, the microphone picks up a well-balanced blend of all the parts of the guitar—strings, soundboard, and sound hole.

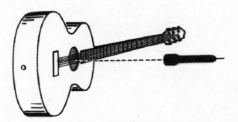

Figure 8.14 Acoustic guitar miking 1½ feet from the sound hole.

Try a closer placement for a bright, realistic sound: 6 inches over the top, over the bridge, and even with the front soundboard (see Figure 8.15). You may be pleasantly surprised with the sound you get.

Figure 8.15 Acoustic guitar miking 6 inches over the top, over the bridge, and even with the front soundboard.

Miking for a Mellow Timbre

A woody, mellow tone quality is picked up by a microphone that is about 4 inches in front of the bridge (see Figure 8.16). Here, the vibrations of the soundboard are emphasized, starting around 200 Hz. This position also reduces pickup of string and pick noise.

Figure 8.16 Acoustic guitar miking 4 inches in front of the bridge.

Classical Guitar Solos

When recording a classical guitar solo, use distant microphone placement to capture the room acoustics or reverberation, a desirable part of the sound of classical music. Record in a recital hall or other warmly reverberant room. Place the microphone about 3 to 8 feet away—closer to reduce reverberation, farther to increase it.

For a more realistic sense of space or "air" surrounding the soloist, record in stereo. Angle two cardioid microphones 90 degrees apart and space their grilles about 8 inches apart (see Figure 8.17). If you are forced to record a classical guitar in an acoustically dead room, try miking the guitar as in Figures 8.13, 8.14, or 8.15. Add artificial reverberation at your mixer.

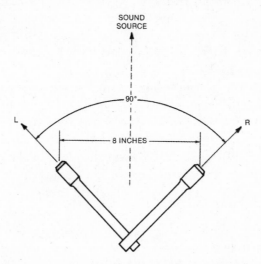

Figure 8.17 A stereo miking technique for acoustic guitar.

Banjo

The banjo uses a drum head to couple the string vibrations to the air. The center of the head vibrates mainly at the head's fundamental frequency; the harmonics of the head vibration are strongest near the edge. Sometimes the lower notes are reinforced by holes in the flange surrounding the head.

To pick up a natural blend of all the parts of the banjo, place a flat-response microphone about 1 foot away. Positioning the microphone close to the center of the head produces a rather harsh, thumpy sound (unless you roll off the bass) but provides good isolation. The sound becomes thinner toward the edge of the head.

You can tape a miniature omni condenser microphone to the drum head about 1 inch in from the bottom edge for maximum isolation, or clip the microphone onto the tailpiece aiming toward the bridge. As a starting placement for a contact pickup, wedge the pickup between the strings and the head behind the bridge. The pickup should be flat against the banjo head.

Violin, Mandolin, Dobro, Fiddle

The violin, mandolin, dobro, and fiddle are constructed in somewhat the same way the acoustic guitar is, so many of the microphone techniques for guitar are applicable.

When played, the fiddle or violin radiates high frequencies primarily upward. Consequently, the audience usually hears a duller sound from the violin than the violinist hears. When close-miking the violin, you can avoid the harsh, bright sound the violinist hears by aiming the microphone at the side of the violin. A microphone response down to 200 Hz is sufficient.

Another technique that works very well is to clip a miniature microphone to the violin's tailpiece and mount it a few inches from an f-hole or over the bridge. You can even clip it to the strings on the player's side of the bridge. A suggested pickup placement for a fiddle is on the left side of the top (from the player's view), on the player's side of the bridge.

Grand Piano

It's difficult to record the piano so that it sounds realistic. One reason for this is that it's such a big, complex sound source. The natural sound of a piano heard at a distance is a blend of the room acoustics and the individual sounds of its many parts: strings, hammers, soundboard, and lid. Close miking, however, emphasizes the part of the piano that the microphone is near. An unnatural recorded timbre can result.

To further complicate matters, combinations of sounds from various areas and sound reflections from the lid cause acoustic phase cancellations that vary with microphone placement. Lid reflections arrive off-axis to the microphone, sometimes producing coloration. In addition, a piano has sharp attack transients that can saturate the recording tape, unless they are recorded at lower-than-normal levels. All these factors make the piano a challenge to record without distortion or coloration.

Distant Miking

One way to record the piano as an audience hears it is to use the following procedure:

1. Set the piano lid open on the long stick.

2. Place a stereo microphone, or a pair of flat-response cardioid condenser microphones, 6 to 12 feet away from the open lid (refer to Figure 8.17).

3. Place the mics in line with the lid to avoid sound reflections from the lid.

4. Move the mics toward the keys for more treble, or toward the tail for more bass.

This method is useful for taping piano solos or overdubs. A classical piano solo should be recorded in a reverberant locale such as a recital hall or concert hall.

Close Miking

In pop-music recording, the piano is miked closer to reduce pickup of room acoustics and leakage, and to increase clarity. Try not to mike the strings closer than 8 inches away, however, because doing so emphasizes the strings closest to the microphone. You want equal coverage of all the notes the pianist plays.

There are many ways to close-mike a piano. Experiment to see what works best for the particular song and instrument.

Spaced Microphones

One popular method of close-miking a piano uses two spaced microphones inside the piano, with the lid on the long stick or even removed. Place one microphone about 8 inches over the treble strings and about 8 inches horizontally from the hammers. The other microphone is placed over the bass strings, about 8 inches high and about 2 to 4 feet from the hammers (see Figure 8.18, positions A and C). These microphone signals are panned partly toward the left and right for a stereo effect.

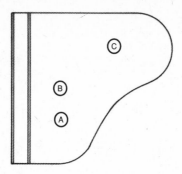

Figure 8.18 Two close-miking positions for piano.

Alternatively, you can tape two boundary microphones to the underside of the piano lid over the bass and treble strings, or taped to the inside of the front edge. Close the lid if necessary for more isolation.

Coincident Microphones

Spaced microphones can cause phase cancellations when mixed to mono, so you might want to try coincident miking. Mount a single microphone or a pair of cardioids crossed at 120 degrees, and position them about 1 foot over the middle of the piano, about 8 inches from the hammers (refer to Figure 8.18, position B). The closer to the hammers the microphones are placed, the more percussive the attack and the greater the isolation. So, if the sound is too "bangy" and lacks tone, move the microphones away from the hammers and toward the tail of the piano.

Again, you might want to tape a boundary microphone to the underside of the piano lid in the middle, and close the lid if leakage is excessive. Special contact pickups for piano are available to further increase isolation.

Achieving a Bright Sound

Often a bright piano sound is desired. You can improve clarity, sharpness, and attack by boosting frequencies around 5 kHz and rolling off around 200 Hz on your mixer, or by using a microphone with a presence peak.

Upright Piano

As with a grand piano, each microphone placement for the upright piano produces a different tone quality. The upright piano is not normally miked at a distance because it is not a classical-music instrument. Distant-miking the upright in a small room tends to sound muddy.

The following close-miking methods provide a variety of piano tonal balances, all with a clear, close-up perspective. Experiment to find the method most suited to the particular song you're recording.

Miking the Panel Area

For a natural sound, remove the panel in front of the piano to expose the strings. Place one mic near the bass strings and one near the treble strings about 8 inches away. Record in stereo and pan the signals left and right for the desired piano width. If you can spare only one microphone for the piano, cover the treble strings or midtreble strings.

Miking the Soundboard

To reduce excessive hammer attack, place a pair of microphones about 8 inches from the soundboard, covering the bass and treble sides. The soundboard should be facing into the room, not into a wall. A boundary mic works well too, placed about 1 foot from the soundboard on the floor, either on the player's side or the back side.

Miking for Isolation

For extra isolation, place two microphones inside the open top. Or tape two mini omni condenser mics to the soundboard and experiment with the position for best results. Another alternative is to tape two boundary microphones to the wall 1 inch from the soundboard.

Strings

Not many home studios record string sections, but if you want to sweeten the sound during an overdub session, here are some suggested techniques.

String Section

Place the strings in a large, hard-surfaced room that has noticeable reverberation, and mike the strings at a distance to pick up a natural acoustic sound. Condenser microphones with a flat frequency response are usually preferred. Use a stereo microphone technique as described in Chapter 7.

If your studio acoustics are dead, you need to mike close and add artificial reverb. For two violins, try one microphone about 6 feet off the floor, aiming down between the players. The viola and cello each can be miked from the side, at about 2 feet from the f-hole. For added definition on the cello, mike it about 1 foot from the bridge.

Large string ensembles can be covered with one microphone for every four violins and violas, one for every two cellos, and one for each acoustic bass.

When you mix all the signals of the strings to stereo, pan them evenly between the monitor speakers. Spread them left, center, and right to achieve a curtain of sound. If you can spare only one track for the strings, you can make that track simulated stereo in the mixdown:

1. Pan the track to the left channel.

2. Simultaneously send it through a 20-millisecond delay.

3. Pan the delayed signal to the right channel.

4. Adjust the relative levels of the direct and delayed signals to achieve a stereo spread from speaker to speaker.

String Quartet

A string quartet can be recorded in stereo using the microphone placement seen in Figure 8.17. Place the microphones about 6 to 10 feet away from the quartet to capture the room ambience. A limited stereo spread, rather than a speaker-to-speaker spread, is sometimes preferred for a string quartet. To reduce the width of the stereo stage, reduce the angle or spacing between the microphones.

Acoustic Bass

The acoustic bass (string bass, double bass, upright bass, bass viol) can be recorded in several ways. This instrument produces frequencies as low as 41 Hz, so use a microphone with an extended low-frequency response. For a well-defined sound, place the microphone a few inches out front, above the bridge. Aim it into the treble f-hole for a fuller sound. As always, watch out for the proximity effect with a closely placed cardioid microphone.

The following are techniques to increase isolation and allow the performer freedom of movement, useful in sound-reinforcement situations:

- Wrap a miniature omni condenser microphone in foam rubber (or in a foam windscreen) and mount it in an f-hole.

- Tape the cable of a mini omni mic to the bridge.

- Wrap a regular microphone in foam padding (except for the front grille) and squeeze it behind the bridge or between the tailpiece and the body.

- Try a direct feed from a pickup. This method provides clarity and "bite," but has an "electric" sound.

Mix a mini omni condenser in the f-hole with a pickup to round out the tone. You may need to roll off the bass of the f-hole mic. Try flipping the polarity of the mic and use the polarity that sounds best.

Bluegrass Band, Old-Time String Band

Bluegrass and similar groups might be covered with a stereo microphone or with two cardioid mics placed as in Figure 8.17, or with a multicapsule mic such as the Soundfield. Arrange the group in a semicircle, with the microphone(s) about 3 feet away. Try to record in an acoustically dead room for clarity, and adjust balances by moving the musicians toward or away from the mics. Typically, though, these groups are recorded with multiple close microphones. The production style aims for a natural sound, usually with no effects except for slight reverberation.

Harp

A harp can be covered by a microphone aiming toward the treble part of the soundboard from the front, about 1½ feet away (if the harp is playing with an orchestra) or at a greater distance (for a harp solo).

For best isolation, tape a mini omni condenser microphone to the soundboard. Miking on the outside of the soundboard sounds more natural; miking on the inside provides more isolation. Also try a bidirectional mic oriented vertically along the axis of the strings, with the side of the mic pointing at the undesired source.

You also can use some C-Ducer tape on the soundboard and add some reverberation in the recording. C-Ducer tape is a strip of plastic that picks up mechanical vibrations and produces a corresponding electrical signal.

Brass Instruments

Brass instruments (trumpets, cornets, trombones, and tubas) radiate strong high-frequency harmonics directly out of the bell, but do not project them to the sides. A microphone placed close to, and in front of, the bell picks up a brighter, more "edgy" tone than the audience usually hears. To soften the tone and restore the natural horn sound, try miking the bell at an angle and distant with a flat-response microphone (see Figure 8.19). You also can mike it on-axis with a ribbon microphone, which typically provides a smooth sound. Use a condenser microphone to reproduce a lot of sizzle or clarity. A tuba often sounds best miked at a distance.

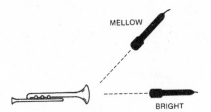

Figure 8.19 Miking for trumpet tone control (top view).

The waveform of a trumpet on-axis has strong spikes that can overload a condenser mic and saturate recording tape. This is another reason for miking the trumpet off-axis. Close microphone placement (about 1 foot) gives a tight sound; distant placement (about 5 feet) yields a fuller, more dramatic sound.

It's common to mike two or more horns with one microphone. Several players can be grouped around a single omnidirectional microphone or around a cardioid microphone placed below the group aiming up. Alternatively, the musicians can play to a boundary microphone taped on the control-room window or on a large panel.

Wind Instruments

With winds (clarinets, oboes, bassoons, flutes), most of the sound radiates not from the bell, but from the holes. So aim a microphone at the holes about 1 foot away. A flat-response dynamic or condenser microphone is typically used.

When miking a wind section within an orchestra, you need to reject nearby leakage from other instruments. To do that, try aiming a bidirectional mic down over the section. The side rejection of the microphone minimizes leakage.

Saxophone

A sax miked very near the bell (see Figure 8.20) sounds bright, breathy, and rather hard. Mike it there for best isolation. A mic placed off to the side picks up a quiet sound with poor isolation. For a natural tonal balance, mike the sax about $1\frac{1}{2}$ feet away, aiming at the player's left hand, about one-third to one-half of the way down the wind column. If you mike too close, the level varies when the player moves and you hear valve clicks. A compromise position for a close microphone might be just above the bell, aiming at the holes. A sax section can be grouped around a single microphone.

Figure 8.20 Two ways to mike a saxophone.

Flute

One effective microphone placement for the flute is a few inches from the area between the mouthpiece and the first set of finger holes (see Figure 8.21). A pop filter may be needed. If you want to reduce breath noises, roll off high frequencies or mike farther away. You also can attach a mini mic to the flute a few inches above the body, between the mouthpiece and finger holes. For classical-music solos, try a stereo pair 5 to 8 feet away.

Figure 8.21 One effective arrangement for flute miking.

Harmonica

A popular technique for recording a harmonica uses a cardioid dynamic microphone with a ball grille placed very close to the harmonica (sometimes held by the player). For a bluesy, dirty sound, use a "bullet" type harmonica mic or play the harmonica through a miked guitar amp. A condenser mic about 1 foot away yields a natural sound.

Vocals

Vocal recording presents a number of problems. Among these are proximity effect, popping, wide dynamic range, sibilance, and sound reflections from the lyric sheet.

Minimizing Proximity Effect

Vocalists on stage have to sing with their lips touching the microphone grille to reduce feedback. Singing or talking close to a cardioid microphone boosts the low frequencies due to proximity effect. The result is a bassy, boomy tone quality that people accept as a standard sound-reinforcement vocal sound.

During a recording session, this effect may add robustness to a weak voice; but usually the vocalist should back off at least 8 inches from the microphone to restore a natural tone quality. Vocals are overdubbed typically from about 8 inches to 2 feet away with a flat-response condenser microphone (see Figure 8.22). Older tube-type condensers are popular for miking vocals.

Figure 8.22 Typical miking technique for a lead vocalist.

Close Miking

If you must record the vocalist simultaneously with the instruments, as in live recording, you probably have to mike them very close so that accompanying musical instruments don't leak into the vocal microphone. A cardioid microphone with a pop filter is useful here. To reduce the boominess caused by close placement, roll off the excess bass on your mixer (typically –8 db at 100 Hz). Some microphones have a built-in bass rolloff switch for this purpose. Aiming the microphone up toward the singer's nose avoids a nasal effect.

Minimizing Pop

Recall from Chapter 6 that when a vocalist sings a word with "p" or "t" sounds, a turbulent puff of air is forced from the mouth. A microphone placed near the mouth is hit by this air puff and generates an undesirable thump called a pop. It can be reduced by placing a foam-plastic pop filter (windscreen) on or in front of the microphone. Some microphones have a built-in ball grille screen for pop suppression.

Although these devices reduce pop, they do little to minimize breathing sounds or lip noises. Distant miking or some high-frequency roll off can help with these problems at the expense of sound quality.

Foam pop filters should be made of special open-cell foam to allow high frequencies to pass through. For this reason, it's better to use a commercially made foam screen than to make one yourself from packing foam, cloth, or socks. Allow a little air space between the foam front and the microphone grille for best pop rejection.

Because most pop filters slightly change the frequency response of a microphone, they should be left off microphones intended for instruments, except for outdoor recording or dust protection.

The most effective pop filter is a hoop with a silk stocking stretched over it. This type is commercially available. Place it between the vocalist and the mic, a few inches from the mic. A separate mic stand can be used for this purpose.

A very effective way to eliminate popping is to place the microphone well above the singer's mouth level (refer to Figure 8.22). This way, the puffs of air shoot under the microphone and miss it. You also can place the microphone off to one side of the mouth (see Figure 8.23).

MUSIC SHEET IS ANGLED AWAY FROM MICROPHONE

Figure 8.23 Miking a vocalist from the side.

Reducing Wide Dynamic Range

Vocalists often sing too loudly or too softly during a song, either blasting the listener or getting buried in the mix. They generally have a wider dynamic range than their instrumental backup. To even out these extreme level variations, the vocalist should use proper mic technique—backing away from the microphone on loud notes, coming in closer for soft ones. Or you can *ride gain* on the vocalist: gently turn the gain down as he or she gets louder, and vice versa. The best solution is to pass the vocal signal through a compressor. (See Chapter 10 for further information.)

A microphone placed close to the mouth is very sensitive to small changes in miking distance. It's better to mike the singer at least 8 inches away because small movements cause less change in loudness at that distance. If you must mike close to prevent leakage, have the singer's lips touch the pop filter to maintain a constant distance to the microphone.

Minimizing Sibilance

Sibilance is the emphasis of "s" or "sh" sounds. These sounds are strongest in the 5 to 10 kHz range, and easily can saturate a tape running at $7\frac{1}{2}$ ips if not controlled.

To reduce excessive sibilance, use a microphone with a flat response—rather than one with a presence peak—or reduce the highs around 5 kHz on your mixer. A *de-esser* device does this automatically whenever sibilant sounds occur. As an alternative, mike the vocalist from the side rather than in front, as in Figure 8.23. The "s" sounds are projected more out front than they are to the sides.

Reducing Reflections from the Lyric Sheet

Sound reflections from the lyric sheet and music stand can bounce into the microphone along with the direct sound from the vocalist (see Figure 8.24). The reflections interfere with the direct sound, creating a colored tone quality similar to mild phasing or flanging.

To eliminate this effect, place or tape the lyric sheet at the rear of the vocalist's cardioid microphone, perpendicular to the microphone axis (refer to Figure 8.22); or mike the vocalist from the side and angle the lyric sheet slightly away from the microphone (refer to Figure 8.23). In the first arrangement, reflections entering the rear of the cardioid microphone are rejected. The second method makes reflections bounce away from the microphone. Try carpet on the music stand, also.

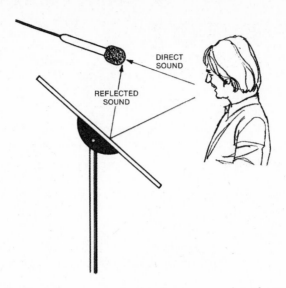

Figure 8.24 Reflections from a music stand can cause interference.

Common Vocal Effects

Some effects often used on lead vocals are reverberation, echo, and doubling. Room reverberation sometimes can be recorded live by miking the singer at a distance in a hard-surfaced, echoey room. Slap echo gives a 1950s rock and roll effect (see Chapter 10 for more information).

Doubling a vocal provides a fuller sound than a single vocal track. Record a second take of the vocal on an empty track at a slightly different miking distance. During mixdown, mix the second vocal take with the original, at a slightly lower level than the original. Or run a single vocal signal through a delay device to double it (as described in Chapter 10).

Vocals typically are boosted slightly in the presence range between 2 kHz and 5 kHz to help them stand out against an instrumental track. This boost may increase sibilance as well.

When recording a classical-music vocalist, place the microphone(s) 3 to 8 feet away to pick up room reverberation. You may want to use a boundary microphone on the floor.

Background Vocals

When overdubbing background vocals, you can group two or three singers in front of a microphone. The farther they are from the microphone, the more distant they sound in the recording. Barbershop or gospel quartets with a good natural blend can be recorded with the stereo setup seen in Figure 8.17 (or with a stereo or bidirectional mic), about 2 to 4 feet away. If their balance is poor, try miking them individually up close, and balance them with your mixer.

In general, if leakage or feedback are problems, place the microphone close to where the sound output is loudest. Otherwise, place the microphone in several different positions until you find a location where you monitor the desired tone quality and amount of ambience.

These microphone techniques are just suggestions to serve as a starting point. After trying them out, invent your own techniques. If you can capture the power and excitement of amplified instruments and drums with fidelity, if you can capture the beautiful timbre of acoustic instruments and vocals, you've made a successful recording.

TAPE RECORDING

Thanks to the tape recorder, a musical performance can be captured permanently and relived again and again. This chapter discusses the equipment and procedures related to tape recording:

- The analog tape recorder—parts and functions
- Operation and preventive maintenance of the recorder
- Noise-reduction systems
- Tape handling, storage, and editing
- The digital tape recorder and DAT

The Analog Tape Recorder

While recording, a tape recorder converts electrical signals into permanent magnetic signals on magnetic tape. The tape itself is a strip of plastic (usually mylar), with a thin coating of ferric oxide or chromium dioxide particles. These particles have a random magnetic orientation, but they can be aligned into magnetic patterns by the external magnetic field applied during recording. During playback, the tape machine converts the magnetic field on tape back into an electrical signal.

The tape recorder has three main parts: the heads, the electronics, and the transport.

The Heads

Professional open-reel tape recorders include three heads (placed left to right: erase, record, and playback (see Figure 9.1). The *erase head* produces an ultrasonic, oscillating magnetic field. As the tape passes over the erase head, the tape is exposed to a gradually decreasing magnetic field. This orients the magnetic particles randomly and erases any signal on tape.

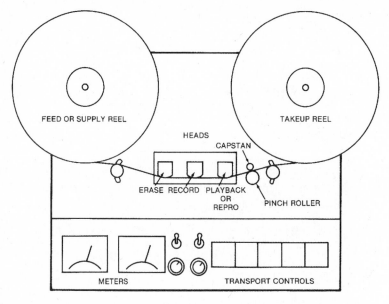

Figure 9.1 Major parts of a typical tape recorder.

The *record head* converts the incoming electrical signal into a magnetic field. The magnetic field varies as the signal does. As the tape passes the record head, the head magnetizes or aligns the tape particles in a pattern that corresponds to the audio signal. This pattern is stored permanently on tape.

The pattern stored on a tape is a magnetic field. As the tape passes the *playback head*, the head picks up this magnetic field and converts it back into a corresponding electrical signal. This signal is amplified and sent to speakers, the mixing console, or another tape deck.

Some semipro open-reel recorders, and most cassette decks, use a single head for both recording and playback.

The *gap* is a vertical line that is the break in the electromagnet. It is located in the center of the head's front face, where it contacts the tape. The record head gap puts the signal on the tape as it passes the head; the playback head gap reads the signal off the tape as it passes the head. Most heads have more than one gap (see Figure 9.2).

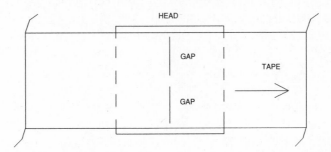

Figure 9.2 Gaps in a tape head.

There are limits to the magnetic signal level that can be recorded on tape. *Tape saturation* occurs when all the magnetic particles are aligned so that further increases in recording level do not increase the magnetic signal on tape. If the recording level is too low, tape noise (hiss) becomes audible because the recorded signal is weak compared to the random noise signals generated by nonaligned magnetic particles.

The Electronics

Tape recorder electronics amplify and equalize the incoming audio signal, send the audio signal to the record head, and amplify and equalize the signal from the playback head.

The equalization provided by the electronics is called *record equalization* and *playback equalization*. Record equalization is a slight boost at low and high frequencies to improve the S/N at these frequencies. Part of the playback equalization is a bass cut to compensate for the bass boost during recording.

During playback, the output from the playback head rises 6 db per octave. To compensate for this rise, playback equalization falls 6 db per octave. The output rises because the faster the magnetic signal varies (the higher the frequency), the higher the output of the head. The head's output doubles (goes up 6 db) with each higher octave.

The magnetism on the tape tends to erase slightly the high frequencies on tape, but playback equalization includes a high-frequency boost to compensate for this, and for high-frequency losses within the head.

The frequency response of the playback equalization has been standardized in the United States to a curve called the NAB (National Association of Broadcasters) curve. Other countries may use different playback equalization.

An ultrasonic oscillator in the electronics drives the erase head. The ultrasonic signal, called *bias*, is also mixed with the audio fed to the record head. The addition of bias is necessary to reduce distortion. The amount of bias, which is adjustable, affects the recording's audio level, frequency response, distortion, and *drop-outs* (temporary signal loss).

The bias setting is critical. Too high a setting reduces the level recorded on tape and rolls off high frequencies. Too low a setting also reduces the level on tape, results in distortion and drop-outs, and raises the high-frequency response. The bias is usually set at the factory for a particular type of tape. That's why it's important to use the type of tape your owner's manual recommends. If your cassette deck has a bias adjustment, set it according to the manufacturer's instruction booklet. Bias setting procedures for professional machines are presented later in this chapter.

The Tape Transport

The job of the transport is to move the tape past the heads. During recording and playback, the transport should move the tape at a constant speed and with constant tape tension. During rewind or fast forward, the tape shuttles rapidly from one reel to the other.

Most professional open-reel machines have three motors in the transport: two for shuttling and tape tension, and a third for driving the *capstan*. The capstan is a post that rotates against a rubber *pinch roller*. The tape is pressed between the capstan and pinch roller. As the capstan rotates, it pulls the tape past the heads. The transport also includes rollers that reduce *wow* (a slow periodic variation in tape speed) and *flutter* (rapid variation in tape speed).

The *tape counter* usually shows the elapsed time on tape. A particular point on tape—for instance, the beginning of a song—can be marked by resetting the tape counter to zero. On some machines, a return-to-zero button shuttles the tape to the zero point and then stops automatically. This function is useful for repeated practices of an overdub or a mix.

A professional open-reel tape deck moves tape at some combination of these speeds: 7½, 15, or 30 ips. Cassette decks run at 1⅞ ips or 3¾ ips. Faster speeds sound better—as tape speed increases, high-frequency headroom increases, tape hiss decreases, and wow and flutter decrease. By contrast, a slower tape speed consumes less tape and allows more running time.

Tracks

A track is a path on tape containing a single channel of audio. The wider the track (that is, the more tape it covers), the greater the S/N. Doubling the track width improves the S/N by 3 db.

Track Width

Tape recorder heads are available in different configurations. Some can erase, record, and play back over the full width of the tape; some have extra gaps so that they can record two or more independent tracks. Figure 9.3 shows some track-width standards for ¼-inch tape. Heads are available in these track formats:

- Full-track mono
- Half-track mono
- 2-track stereo or half-track stereo
- Quarter-track stereo
- Multitrack

A full-track mono head records over nearly the full width of the tape in one direction (see Figure 9.3A).

A half-track mono head records 1 track in one direction and 1 track in the opposite direction when the tape is flipped over (see Figure 9.3B). Each track covers approximately one-third of the tape. The unused third between the tracks is a guard band to prevent crosstalk between tracks.

A 2-track stereo head or half-track stereo head records 2 tracks in one direction (see Figure 9.3B). This format is used for stereo master tapes. Track widths are the same as half-track mono.

A quarter-track stereo head records 2 tracks in one direction and 2 tracks in the opposite direction when the tape has been flipped over (see Figure 9.3C). Consumer stereo cassette decks use this format on ⅛-inch tape.

A multitrack head records 4 or more tracks in one direction (see Figure 9.3C). Depending on the width of the tape, the number of tracks can be 4, 6, 8, 12, 16, 24, 32, or 48. Recorder-mixers use this tape format (4, 6, 8, or 12 tracks only).

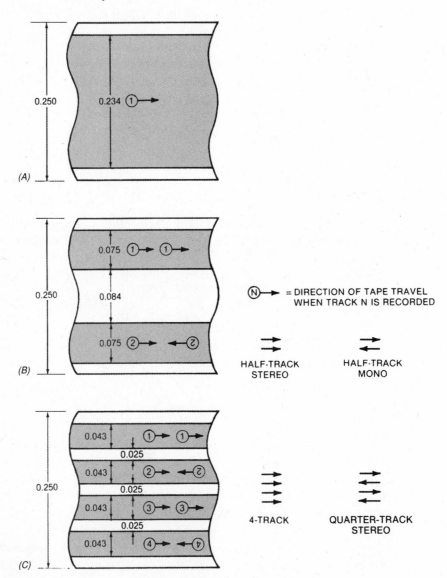

Figure 9.3 Some track-width standards for ¼-inch tape.

Tape Widths

Magnetic recording tape comes in various widths to accommodate the track formats:

- $\frac{1}{8}$-inch for $\frac{1}{4}$-track stereo, 4-track, and 8-track cassette
- $\frac{1}{4}$-inch for full-track mono, half-track mono, quarter-track stereo, 2-track stereo, 4-track, and 8-track
- $\frac{1}{2}$-inch for 4, 8, or 16 tracks
- 1-inch for 8, 16, or 24 tracks
- 2-inch for 16, 24, 32, or 48 tracks

Cassette Deck

The cassette deck from a home stereo provides a low-cost, convenient means of mastering. Excellent units are available from $200 up. A good deck should have Dolby C or dbx (which reduces tape hiss), and, if possible, Dolby HX (which reduces high-frequency distortion). Adjustable bias also is a useful feature.

The sound reproduction of a cassette deck is adequate for demo tapes, but not for masters that will be duplicated commercially. A drawback of cassettes is that you can't edit the tape to resequence the songs or add blank leader tape between them.

Multitrack and Synchronous Recording

Multitrack machines are available that record 4, 6, 8, 12, 16, 24, 32, or 48 tracks on a single tape. Each track contains the signal of a different instrument, or a different mix of instruments. The tracks can be recorded all at once, one at a time, or in any combination. After the tracks are recorded, they are combined and balanced through a mixing console. Unlike 2-track recording, multitrack recording lets you fine-tune the mix after the recording session. You can practice the changes in the mix until you get them right.

The multitrack recorder can be either a stand-alone unit or can be built into a recorder-mixer. Chapter 2 describes the features of the multitrack recorders used in recorder-mixers. The stand-alone multitrack recorder can be analog or digital. A digital recorder offers higher sound quality—as good as a compact disc—but costs more. One example of a multitrack digital recorder is the Alesis ADAT, an 8-track unit selling for under $4,000.

Multitrack recording offers the potential of clearer sound than recording live to 2-track because you can overdub instruments without microphone leakage, rather than recording them all at once. If you record several instruments and vocals simultaneously, leakage or off-mic sound can yield a muddy, loose sound in the mix. When you overdub there is no leakage, so the final mix can be cleaner.

Multitrack recording requires an extra generation because you must record the multitrack mix onto a 2-track tape. Each generation or tape copy adds at least 3 db of tape hiss (unless you use a DAT recorder, covered later). In addition, every time the number of tracks used in the mix doubles, the noise increases 3 db. This is not a lot, but it is audible.

Another trade-off of multitrack recording is that the recording process takes much longer. With live-to-2-track recording, the recording is done when the performance is done, but with multitrack recording, you must record and do a mixdown. Overdubbing is optional, but is the norm, and it adds more time.

Multitrack equipment also is more complicated and expensive, and is more time-consuming to set up. Still, the ability to fine-tune the mix after the session makes multitrack the preferred choice for pop-music recording.

One advantage of multitrack recorders is that tape tracks can be recorded at different times. For instance, a musician can listen to recorded tracks off the playback head and overdub a new part. During playback, the new part is delayed relative to the original tracks because the playback head is located a small distance from the record head.

To remove the delay caused by overdubbing and to synchronize the original tracks with the overdub, most professional open-reel decks allow the original tracks to be played through the record head temporarily. At the same time, the record head records the overdub on an open track. This process is called *simulsync*, *selsync*, or *synchronous recording*. It's usually enabled by setting each track's tape monitor switch to the SYNC position. When you play a tape through the record head, the signal loses highs but is adequate for synching.

Semipro tape decks and recorder-mixers that combine the record and playback functions in one head do not have a sync problem; previously recorded tracks and overdubs are always synchronized.

Meters and Level Setting

Meters on the tape recorder (one per track) show the record and playback levels. These meters may be VU meters, VU meters with built-in peak LEDs, or LED bargraph indicators showing peak levels.

The VU Meter

A VU meter is a voltmeter that shows approximately the relative volume or loudness of the audio signal. The meter is calibrated in VU or Volume Units. The Volume Unit corresponds to the decibel only when measuring a steady-state sine-wave tone. That is, 1 VU = 1 db only when a steady tone is applied.

A *0 VU recording level* (0 on the record level meter) is the normal operating level of a recorder. It indicates that the magnetic signal is being recorded on tape at the optimum level.

Excessive recording levels (greater than +3 VU) saturate or overload the tape, causing distortion. Levels that are too low (for instance, consistently below –10 VU) result in audible tape hiss.

When a complex waveform is applied to a VU meter, the meter reads less than the peak voltage of the waveform because the response of a VU meter is not fast enough to track rapid transients accurately.

This inaccuracy can cause problems with level setting. For example, if you record drums at 0 VU on the meter, peaks may be 8 to 14 db higher, resulting in tape distortion. So, whenever you record instruments having sharp attacks or a high peak-to-average ratio (such as drums, piano, percussion, or horns), record at –6 to –8 VU to prevent tape distortion. In some instances (with drums, for example), mild distortion on peaks (recording "hot") may give a desirable effect. Instruments with a low peak-to-average ratio (such as organ or flute) can be recorded around +3 VU without audible distortion.

Peak Indicators

Unlike the VU meter, the peak indicator shows peak recording levels more accurately because it responds very rapidly. If your recorder has LED peak indicators, set the levels for all the tracks so that the LEDs flash only occasionally. For setting recording levels, an LED flash takes precedence over the VU meter reading. If the recorder has LED bargraph peak indicators, set all tracks to peak at 0 to +6 db, depending on the sound source.

Judging Machine Specifications

When considering the requirements for a quality analog tape recorder, whether open-reel or cassette, obtain the published specifications for the deck you want to buy or use, and look for the specs given in the next three sections.

Wow and Flutter

If wow and flutter are excessive, they wobble the pitch of recorded instruments. The lower the wow and flutter spec, the steadier the reproduced pitch. Watch for the following:

0.04% RMS weighted (or WRMS) is excellent.
0.05% RMS weighted (or WRMS) is very good.
0.1% IEC/ANSI peak weighted is very good.

Higher values than these are not as good, and mean that you may hear the pitch wobble on recordings of fretted stringed instruments or piano.

Signal-to-Noise Ratio

Recall from Chapter 3 that this is the ratio, expressed in db, between the maximum undistorted recorded signal level and the noise level. The higher the S/N, the more noise-free the recording. All the following specs are measured with noise reduction:

90 db is excellent (typical of dbx).
85 db is excellent (typical of Dolby S or SR).
70 db is very good (typical of Dolby C).
65 db is good.
55 db is fair.

These specs are A-weighted, which means that the measurement includes the effect of the frequency response on the human ear. When comparing two different decks, be sure that both signal-to-noise specs are A-weighted.

Record/Play Response

The record/play response is the range of frequencies that the recorder records and plays back at an equal level, within a tolerance (such as ±3 db). The lower the lower frequency, and the higher the upper frequency, the better the fidelity. Watch for the following specs:

40 Hz-18 kHz (±3 db) is excellent for a cassette deck.
40 Hz-18 kHz (±1 db) is excellent for an open-reel deck.
40 Hz-14 kHz (±3 db) is good.
40 Hz-12.5 kHz (±3 db) is fair.

Operating Precautions

There are several things that can go wrong during a recording session, rendering your tape unusable and the session a waste of time. The following are tips that may prevent some accidents:

- Don't put the machine in record mode until levels are set. If you record an extremely high-level high-frequency signal, the crosstalk within the head might erase other tracks.

- Keep tape away from recorder heads when turning the machine on or off, or you may put a click on tape.

- Keep degaussers and bulk tape erasers several feet from tapes you don't want to erase.

- Before you start recording on a track, make sure you won't be erasing something you want to keep. Listen to the track first and refer to your track sheet.

- Edge tracks of multitrack tapes are prone to drop-outs due to edge damage. Because drop-outs occur mostly at high frequencies, use the edge tracks only to record instruments with little high-frequency output (such as bass or kick drum).

- Repeated passes of a recording past the heads may erase high frequencies gradually. You may want to make a copy of the multi-track tape (or a quick 2-track mix) for musicians to practice over-dubs with and then go back to the original tape when the musicians are ready to record.

- Bouncing or ping-ponging tracks tends to lose high-frequency response and increases tape hiss, so try to limit bounced tracks to bass or midrange instruments.

Noise Reduction

The analog tape recorder adds undesirable tape hiss and *print-through* to the recorded signal, degrading its clarity. Print-through is the transfer of a magnetic signal from one layer of tape to the next, causing an echo. Tape hiss becomes especially audible during a multitrack mixdown because every track mixed in adds to the overall noise level. Noise increases 3 db whenever the number of tracks in use doubles, assuming they are mixed at equal levels.

Fortunately, noise-reduction devices such as Dolby or dbx are available to reduce tape hiss and print-through. However, these units do not remove noise in the original signal from the mixing console. If your signal is noisy before you record it, Dolby or dbx does not remove this noise. They work only on tape noise.

One channel of noise reduction is needed per tape track. Noise-reduction units connect between the mixer output buses and the corresponding tape-track inputs, and also between the tape-track outputs and the mixer tape inputs (see Figure 9.4). Some open-reel recorders and most cassette recorders have built-in noise reduction; it is permanently connected.

These noise-reduction devices compress the signal during recording and expand it in a complementary fashion during playback. The compressor part of the circuit boosts the recorded level of quiet musical passages. The expander part works in a complementary way during playback, turning down the volume during quiet passages, thereby reducing noise added by the tape. During loud passages (when noise is masked by the program), the gain returns to normal.

A compressed tape is described as *encoded*; the expanded tape is called *decoded*. If an encoded tape is played without decoding, the dynamic range and frequency response are altered.

It's important that the encode and decode sections track each other. For example, a 10 db level change at the input of the encode section should yield a 10 db level change at the output of the decode section. Otherwise,

dynamics sound unnatural. To avoid this problem, avoid excessive recording levels and adjust the noise-reduction unit for correct tracking if it
can be adjusted (see the operating manual for instructions).

Two types of noise-reduction systems have become standard in the
home and pro recording industry: dbx and Dolby.

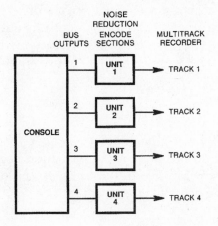

(A) Recording.

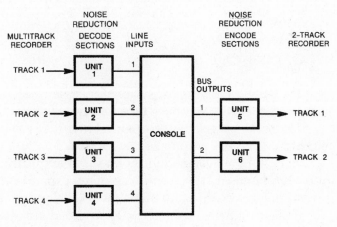

(B) Mixdown.

Figure 9.4 Noise reduction applied to multitrack tape and to 2-track master
tape.

dbx

With dbx noise reduction, the compression ratio is 2:1. That is, a program with a 90 db dynamic range is compressed to 45 db, which is easily handled by a tape recorder with a 60 db S/N. During playback, the dynamic range is expanded back to the original 90 db. Use of dbx improves S/N by 30 db and increases headroom by 10 db. The dbx circuit also includes preemphasis (treble boost) of 12 db during recording and complementary deemphasis (treble cut) during playback to reduce modulation noise. dbx operates at all signal levels and across the entire audible spectrum.

Dolby

Dolby operates only on quiet passages—those below –10 VU. High-level passages do not need noise reduction because the program masks the noise. There are five different types of Dolby noise reduction (listed in increasing order of effectiveness):

- Dolby B
- Dolby C
- Dolby A
- Dolby S
- Dolby SR

Dolby B is a lower-cost system for cassette decks, and operates only at high frequencies to reduce tape hiss by up to 10 db.

Dolby C, for cassette and open-reel, works over a slightly wider range and reduces noise by up to 20 db.

The Dolby A system divides the audible spectrum into four separate frequency bands that are compressed and expanded independently. This system reduces noise by 10 db below 5 kHz, and up to 15 db at 15 kHz.

Dolby S reduces tape hiss by 24 db and low-frequency noise by 10 db.

Dolby SR (Spectral Recording) is the most effective Dolby system, reducing noise by more than 25 db over most of the audible spectrum. As a result, a recorder operated at 15 ips with Dolby SR can have a maximum S/N exceeding 105 db. During recording, Dolby SR boosts the gain of regions of the spectrum that are low-to-medium in level. During playback, it reduces the gain of the same regions in a complementary fashion.

Dolby A, S, and SR are only for open-reel units. When using Dolby A, you must record a calibration signal called a *Dolby tone* on tape before the regular program. This tone is generated by an oscillator in the Dolby unit. During playback, the level of the recorded Dolby tone is indicated on a Dolby meter. You set the Dolby input level so that the meter indication lines up with the Dolby-level mark on the meter. Then the expander circuitry tracks the recording properly.

If the level is set improperly, the frequency response and dynamic range are slightly altered. Fortunately, there is room for some error, because these alterations occur in low-level signals and consequently are hard to hear.

Dolby versus dbx

Both Dolby and dbx have advantages and disadvantages. Compared to Dolby, dbx provides more noise reduction. On the other hand, dbx exaggerates drop-outs more than Dolby does. dbx-encoded tapes have some "breathing"—hiss or fuzziness that varies with the signal level, especially on bass or percussion tracks. Recordings made with Dolby are free of breathing; dbx can change the dynamics at low frequencies.

Many professional engineers record at 30 ips, without noise reduction, or use Dolby SR.

Dolby-encoded and dbx-encoded tapes are not compatible with each other, and cannot be played properly without decoding through the appropriate unit. So, if you plan to send your tapes to another studio, check that the studio has the same type of noise reduction that you want to use. If you're unsure what type of noise reduction to use on mass-produced cassettes, use Dolby B because all consumer stereo cassette decks have it. You can use whatever you want on your multitrack tape.

When using noise reduction, avoid saturating the tape while recording. Otherwise, the attack transients may be altered during playback through the noise-reduction unit. If you are using noise reduction, you can record at 3 VU lower than normal for 3 db more headroom. When you copy a tape, switch in the noise reduction on the playback deck (if it has been recorded with noise reduction), and also on the recording deck. Be sure to copy the Dolby tone if the master tape has one.

Matching Mixer and Recorder Meters

In a recorder-mixer, the mixer meters and recorder meters are the same, but if you're using a separate mixer and recorder, it's common practice to set the mixer meters and recorder meters to match each other. That way you have to watch only the mixer meters while recording. Also, when the mixer and recorder are both peaking around 0 VU, this prevents excessive noise and distortion in both units.

Ideally, meter matching is done with a steady tone from a signal generator or a synthesizer note (C or B two octaves above middle C). Otherwise, hum a steady tone into a microphone plugged into your mixer, and set the levels on the mixer and tape deck to 0.

If your tape deck meters move faster or slower than your mixer meters, you have to watch the tape deck meters while recording.

If dbx noise reduction is used, matching the meters becomes confusing because the encoded signal from the dbx is compressed. The recorder meters wiggle less than the mixer meters. Follow the calibration instructions in the dbx instruction manual, and watch the recorder meters while recording.

Once the mixer and recorder are calibrated to match each other at 0 VU, leave the recorder controls alone. Set levels with the mixer faders only.

Preventive Maintenance

The analog tape recorder needs periodic maintenance—cleaning, demagnetizing, alignment, and calibration—to ensure optimum performance.

Cleaning the Tape Path

Over time, dust and oxide shed from the tape and build up on your deck's heads. This layer of deposits separates the tape from the heads, causing high-frequency loss (a dull, muffled sound) and drop-outs (quick level drops). In addition, buildup of oxide on the tape guides, capstan, and pinch roller can cause wobbly pitch. It's very important to clean the entire tape path before every recording session.

Use the cleaning fluid recommended in your recorder manual. Denatured alcohol (or a freon-based cleaner) and a dense-packed cotton swab are often used. Don't use rubbing alcohol or isopropyl alcohol because they can leave a film on the head, and they contain water. Allow the cleaning fluid to dry before putting in a cassette or threading on a tape.

Demagnetizing the Tape Path

Tape heads and tape guides build up a magnetic field that can partly erase high frequencies, add tape hiss, and cause clicks at splices. You can get rid of this magnetism with a tape head *demagnetizer* or *degausser*. Generally, only the gapped types are strong enough to be effective; the pencil-shaped types may cost less but don't work as well.

Essentially an electromagnet with a probe tip, the demagnetizer produces a rapidly vibrating magnetic field. Touch the probe tip to the head in order to magnetize it; then slowly pull the tip away so that the magnetism tapers off until none is left.

The technique of using a demagnetizer is critical:

1. If necessary, cover the probe tip with electrical tape or a handkerchief to avoid scratching the heads.

2. Turn off your recorder-mixer. Be sure that no tapes are near the demagnetizer.

3. With the demagnetizer at least 1 foot from your recorder-mixer, plug it in.

4. Bring the demagnetizer slowly to the part to be demagnetized.

5. After touching the part with the probe tip, remove the demagnetizer slowly to at least 1 foot away and unplug it. In this way, the induced magnetic field diminishes to zero gradually.

Move slowly. If you touch the demagnetizer to a head and quickly remove it, you magnetize the head worse than when you started! Demagnetize each tape head and tape guide in this manner—one at a time. Demagnetize your machines after every eight hours of use and before playing an alignment tape. The same precautions about slow operation apply to a bulk tape eraser as well.

Alignment and Calibration for a Cassette Deck

For the best high-frequency response (brilliance and clarity), the gap in each head must be exactly at a right angle to the tape edge. This is called *azimuth alignment* (see Figure 9.5). The azimuth is the left-right head angle relative to the tape edge. Cassette deck heads are aligned at the recorder factory, and usually stay aligned if you treat the recorder gently and avoid bumping it. In professional studios, however, the heads are aligned periodically with the aid of a *standard alignment tape* (described later).

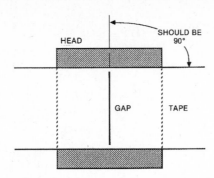

Figure 9.5 Azimuth alignment.

In a home studio, if you clean and demagnetize the heads, and still think that the high-frequency response of your recorder is diminished, consider aligning the heads yourself or letting a professional technician do it. You need either a standard alignment tape or a commercially recorded cassette. You may need to remove the cassette door cover first.

Look for a small spring-loaded screw next to the record/playback head. This screw affects the azimuth. If you have an alignment tape, put it in your cassette deck and play the 15 kHz tone. Adjust the azimuth screw for maximum signal level as shown on your meters.

If you lack an alignment tape, put on a good commercially recorded cassette that has lots of cymbals or high-hat. Adjust the azimuth screw to the point where these instruments sound the most crisp and clear. You'll find a peak in the clarity at a certain screw rotation, and a duller sound on either side of that.

Before a cassette deck or recorder-mixer is shipped to your dealer, its electronics are factory calibrated—adjusted for optimum performance from a certain brand of tape. If your machine is calibrated correctly, the playback signal should sound like the input signal (except for some added tape hiss, and perhaps a little loss of clarity or high end). The calibration is usually left alone, and you use the brand of tape for which the machine was adjusted.

Occasionally, these circuit adjustments drift, so the circuit may need to be recalibrated. It's a complicated procedure best left to a service technician. In fact, some home and semipro recorders are not designed for easy calibration. The internal parts to be adjusted may not be easily accessible.

Alignment and Calibration for Professional Tape Machines

Professional recording engineers align and calibrate their machines periodically to ensure flat frequency response, maximum S/N, and lowest distortion. They also align and calibrate to correctly reproduce tapes made at other studios, using the alignment tones on those tapes.

To perform a complete alignment, you need

- A small screwdriver

- An audio-frequency generator

- A standard playback alignment tape

Information about standard playback alignment tapes is available from various tape recorder manufacturers, and from Ampex (2201 Lunt Ave., Elk Grove Village, IL 60007) and Magnetic Reference Laboratory (999 Commercial St., Palo Alto, CA 94303).

Follow the tape recorder instructions regarding calibration—be sure to clean and demagnetize the tape heads before starting. Basically, you follow these steps:

1. Using the alignment tape, play the 15 kHz tone and adjust the playback head azimuth for maximum output or for best phase match between channels (using an oscilloscope).

2. Adjust the high-frequency playback equalization (if any) to achieve the same output level at 700 Hz and 10 kHz. Or try for the flattest overall response if several tones are on the tape. Don't adjust the low-frequency equalization yet.

3. The magnetic field strength on tape (the fluxivity) is measured in nanowebers per meter (nwb/m). If you're using an alignment tape that has a standard operating level of 185 nwb/m (old Ampex standard level), set the playback level to read –3 VU or –6 VU as recommended by the recording tape manufacturer. If you're using an elevated-level alignment tape that uses a standard operating level of 250 nwb/m or 320 nwb/m, set the playback level to read 0 VU (or as recommended by the recording tape manufacturer and recorder manufacturer). Do not touch the playback level for the rest of the calibration.

4. Thread on some blank tape of the desired brand.

5. Record a 15 kHz tone and adjust the record head azimuth for maximum playback output, or for best phase match between channels. (Skip this step if your recorder combines the record and playback functions in a single head.)

6. While recording a 1 kHz tone, set the bias to achieve maximum playback level. Then go back to 10 kHz, and turn up the bias past that point (*overbias*) until the output drops 0.5 to 1 db. Overbiasing reduces drop-outs and modulation noise. Consult the tape manufacturer's directions for alternative overbias settings.

7. While recording tones of 10 kHz, 100 Hz, and 700 Hz, adjust the high-frequency record equalization and low-frequency playback equalization (if any) to achieve the same playback output level at all frequencies. Or use many tones to achieve the flattest overall response. Record the tones at 0 VU for 15 ips, –10 VU for 7 ½ ips, and –20 VU for cassettes. The slower tape speeds need lower recording levels to prevent tape saturation at high frequencies.

8. Feed a 1 kHz tone at 0 VU from the mixing console to the recorder. Record the tone. Set the record level so that the recorder reads 0 VU on playback.

9. Set the "record cal" or "meter cal" so that the meter reads 0 VU on "input" or "source."

After calibration, your tape machine will operate as well as possible with the particular type of tape you're using. The playback signal should sound virtually identical to the input signal (except for some added tape hiss).

Using Magnetic Tape

Now that you have been introduced to tape recording hardware, it's time to consider the tape itself—its editing, handling, and storage.

Editing and Leadering

Recall from Chapter 2 that editing is the cutting and rejoining of open-reel magnetic tape to delete unwanted material, insert leader tape, or rearrange material into the desired sequence. If you're doing all your work on cassettes, you can skip this section.

Equipment and Preparation

Editing requires the following materials: demagnetized single-edge razor blades, a light-colored grease pencil, splicing tape, *leader tape*, and an *editing block*.

Leader tape is plastic or paper tape without an oxide coating, which is used for a spacer between takes (silence between recorded songs). Plastic leader is preferred over paper because paper can absorb humidity during long storage and can become warped. An editing block holds the tape during the splicing operation. It's easier to use than a tape splicer with hold-down tabs and allows more precise cuts.

Before editing, wash your hands to avoid getting oily spots on the tape. Cut several 1-inch pieces of splicing tape and stick them on the edge of the tape deck or table. Cut several sections of leader at the 45-degree slot in the editing block. A typical leader length between songs is 4 seconds, which is 60 inches long for 15 ips or 30 inches long for $7\frac{1}{2}$ ips. While editing, try to hold the magnetic tape lightly by the edges.

Leadering

Suppose you've recorded a reel full of takes and you want to remove the outtakes, count-offs, and noises between the good takes. You also want to insert leader between each song. This process, called *leadering*, can be done with the following steps:

1. Wind several turns of leader onto an empty take-up reel and cut the leader at the 45 degree slot.

2. Remove this take-up reel, put on an empty one, and play the tape to be edited.

3. Locate the beginning of the first song's best take. Stop the tape there.

4. Put the machine in cue or edit mode so the tape presses against the heads.

5. While monitoring the tape recorder output, rock the tape back and forth over the heads by rotating both reels by hand—first rapidly and then more and more slowly. You'll hear the music slowed down and low in pitch.

6. Find the exact point on tape where the song starts, that is, where it passes over the playback head gap. Align the beginning sound with the gap.

7. Using the grease pencil, mark the tape about 1/2-inch to the right of the gap, that is, at a point on tape just before the song starts.

8. Loosen or "dump" the tape by rotating the supply reel counter-clockwise and the take-up reel clockwise simultaneously.

9. Remove the tape from the tape path and press it into the splicing block, oxide side down.

10. Align the mark with the 45 degree angled slot (see Figure 9.6).

11. Slice through the tape with a razor blade, drawing the blade toward you. Don't use the 90 degree slot because such an abrupt cut can cause a pop noise at the splice.

12. Remove the unwanted tape to the right of the cut and put the take-up reel aside.

13. Slide the cut end of the tape to the right of the editing-block slot (see Figure 9.7).

14. Put on the take-up reel containing the turns of leader tape, and insert the end of the leader into the right half of the block.

15. Slide together the ends of the leader tape and magnetic tape so that they butt or touch together with no overlap.

16. Take a piece of splicing tape and stick a corner of it onto a hand-held razor blade.

17. Align the splicing tape piece parallel to the recording tape.

18. Apply the piece over the cut onto the nonoxide side, and stick it down by rubbing with your fingernail.

19. Slide the splice out of the block. Gently pop the tape out of the block by pulling up on the ends of the tape extending from both sides of the block. Twist the tape toward you while pulling.

20. Check that there is no gap or overlap at the splice.

21. Wind the tape onto the take-up reel and locate the ending of the first song.

22. As it ends, turn up the monitors and listen for the point where the reverberant tail of the music fades into tape hiss. Stop the tape there and mark it lightly at the playback head gap (at the center line of the head).

23. After pressing the tape into the block, cut the tape at the mark. Remove the tape to the left of the cut.

24. Splice the end of the first song to a 4-second length of leader and again check the splice.

25. Wind the first song and the leader onto the take-up reel and remove it.

26. Put on the take-up reel containing unwanted material you set aside previously. Splice it to the rest of the master tape.

27. Locate the beginning of the next good take you want in the program. Mark it and cut the tape.

28. Put the reel containing the first song on the take-up spindle.

29. Splice the tail end of the leader onto the beginning of the second song and then wind the second song onto the take-up reel. You now have two songs joined by leader tape.

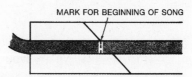

(A) Mark for beginning of song.

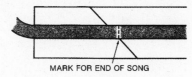

(B) Mark for end of song.

Figure 9.6 Aligning edit marks with cutting slot.

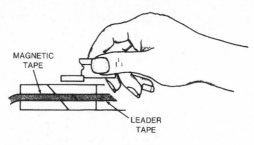

Figure 9.7 Applying splicing tape.

Repeat these steps until all the good takes are joined by leader. You then have a reel of tape with several songs separated by white leader, which makes it easy to find the desired selections

Joining Different Takes

What if you want to join the verse of Take 1 to the chorus of Take 2? You have to cut into both takes at the same point in the song and then join them. It takes practice to make an inaudible splice in this manner, but it's done every day in professional studios.

The two takes must match in tempo, balance, and level for the edit to be undetectable. To mask any clicks occurring at the splice, cut the tape just before a beat—at the beginning of a drum attack, for instance. An alternative is to cut into a silent pause. If you cut into a continuous sound, such as a steady chord, a cymbal ring, or reverberation, the splice is noticeable.

Follow these steps to join different takes:

1. Play Take 1 and locate the point where you want Take 1 to stop and Take 2 to start—at the beginning of the chorus, for instance. Stop the tape there.

2. Put the recorder in cue or edit mode, rock the tape, and try to identify a beat or attack transient.

3. At the point on tape where this beat just starts to cross the play-back head gap, mark the tape.

4. Cut the tape at the mark and remove the take-up reel containing the verse of Take 1.

5. Put on an empty take-up reel, thread the master tape, and fast-wind to Take 2.

6. Find the same spot in Take 2 that you marked in Take 1. Mark and cut it.

7. Using splicing tape, join Take 2 (in the supply reel) to Take 1 (in the take-up reel you just set aside). Again, check that there is no gap and no overlap at the splice.

Play the spliced area to see if the edit is detectable. If not, congratulations! It should sound like a single take. If Take 2 comes in a little late, carefully remove the splice and cut out just a little tape surrounding the cut. Resplice and listen again.

Suppose you record most of a good take, but the musicians make a mistake and stop playing. Rather than repeating the entire song, the musicians can start playing a little before the point where they stopped and then finish the song. You splice the two segments into a complete and perfect take. Editing is also useful for inserting sound effects in the middle of a song, or for making tape loops. You even can record a difficult mixdown in segments and then edit the segments together.

Reducing Print-Through

If print-through follows the program, it is called *post-echo*. If it precedes the program, it is called *pre-echo*. Print-through is especially audible in recordings with many silent passages, such as narration. To minimize print-through:

- Demagnetize the tape path (stray magnetic fields increase print-through).

- Use 1½-millimeter tape (thinner tapes increase print-through). C-60 cassette tape is thicker than C-90, so C-60 is preferred.

- Use noise-reduction devices (discussed earlier in this chapter).

- Store tapes at temperatures under 80 degrees Fahrenheit, and don't leave tapes on a hot machine (heat increases print-through).

- Rewind tapes in storage at least once a year. This action allows print-through to decay by separating and realigning adjacent layers of tape.

- Store tapes tail out. That is, after playing or recording a tape, leave it on the take-up reel. Rewinding a tape about 15 minutes before playing helps to reduce print-through that may have occurred during storage. (This measure becomes less effective as the storage time increases.) In addition, tail-out storage results mainly in post-echo, which is less audible than the pre-echo that is emphasized in tapes that are rewound before being stored.

Tape Handling and Storage

Careful handling and storage of tape reels is essential to avoid damaging the tape and the signals recorded on it.

If you examine a reel of used recording tape, you may see some edges or layers of tape sticking out of the tape pack. These edges can be crushed by pressure from the reel flanges, causing drop-outs and high-frequency loss. For this reason, never hold a reel of tape by squeezing the flanges together. Instead, hold the reel in one hand by putting your fingers in the hub and your thumb on the flange edges (see Figure 9.8). When using two hands, hold the reel with extended fingers on the flange edges.

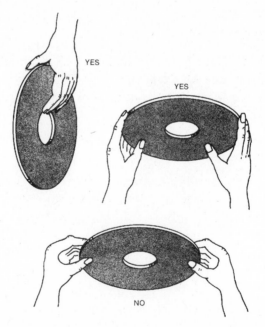

Figure 9.8 Handling tape reels.

To prevent edge damage during storage, leave tapes tail out after playing or recording to ensure a smooth tape pack. Repair or discard reels with a bent flange. Reels left out in the open can collect dust, so keep them in boxes. Store tape boxes vertically, not stacked. The preferred storage conditions are 60 to 75 degrees Fahrenheit and 35 to 50 percent relative humidity. Keep tapes away from magnetic fields, such as those caused by speakers, headphones, or telephones.

The Digital Tape Recorder

The types of recorders described so far were analog recorders. That is, the magnetic particles on tape are oriented in patterns analogous to the audio waveform. The drawbacks of this system are tape hiss, tape distortion, frequency-response errors, wow, and flutter. Digital recorders eliminate these problems. A full discussion of the digital recorder is beyond the scope of this book, but the following is a brief overview of the process:

1. The signal (varying voltage) from the mixer is run through a lowpass filter that removes all frequencies above 20 kHz.

2. The filtered signal then passes through an *analog-to-digital (A/D) converter* (see Figure 9.9A). This converter measures the voltage of the audio waveform several thousand times a second (see Figure 9.9B).

3. Each time the waveform is measured, it is quantized, that is, a binary number (made of 1s and 0s) is generated that represents the voltage of the waveform at the instant it is measured (see Figure 9.9C). Each 1 and 0 is called a *bit*, which stands for binary digit.

4. In a digital tape recorder, these binary numbers are stored magnetically on tape in the form of a modulated square wave, recorded at maximum level (see Figure 9.9D).

The playback process is the reverse:

1. The binary numbers are read from tape (or, in a sampler, from memory).

2. The *digital-to-analog (D/A) converter* translates the numbers back into an analog signal made of voltage steps.

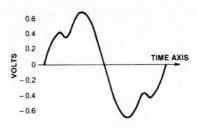

(A) The audio waveform enters the A/D converter.

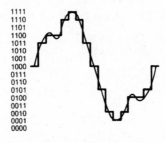

(B) The voltage is measured at regular intervals.

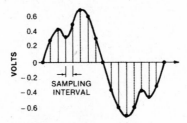

(C) The voltage measurements are quantized.

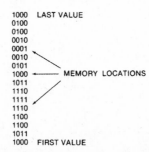

(D) The binary numbers are stored in memory or on tape.

Figure 9.9 Digital recording.

3. An anti-imaging filter smooths the steps in the analog signal, resulting in the original analog signal. Because the digital playback head reads only two binary numbers, it is insensitive to tape hiss and tape distortion. Numbers are read into a buffer memory and read out at a constant rate, eliminating speed variations.

The resulting freedom from noise, distortion, print-through, wow, and flutter makes digital recordings sound extremely clean and clear. Unlike analog recordings, digital recordings can be copied with little or no degradation in quality. Lost data is usually restored by error-correction circuitry.

Two other digital recording devices are a *computer hard-disk drive* and a *sampler*. They use the same A/D-D/A conversion processes just described. In a hard-disk drive, the binary numbers are stored on the hard magnetic disk. In a sampler, they are stored in random access memory (RAM)—a group of integrated circuit chips, each containing thousands of solid-state switches. Because RAM memory is limited, a sampler records only short sound events, such as a single note from an instrument. More on samplers in Chapter 15.

Recall that the audio signal is measured several thousand times a second to generate a string of binary numbers. The longer each binary number is (the more bits it has), the greater the accuracy of the measurement. In other words, short binary numbers provide poor resolution of the waveform's amplitude or voltage; long binary numbers provide good resolution. A *quantization* of 16 bits is adequate for high-fidelity reproduction. It is the current standard for digital tape recording and compact discs.

Don't confuse quantization with sequencer quantizing, which makes musical performances precise rhythmically.

Sampling Rate

The rate at which the waveform is measured is called the sampling rate, measured in samples/second. At a sampling rate of 40 kHz, 40,000 measurements are generated for each second of sound.

The higher the sampling rate, the wider the frequency response of the recording. The upper frequency limit is slightly less than half the sampling rate. If the sampling rate is 44.1 kHz, this is adequate for high-fidelity reproduction up to 20 kHz.

A rate of 44.1 kHz is the current standard for compact discs; 48 kHz is standard for open-reel digital audio tape. Sampling rates are selectable.

DAT Recorder

Currently, open-reel digital recorders are quite expensive. For stereo mastering, there's an alternative to an open-reel digital recorder: a DAT or R-DAT (Rotating-head Digital Audio Tape) recorder. Costing $800 and up, a DAT recorder (see Figure 9.10) records audio digitally on a small cassette. Its sound quality is as good as a compact disc. What you put in, you get out—with virtually no added hiss, distortion, wow, or flutter.

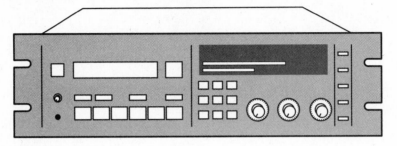

Figure 9.10 A DAT recorder.

A DAT cassette is about half the size of a standard analog cassette, measuring 73 by 54 by 10.5 millimeters. Its tape is 3.81 millimeters (⅛-inch) wide. The shell has a hinged door that flips open to expose the tape, much like a video cassette.

When you load the cassette, two spindles enter the two hubs from below the cassette and lock it into place. Then the tape is drawn into the machine and wraps around a rotating drum, which holds the record and playback heads.

The digital signal is recorded on tape in diagonal tracks. (The tracks laid down by the rotating head are thinner than a human hair!) Although the linear tape speed is slow, the tape speed as seen by the record head is very high so that the ultrasonic digital signal can be recorded. Tape dropouts can cause data losses, but most of these are reconstructed by error-correction circuitry.

DAT tapes can record up to two hours of audio on a tape about 60 meters long. Blank tapes use a metal-powder oxide; prerecorded tapes use a barium-ferrite oxide. The cassette includes a sliding tab on one end to prevent accidental erasure. The DAT transport is very fast. A 2-hour tape winds in about 45 seconds.

A major drawback of DAT tape is that you can't resequence the tape by splicing it. Instead, you must copy from one DAT machine to another, changing the order of selections during the copying process.

Another drawback is that you can't leader the DAT tape to provide silent spaces between songs. On an open-reel machine, you can. There are low-tech ways around the leadering problem; they are covered in Chapter 13.

You *can* resequence, add spaces between songs, and perform tight edits with a digital-audio editing system. You play your DAT tape, record it on hard disk, use a mouse and computer screen to edit the selections, and record a new edited DAT tape off the hard disk. Some editors are Digidesign Audiomedia, Digidesign Sound Tools, Sonic Solutions Sonic System, and the Turtle Beach 56K system.

There are other problems with mastering to DAT machines. In some units, the quality of the analog electronics and D/A converters is relatively poor, and the archival ability of DAT tape is not established clearly.

Some DAT machines come in two parts: a tape transport and a digital audio processor. Most DATs have conventional cassette transport controls, plus a number of unique features, indicators, and controls. Some of these are described in the next four sections.

Subcodes

This is information written on tape, independent of the audio signal, that tells the machine the number of each selection or program, where each selection starts, and whether or not to play each one. Subcodes can be recorded easily or erased without altering the audio program. The three main types of subcodes are

- Program numbers
- Skip ID
- Start ID

Program numbers are assigned to selections in order, and can then be used to locate them.

A Start ID marks the beginning of each selection. It can be written manually or automatically. Manual Start IDs can be placed anywhere, to mark cues, for instance. Automatic Start IDs are put on tape whenever there is enough signal applied, after a silence of three or more seconds. Record manual Start IDs after recording all your mixes onto a DAT tape.

As with other subcodes, Start IDs can be recorded or erased without altering the audio program, and you can enter them during recording or playback. If the cassette's safety tab is set to prevent accidental erasure, you can't record or erase subcodes.

A Skip ID makes the machine skip the selection. This ID can be written only manually. Whenever the machine senses a Skip ID during playback, it stops and fast-winds to the next Start ID, and begins playing. This function can be turned on and off.

DAT Features

Some DAT machines include these features:

- Search
- Memory rewind or return-to-zero
- SMPTE time code
- Digital inputs and outputs

When you enable the search function, the machine fast-winds to the selected program number.

When enabled, memory rewind or return-to-zero rewinds the tape to a preset 0 position on the tape counter.

SMPTE time code is available on a few models, digitally encoded as part of the subcode.

Digital inputs and outputs allow copies to be made in the digital domain with no A/D-D/A converters required. A copy made from a digital in/out is a clone of the original recording, with no loss in sound quality. The digital connectors are either consumer type (IEC 958 or SPDIF) or professional type (AES/EBU or SDIF-2).

Other features might include a built-in monitor speaker, a time-clock/calendar, phantom power for condenser microphones, input attenuator to prevent overload, and a stereo microphone. Portable units run off battery power as well as AC.

DAT Indicators

DAT indicators include

- LED or LCD display window
- Error indicator
- Sampling frequency indicator
- Subcode information indicator
- Search mode indicator

The LED or LCD display window displays tape running time, absolute time, remaining time on the tape, or elapsed time for the current selection. Peak-reading bargraph meters are also included. Unlike with an analog tape deck, 0 on the meter is absolute maximum recording level. If your peaks are reaching 0, that level is too high.

The error indicator shows a loss of data. Usually the electronics can correct for this loss.

The sampling frequency indicator shows the frequency at which the machine is sampling audio signals, such as 44.1 kHz.

The subcode information indicator shows subcode information (program numbers, Start ID, and Skip ID).

The search mode indicator shows whether the search mode is activated.

DAT Controls

DAT controls include

- Sampling frequency
- Numeric keypad
- Analog/digital input selector
- Emphasis
- Copy inhibit

Sampling frequency is the rate at which the DAT's A/D convertor samples or measures the analog waveform. If you have a professional DAT recorder, you can set the sampling frequency to 44.1, 48, or 32 kHz. A 32 kHz sampling rate, available in some models, provides either longer playing time or four channels.

A rate of 44.1 kHz is preferred if your tapes will be duplicated on compact disc because no sample-rate conversion is necessary. Older consumer DAT machines record only at a 48 kHz sampling frequency, but a CD requires a sampling rate of 44.1 kHz. If you have a consumer DAT deck and want to do a digital-to-digital transfer to CD, the mastering engineer must use a sampling-rate converter. Most CD manufacturers can convert a 48K tape to 44.1K, but check with them first. The mastering engineer can avoid sampling-rate conversion if the DAT's analog outputs are used.

The numeric keypad is used to enter subcodes.

The analog/digital input selector chooses between analog or digital input signals.

Used in consumer DAT recorders, emphasis boosts high frequencies during recording and attenuates them during playback. The result is lower noise.

Copy inhibit prevents dubbing any material that is copy protected. A DAT deck identifies data that has been recorded with a copy inhibit flag in its subcode, and does not copy that recording digitally. (Be sure copy inhibit is off if you want to duplicate your DAT master digitally.)

Consumer DAT machines have a copy inhibit system called SCMS (Serial Copy Management System). This feature lets you make a digital-to-digital recording of a commercial DAT or CD, but prevents regenerations from that copy. That is, you can't make subsequent digital copies of the copy. SCMS does *not* prevent digital duplication of DAT recordings of your mixer output or other analog source.

Thanks to digital recording, the original goal of tape recording has finally been achieved: to accurately store and reproduce your audio creations.

SIGNAL PROCESSORS AND EFFECTS

With effects, you can modify or enhance the basic sounds of recorded instruments and voices. For example, you can put a studio-recorded instrument in a concert hall with reverberation, or add a moving, shimmering effect with stereo chorus.

Effects are created by electronic devices called signal processors (see Figure 10.1). Usually external to the mixing console, this outboard equipment takes a signal fed from the console and modifies it in a controlled way. Then the modified signal returns to the console for routing to the appropriate channels. The result is a recording that sounds more like a professional production and less like a bland documentation.

Figure 10.1 A signal processor.

Used on most pop records, effects such as reverberation, echo, and chorus add spaciousness and excitement. The signal processors that produce such effects cost $125 and up. They really are a worthwhile investment if you want to produce a commercial sound. Recordings that include the natural room acoustics, such as recordings of classical-music ensembles or some folk groups, need no signal processing.

This chapter describes the most popular signal processors and tells how to use them.

The Equalizer

Recall from Chapter 2 that an equalizer (usually in the mixer) is a sophisticated tone control, something like the bass and treble controls in a hi-fi set. Equalization (EQ) lets you improve on reality—make an instrument sound warmer or less harsh, remove noises, add punch.

EQ adjusts the bass, treble, and midrange of a sound by turning up or down certain frequency ranges. To do this, it operates on the spectrum of the sound source—its fundamental and harmonic frequencies. The spectrum helps give the instrument its distinctive tone quality or timbre.

If some of these frequencies change in level, the tone quality changes. An equalizer raises or lowers the level of a particular range of frequencies (a frequency band), and so controls the tone quality. That is, it alters the frequency response. For example, a boost (level increase) in the range centered at 10 kHz makes percussion sound bright and crisp. A cut at the same frequency dulls the sound.

Types of EQ

The most basic type of EQ is a *bass and treble control* (often labeled LF EQ and HF EQ). Its effect on frequency response is shown in Figure 10.2. Typically, this type provides up to 15 db of boost or cut—at 100 Hz (for the low-frequency EQ knob) and at 10 kHz (for the high-frequency EQ knob).

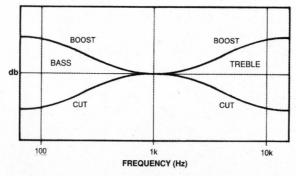

Figure 10.2 The effect of the bass and treble control.

You have more control over tone quality with a *multiple-frequency equalizer*; you can boost or cut several frequency bands (see Figure 10.3).

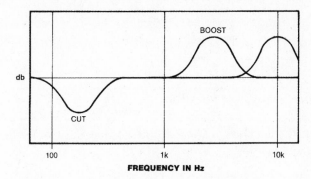

Figure 10.3 The effect of multiple-frequency equalization.

Recall that sweepable EQ is even more flexible. You can tune in the exact frequency range needing adjustment (see Figure 10.4). Sweepable EQ is often incorrectly called parametric. You won't find a true parametric equalizer in home-studio equipment.

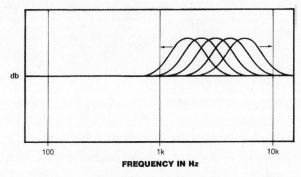

Figure 10.4 The effect of sweepable equalization.

The parametric equalizer allows continuous adjustment of frequency, boost or cut, and *bandwidth*—the range of frequencies affected. Figure 10.5 shows how a parametric equalizer varies the bandwidth of the boosted portion of the spectrum.

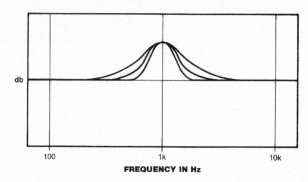

Figure 10.5 Curves that illustrate varying the bandwidth of a parametric equalizer.

A *graphic equalizer* is usually external to the mixing console (see Figure 10.6). This type has a row of slide potentiometers dividing the audible spectrum into 5 to 31 bands. When the controls are adjusted, their positions indicate graphically the equalizer's frequency response. Usually, a graphic equalizer is used for monitor-speaker equalization.

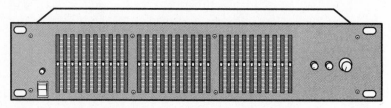

Figure 10.6 A graphic equalizer.

Equalizers also can be classified by the shape of their frequency response. A *peaking equalizer* creates a response in the shape of a hill or peak when set for a boost (see Figure 10.7). With a *shelving equalizer*, the shape of the frequency response resembles a shelf (see Figure 10.8).

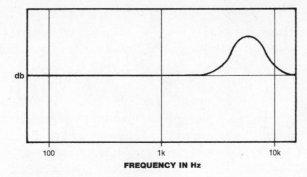

Figure 10.7 Peaking equalization at 7 kHz.

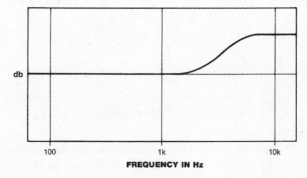

Figure 10.8 Shelving equalization at 7 kHz.

Recall that a filter is a special type of equalizer, found only in some mixing consoles, that causes a roll off at the frequency extremes. It sharply rejects (attenuates) frequencies above or below a certain frequency. Figure 10.9 shows a lowpass filter.

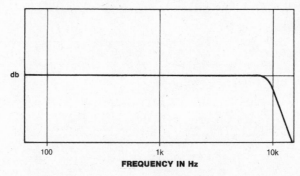

Figure 10.9 A 10 kHz lowpass filter (–3 db at 10 kHz).

225

A 10 kHz lowpass filter (high-cut filter) removes frequencies above 10 kHz. Its response is down 3 db at 10 kHz and more above that. This reduces hiss-type noise without affecting tone quality as much as a gradual treble roll off would. A 100 Hz highpass filter (low-cut filter) attenuates frequencies below 100 Hz. Its response is down 3 db at 100 Hz and more below that. This removes low-pitched noises such as room rumble, microphone handling noise, and microphone breath pops. A 1 kHz bandpass filter attenuates frequencies above and below a frequency band centered at 1 kHz.

The crossover filter in most monitor speakers consists of lowpass, highpass, and bandpass filters that send the lows to the woofer, mids to the midrange, and highs to the tweeter. A filter is named for the steepness of its roll off: first-order (6 db per octave), second-order (12 db/octave), third-order (18 db/octave), and so on.

How To Use EQ

If your mixer has bass and treble controls, their frequencies are preset (usually at 100 Hz and 10 kHz). Set the EQ knob at 0 to have no effect ("flat" setting). Turn it clockwise for a boost; turn it counter-clockwise for a cut. If your mixer has multiple-frequency EQ or sweepable EQ, one knob sets the frequency range and another sets the amount of boost or cut.

Table 10.1 shows the fundamentals and harmonics of musical instruments and voices. The harmonics given represent an approximate range. For any particular instrument, turn up the lower end of the fundamentals for warmth and fullness; turn down the fundamentals if the tone is too bassy or tubby. Turn up the harmonics for presence and definition; turn down the harmonics if the tone is too harsh or sizzly.

Table 10.1 Frequency ranges of musical instruments and voices.

Instrument	Fundamentals	Harmonics
Flute	261-2349 Hz	3-8 kHz
Oboe	261-1568 Hz	2-12 kHz
Clarinet	165-1568 Hz	2-10 kHz
Bassoon	62-587 Hz	1-7 kHz
Trumpet	165-988 Hz	1-7.5 kHz

Instrument	Fundamentals	Harmonics
French horn	87-880 Hz	1-6 kHz
Trombone	73-587 Hz	1-7.5 kHz
Tuba	49-587 Hz	1-4 kHz
Snare drum	100-200 Hz	1-20 kHz
Kick drum	30-147 Hz	1-6 kHz
Cymbals	300-587 Hz	1-15 kHz
Violin	196-3136 Hz	4-15 kHz
Viola	131-1175 Hz	2-8.5 kHz
Cello	65-698 Hz	1-6.5 kHz
Acoustic Bass	41-294 Hz	1-5 kHz
Electric Bass	41-300 Hz	1-7 kHz
Acoustic Guitar	82-988 Hz	1-15 kHz
Electric Guitar	82-1319 Hz	1-3.5 kHz (through amp)
Electric Guitar	82-1319 Hz	1-15 kHz (direct)
Piano	28-4196 Hz	5-8 kHz
Bass (voice)	87-392 Hz	1-12 kHz
Tenor (voice)	131-494 Hz	1-12 kHz
Alto (voice)	175-698 Hz	2-12 kHz
Soprano (voice)	247-1175 Hz	2-12 kHz

Avoid excessive boost because it can distort the signal. Try cutting the lows instead of boosting the highs.

Here are some suggested frequencies to adjust for specific instruments. If you want the effects described below, apply boost. If you don't, apply cut. Try these suggestions and accept only the sounds you like:

Bass	Full and deep at 60 Hz, growl at 600 Hz, presence at 2.5 kHz, string noise at 3 kHz and up
Electric guitar	Thumpy at 60 Hz, full at 100 Hz, honky at 600 Hz, presence at 2-3 kHz, sizzly and raspy above 6 kHz

Drums	Full at 100 Hz, wooly at 250-600 Hz, trashy at 1-3 kHz, attack or snap at 5 kHz, sizzly and crisp at 10 kHz
Kick drum	Full and powerful below 60 Hz, papery at 300-800 Hz (cut at 400-600 Hz for better tone), click or attack at 2-6 kHz
Sax	Warm at 500 Hz, harsh at 3 kHz, key noise above 10 kHz
Acoustic guitar	Full or thumpy at 80 Hz, presence at 5 kHz, pick noise above 10 kHz
Voice	Full at 100-150 Hz (males) and 200-250 Hz (females), honky or nasal at 500 Hz-1 kHz, presence at 5 kHz, sibilance above 6 kHz

Setting EQ by Ear

You also can set an equalizer by ear. One way is to tune the equalizer to the approximate frequency range you need to work on (you'll soon know where by experience). Then apply full boost or cut so the effect is easily audible. Finally, fine-tune the frequency and amount of boost or cut until the tonal balance is the way you like it.

For example, if a close-miked vocal sounds unnaturally bassy, reach for the low-frequency equalization knob (100 Hz, for example) and turn it down, adjusting the amount of cut for the desired tonal balance.

If you hear a coloration in the tone quality of an instrument, set a sweepable equalizer for extreme boost. Then sweep the frequencies until you find the frequency range matching the coloration. Cut that range by the amount that sounds right. For example, a piano miked with the lid closed might have a tubby coloration—excessive output around 300 Hz, for example. Set your low-frequency EQ for boost, and vary the center frequency until the tubbiness is exaggerated. Then cut at that frequency until the piano sounds natural.

When To Use EQ

Before using EQ, try to get the desired tone quality by changing the microphone or its placement. This gives a more natural effect than EQ.

Should you apply equalization during recording, mixdown, or both? If you mix more than one instrument to the same track, you can't EQ them independently during mixdown unless their frequency ranges are far apart. Suppose a recorded track contains lead guitar and vocals. If you add a midrange boost to the guitar, you hear it on the vocals too. The only way around this is to EQ the lead guitar independently when you record it.

If a track contains bass and cymbals, however, you can EQ the low end of the bass without affecting the cymbals much. That's because the bass produces mostly low frequencies, and the cymbals produce mostly high frequencies.

If you assign each instrument to its own track, you can keep things simple by recording flat (without EQ). Then equalize the track during mixdown.

Here's one reason to record with EQ. If the monitor mixer in your board has no EQ, and you play back the multitrack recording through the monitor mixer, it won't sound right unless the tracks are already equalized. Later, when you start to mix down, the tracks already sound good and don't need much EQ.

If you're using a bass cut or treble boost, you can get a better signal-to-noise ratio (S/N) by applying this EQ during recording, rather than during mixdown. If the equalization used is a treble cut, however, applying it during mixdown reduces tape hiss.

Uses of EQ

EQ comes in handy in the following applications:

- Improving tone quality
- Special production effects
- Reducing noise and leakage
- Compensating for the Fletcher-Munson effect
- Making a pleasing blend
- Compensating for response deficiencies
- Compensating for microphone placement

Improving tone quality is the main use of EQ. For example, you might use a high-frequency roll off on a singer to reduce sibilance, or on a direct-recorded electric guitar to take the edge off the sound. Boosting 100 Hz on a floor tom gives a fuller sound; cutting around 250 Hz on a bass guitar aids clarity. The frequency response and placement of each microphone affect tone quality as well.

Extreme equalization reduces fidelity, but it also can make interesting sound effects. Sharply rolling off the lows and highs on a voice, for instance, gives it a "telephone" sound. A 1 kHz bandpass filter does the same thing. An extreme boost at 5 kHz accents the impact of a snare drum.

You can reduce unwanted low-frequency sounds—bass leakage, air-conditioner rumble, mic-stand thumps—by turning down low frequencies below the range of the instrument you're recording. For example, a fiddle's lowest frequency is about 200 Hz, so set the equalizer's frequency range to 40 or 60 Hz and apply cut. This roll off doesn't change the fiddle's tone quality because the roll off is below the range of frequencies that the fiddle produces.

Similarly, a kick drum has little or no output above 5 kHz, so you can filter out highs above 5 kHz on the kick drum to reduce cymbal leakage. If this filtering is done during mixdown, it also reduces tape hiss. Filtering out frequencies below 80 Hz on most instruments reduces air-conditioning rumble and muddy bass.

Recall from Chapter 4 that the Fletcher-Munson effect states that the ear is less sensitive to bass and treble at low volumes than at high volumes. Therefore, when you record a very loud instrument and play it back at a lower level, it might lack bass and treble. To restore these, you may need to boost the lows (around 100 Hz) and the highs (around 4 khz) when recording loud rock groups. The louder the group, the more boost is needed. As an alternative, use cardioid microphones with proximity effect (for bass boost) and a presence peak (for treble boost).

When several instruments are heard together, they sometimes crowd or overlap each other in the frequency spectrum. That is, it may be difficult to distinguish the instruments by tonal differences. By equalizing various instruments at different frequencies, you can make their timbres distinct, which results in a more pleasing blend. This procedure also evens out the contribution of each frequency band to the total spectrum, yielding a mix that is well balanced tonally.

If you have two instruments that sound alike, such as lead guitar and rhythm guitar, you can make them more distinct by equalizing them differently. You might make the lead guitar edgy by boosting 2 to 3 kHz, and make the rhythm guitar mellow by cutting 2 to 3 kHz. The same philosophy applies to bass guitar and kick drum. Because they occupy about the same low-frequency range, they tend to mask or cover each other. To make them distinct, either fatten the bass and thin out the kick a little, or vice versa.

The microphones, tape recorder, monitor speakers, and the mixing board itself may not have a flat frequency response. Equalization can compensate partly for these deficiencies. If a microphone has a gradual high-frequency roll off, for example, a high-frequency boost on the console may help restore a flat response. On the other hand, if a microphone "dies" above a certain frequency, no amount of boost can help it. Some directional microphones have proximity effect—a bass boost when used up close. A bass roll off on the console can compensate for this boost.

Many purists shun the use of EQ, complaining of excessive phase shift or ringing caused by the equalizer. Instead, they use high-quality microphones, carefully placed, to achieve a natural tonal balance without EQ. The resulting sound is said to be less strained, more natural.

Often you must place a microphone very close to an instrument to reject background sounds and leakage. Unfortunately, this emphasizes the part of the instrument the microphone is near; the tone quality picked up may not be the same as that of the instrument as a whole. Equalization can compensate partly for this effect.

For example, an acoustic guitar picked up with a mic next to the sound hole sounds bassy because the sound hole radiates strong low frequencies, but a complementary low-frequency roll off on your mixer can restore the natural tonal balance.

This use of EQ can save the day by helping poorly recorded tracks in live concert recordings. During a concert, the stage monitors might be blaring into your recording/P.A. microphones, so you're forced to mike close in order to reject monitor leakage and feedback. This close placement, or the monitor leakage itself, can give the recording an unnatural tone quality. In this case, EQ is the only way to get usable tracks.

The Compressor

The compressor is a form of automatic volume control. Sometimes vocalists sing too softly and get buried in the mix; other times they hit loud notes, blasting the listener and saturating the tape. Sometimes they move toward and away from the microphone while singing, causing the average recording level to fluctuate.

To control these problems, you can ride gain on the vocalists—turn them down when they get too loud, up when they get too quiet. It's hard to anticipate these changes, however, so it's better to use a compressor, an amplifier that performs the same function automatically. It reduces the gain (amplification) when the input signal exceeds a preset level (called the *threshold*). The greater the input level, the less the gain. Quiet passages are made louder, loud passages are made softer, and the dynamic range is reduced (see Figure 10.10).

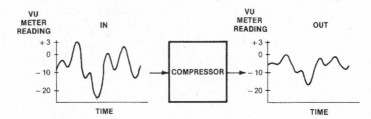

Figure 10.10 Compression.

Compression keeps the level of vocals or instruments more constant, making them easier to hear throughout the mix and preventing loud notes that may saturate the tape. With extreme control settings, a compressor also can be used for a special effect—to make drums sound "fatter," for example. In professional studios, compression is applied nearly always to vocals, often to bass guitar and drums, and sometimes to piano and lead guitar.

You might be able to get by without a compressor if the vocalists use proper mic technique—backing away from the mic on loud notes, and coming in close on soft notes. To tell whether you need a compressor, listen to your finished mix. If you can understand the words throughout the song without the loud vocal notes being too loud, you probably can do without a compressor.

Using a Compressor

Normally, you compress individual instruments or tracks rather than the entire mix. That procedure makes the effect less audible by applying compression only to those instruments needing it. You also can compress the entire mix slightly to add punch.

Compressing instrument signals during recording improves the S/N of the tape tracks, but forces you to decide on compressor settings during the recording session. Compressing tape tracks during mixdown allows you to change the settings at will, but can make tape hiss audible by raising the gain during quiet passages.

Several controls on the compressor need careful adjustment. Some of the parameters in the next sections are preset internally on various models.

Compression Ratio or Slope

Compression ratio or slope is the ratio of the change in input level to the change in output level. For example, a 2:1 ratio means that for every 2 db change in input level, the output changes 1 db. A 20 db change in input level results in a 10 db change in the output, and so on. Ratio settings of 1.5:1 to 4:1 are typical.

A "soft knee" or "over easy" characteristic is a low compression ratio for low-level signals and a high compression ratio for high-level signals. Some manufacturers say that this characteristic sounds more natural than a constant compression ratio.

Gain Reduction

Gain reduction is the number of db that the gain or level is reduced by the compressor. It varies with the input level. You set the ratio and threshold controls so that the gain is reduced on loud notes by an amount that sounds right, or looks right on the gain reduction meter.

Attack Time

The attack time setting controls how fast the gain reduction occurs in response to a musical attack. Typical attack times range from 0.25 to 10 milliseconds. Some compressors adjust attack time automatically to suit the program material; others have a factory-set attack time. The longer the attack time, the larger the peaks that are passed before gain reduction occurs. Thus, a long attack time sounds punchy; a short attack time reduces punch by softening the attack.

Release Time

The release time or recovery time control affects how fast the gain returns to its normal value after a loud passage. It can be adjusted from about 50 milliseconds to several seconds. Release time must be longer than about 0.4 second for bass instruments to prevent harmonic distortion.

As the gain returns to normal, noise is increased along with the signal, resulting in a "pumping" or "breathing" sound. Release time usually is set for the least objectionable effect, depending on program material. Shorter release times make the compressor follow faster dynamic changes in the music, and keep the average level higher. In some units, the release time is adjusted automatically, or is factory-set to a useful value.

233

Threshold

Set the threshold high (near 0 VU) to compress only the loudest notes; set it low (–10 or –20 VU) to bring up quiet passages as well as softening loud ones. If the compressor has a fixed threshold, the input level control is used to adjust the amount of compression.

Output Level Control

The *output level control* sets the signal strength coming out of the compressor to the proper level for the input section of the console (usually around 1.23 volts). Some units maintain a constant output level automatically when other controls are varied.

Connecting a Compressor

Connect a compressor, in series with the signal you want to compress, in one of the following ways:

- If you want to compress a single instrument or voice, and your mixer has access jacks, locate the mixer input module controlling the instrument you want to compress. Connect the compressor between the access jacks.

- If you want to compress the signal of a console output channel (bus) while recording, locate the bus output containing the signal of the instrument(s) you want to compress. Connect this output to the compressor input. Connect the compressor output to the desired tape-track input.

- If you want to compress a particular tape-track during mixdown, connect the tape-track output to the compressor input. Connect the compressor output to the console line input normally used for that track. Alternatively, locate that track's input module in the console, and connect the compressor between the access jacks for that input module.

The Limiter

A *limiter* is an amplifier whose output is practically constant above a preset input level. The compression ratio in a limiter is very high—10:1 or greater—and the threshold is usually set just below the point of tape saturation or amplifier clipping. The output of the limiter is virtually constant for input signals above that level so that the limiter can prevent tape saturation or amplifier clipping.

A compressor reduces the overall dynamic range of the program, but a limiter controls only the level of attack transients or peaks (see Figure 10.11). To act on these rapid peaks, limiters have a much faster attack time than compressors—typically 1 microsecond to 1 millisecond.

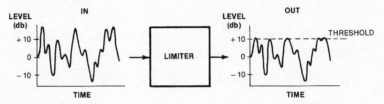

Figure 10.11 Limiting.

Compressors are sometimes called limiters, but the setting of the ratio or slope tells what the device is really doing. A compressor/limiter combines both functions by compressing the average signal levels over a wide range, and by limiting peaks to prevent overload. It has two thresholds: one relatively low for the compressor and one relatively high for the limiter.

The Noise Gate

A noise gate acts like an on-off switch to eliminate noises during pauses in an audio signal. It does this by reducing the gain when the input level falls below a preset threshold. That is, when an instrument stops playing momentarily, the signal level is low enough so that the noise gate turns off—removing any noise and leakage during the pause (see Figure 10.12).

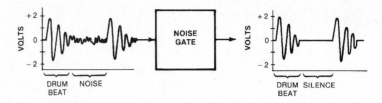

Figure 10.12 Noise gating.

During recording, you patch a noise gate between a mixer direct out or bus out and a tape-track input. During mixdown, you patch it between a tape-track output and a mixer tape input.

The noise gate helps to clean up drum tracks by removing leakage between beats. It also can be used for special effect to shorten the decay time of the drums, giving a very tight sound. During a mixdown, a gate is sometimes used on each output of the multitrack recorder to reduce tape hiss. The noise gate threshold should be set high enough to chop off tape hiss during pauses, but low enough not to remove any program material (unless that is the desired effect). The release time should be very fast for drums and longer for more sustained instruments.

Very adequate demo tapes can be made without gating. But for those who want a little tighter, cleaner sound, gates are worthwhile. Some signal processors combine compression, limiting, and noise gating in a single package.

The Delay Unit

A wide variety of special effects can be created by delaying a signal. Some of these effects are echo, multiple echo, doubling, chorus, and flanging.

Recall from Chapter 2 that a delay unit or digital delay accepts an input signal, holds it in an electronic memory and then plays it back after a short delay—about 1 millisecond to over 10 seconds (see Figure 10.13). Delay is the time interval between the input signal and its repetition at the output of the delay device.

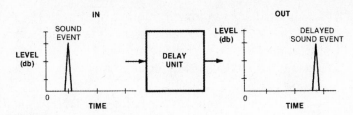

Figure 10.13 Delaying the signal.

Delay Unit Specifications

The bandwidth of the delay unit is the frequency range or upper frequency limit of the delayed signal. A 12 kHz bandwidth is good, 16 kHz is excellent, and 20 kHz is icing on the cake.

The S/N of the delay unit is the ratio in db between the delayed signal's level and the noise level. In general, the longer the delay, the poorer the S/N. A ratio of 70 db is considered fair for delay units, 80 db is good, and 90 db is very good.

Echo

Delay by itself is not an audible effect. However, if you delay the incoming signal by 50 milliseconds to 1 second, and combine the undelayed and delayed signals, you hear two distinct sounds: a signal and an echo (see Figure 10.14). Echoes occur naturally when sound waves travel to a room surface, bounce off, and return later to the listener—repeating the original sound. A delay unit can mimic this effect.

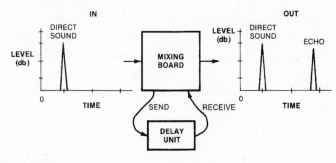

Figure 10.14 Echo.

The undelayed ("dry") and delayed ("wet") signals can be combined in the delay device by setting its direct/delay mix control (dry/wet control) part-way up. A delay around 50 to 200 milliseconds results in a slap echo or slapback echo, often used in 50s rock and roll tunes, and still used today.

Many delay units have a feature called *recirculation* or *regeneration*. With this feature, some of the delayed output is fed back into the input, so that the signal is redelayed many times. This creates a *multiple echo—* several repetitions that are evenly spaced in time (see Figure 10.15). Recirculate the delayed sound by turning up the recirculation or regeneration control on the delay unit. The higher the recirculation level, the longer the repeats last.

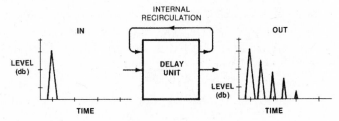

Figure 10.15 A multiple echo from a delay unit.

Multiple echo is most musical if you set the delay time to create an echo rhythm that fits the tempo of the song. A slow repeating echo—0.5 second between repeats, for example—gives an outer space or haunted house effect.

Doubling

If the delay is set around 15 to 35 milliseconds, the effect is called *doubling* or *automatic double tracking (ADT)*. It gives an instrument or voice a fatter, stronger sound, especially if the original signal is panned left and the delayed signal is panned right, or vice versa. The short delays used in doubling sound like early sound reflections in a studio—thus they add a sense of "air" or ambience to close-miked instruments that would otherwise sound too dead.

Doubling a vocal can be done without a delay unit as follows:

1. Record a vocal part.

2. Rewind the tape to the beginning.

3. Set the tape recorder in sync mode so that the singer can hear the performance just recorded and sing along with it.

4. On an unused track, record another performance of the same vocal part.

5. Rewind the tape and play back the two synchronized performances. The doubled vocal sounds fuller than a single vocal track. (This method was often used by the Beatles.)

Chorus

If the delay used in doubling is modulated (varied at a slow rate), this produces a wavy or shimmering effect called *chorus*. The time modulation of the delayed signal causes frequency modulation (pitch bending) as a side effect. The slight pitch bending or detuning of the delayed signal creates the wavy effect.

Stereo Chorus

Stereo chorus is an especially beautiful effect. In one channel, a delayed signal is combined with the dry signal in the same polarity. In the other channel, the delayed signal is inverted in polarity and then combined with the dry signal. Thus, the right channel has a series of peaks in the frequency response where the left channel has dips, and vice versa.

Bass Chorus

The bass chorus includes a high-pass filter so that low frequencies are not chorused, but higher harmonics are. It's used to add spaciousness to bass guitar.

Flanging

If the delay is set around 0 to 20 milliseconds, the ear is usually unable to resolve the direct and delayed signals into two separate and distinct sounds. Instead, a single sound with an unusual frequency response is heard. Due to phase cancellations of the direct and delayed signals combined, there are a series of peaks and dips in the net frequency response—the comb-filter effect discussed in Chapter 2 (see Figure 10.16). It gives a very colored, filtered tone quality. The shorter the delay, the farther apart the peaks and dips are spaced in frequency.

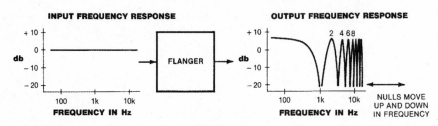

Figure 10.16 Flanging (or positive flanging).

With the *flanging* effect, the delay is varied (swept) automatically from about 0 to 20 milliseconds. This causes the comb-filter nulls to sweep up and down the spectrum. The resulting sound quality is hollow, swishing, and ethereal, as if the music were playing through a variable-length pipe. Flanging is applied most effectively to broad-band signals such as cymbals, but can be used on any instrument or the entire mix.

Used most often in psychedelic music, flanging can be heard on many Jimi Hendrix recordings, as well as the song "Itchycoo Park" by the Small Faces.

Positive and Negative Flanging

Positive flanging refers to flanging in which the delayed signal is the same polarity as the direct signal. With *negative flanging*, the delayed signal is opposite in polarity to the direct signal, creating a stronger effect. The low frequencies are canceled (the bass rolls off), and the "knee" of the bass roll off moves up and down the spectrum as the delay is varied. The high frequencies still are comb-filtered (see Figure 10.17). (Negative flanging makes the music sound as if it is turning inside out!)

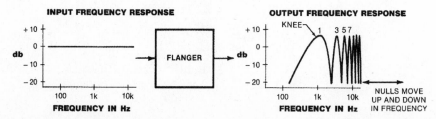

Figure 10.17 Negative flanging.

Resonant Flanging

By feeding some of the output of the flanger back into the input, the peaks and dips are reinforced, creating a powerful science fiction effect called *resonant flanging*.

Phasing

Phasing is similar to flanging except that a phase-shift network replaces the delay circuit. The resulting peaks and dips are spaced more widely and irregularly in the frequency spectrum.

The Reverberation Unit

Recall that a reverberation unit adds a sense of room acoustics, ambience, or space surrounding instruments and voices. This effect is a necessity; reverb should be the first signal processor you buy.

Acoustic reverberation is a series of multiple sound reflections that makes the original sound persist and die away gradually or decay. These reflections tell the ear that you're listening in a large or hard-surfaced room. An artificial reverberation unit simulates the sound of an acoustic environment—a club, auditorium, or concert hall—by generating random multiple echoes that are too numerous and rapid for the ear to resolve. Reverberation is illustrated in Figure 10.18.

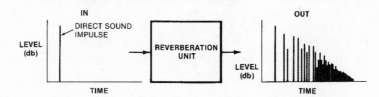

Figure 10.18 Reverberation.

A digital reverb unit offers a wide variety of reverberation patterns. It uses sophisticated programs that mimic the early and late sound-reflection patterns of various-size rooms. It even can duplicate the bright sound of a metal-foil plate, which used to be the most popular type of reverb device in professional studios.

Some units let you adjust tone quality, decay time, and other parameters. Unnatural effects are also available, such as nonlinear decay, reverse reverberation (that builds up before decaying), and *gated reverb*. With gated reverb, the reverberation suddenly cuts off shortly after a note is hit. It's often used with snare drums. A good example is the song "You Can Call Me Al" on Paul Simon's album, *Graceland*. To produce this effect, use either a reverberation unit with a gated reverb program, or feed the reverberation-return signal through a noise gate set to cut off the end of the reverberant "tail."

Another feature in some units is *predelay* (prereverb delay). This is a short delay (30 to 100 milliseconds, for example) before the reverberation to simulate the delay that occurs in real rooms before the onset of reverberation. The longer the predelay, the greater the sense of room size. If your reverb unit does not have predelay built in, you can create it by connecting a delay unit or tape machine between the console aux-send output and the reverb-unit input.

Digital reverb is available either in a stand-alone unit, or as part of a multieffects processor. Stand-alone reverbs include the Lexicon LXP-1 and the Alesis Microverb II and III. Follow these steps to connect a reverb unit to your mixer:

1. Connect a cable from the mixer aux-send (effects-send) output to the reverb input.

2. Connect a cable (two for stereo) from the reverb outputs to the mixer aux returns (effects returns or bus inputs).

3. Set the mix control on the reverb unit all the way to "wet" or "reverb."

4. Turn up the mixer's aux-return or bus in knobs (if any) about 3/4 up and then adjust the amount of reverb on each track with the aux-send knobs.

The Enhancer or Exciter

If your recording sounds dull or muffled, you can run it through an *enhancer*, which puts brilliance, sparkle, and clarity back into it—without adding noise as EQ can. It works either by adding slight distortion and phase shift (as in the Aphex Aural Exciter) or by boosting the treble when the signal has high-frequency content (as in the Alesis Micro Enhancer and the Barcus Berry Electronics 402 Sonic Maximizer).

This last device also divides the frequency range into three bands: the lows are delayed about 1.5 milliseconds, the midrange is delayed about 0.5 millisecond, and the highs are delayed only a few microseconds. Thus, harmonics and fundamentals are realigned in time, which is claimed to aid clarity.

The Octave Divider

This unit accepts a signal from a bass guitar and provides deep, growling bass notes 1 or 2 octaves below the pitch of the bass guitar. It does this by dividing the incoming frequency by 2 or 4; if you put 82 Hz in, you get 41 Hz out.

Here's another way to achieve a similar effect: Connect a bass guitar to a guitar-to-MIDI converter, and use it to drive a MIDI sound module set to a deep-bass patch.

The Harmonizer

Basically a delay unit with time modulation, a *harmonizer* produces a wide variety of pitch-shifting effects. It can create harmonies, change pitch without changing the duration of the program, change duration without changing pitch, and many other oddities. You've heard harmonizers on radio station breaks when the announcer's voice sounds like a munchkin or Darth Vader.

Preverb

With the *preverb* effect, you can make echo or reverberation precede the attack of each note. This can make a snare drum hit sound like a whip. It also is called *reverse echo*. Currently, a signal processor cannot create this effect; you create it with a multitrack tape recorder (see Figure 10.19). Suppose you want to add preverb to a drum track. The track format might be as shown in Figure 10.19A. Follow these steps:

1. On your multitrack machine, reverse the tape reels so that the tape plays backwards. That is, put the take-up reel where the supply reel was, and vice versa. Play the tape in sync mode. You'll hear the tracks playing backwards (see Figure 10.19B). Because the tape is upside down, the instruments are on different tracks than they were originally.

2. Add reverberation or echo to the desired track, and record the reverberated signal on an open track (see Figure 10.19C).

3. Again reverse the reels and play the desired track along with the newly recorded reverberation track (see Figure 10.19D).

Some signal processors have a *reverse reverb* effect in which the reverb comes after the note that produced it, but builds up instead of fading out. This is not quite the same as preverb. Reverse reverb can upset the musical timing; preverb doesn't.

The Multieffects Processor

Effects are available either with one effect per unit, or with several effects in a multieffects processor, such as the Yamaha SPX1000, Alesis Quadraverb, or DigiTech DSP-128 Plus. Some units let you modify the preset effects and save them; others also let you combine up to five effects at once.

A multieffects processor uses a custom digital signal processing chip and memory (RAM). The amount of memory is limited, so the more memory that one effect uses, the less is available for other effects. For example, suppose you're combining reverb and echo. If you use a reverb with a long decay time (which takes a lot of memory), you may have to settle for an echo with a short delay.

Most such units have a frequency response up to 20 kHz and at least 16-bit resolution. They offer 100 or more programmable presets with MIDI control over any parameter. For example, with some units you can place an instrument in a simulated room, and use a MIDI controller to change the size of that room continuously.

MIDI Automation of Effects

Many signal processors can be controlled by MIDI program change commands (see Chapter 15). You can change the type of effect—or various parameters of an effect—quickly with certain program changes entered into a sequencer.

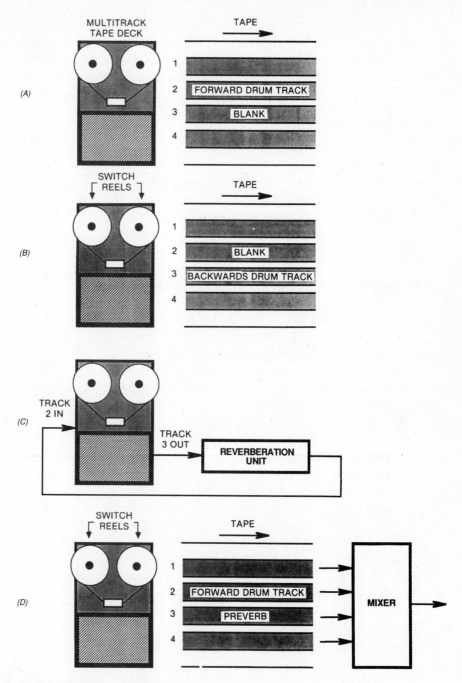

Figure 10.19 Setup for preverb.

Suppose you want each tom-tom hit in a drum fill to have a different size room added to it. You could make the high rack tom sound as if it's in a small room, put the low rack tom in a concert hall, and put the floor tom in a cave. To do this, first assign a different program number (patch or preset number) to each effects parameter. This is done with the effects device. Then, using the sequencer, punch in the appropriate program number for each note.

A MIDI program-change footswitch lets guitarists call up different programs on MIDI signal processors. By tapping a footswitch, they can get fuzz, flanging, wah-wah, and so on.

Using a MIDI mapper, you can control certain effects parameters with any controller—for example, varying reverb decay time with a pitch wheel, or varying a filter with key velocity.

Which Effects Do You Need?

The first signal processors a home studio owner should purchase are a reverberation unit and a compressor. These devices are practically indispensable for producing a commercial sound.

Rock music uses all the effects discussed in this chapter, although certain ones go in and out of style. The guitar in rock, jazz, or New Age music often benefits from chorus. Pop and country music use reverb and echo. EQ and reverberation are useful for all types of music. The same is true of the enhancer if the recording lacks brilliance. Compression is needed mainly for vocals, or for any instrument that varies too widely in loudness.

All these signal processors produce sonic effects that may be difficult to describe in technical terms. For example, what equalization should be used to get a "fat" sound or a "thin" sound? What physical conditions may be causing a "muddy" sound or a "metallic" sound? In general, which knob do you turn to achieve a certain sonic effect?

Table 10.2 answers these questions. It translates audio-engineering terms (such as equalization settings) into subjective descriptions of sound quality. These definitions are not agreed upon universally, but they are some of the most common meanings. The positive terms are used when you like the effect; the negative terms are used when you don't!

Table 10.2 Subjective translation of audio engineering terms.

Low-Frequency Boost (Below 500 Hz)

Positive	*Negative*
Powerful (under 200 Hz)	Muddy
Ballsy (under 200 Hz)	Tubby (200-300 Hz)
Heavy (under 200 Hz)	Thumpy
Fat	Boomy
Thick	Barrelly
Warm	Woody (200-400 Hz)
Robust	
Mellow	
Full	
Woody (200-400 Hz)	

Flat, Extended, Low Frequencies

Positive	*Negative*
Full	Rumbly
Full-bodied	
Rich	
Solid	
Natural	

Low-Frequency Roll Off

Positive	*Negative*
Clean	Thin
	Cold, cool
	Tinny
	Anemic

continues

Table 10.2 Continued

Midfrequency Boost (500 Hz to 7 kHz)

Positive	Negative
Present (Presence)	Hollow, muffled (500 Hz)
Punchy	Puffy, hornlike (500 Hz)
Edgy	"Aw" sound (500-800 Hz)
Clear	Tinny, telephonelike (1 kHz)
Intelligible	"Er" sound (1.5 kHz)
Articulate	Nasal, honky (500 Hz to 3 kHz)
Defined	Hard (2-4 kHz)
Projected (2-3 kHz)	Harsh, strident, piercing (2-5 kHz)
Forward (2-3 kHz)	Metallic (3-5 kHz, especially 3 kHz)
	Twangy (3 kHz)
	Edgy (3-7 kHz)
	Sibilant (4-7 kHz)

Flat Midfrequencies

Positive	Negative
Natural	No Punch
Neutral	"Flat" (lacking character or color)
Smooth	
Musical	

Midfrequency Dip

Positive	Negative
Mellow	Hollow (500-1000 Hz)
	Disembodied (500-1000 Hz)
	Muffled (5 kHz)
	Muddy (5 kHz)

High-Frequency Boost (Above 7 kHz)

Positive	Negative
Trebley	Trebley
Bright	Sizzly (voice)
Crisp	Edgy
Articulate	Glassy
Etched	"Essy" Sibilant
Hot	Steely
Sizzly (cymbals)	String Noise

Flat, Extended High Frequencies

Positive	Negative
Open	Too detailed
Airy	Too close
Transparent	
Clear	
Natural	
Neutral	
Smooth	
Effortless	
Detailed	

High-Frequency Roll Off

Positive	Negative
Mellow	Dull
Round	Restricted
Smooth	Muffled
Easy-on-the-ears	Veiled

continues

Table 10.2 Continued

Positive	Negative
Like a concert hall	Muddy
Dark	Distant

Overall Response

Positive (all flat response)	Negative
Natural	Rough, peaky, harsh, colored (nonflat, peaks and dips)
Accurate	
Neutral	Phasey (sharp dips)
Smooth	Cheap (narrow-band)
Transparent	Flat (lacking character—too neutral)
Effortless	
Musical	
Uncolored	
Liquid	

Reverberation or Leakage

Too Little	Well-Controlled	Pleasant	Too Much
Sterile	Clean	Warm	Echoey
Dry	Tight	Rich	Bathroom-sound
Dead		Sumptuous	Muddy
Muffled		Airy	Loose
Thin		Having depth	Washed-out
		"Live"	Barrel-like
		Spacious	Cavernous
		Open	In another room
		Full	Distant
		Bright	Trashy

Noise and Distortion

Absent	Present
Clean	Veiled (mild distortion)
Clear	Hard
Smooth	Harsh
Open	Grainy
Sweet	Gritty
	Dirty (positive or negative)
	Distorted
	Fuzzy
	Sputtering
	Raunchy
	Noisy
	Hissy

Transient Response

Good	Bad
Clean	Smeared
Tight	Blurred
Crisp	Veiled
Sharp	Muffled

Stereo Imaging

Sharp	Diffuse
Focused	Vague
Pinpointed	Unfocused
Easy-to-localize	Hard-to-localize
Fused	Smeared
Defined	Spread

continues

Table 10.2 Continued

Sharp	*Diffuse*
Pan-potted	Directionless
	Spacious
	Hole-in-the-middle
	Phasey
	Fat
	Big

Relative Loudness in the Mix

Loud	*Quiet*
Up front	Distant
On top	Subtle
Present	In the background
Hot	Recessed
Forward	Lost
Dominating	Covered
Covering	

Special effects help define the characteristic recorded sound of an era. The '50s had the "tube sound" and slap echo; the '60s used fuzz, wah-wah, and flanging; the early '70s sounded rather dead; the early '80s introduced delay units and enhancers. Today's sound emphasizes MIDI keyboards, drum machines, and digital reverb effects. You make contemporary-sounding recordings by using the latest effects and musical instruments on the market, and by inventing new sounds. Using these effects creatively—combining and manipulating them in unusual ways—leads to ear-grabbing recordings.

MIXING CONSOLES AND RECORDER-MIXERS

In a recording studio, you do most of the work with a mixer and a multitrack tape machine. The mixer accepts microphone or line-level signals and amplifies them up to the level needed by the tape machine; the multitrack tape machine records several tracks on tape. One track might be a lead vocal, another track might be a saxophone, and so on.

A recorder-mixer combines a mixer and a multitrack recorder in a single portable chassis. This convenient unit is also called a *ministudio* or *portable studio*. Most recorder-mixers record 4 tracks, but high-end units record 8 or more tracks. This chapter covers both mixers and mixing consoles, first describing typical features of both and then explaining additional features found only in mixing consoles.

Stages of Recording

Recall from Chapter 2 that there are three stages in making a multitrack recording: recording, overdubbing, and mixdown.

First, you record one or more instruments onto 1 or more tracks. Next, while listening to prerecorded tracks (over headphones), the musician records new parts on open (unused) tracks.

After all the tracks are recorded, you mix or combine them into 2-track stereo (along with effects and any sequenced tracks of MIDI instruments).

This stereo mix is recorded onto an external 2-track recorder, such as a cassette deck, open-reel deck, or DAT machine. This recording is the final master tape, which can be duplicated on cassettes, records, or compact discs.

Mixer Features

Although the knobs and meters on a mixer may appear intimidating, they can be understood if you read the manual and practice with the equipment. A mixer is rather complicated because it lets you control many aspects of sound:

- The loudness of each instrument (to control the balance among instruments in the mix)

- The tone quality of each instrument (bass, treble, midrange)

- The room that the instruments are in (reverberation)

- The left-to-right position of each instrument (panning)

- Special effects (flanging, echo, chorus, etc.)

- Track assignments (sometimes more than one instrument on each track)

- Recording level (to reduce distortion and/or noise)

- Monitor selection (what you're listening to during recording, the mixed tracks during playback, the prerecorded tracks mixed with a live instrument during overdubbing, all tracks mixed to 2-channel stereo during mixdown)

Inputs and Outputs

A mixer or console can be specified by the number of inputs and outputs it has. For example, an 8 in, 2 out mixer (8x2 mixer) has 8 signal inputs, which can be mixed into 2 output channels (buses) for stereo recording. Similarly, a 16 in, 8 out (16x8) mixing board has 16 signal inputs and 8 output channels for multitrack recording. A 16x4x2 mixer has 16 inputs, 4 submixes (explained later), and 2 main outputs. There also may be connectors for external equipment, such as reverberation units and monitor amplifiers.

The mixer is typically organized in three sections:

- Input modules
- Output section
- Monitor section

Input Modules

A mixer is made of groups of controls called *modules*. An *input module* (see Figure 11.1) affects a single input signal—from a microphone, for instance. The module is usually a narrow vertical strip, one per input. Several modules are lined up side-by-side. Each input module is the same, so if you know one, you know them all.

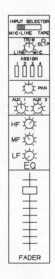

Figure 11.1 A typical input module.

The more inputs your mixer has, the more instruments you can record at the same time. If you're recording only yourself, you may need only two inputs. Each input module typically has these parts:

Input connector	Accepts the signal from a microphone, a direct box, an electric musical instrument, or a multitrack tape recorder

Preamp	Amplifies your input signal
Gain or trim control	Adjusts the level of the input signal so that it doesn't distort
Input selector	Allows you to choose which input signal you want to work with
Fader	Adjusts the recording level, and adjusts the balance between tracks during mixdown
Equalizer	Adjusts the tone quality (bass, treble, and midrange)
Aux send (effects send)	Controls how much effects (reverb, chorus, etc.) are added to each input signal
Assign switch	Allows you to select which tape track to send the signal to for recording (usually used in combination with the pan pot)
Pan pot	Places various sounds where desired between your stereo speakers (often used with the assign switch to send signals to the desired tracks)

Figure 11.2 shows the signal flow from input to output through a typical input module.

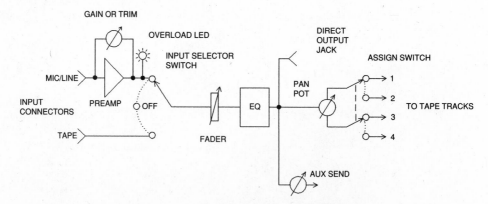

Figure 11.2 Signal flow through a typical input module.

Input Connectors

Input connectors are for microphones, direct boxes, electric musical instruments, or an external multitrack tape recorder. The following are labels for each connector:

- MIC (for mic-level signals: microphones and direct boxes)
- LINE (for line-level signals: a synth, drum machine, or electric guitar)
- TAPE (for line-level signals from an external multitrack tape recorder)

In some recorder-mixers, a single $1/4$-inch phone jack is used both for mic-level and line-level signals. A mic-level signal is typically about 1 to 2 millivolts. A line-level signal is about 0.3 to 1.23 volts. The two levels are handled either by a MIC/LINE switch, a HI-LO GAIN switch, or a TRIM control.

Some units have separate jacks for mic and line inputs. The mic input is either an unbalanced $1/4$-inch phone jack (a $1/4$-inch hole) or an XLR-type connector (with three small holes). The line input is either a $1/4$-inch phone jack, an RCA phono jack (such as that on a stereo system), or an XLR-type connector (in a mixing console). You can plug an electric instrument directly into a phone-jack input without using a direct box if the cable is under 10 feet; a longer cable may pick up hum.

Some newer recorder-mixers also have a *sync input*. It goes into track 4, and is used for recording a special tape-sync tone from a computer running a sequencer program. The sync tone synchronizes tape tracks with MIDI sequencer tracks. It also lets you overdub 2 or more sequencer tracks onto tape by keeping them synchronized. On an 8-track cassette or open-reel machine, use track 8 as the sync track.

Phantom Power (P48, +48)

The phantom power switch is found only in elaborate units and turns on phantom power to condenser microphones. This is 12 to 48 volts DC voltage applied through resistors equally to pins 2 and 3 of XLR-type mic-input connectors. The microphone receives phantom power and sends audio along the same two conductors. Each input module has its own phantom power switch.

Input Selector

The input selector switch selects the input you want to process: mic, line, or tape. The switch might be labeled in one of these ways:

Mic/line

Mic/line/tape

Mic/line/remix

Mic-line/off/tape

Input/off/tape

Input/mute/track

Input/off/line

The following list explains how each switch position works:

Mic	The mic signal enters the mixer.
Line	The line or tape signal enters the mixer.
Mic-line or Input	Either the mic signal or the line signal enters the mixer, depending on what is plugged into that input.
Tape, Track, or Remix	The tape-track signal enters the mixer (for overdubbing or mixdown).
Off or Mute	No signal is processed. During mixdown, it's a good idea to mute tracks that have nothing playing at the moment to reduce tape hiss.

Using the input selector is simple. If you plugged in a microphone or direct box to record its signal, set the input selector to "mic" or "input." If you plugged in a synth, drum machine, or electric guitar, set the selector to "line" or "input."

Mic Preamp

After entering the mic connector and input selector switch, a microphone signal goes into a mic preamplifier inside the mixer. The preamp boosts or amplifies the weak microphone signal up to a higher voltage, making it a line-level signal.

Trim (Gain)

If a microphone is picking up a loud instrument or vocal, the mic signal is very strong. This signal can overload the mic preamp, causing distortion—a gritty sound.

You can prevent overload with the trim or gain control. In some mixers, in each input module, there's a tiny light (LED) labeled "clip" or "peak." It flashes when the mic preamp is distorting. If this light flashes when you're picking up an instrument or vocal, gradually turn down the TRIM control just to the point where the light stays off.

If your mixer lacks such an indicator, you can prevent the input-overload distortion by setting the *master fader(s)* within the shaded portion of its travel (sometimes at 0, about ¾ up). Do the same for the *input fader* (discussed next). Assign the signal to a tape track, and adjust the trim control so that the meter peaks around 0.

Another way to adjust the trim control is by ear. First, turn it full counterclockwise. Then turn it clockwise until the signal distorts. Then slowly turn it back down until you hear no trace of distortion.

Inexpensive recorder-mixers do not have an overload LED or a trim control. The input fader serves this function.

Input Fader

After the microphone signal is amplified by the preamp, it goes to the input fader. This is a sliding volume control for each input signal. You use it during recording to set recording levels on tape, and during mixdown to set the relative loudness balance among instruments.

Direct Out

Found only in fancier units, the direct out is an output connector following each input fader. The signal at the direct-out jack is an amplified version of the input signal. The fader controls the level at the direct-out jack. Use the direct-out jack when you want to record one mic per track on an external multitrack recorder or affect the direct out before the tape track. You connect the direct-out jack to a tape-track input. Because the direct out bypasses the mixing circuits farther down the chain, the result is a cleaner signal.

If a mixer has eight inputs with a direct-out jack for each input, you can use the mixer with an 8-track recorder—even if the mixer has only 2 or 4 outputs.

EQ (Equalization)

The signal from the input fader goes to an equalizer, which is a tone control. With EQ you can make an instrument sound more or less bassy and more or less trebley, by boosting or cutting certain frequencies.

Equalizers cover two or three bands of the audible spectrum. Inexpensive units have a simple two-knob bass and treble control; you can boost or cut the treble or bass. Fancier models have a sweepable EQ (sometimes called semiparametric EQ) that lets you "tune in" the exact frequency range to work on. This feature adds cost and complexity, but gives you more control over the tone quality.

In some low-cost recorder-mixers, the EQ works on 2 tracks at a time during recording, and on the stereo mix during mixdown. This is less flexible than a unit with EQ on each input.

Assign Switch

The equalized signal goes to the *assign switch* (sometimes called track selector switch). It lets you send the signal of each instrument to the tape track you want to record that instrument on.

Some units have assign switches labeled 1, 2, 3, or 4. If you want to record bass on track 1, for instance, find the assign switch for the input module the bass is plugged into, and push switch 1. If you want to record four drum mics on track 2, push assign switch 2 for all those input modules.

Other recorder-mixers assign tracks with two controls: a selector switch and a pan pot (described next).

Pan Pot

A pan pot is a device that sends a signal to 2 channels. By rotating the pan pot knob, you control how much signal goes to each channel. Set the knob all the way left and the signal goes to 1 channel. Set it all the way right and the signal goes to the other channel. Set it in the middle and the signal goes to both channels.

Here's how you might use a pan pot to assign an instrument to a track. The track-selector switch (assign switch) might have two positions labeled 1-2 and 3-4. If you turn the pan pot left, the signal goes to odd-numbered tracks (either 1 or 3, depending on how you set the assign switch). If you turn the pan pot right, the signal goes to even-numbered tracks (2 or 4).

Suppose you want to assign the bass to track 1. Set the assign switch to 1-2, and turn the pan pot far left to choose the odd-numbered track (track 1).

The pan pot has a different function during mixdown. It places images between your speakers. An image is an apparent source of sound, a point between your speakers where you hear each instrument or vocal. Set the pan pot to locate each instrument at the left speaker, right speaker, or anywhere in between.

Aux (Effects or FX)

The aux or aux-send feature (see Figure 11.3) can be used in two ways:

- To set up a monitor mix—a balanced blend of input signals you hear over speakers or headphones

- To set the amount of effects (reverb, echo) heard on each instrument in a mix

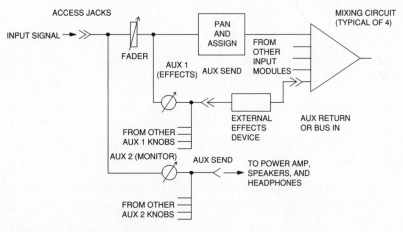

Figure 11.3 Auxiliary and output sections.

Some recorder-mixers have no aux sends. Some have one aux-send control per module; some have two (labeled aux 1, aux 2, or cue send). The more aux sends you have, the more you can play with effects, but the greater the cost and complexity. The aux number (1 or 2) is not necessarily assigned a specific function; you decide what you want aux 1 and aux 2 to do.

261

During recording and overdubbing, the aux knobs or cue send knobs of all the input modules are usually used to create a *monitor mix*.

The monitor mix that you create with the aux knobs is independent of the levels going on tape. You use the faders during recording to set recording levels, and you use the aux knobs to create an independent mix that is heard over your monitor system.

In Figure 11.3, the aux 1 send control is just before the fader. In this mixer, the signals from all the aux 1 knobs in the mixer combine at a connector jack labeled "aux 1 send" or "monitor." You can connect that jack to your power amplifier, which drives monitor speakers and head-phones.

The aux 2 send control is just after the fader. In this mixer, during mixdown, each aux 2 knob controls how much effects (reverb, echo) you hear on each track. The aux knob controls the level of each input signal sent to an external effects device, which adds echo, reverb, or some other effect. The effects signal returns to the mixer's aux-return or bus in jacks. Inside the mixer, the effects signal blends with the original signal, adding spa-ciousness or ambience to an otherwise "dry" track.

A few recorder-mixers have an aux-return control (also called aux receive or bus in) that sets the overall effects level returning to the mixer.

Follow these steps to use the aux controls to adjust the amount of effects heard on each track:

1. Patch an effects unit between your mixer's aux-send and aux-return (bus in) jacks.

2. On the effects unit, set the dry/wet mix control all the way to "wet" or "effect."

3. If your mixer has aux-return (bus in) knobs, turn them about ¾ up and pan their signals hard left and right.

4. Turn up the aux-send knob for each input, according to how much effect you want to hear on that input signal.

Suppose you're using reverb as an effect. You might turn it up by different amounts for the vocals, drums, and lead guitar, and leave it turned down for the bass and kick drum. As you're setting the aux levels, check the overload indicator on the reverb unit. If it's flashing, turn down the input level on the reverb unit just to the point where the overload light stops flashing. Then turn up the output level on the reverb unit (or turn up the aux return on the mixer) to achieve the same amount of reverb you heard before.

There might be a *pre/post switch* next to the aux-send knob. When an aux knob is set to pre (prefader), its level is not affected by the fader setting. You use the pre setting for a headphone mix during recording or overdubbing because you don't want the fader settings to affect the monitor mix.

The post setting (postfader) is used for effects during mixdown. In this case, the aux level follows the setting of the fader. The higher you set the track volume with the fader, the higher the effects level is.

Access Jacks (Insert Jacks)

The access jacks on the mixer let you plug a compressor in series with an input module's signal for automatic volume control. Inexpensive units omit this feature. Some units have access jacks on only two inputs.

The access jacks also can be used to insert any other signal processor (reverb/delay, for instance) into the signal path of 1 track. This way, if all your aux sends are tied up, you can add another signal processor. On the reverb/delay unit, set the dry/wet mix control for the desired amount of effect.

Output Section

The output section is the final part of the signal path, the section that feeds signals to the tape tracks. It includes mixing circuits, submaster faders (sometimes), master faders, and meters (see Figure 11.4).

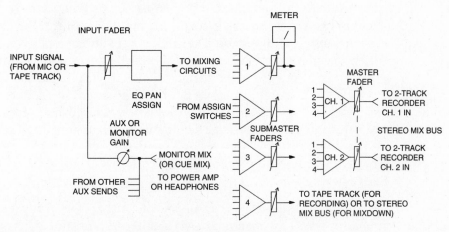

Figure 11.4 Output and monitor sections of a mixer.

Mixing Circuits (Active Combining Networks)

The mixing circuits are near the right side of Figure 11.4; they are part of the output section (not shown). Recall that you use the assign switches to send each input signal to the desired channel or bus, and each bus feeds a different tape track. A bus is a channel in a mixer containing an independent mix of signals. The bus 1 mixing circuit accepts the signals from all the inputs you assigned to bus 1 and mixes them together to feed track 1 of the tape recorder. The bus 2 mixing circuit mixes all the bus 2 assignments, and so on. Mixing circuits also accept the effects-return signals, such as the reverberated signal from an external digital reverb unit.

A four-bus mixer provides 4 independent output channels or buses; each bus carries a signal that may contain the sounds from one or more musical instruments. The four buses could feed a 4-track cassette recorder. A mixer with only two output buses can be used with a 4-track recorder by recording 2 tracks at a time.

Master and Submaster Faders

Located toward the right side of your mixer, the *stereo master faders* are one or two sliding volume controls—or a knob—that affects the overall level of the stereo output channels or buses. Usually, you set the master fader(s) within "design center," the shaded area about ¾ up on the scale. This setting minimizes mixer noise and distortion. You can fade out the end of a mix by turning down the master faders gradually.

Elaborate mixers also have faders that control the level of each bus independently, called *submaster*, *bus master*, or *group faders*. You might create a drum submix, or keyboard submix, and control the overall level of each submix with a submaster fader. Set submasters to design center initially, set the recording level and submix balances with the input faders, and then fine-tune each overall submix level with the submaster faders.

The submasters can serve double duty as master faders if you use only two of them. Then you can take your stereo mix from the bus 1 and 2 outputs. The noise is less there than after the master faders.

Meters

Meters are an important part of the output section. They measure the voltage or level of various signals. Usually, each output bus has a meter to measure its signal level. Because these buses feed the tape tracks, you use the meters to set the recording level for each track. Your recorder-mixer has one of three types of meters:

VU	A voltmeter that shows approximately the relative loudness of various audio signals. Set the record level so that the meter needle reaches +3 VU maximum for most signals, and about –6 VU maximum for drums, percussion, and piano. That's necessary because the VU meter responds too slowly to show the true level of percussive sounds.
LED bargraph level indicator	A column of lights (LEDs) that shows peak recording level. For all instruments, set the level to peak at 0 to +6 db maximum, according to the manufacturer's recommendations.
LED peak indicator	A light mounted in a VU meter. It flashes when peak recording levels are excessive. If you have this type of meter, set the level as high as possible, but not so high that the LED flashes.

Tape-Out Jacks

Tape-out jacks are sometimes included in the output section of recorder-mixers. These are connected to the tape-track outputs, and are used for copying your 4-track cassette recordings onto a multitrack studio recorder for further overdubs and processing.

Monitor Section

The monitor section controls what you're listening to. It lets you select what you want to hear, and lets you create a mix over headphones or speakers to approximate the final product. This monitor mix has no effect on the levels going on tape. Your mixer might have a small group of knobs called a *monitor mixer* (*monmix* or *tape cue*), or it might be a row of monitor knobs, aux knobs, or output knobs, one in each input module. In either case, these knobs control the mix you hear as you're recording.

The monitor mixer is made of several *monitor gain* controls, plus mixing circuits that feed headphones or an external stereo amplifier and speakers. The gain knob controls how loud each live instrument or track is in the monitor mix. Some monitor mixers also have *monitor pan* and monitor effects controls. The pan knob controls the left-right position of the instrument or track between your stereo speakers or headphones.

The monitor mixer is also used to blend prerecorded tape tracks and live microphone signals into a cue mix that is sent to headphones. You overdub new parts while listening to the cue mix. In most recorder-mixers, the monitor mix and cue mix are identical.

The Tascam Midistudio recorder-mixers have several extra inputs for MIDI instruments, along with aux or monitor knobs for these instruments so you can add them to the monitor mix. Because of this feature, you can use the recorder-mixer to mix tape tracks and sequencer tracks; you don't need to purchase an extra mixer to do this.

Remember that the auxiliary (aux) sends in the mixer can serve multiple duty as controls for a monitor mix, headphone mix, or effects sends.

Monitor Select Buttons

Another feature of the monitor section is the *monitor select buttons*. They let you choose what signal you want to monitor or listen to. Because the configuration of these buttons varies widely among different recorder-mixers, they are not shown in Figure 11.3. The following are some of the monitor select buttons you may find:

- Monitor Track 1, 2, 3, 4
- Tape/bus 1, 2, 3, 4
- Tape/bus stereo/aux or Tape-bus/2-tr/aux
- Remix/cue/aux
- Line/mixdown

With the Monitor Track 1, 2, 3, and 4 buttons, you select which track or combination of tracks you want to hear.

With the Tape/bus 1, 2, 3, and 4 buttons, you select signals from tape tracks 1, 2, 3, or 4 or from buses 1, 2, 3, or 4. Select "tape" to hear a playback, or for hearing previously recorded tracks during an overdub. Select "bus" to hear the live signal that you're recording.

The "stereo" or "2-tr" switch position of the Tape-bus/stereo/aux button gives you the 2-channel stereo mix during mixdown. The "aux" position is used to hear the aux signal (effects or headphone mix).

The "Remix" position of the Remix/cue/aux button is the 2-channel stereo mix you want to hear during mixdown. "Cue" is the headphone mix. "Aux" is the effects-signal mix.

The "Line" position of the Line/mixdown button is for overdubbing. It's a mono mix of live signals and tape signals over headphones for selected tracks. "Mixdown" is used during mixdown to hear a stereo mix of all 4 tracks.

Some units have no monitor-select switches. Instead, you always monitor the 2-channel stereo monitor mix.

Additional Features Found in Mixing Consoles

Mixing consoles have more features than recorder-mixers do. If you're working only with a recorder-mixer, you might want to skip this section. The extra features of mixing consoles include:

- I/O Design
- Pre/post switch
- Foldback (cue, or headphone mix)
- Solo (PFL)
- Phase (polarity invert)
- Automated mixing controls
- Effects panning
- Foldback connectors
- Bus trim
- Bus/monitor/cue switch for effects return
- Meter switches
- Dim
- Effects return to cue
- Effects return to monitor

- Talkback

- Slate

- Oscillator or tone generator

Some consoles use an Input/Output (I/O) type of construction (also called in-line). In this type of console, each module (other than the monitor section) contains 1 input channel and 1 output channel.

When used with an effects-send pot, the Pre/post switch selects whether the effects send is derived prefader (before the fader) or postfader (following the fader). A prefader effects send is not affected by the input's fader—if you turn down the input fader, the effect remains. A postfader effects send follows the fader action—if you turn down the fader, the effects-send level goes down.

The SOLO button in an input module lets you monitor only that input without affecting other console functions. More than one input can be soloed at one time. On British consoles, the SOLO function is called "PFL" or "AFL," which stand for Pre-Fader Listen and After-Fader Listen (postfader), respectively. You listen to or monitor the signal before or after the fader.

In consoles that have both PFL and SOLO, PFL is prefader and is used mainly to listen for distortion during recording; SOLO is postfader and is used for listening to 1 track during mixdown.

Suppose you hear a buzz in the audio and suspect it may be in the bass guitar signal. If you push the SOLO button in the bass guitar's input module, you monitor only the bass guitar. Then you can easily hear whether the buzz is in that input.

Used only with balanced lines, the Phase (polarity invert) switch inverts the polarity of the input signal. That is, it switches pins 2 and 3 to flip the phase 180 degrees. You might use it to correct for a miswired microphone cable whose polarity is reversed. If you mike a snare drum top and bottom, you need to invert the polarity of the bottom mic.

Automated mixing controls (Read, Write, Update, etc.) are beyond the scope of this book. Basically they control the functions of a computer-assisted mixing system. The computer memory remembers and updates console settings so that a mix can be performed and refined in several stages and remembered later.

The Effects panning feature places the images of the effects signals wherever desired between the monitor speakers. Some consoles let you pan effects in the monitor mix as well as in the final program mix.

Foldback connectors are in parallel with the TAPE IN jacks. The output of each tape track is connected to a TAPE IN jack, so the FOLDBACK connector parallels, or "mults," the tape-machine output. The FOLDBACK jacks can be be used to send the tape outputs to an outboard device in addition to the console, such as an external cue mixer.

The Bus trim rotary pot provides variable gain reduction on the bus, used in addition with the bus master (or submaster) fader.

The Bus/monitor/cue switch for effects return feeds the effects-return signal to your choice of destinations: program bus (for mixdown), monitor mix, cue mix, or any combination of the three.

In many consoles, the VU meters can measure signal levels other than console output levels. Switches near the meters can be set so that the meters indicate bus level, aux-send level, aux-return level, monitor-mix level, etc.

Those readings help you set optimum levels for the outboard devices receiving those signals. Too low a level results in noise; too high a level causes distortion in the outboard unit. For example, if the aux-return signal sounds garbled or distorted, the cause may be an excessive aux-send level. That condition can be verified by checking the VU meters switched to read the aux or effects bus.

The Dim switch reduces the monitor level by a preset amount (as in "Dim the lights").

The Effects return to cue is an effects-return level control that affects the amount of effects heard in the studio headphone mix. These monitored effects are independent of any effects being recorded on tape.

The Effects return to monitor effects-return control adjusts the amount of effects heard in the monitor mix. These monitored effects are independent of any effects being recorded on tape.

The Talkback function lets the people in the control room talk to the musicians in the studio. A small microphone often is built into the console for this purpose.

The Slate function routes the control-room microphone signal to all the buses for announcing on tape the name of the tune and take number. In some consoles, a low-frequency tone is recorded on tape during slating; then the beginning of the take can be quickly located by listening for tape tones during fast-forward or rewind.

An Oscillator or tone generator is used to put alignment tones on tape, and to reference the tape recorder's meters to those on the console. You also can use it to check signal path, levels, and channel balance.

Now that you understand the typical features of mixers and mixing consoles, you are ready to learn how to use them.

OPERATING THE MULTITRACK RECORDER AND MIXER

Get your hands on those knobs. You're going to operate a mixer as part of a recording session. This will be a basic run-through—detailed session procedures are described in Chapter 13.

First, recall the stages in making a recording:

1. Recording

2. Punching in

3. Overdubbing

4. Bouncing tracks

5. Mixdown

This chapter considers each stage in turn.

Recording

Before making a recording, it's important to clean your multitrack deck. Dust or tape oxide can accumulate on the tape heads, making the sound dull. So clean the tape heads, tape guides, and rubber pinch roller with a cotton swab and the cleaner recommended by the manufacturer. A typical cleaner is denatured alcohol, available at hardware stores. Freon-based cleaners are also available. Don't use rubbing alcohol or isopropyl because they can leave a film on the heads, and they contain water.

When the heads are dry, thread on some blank recording tape or insert a cassette. High-bias (chrome or metal) cassette tape provides better high-frequency response than ferric, and C-60 or C-90 lengths record bass sounds better than longer lengths.

For open-reel recorders, low-noise, high-output tape is best. With high-bias cassette tape and high-quality reel tape, you can record with a higher S/N ratio.

If you plan to use a tape-sync signal to synchronize your recorder with MIDI equipment, record it for the entire length of the song before recording any other tape tracks. Usually the sync tone is recorded on track 4 of a 4-track recorder or track 8 of an 8-track recorder. This procedure is detailed in Chapter 15.

In planning your track assignments, remember that when several instruments are assigned to the same track, you can't separate their images in the stereo stage. That is, you can't pan them to different positions; all the instruments on 1 track sound as if they're occupying the same point in space. For this reason, you may want to do a stereo mix of the rhythm section on, for instance, tracks 1 and 2. Then overdub vocals and solos on tracks 3 and 4.

Starting Up

To start the process, first zero or neutralize the mixer by setting all the controls to "off," "flat," or "zero" to establish a point of reference and avoid surprises later on.

If you have a separate mixer and multitrack recorder, you need to make their meter readings match. To do this, play a steady tone into the mixer to get a 0 reading on the meters for all tracks. Then set the multitrack recorder's record level (if any) to get 0 readings on all the tracks.

Suppose you're ready to record a vocal or an acoustic instrument. Place the microphone and plug it into a mic input. If you want to record a synth or drum machine on tape, connect a cable between the instrument's output and a line input on the mixer.

Attach a strip of masking tape or white removable tape along the bottom of the faders, and label each fader according to what instrument you plugged into that input. Be sure that all the faders are down.

Set the input selector to "input," "mic," or "line" depending on what is plugged into each input. If there is no input selector, turn down the TRIM control for line-level signals.

Plug in headphones to hear what you're recording. Turn up the headphone volume control or, if you're in a control room and the musicians are in a studio, turn up the monitor level to listen over the monitor loudspeakers. Set the MONITOR SELECT switch and turn up the musicians' cue-mix.

Set the master faders about ³/₄ up (at 0), or within the shaded portion of fader travel. Recall from Chapter 12 this is design center. Later, you do the same for the input fader in use (see Figure 12.1). These settings give the least noise and distortion.

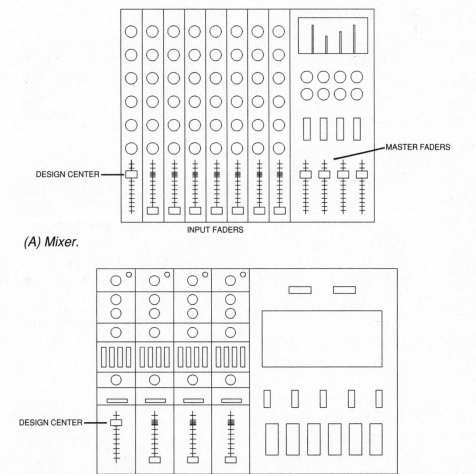

(A) Mixer.

(B) Recorder-mixer.

Figure 12.1 Setting faders at design center.

273

Assigning Signals to Channels

Assign each input signal to the desired output channel (bus) as specified on your track sheet. Each channel is connected to the corresponding numbered tape track on the multitrack recorder.

If only one instrument is assigned to a track, you can eliminate the noise of the console combining amplifier by patching the instrument's signal directly to the tape track. To do this, locate the direct output jack of the input module for that instrument and patch it to the desired track. Some mixing boards also require pressing a direct button on the input module.

Setting Trim

Have the musician sing or play the loudest part of the music. Slowly bring up that fader to design center. If your recorder-mixer has a TRIM control, gradually turn it down just until the input-overload (clip) light stops flashing. You also can set the TRIM control so that the meter peaks around 0 maximum, or gradually turn it down until you hear no trace of distortion.

Setting Record Level

Now you're ready to "get a level." Have each instrument play, one at a time. Using the fader on the instrument's input module, set the recording level as high as possible without causing tape distortion. The recording level should be 0 to +6 db for a peak-reading LED bargraph meter or 0 VU for a VU meter. When you record percussive instruments, a peak-reading LED meter should peak around 0 to +6 db, but a VU meter should peak around –6 to –8 VU to allow for the slow meter movement. If your VU meter contains a peak LED light, set the recording level so that the peak LED flashes only occasionally.

If you have a separate mixer and multitrack recorder, which meters should you watch? Usually you watch the mixer meters to set levels because you previously matched the recorder meters to the console meters. You have to watch the recorder meters for tracks that are patched direct or if you're using dbx noise reduction.

Setting EQ

You may want to apply equalization at this point to each instrument heard individually. If necessary, filter out frequencies above and below the range of the instrument. However, don't spend too much time on equalization until all the instruments are mixed together because the equalization that sounds right on an individual instrument may not sound right when all the instruments are heard together. In creating the desired tonal balance, use equalization as a last resort after experimenting with microphone selection and placement. You also can apply the same EQ during playback/mixdown. This may be preferable in many cases because EQ applied when recording cannot always be undone if you're unhappy with it.

Next, set the track you want to record to "record ready" mode, and set the tape counter to 0. Now start recording. "Slate" the tape: announce on tape the name of the tune and the take number. Then record a two-measure count-off. This is done to set the tempo for overdubs. For example, if the time signature is ⁴/₄, you say, "1, 2, 3, 4, 1, 2, (rest) (rest)." The rests are silent beats—you need some silence before the song starts to make editing easier later on. If your recorder-mixer is part of a MIDI tape sync system, the count-off is unnecessary because your MIDI sequencer sets the song tempo.

After recording the track, rewind the tape using the return-to-zero function. Set the monitor selectors to "tape," "track," or "remix," and play back the recording to check the performance and sound quality. You can set a rough mix with the monitor mix (aux) knobs.

Punching In

You might want to correct musical errors in a track by punching in. Follow these steps:

1. Set the tape counter to 000 a few seconds before the part that needs correction.

2. Play the tape track to the musician over headphones.

3. During a rest (a pause in the track) just before the part needing correction, punch in the record button (or use a footswitch). Have the musician record the corrected musical part.

4. Immediately after the corrected part is played, punch out of record mode (or use the footswitch) to avoid erasing the rest of the track.

5. Using the return-to-zero function, rewind the tape and play it back. If necessary, you can rerecord the punch.

Often it's difficult for a musician to get all the way through a long, difficult solo or musical line without making a mistake. In this case, you can punch in and out to record the part in successive segments.

With care, you can punch in additional instruments on a completely full tape by recording them in the pauses on previously recorded tracks. For example, suppose all the tracks are full but you want to add a cymbal roll at the beginning of the chorus. Find a track that has a pause at that moment, and punch in the cymbal roll there.

Overdubbing

After your first track is recorded, you might want to add more musical parts. This procedure is called overdubbing. When you overdub, you listen to tracks you've already recorded, and record a new part on an unused track.

First, locate the monitor mixer section. It is a row or group of knobs called "monmix," "monitor," "submix," "aux," or "tape cue." Find the monitor mixer input selectors for the recorded tracks you want to listen to. Set them to "tape" or "track" so you can monitor them. Also, set the MONITOR SELECT switch to aux1, aux2, or whatever bus the monitor controls are affecting.

Plug in a pair of headphones. Play the tape and set up a blend of the tracks using the monitor-level and PAN controls in the monitor mixer.

Next, plug in the mic or instrument you want to record and assign it to an open (unused) track. Find the input-selector switch for the input signal you're recording. Set it to "mic," "line," or "input" as required. Do the same in the monitor mixer. Turn up the monitor-level control for the live signal so you can hear it.

Have the musician play the instrument or sing into the mic. Set the TRIM (INPUT ATTEN or GAIN) to prevent distortion as described before. Then set the recording level with the fader.

Create a monitor mix of the recorded tracks and the live signal. Play the tape and have the musician play or sing along with it. Both the recorded tracks and the live signal can be heard in the musician's headphones. Adjust the monitor-level controls to get a good mix of the recorded tracks and the live signal.

When you're ready to record the new part, rewind to the beginning of the song. Set the recorded tracks to "safe" and set the track you're recording on to "record ready." Start recording and have the musician play along with the tracks being monitored. If the musician makes a mistake, it can be rerecorded or punched in without affecting the parts already on tape.

If an overdub occurs only in the middle of a song, you don't need to rewind to the beginning. Set the tape counter to 000 a few seconds before the overdub point, and use the return-to-zero feature to practice the overdub.

If there are other parts to add, overdub them too. But you might want to leave one or two tracks open for bouncing.

Bouncing Tracks

Recall that if your recorder has too few tracks for all the parts you want to overdub, you can bounce tracks—mix several tracks to one or two open tracks, and record the mix on that track. Then you can erase the original tracks, freeing them for more overdubs.

Suppose you want to bounce tracks 1, 2, and 3 to track 4. Follow these steps:

1. Monitor only track 4.

2. Assign input modules 1, 2, and 3 to track 4.

3. Set all tape deck tracks to "play" or "safe" mode.

4. Set the input selector switches for input modules 1, 2, and 3 to "tape."

5. Play the tape.

6. Using input faders 1, 2, and 3, mix the tracks as desired and set the recording level to peak around 0 on track 4.

7. When you're happy with the mix, rewind to the beginning of the song.

8. Set only tape track 4 to "record ready" mode.

9. Start recording. The mix of tracks 1, 2, and 3 record on track 4.

You can add live mic or instrument signals while you're bouncing by plugging them into input 4, and assigning input 4 to track 4. In this way, you can record up to 10 tracks on a 4-track machine while bouncing tracks. Table 12.1 shows this bouncing procedure. Each track with an asterisk is a live instrument or microphone signal. Tracks without an asterisk are already recorded on tape.

Table 12.1 Bouncing procedure for recording 10 tracks with a 4-track recorder.

Step 1 Track	Step 2 Track	Step 3 Track	Step 4 Track	Step 5 Track	Step 6 Track	Step 7 Track
1 A*	1	1 E*	1	1 H*	1	1 J*
2 B*	2	2 F*	2	2	2 HI*	2 HI
3 C*	3	3	3 EFG*	3 EFG	3 EFG	3 EFG
4	4 ABCD*	4 ABCD	4 ABCD	4 ABCD	4 ABCD	4 ABCD

Follow these steps to execute this bouncing procedure:

1. Record three instruments (A, B, C) on tracks 1, 2, and 3.

2. Mix these three tracks with a live instrument signal and record the result on track 4.

3. Record two more instruments on tracks 1 and 2.

4. Bounce tracks 1 and 2 onto track 3 while mixing in another live instrument.

5. Record one more instrument on track 1.

6. Bounce track 1 to track 2 while mixing in another live instrument.

7. Record one more instrument on track 1.

You can continue this process to add even more instruments, but every rerecording adds noise, distortion, and frequency-response errors. This signal degradation is called *generation loss*.

Try a similar procedure for other track-bouncing combinations, setting up your recorder-mixer appropriately for the desired track assignments.

Mixdown

After all your tracks are recorded (maybe with some bouncing), it's time to mix or combine them to 2-track stereo. Use the mixer faders to control the relative volumes of the instruments, use panning to set their stereo position, use EQ to adjust their tone quality, and use the aux knobs to control effects.

If you're mixing only tape tracks (no live sequencer tracks), use the mixing console or recorder-mixer, but if you're synching a sequencer to your recorder, mix the tape tracks and sequencer tracks with an outboard mixer that is not part of the console or recorder-mixer. Some newer recorder-mixers, such as some of the Tascam Midistudios, have extra line inputs for MIDI instruments so that you can do the entire mix with the recorder-mixer.

Setting Up the Mixer and Recorders

To perform a mixdown, first locate the jacks for output channels 1 and 2—they might be called "Bus 1 and 2," or "Stereo mix bus"—on the back of the mixer. Plug these outputs into the line or aux inputs of your 2-track recorder (see Figure 12.2).

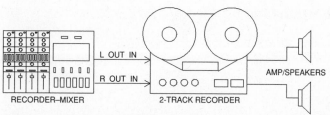

Figure 12.2 Connections for mixdown.

Clean and demagnetize the tape machines. Set all the controls to "off," "zero," or "flat." You should start from ground zero in building a mix.

Tape a strip of paper along the front of the mixer to write which instrument(s) each fader affects. Keep this strip with the multitrack master tape so that you can use it each time the master is played.

Set the input-selector switches on the mixer to "tape" (or "track" or "remix") because you're mixing down the multitrack tape. Monitor the 2-track stereo mix bus.

Position the master faders (output faders) ¾ up (at 0 or at the shaded portion of fader travel).

Assign each track to channels 1 and 2, and use the pan pots to place each track where desired between your stereo speakers. Typically, bass, kick drum, and vocals go to center; keyboards and guitars can be panned left and right.

Erasing Unwanted Material

Play the multitrack tape and listen to each track alone. Erase unwanted sounds, outtakes, and entire segments that don't add to the song. To avoid mistakes, it's best to do this while the musicians are around.

If a noise occurs just before the musician starts playing and you try to erase the noise, you might erase the beginning of the track. To prevent this, turn the cassette tape upside down or reverse the multitrack tape reels. Then find the track of the desired instrument playing backwards. Play the tape section that comes just after the noise; you hear it playing in reverse. Just after the reverse part ends, punch that track into record mode to erase the noise. It might be safer to mute the track during mixdown and then unmute it just before the musician plays.

Compressing the Vocal Track

Sometimes the vocal track might be too loud or too quiet relative to the instruments because vocals have a wider dynamic range than instruments. You can prevent this by running the vocal track through a compressor. This device keeps the volume of the vocals more constant, making them easier to hear throughout the mix. Patch the compressor into the access jacks for the input module of the vocal and set it for the desired amount of compression. (For more information, see Chapter 10.)

Setting a Balance

Using the input faders, adjust the volume of each track for a pleasing balance among instruments and vocals. You should be able to hear each instrument clearly. In some units, use the MONMIX controls for this function.

As a starting point, you may want to set the mix so that all the instruments and vocals sound equally loud and then turn up the most important tracks and turn down background instruments. Or you can bring up one track at a time and blend it with the other tracks. For example, first bring up the kick drum; then add bass and balance the two together. Next add drums, guitars, keyboards, and then vocals.

One method of setting balances for pop music is to set the kick drum level to –10 VU on the VU meters. Turn up the monitor level until the kick drum is as loud as you like to hear it and then leave the monitor level alone. Bring up the other tracks one at a time and mix them relative to the kick drum. For example, first bring up the kick drum; then add bass and balance the two together. Next add drums and balance them with the kick drum and bass. Then add guitars, keyboards, and vocals.

There is another method of setting balances, often used in country music, where the vocal is most prominent. Set the lead vocal level to peak at –5 VU. Bring up the monitor level so that the vocal is as loud as you like to hear it and then leave the monitor level alone. Bring in the other tracks one at a time and mix them relative to the vocal track.

When the mix is right, everything can be heard clearly, yet nothing is obtrusive. The most important instruments or voices are loudest; less important parts are in the background. Note that there's a wide latitude for musical interpretation and personal taste in making a mix. Sometimes you don't want everything to be clearly audible. In rare occasions you may want to mix in certain tracks almost inaudibly for a subtle effect.

Mixing is a dynamic process. You change the mix continuously to highlight certain instruments according to the demands of the music. To reduce tape noise, mute all tracks that have nothing playing at the moment. That is, if there is a long silence during a track, mute that silent portion. Unmute these tracks just before their instruments start playing. Mute unrecorded tracks as well.

Monitor frequently in mono to judge the singer/ensemble balance or soloist/ensemble balance.

To test your mix, occasionally play the monitors very quietly, and see if you can hear everything. Switch from large monitors to small, and make sure nothing is missing.

Setting EQ

Adjust the equalization (EQ) for the desired tonal balance on each track. If a track sounds too dull, turn up the treble or high frequencies. If a track sounds too bassy, turn down the bass or low frequencies, and so on. EQ is covered in detail in Chapter 10.

Each track can be equalized independently. For example, you can add crispness (high frequencies) to the cymbals without affecting the tone quality of the vocals. You can remove a "tubby" tone from the kick drum without affecting the keyboards, if they are recorded on separate tracks. EQ can change the balance among tracks, so you may need to reset the fader levels after EQ is added.

Setting Effects

You might want to plug in an external reverb or delay unit to add spaciousness to the sound. (See Chapter 10.) This device connects between your mixer's aux-send and aux-receive jacks (or aux-send and bus in jacks). If your recorder-mixer has an AUX RETURN or BUS IN control, set it ¾ up. If the return is stereo, pan it far left and right. Using the AUX knobs on the mixer, adjust the amount of delay or reverb for each track as desired. AUX might be labeled EFFECTS or FX on your recorder-mixer.

Setting Recording Level

As you're mixing, be sure to keep the recording level peaking around 0 by adjusting the input faders, with the master faders remaining about ¾ up. The meters in the multitrack recorder-mixer, and in the 2-track recorder, should all peak around 0 (–3 db maximum for a DAT machine).

Making a Cue Sheet

If level changes are required during the mixdown, mark the settings for each change by the faders. Use white tape or masking tape for marking.

Make a *cue sheet* that notes the mixer changes needed at various tape-counter times. For example:

1:10 Lead guitar +3 db

1:49 Lead guitar –2 db

2:42 Synth +6 @ 12 k

3:05 Fade, out at 3:15

Judging the Mix

When you mix, listen briefly to each instrument in turn, and to the mix as a whole. If you hear something you don't like, fix it. Is the vocal too tubby? Roll off the bass on the vocal track. Is the kick drum too quiet? Turn it up. Is the lead guitar solo too dead? Turn up its aux send.

Set the balances, EQ, and effects to sound like commercial recordings you've heard through the monitors you're using. It's a good idea to play a recording with similar tunes to those you are recording to hear a typical mix.

The producer of a recording is the musical director and decides how the mix should sound. Ask to hear recordings having the kind of sounds the producer desires. Try to figure out what techniques were used to create those sounds.

Also try to translate the producer's sound quality descriptions into control settings. If the producer asks for a "warmer" sound on a particular instrument, turn up the low frequencies. If the lead guitar needs to be "fatter," try a stereo chorus on the guitar track. If the producer wants the vocal to be more "spacious," try adding reverb, and so on.

The mix must be appropriate for the style of music. For example, a mix that's right for rock music usually won't work for folk music or acoustic jazz. Rock mixes typically have lots of production EQ, compression, and effects, and the drums are up front in the mix. On the other hand, folk or acoustic jazz is usually mixed with no effects other than slight reverb, and the recorded timbres of instruments and vocals are natural. Rock guitars usually sound bright and distorted; jazz guitars usually sound mellow and clean.

If a realistic, natural sound is desired, adjust the controls to create the illusion of live musicians playing in front of you. To do this you must be familiar with the sound of real instruments. Manipulate the recorded tracks until they sound like your memory of the real thing.

Try to keep the mix clean and clear. A clean mix is one that is uncluttered, free of excess instrumentation. This is achieved by arranging the music so that similar parts don't overlap. Usually, the fewer the instruments, the clearer the sound. Mix selectively so that not too many instruments are heard at the same time.

In a clear-sounding recording, instruments do not "crowd" or mask each other's sound. They are separate and distinct, and blend well. Clarity arises when instruments occupy different areas of the frequency spectrum. For example, low frequencies are provided by the bass, midbass is emphasized by the keyboards, upper midrange is provided by lead guitar, and highs are filled in by the cymbals.

Rhythm guitar often occupies the same frequency range as piano, so they tend to mask each other's sound. You can increase clarity by boosting the guitar at 2 kHz, for instance, and boosting the piano around 5 kHz. It also helps to pan them to opposite sides.

See Chapter 18 for more information about the technical problems of mixdown and sound production values.

Calibration Tones

If your master tape is open-reel, you should record calibration tones on the master tape just before recording the mixes. Record the following tones on both channels simultaneously with no noise reduction (20 seconds each):

- 1 kHz at 0 VU

- Optionally, 15 kHz for azimuth alignment at OVU for 15 or 30 ips; –10 VU for 7 1/2 ips to prevent tape saturation

- 1 kHz, 10 kHz, and 100 Hz (record at 0 VU for 15 or 30 ips; –10 VU for 7 1/2 ips)

- If Dolby-A is used, record an encoded Dolby tone at 0 VU, followed by an encoded 1 kHz tone at 0 VU (Dolby-A tones should be generated by each track's encoder)

- If dbx Type 1 is used, record an encoded 1 kHz tone at 0 VU; if a zero offset is used, note the offset level (for example, 0 VU program = –3 VU on tape)

The duplicating engineer or CD-mastering engineer uses the 15 kHz tone to align the repro head, the 1 kHz 0-VU tone to set overall level and channel balance, and the other tones to set playback EQ. Then the engineer's tape machine plays back the same tonal balance and stereo balance that you recorded during mixdown.

If you don't have access to a multifrequency generator, record a 1 kHz tone or a sine-wave synthesizer note (2 octaves above middle C) at 0 VU, both channels.

Recording the Mix

When you're satisfied with the mix, sound quality, and recording levels, slate the tape and record the mix on your 2-track machine. An especially difficult mix can be recorded a section at a time, and the sections can be edited together.

If you want to fade out the end of the tune, pull down the master faders slowly and smoothly. Try to have the music faded out by the end of a phrase in the lyrics. The slower the song, the slower the fade should be. Play back the mix to listen for dropouts and errors.

The mixdown is now complete. Repeat these mixdown procedures for the rest of the good takes. Some engineers record several mixes of the same tune and choose the best one.

After a few days, listen to the mix—perhaps on car speakers, a boom box, or a home system. The time lapse between mixdown and listening allows you to hear with fresh ears. See if there's anything you want to change.

The following are summaries of the procedures for recording, over-dubbing, and mixdown. Use these steps for easy reference.

Recording

1. Turn up the headphone or monitor volume control. Monitor the aux bus you're using for the monitor mix.

2. Assign instruments to tracks.

3. Turn up the submaster and master faders to design center (the shaded portion of fader travel, about ¾ up).

4. Adjust the input attenuators (trim) and bring up the input faders to design center.

5. Set the submixes and recording levels.

6. Set the cue mix.

7. Record onto the multitrack tape.

Overdubbing

1. Assign the instruments or vocals to be recorded to open tracks. An open track is blank or has already been bounced.

2. Turn up the cue system.

3. Turn up the submasters and master to design center.

4. Play the multitrack tape in sync mode and set up a cue mix of already-recorded tracks.

5. While a musician is playing, adjust the input attenuation and recording level.

6. Set the cue-monitor mix to include the sound of the instrument or vocal being added.

7. Record the new parts on open tracks.

8. Punch in and bounce as needed.

Mixdown

1. Set the input selectors to accept the multitrack tape signals.

2. Monitor buses 1 and 2 (stereo mix bus).

3. Assign tape tracks to buses 1 and 2.

4. Turn up the master fader to design center. In some mixers, the submasters should also be up.

5. Set a rough mix with the input faders.

6. Set equalization, reverb, panning, and effects.

7. Perfect the mix and set recording levels.

8. Record onto the 2-track tape.

The next chapter gives detailed session procedures, including how to assemble the master reel.

13

SESSION PROCEDURES

"We're rolling. Take One." These words begin the recording session. It can be an exhilarating or an exasperating experience, depending on how smoothly you run it.

The musicians need an engineer who works quickly yet carefully. Otherwise, they may lose their creative inspiration while waiting for the engineer to get his act together. And the client, paying by the hour, wastes money unless the engineer has prepared for the session in advance.

This chapter describes how to conduct a multitrack recording session. These procedures should help you keep track of things and run the session efficiently.

There are some spontaneous sessions—especially in home studios— that just "grow organically" without advance planning. The instrumentation is not known until the song is done! You just try out different musical ideas and instruments until you find a pleasing combination.

In this way, a band that has its own recording gear can afford to take the time to find out what works musically before going into a professional studio. In addition, if the band is recording itself where it practices, the microphone setup and some of the console settings can be more-or-less permanent. This chapter, however, describes procedures usually followed at professional studios, where time is money.

Preproduction

Long before the session starts, you're involved in *preproduction*—planning in advance what you're going to do at the session in terms of overdubbing, track assignments, instrument layout, and microphone selection.

Instrumentation

The first step is to find out from the producer or the band what the instrumentation is and how many tracks are needed. Make a list of the instruments and vocals to be used in each song. Include such details as the number of tom toms, whether acoustic or electric guitars will be used, and so on.

Recording Order

Next, decide which of these instruments will be recorded at the same time and which will be overdubbed one at a time. It's common to record the instruments in the following order, but there are always exceptions:

1. Loud rhythm instruments—bass, drums, electric guitar, electric keyboards
2. Quiet rhythm instruments—acoustic guitar, piano
3. Lead vocal and doubled lead vocal (if desired)
4. Backup vocals (in stereo)
5. Overdubs—solos, percussion, synthesizer, sound effects
6. Sweetening—horns, strings

The lead vocalist usually sings a reference vocal or *scratch vocal* along with the rhythm section so that the musicians can get a feel for the tune and keep track of where they are in the song. In this case, the vocalist's performance is recorded but probably is redone later.

In a MIDI studio, a typical order might be:

1. Drum machine (playing preprogrammed patterns)
2. Synthesizer bass sound
3. Synthesizer keyboard sound (chords)
4. Synth melody

5. Synth solos, extra parts

6. Tape-recorded vocals and solos

Track Assignments

Once the instrumentation and the order of recording are understood clearly, you can plan your track assignments. Decide what instruments go on which tracks of the multitrack recorder. The producer may have a fixed plan already. The outer tracks are most prone to dropouts at high frequencies, so they are usually reserved for bass, kick drum, or SMPTE time code.

You may have more instruments than tracks, in which case you have to decide what groups of instruments to put on each track. In a 4-track recording, for example, you might record a stereo mix of the rhythm section on tracks 1 and 2 and then overdub vocals and solos on tracks 3 and 4. Or you might put guitars on track 1, bass and drums on track 2, vocals on track 3, and keyboards on track 4.

Remember that when several instruments are assigned to the same track, you can't separate their images in the stereo stage. That is, you can't pan them to different positions; all the instruments on one track sound as if they are occupying the same point in space. For this reason, you may want to do a stereo mix of the rhythm section on tracks 1 and 2, for instance, and then overdub vocals and solos on tracks 3 and 4.

It's possible to overdub more than four parts on a 4-track recorder. To do this, bounce or ping-pong several tracks onto one (see Chapter 12).

If you have many tracks available, leave several tracks open for experimentation. For example, you can record several takes of a vocal part using a separate track for each take so that no take is lost. Then combine the best parts of each take into a single final performance on one track. It's also a good idea to record the monitor mix on one or two unused tracks. The recorded monitor mix can be used to make a work-print tape for the client to take home and evaluate, or for a cue mix for overdubs.

Session Sheet

Once you know what you're going to record and when, you can fill out a session sheet (see Figure 13.1). This simple document is adequate for home studios. On the session sheet is the song title, a list of track numbers, what goes on each track, whether each track is an overdub (OD), and what mic you want to use on each instrument. You also note how many takes you recorded, and circle the best one.

```
SONG: Escape to Air Island

TRACK  INSTRUMENT         MICROPHONE
1      Kick               AKG D-112
2      Drums              Crown GLM-100
3      Lead Voc   OD      Neumann U-87
4      Harm Voc   OD      Neumann U-87
5      Lead Guit  OD      Shure SM-57
6      Keys L             Direct
7      Keys R             Direct
8      Bass               Direct

TAKES:  1, 2, ③
```

Figure 13.1 A session sheet for a home studio.

Production Schedule

In a professional recording studio, the planned sequence of recording basic tracks and overdubs is listed on a *production schedule* (see Figure 13.2).

```
Tape Speed:  15 ips               Artist:  Muffin
8 Track                           Producer:  B. Brauning
Noise Reduction:  dbx


1.  Song:  "Mr. Potato Head."
    Instrumentation:  Bass, drums, electric rhythm guitar,
    electric lead guitar, acoustic piano, sax, lead vocal.
    Comments:  Record rhythm section together with reference
    vocal. Overdub sax, acoustic, piano, and lead vocal later.

2.  Song:  "Sambatina."
    Instrumentation:  Bass, drums, acoustic guitar, percussion,
    synthesizer.
    Comments:  Record rhythm section with scratch acoustic
    guitar. Overdub acoustic guitar, percussion, and
    synthesizer.

3.  Song:  "Mr. Potato Head."
    Overdubs:  (1) acoustic piano, (2) lead vocal, (3) sax.

4.  Song:  "Sambatina."
    Overdubs:  (1) acoustic guitar, (2) synthesizer,
    (3) percussion.

5.  Mix:  "Mr. Potato Head."
    Comments:  Add 80-msec delay to toms.
               Double lead guitar in stereo.
               Increase reverb on sax during solo.

6.  Mix:  "Sambatina."
    Comments:  Add flanger to bass on intro only.
               Manually flange percussion.
```

Figure 13.2 A production schedule.

Track Sheet

Another document used in a pro studio is the track sheet (see Figure 13.3). Write down which instrument or vocal goes on which track. The track sheet also has blanks for the date, tape used, and so on.

TRACK SHEET

Studio: SUBLIMINAL SOUND
Client: MR. PACKETS PRODUCTIONS
Artist: THE TROLLS
Producer: FLAKEY FOONT
Engineer: B. BARTLETT
Album title: SIT-DOWN MUSIC
Speed: 15 IPS
Noise reduction: DOLBY C

Song title: DIG UP NEBRASKA

Track 1: BASS
    2: RHYTHM GUITAR
    3: LEAD GUITAR
    4: PIANO
    5: LEAD VOCAL
    6: DRUMS L
    7: DRUMS R
    8: KICK

Song title: SIDEWALK BLUES (EXPERIMENTAL)

Track 1: BANJO-BASS
    2: VOCAL
    3: DOUBLED VOCAL
    4: EXPONENTIAL HORNS
    5: TINKER TOYS (PERCUSSION)
    6: SLINKY (PERCUSSION)
    7: FOOT STOMPS
    8: SPARE

Figure 13.3 A track sheet.

Microphone Input List

Make up a microphone input list similar to the following:

Input	Instrument	Microphone
1	Bass	Direct
2	Kick	EV RE-20
3	Snare/Hi-Hat	AKG C451
4	Drums Overhead L	Shure SM81
5	Drums Overhead R	Shure SM81

Input	Instrument	Microphone
6	Hi Toms	Sennheiser MD 421
7	Low Toms	Sennheiser MD 421
8	Electric Lead Guitar	Shure SM57
9	Electric Lead Guitar	Direct
10	Piano L	Crown PZM-30R
11	Piano R	Crown PZM-30R
12	Scratch vocal	Beyer M500

Write down a column of numbers at the left side of the list corresponding to each numbered console input. Next to each input number write the name of the instrument assigned to that input. Finally, write down next to each instrument the microphone(s) or direct box you plan to use on that instrument.

Be flexible in your microphone choices—you may need to experiment with various microphones during the session to find one giving the best sound with the least console equalization. During lead guitar overdubs, for example, you can set up a direct box, three close-up microphones, and one distant microphone—then find a combination that sounds best.

Find out what sound the producer wants: a "tight" sound; a "loose, live" sound; an accurate, realistic sound. Ask to hear recordings having the kind of sound the producer desires. Try to figure out what techniques were used to create those sounds, and plan your microphone techniques and effects accordingly. Tips on choosing a microphone are given in Chapter 6.

Instrument Layout Chart

Work out an instrument layout chart, indicating where each instrument will be located in the studio, and where baffles and isolation booths will be used (if any). In planning the layout, make sure that all the musicians can see each other and are close enough together to play as an ensemble.

Setting Up the Studio

About an hour before the session starts, clean up the studio to promote a professional atmosphere. Lay down rugs and place AC power boxes according to your layout chart.

Now position the baffles on top of what has gone before. Put out chairs and stools according to the layout. Add music stands and music stand lights. Run cue cables from each artist's location to the cue panel in the studio.

Place microphone stands approximately where they will be used. Wrap one end of a microphone cable around each microphone-stand boom, leaving a few extra coils of cable near the microphone-stand base to allow slack for moving. Run the rest of the cable back to the microphone input panel or snake box. Plug each cable into the appropriate wall panel or snake box input, according to your microphone input list.

Some engineers prefer to run cables in reverse order, connecting to the input panel first and running the cable out to the microphone stand. That procedure leaves less of a confusing tangle at the input panel where connections might be changed.

Now set up the microphones. Check each microphone to make sure its switches are in the desired positions. Put the microphones in their stand adapters, connect the cables, and balance the weight of the boom against the microphone.

Finally, connect the musicians' headphones for cueing. Set up a spare cue line and microphone for last-minute changes.

Setting Up the Control Room

Having prepared the studio, run through this checklist to make sure the control room is ready for the session:

- Pull all the patch cords from the patch panel.

- If necessary, patch console bus 1 to tape track 1, bus 2 to track 2, and so on.

- Check out all the equipment to make sure it's working.

- Clean and demagnetize the tape machines.

- Thread on some blank tape.

- Put calibration tones on tape.

- Normalize or zero the console by setting all switches and knobs to "off," "zero," or "flat" so as to have no effect. This establishes a point of reference and avoids surprises later on.

- Feed a 1 kHz tone to all the console outputs so that the console meters read 0 VU. Adjust the multitrack machine's record levels so the recorder meters also read 0 VU. This procedure matches the recorder meters to the console meters, so you have to watch only the console meters while recording. If you're using noise-reduction equipment, refer to Chapter 9 for meter calibration and Dolby-tone recording.

- Switch on phantom powering for condenser microphones.

- Set the console input-selector switches to "mic."

- Attach a *designation strip* of paper leader across the front of the console to write down the name of the instrument each fader affects. Also label the submasters and monitor mixer pots according to what is assigned to them.

- Turn up the monitor system. Carefully bring up each fader one at a time and listen to each microphone. You should hear normal studio noise. If you hear any problems such as dead or noisy microphones, hum, bad cables, or faulty power supplies, correct them before the session.

- Verify the microphone input list. Have an assistant scratch each microphone grille with a fingernail and identify the instrument the microphone is intended to pick up.

- Check all the cue headphones by playing a tone through them and listening while wiggling the cable.

After the musicians arrive, they typically are allowed one-half to one hour free setup time for seating, tuning, and microphone placement. Show them where to sit, and work out new seating arrangements if necessary to make them more comfortable.

Once the instruments are set up, you may want to listen to their live sound in the studio and do what you can to improve it. A dull-sounding guitar may need new strings; a noisy guitar amp may need new tubes, and so on. Adjust the studio lighting for the desired mood.

Session Overview

Usually, the sequence of events in the control room is as follows:

1. For efficiency, record the basic rhythm tracks for several songs on the first session.

2. Do the overdubs for all the songs in a dubbing session.

3. Mixdown all the tunes.

4. Assemble and leader the master tape.

Recording

Follow the mixer recording procedures described in Chapter 12. Before you start recording, make connections to record a work-print tape of the studio monitor mix, either on two leftover tracks or on a cassette deck. This tape is for the producer to take home to evaluate the performance.

When you're ready to record the tune, briefly play a metronome to the group at the desired tempo, or play a click track (an electronic metronome) through the cue system. Or just let the drummer set the tempo with stick clicks.

Start the tape in record mode. Hit the slate button and announce the name of the tune and the take number.

Have someone play the keynote of the song (for tuning other instruments later). Then the group leader or the drummer counts off the beat, and the group starts playing.

The producer listens to the musical performance while the engineer watches levels and listens for audio problems. As the music progresses, you may need to make small level adjustments. As stated before, the recording levels are set as high as possible without causing distortion. Balancing the instruments at this time is done with the monitor mixer. The monitor mix affects only what is being heard, not what is going on tape.

The assistant engineer (if any) keeps track of the takes on a *take sheet*, noting the name of the tune, the take number, and whether the take was complete (see Figure 13.4). A code is often used to indicate whether the take was a false start, nearly completed, a "keeper," and so on.

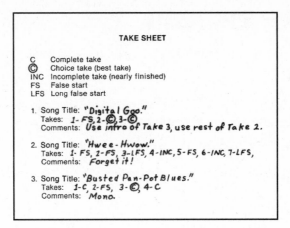

Figure 13.4 A take sheet.

While the song is in progress, don't use the solo function because the abrupt monitoring change may disturb the producer. The producer should stop the performance if a major fluff (mistake) occurs but should let the minor ones pass.

At the end of the song, the musicians should be silent for several seconds after the last note. Or, if the song ends in a fade-out, the musicians should continue playing for about a minute so there is enough material for a fade-out during mixdown.

After the tune is done, you either can play it back or go on to a second take. Set a rough mix with the aux or monitor mix knobs. The musicians catch their fluffed notes during playback; you just listen for audio quality.

Now record other takes or tunes. Pick the best takes. It's usually less tiring to do only three or four takes of a single song and then run through another song. If a song is not working, you can come back to it later. Try to limit tracking sessions to four hours or less—five hours maximum.

Overdubbing

After the basic or rhythm tracks for all the tunes are recorded, overdubs are added. A musician listens to previously recorded tracks over headphones, and records a new part on an open track. Follow the overdubbing procedures in Chapter 12.

Composite Tracks

If several open tracks are available, you can record a solo overdub in several takes, each on a separate track. This is referred to as recording *composite tracks*. After recording all the takes, play back the solo (in sync mode) and assign all the overdubbed tracks to a remaining open track set in record mode. You bounce all the solo tracks to a composite track. Match the levels of the different takes. Then switch the overdubbed tracks on and off (using muting), recording just the best parts of each take. Finally, erase the old overdubbed tracks to free them up for other instruments.

Drum Overdubs

Drum overdubs are usually done right after the rhythm session because the microphones are already set up, and the overdubbed sound will match the sound of the original drum track.

Overdubbing in the Control Room

To aid communications among the engineer, producer, and musician, have the musician play in the control room while overdubbing. A synthesizer or electric guitar can be patched into the console through a direct box. The guitar's direct signal can be fed to a guitar amp in the studio via a cue line. Pick up the amp with a microphone, and record and monitor the micro-phone's signal.

Breaking Down

When the session is over, tear down the microphones, microphone stands, and cables. Put the microphones back in their protective boxes and bags. Wipe off the cables with a damp rag if necessary.

Wrap each cable around your arm (between palm and elbow) and coil the last two feet or so around the cable loops. Some studio engineers hang the cable in big loops on the microphone stand. Other engineers wrap the cable "lasso style" with every other loop reversed. You learn this on the job.

Put the track sheet and take sheet in the multitrack tape box along with the tape (stored tail out). Label the box and the tape for their contents. Normally the studio keeps the multitrack master unless the group wants to buy or rent it.

You may want to edit out the outtakes and splice them together on a separate reel. Then put one or more feet of paper leader between each of the master tape's keeper takes. Write new tape logs indicating the reels' contents.

Log the console settings by writing them in a notebook or reading them slowly into a portable cassette recorder. At a future session, you can play back the tape and reset the console the way it was for the original session.

Mixdown

After all the parts are recorded, you're ready for mixdown. Prepare the console and tape decks, record tones, erase noises, and play the multitrack tape through the console while adjusting balances, panning, equalization, reverberation, and effects. Once you've rehearsed the mix to perfection, record it onto a 2-track recorder. Follow the mixdown procedures in Chapter 12.

Calibration tones should be recorded on the $1/4$-inch master tape just before recording the mixes. (See Chapter 12 for more information.)

Assembling the Master Reels

Now you're ready to assemble the 2-track open-reel tape into a finished format for tape or CD duplication. It will contain the songs in the desired order, plus leader tape for separating the songs with silence. It also has calibration tones. The cassette/CD mastering engineer will use those tones to align the playback deck for flat response from your tape.

Sequencing the Songs

Consider and discuss in what sequence you want the songs on the recording. For the first song on Side 1, use a strong, accessible, up-tempo tune. Follow it with something quieter. Consider alternating keys or tempos from song to song. The last tune should be as good as or better than the first to leave a good final impression.

Try to keep the total times for Side 1 and Side 2 about equal to conserve cassette tape. Side 1 should be slightly longer than Side 2 so that any blank cassette tape is at the end of Side 2.

Leader Length

The length of leader between songs depends on how long a pause you want between them. Four seconds is typical. Use longer leader if you want the listener to get out of the mood of the piece he or she just heard before going on to the next. Use shorter leader either to change the mood abruptly or to make similar songs flow together. Short leader also works well after a long fade-out because the fade-out itself acts like a long pause between songs.

What if you want to crossfade between two songs? Follow these steps:

1. Use two 2-track recorders. Put song 1 on one recorder and song 2 on another.

2. Feed both recorders into your mixer, and connect the mixer output to a third 2-track recorder. Match the levels and noise reduction on all the recorders.

3. Play song 1. Near the end of the song before the crossfade, start recording the mix on the third machine.

4. As song 1 fades out, start song 2 and fade it up.

5. After recording this crossfade on the third machine, edit the crossfade into the rest of the program.

Master Reel Assembly

If the recording is too long to fit on a single reel, make a separate reel for Side 1 and Side 2 of the cassette. To assemble the master tapes, wind onto the take-up reel the following material in this order:

1. At least 15 seconds of leader or blank recording tape

2. Tones

3. At least 10 seconds of leader

4. First song

5. Leader

6. Second song

7. Leader, etc.

8. Last song on Side 1 of album

9. At least 15 seconds of leader

Then rewind the tape. Play it and time it from the beginning of the first song to the end of the last song (including the leaders between songs). This is called the *running time*. Also note the start and stop times of each selection.

Using a piece of masking tape, fasten the leader tail to the reel and print "TAIL OUT" on the masking tape, or use blue leader tape for tails out, red for heads out. Type or print a neat label for the tape reel including title, artist, "Side 1," and the running time.

Using another take-up reel, assemble Side 2 of the album (but without tones). Time Side 2 and label the reel.

Recording Mixdowns on DAT

Because DAT has the highest sound quality, you might prefer to master on DAT rather than open-reel tape or cassette. This section describes how to mix sequencer tracks and tape tracks through a mixer to a DAT machine.

Cassette or CD Duplication?

First, decide whether you want your finished master tape to be duplicated on cassette or compact disc.

If you want cassettes, note that the duplicators seldom edit your tapes. They want a finished, edited, and sequenced tape, ready for a simple transfer.

If you want compact disc duplication, or if you want to edit the recording yourself with a digital audio workstation, you should put long silent spaces between mixed songs—20 seconds, for instance. This makes editing easier.

By editing your DAT tape digitally, the mastering engineer can make cleaner, more consistent silences between songs than you can by tightly cueing the DAT machine during mixdown. In addition, the mastering engineer can resequence your songs if necessary. This work is well worth the price for professional results. Typically, editing charges for an album are only $400 to $500, a small fraction of the total project costs.

DAT Mastering for Cassette Duplication

When you're ready to mixdown to DAT, follow this procedure; it makes your DAT master sound like a finished album, with a short pause between songs.

1. Record a 30-second 1 kHz tone at the head of the DAT tape at 0 db; record 20 seconds of silence and then hit STOP. This tone will be used by the cassette duplicator to set levels and match channel levels.

2. On your multitrack tape, find the song you want to be first on the master tape.

3. Set the tape counter to zero.

4. Play the song several times to practice the mix.

5. The DAT has a peak-reading recording-level meter. Set the DAT machine in record and pause mode, and set the recording level so that the DAT meter peaks around –3 db maximum. Unlike the meters on an analog tape deck, "0" on the DAT meter shows the absolute maximum recording level. If your peaks are reaching 0, that level is too high.

6. Rewind the multitrack tape to the beginning of the song.

7. Zero the DAT tape counter.

8. Play the multitrack tape. Before zero appears on the multitrack tape counter, and just after the count-off, tap the PAUSE button on the DAT recorder to start recording. Note that the PAUSE button is a toggle—tap it once to stop tape motion, tap it again to release it and start tape motion.

9. When the song is done, or fades into silence, hit PAUSE on the DAT machine to stop recording.

Now add a silent space between songs. If you want 3 seconds of silence, press PAUSE to record, wait 3 seconds, and press STOP. This process is imprecise, so you may need to experiment.

Finally, cue up the multitrack tape to the next song you want to mix, and go to step 3. Repeat this procedure for all the songs you want to mix to DAT.

If you have to rerecord a mix, follow this procedure:

1. Find and play the end of the last mix you recorded on DAT.

2. As soon as the song stops, hit PAUSE.

3. Hit RECORD and PLAY while in pause mode.

4. For a 3-second space between songs, hit PAUSE, wait 3 seconds, and hit PAUSE again.

5. Play the multitrack tape. Just before "0" appears on the multitrack tape counter, hit PAUSE on the DAT machine to release it and start recording the mix.

Using PAUSE and STOP sometimes makes slight noises on the DAT tape, but you have to live with them. Some DAT machines are quieter than others in this regard. (Many CD mastering plants reject a master DAT tape if it has such noises.) You could run the program through a noise gate between songs to remove the clicks, and copy the program onto another DAT tape.

DAT Mastering for CD Duplication

Before getting into this procedure, you need to understand the copy-inhibit feature in recent consumer DAT machines. This feature lets you make a digital-to-digital recording of a commercial DAT or CD, but prevents regenerations from that copy. That is, you can't make subsequent digital copies of the copy.

Suppose you intend your DAT tape to be duplicated digitally on compact disc. Does the SCMS (Serial Copy Management System) copy-protection scheme prevent this? No.

The copy-inhibit information is picked up from the CD you're copying—it is not generated by your DAT recorder. It does not appear on recordings made from your mixer output. This means that any DAT recording you make of your own material can be duplicated digitally by a CD mastering house.

If you plan to have a CD mastering house edit in the silent spaces between selections, or if you plan to do it yourself with your computer, leave long spaces between selections when you mix to DAT. Follow this procedure:

1. First, set the DAT controls. If you have a professional DAT recorder, you can set the sampling frequency to 44.1 or 48 kHz. A

rate of 44.1 kHz is preferred if your tapes will be duplicated on compact disc, because no sample rate conversion is necessary. Be sure copy-inhibit is off if you want to duplicate your DAT master digitally.

2. Some engineers don't bother recording a calibration tone on DAT tape. That's because the CD mastering engineer looks for the peak program level on your DAT tape to set the recording level, rather than using a tone. On your tape log, note the DAT tape-counter time at the loudest part of your program. If you want to record a 1 kHz tone, a suggested level is 0 db.

3. Record about 20 seconds of silence at the head of the DAT tape.

4. On your multitrack tape and sequencer, find the song you want to mix. Play the song several times to practice the mix.

5. Set the DAT machine in record and pause mode, play the multi-track tape, and set the DAT recording level to peak around –3 db maximum.

6. Cue the multitrack tape to the beginning of the tape-sync tone for the song (if any).

7. Zero the DAT tape counter.

8. Hit PAUSE to start recording on the DAT machine; wait a few seconds for the DAT machine to get up to speed, and play the multitrack tape.

9. When the song is done, or it fades into silence, stop the multitrack machine, and record about 20 seconds of silence on the DAT tape before you start on the next tune.

Making Your Own CD Premaster on DAT

You can edit and resequence your DAT master digitally by using a personal computer, 2-track digital-audio-editing software, and a special plug-in card. You can take a rough DAT mixdown master and create from that a polished CD premaster on another DAT cassette. Some examples of digital editing systems are the Digidesign Sound Tools system and the Turtle Beach 56K system.

Play your DAT mixdown master into your computer and copy it onto hard disk. Then, using your computer screen and mouse, you can edit the program: reorder songs, reorder or copy sections within each song, add silences between songs, make level changes, crossfade, compress, expand, limit, noise-gate, sync to SMPTE, change the playing time of each selection, and more. Finally, you dump the edited program onto DAT, and that is your CD premaster. Record about 1 minute of silence at the beginning of the DAT tape before recording the program.

If your DAT machine has SMPTE time code, a compact disc can be mastered directly from your DAT tape. Machines that record SMPTE time code have SMPTE in and out connectors, and record the SMPTE time code in the DAT subcode area. The Sony machines use the proposed IEC time code standard for DAT.

Here's how to make an SMPTE-striped CD premaster on DAT:

1. Start with an edited, sequenced DAT master tape.

2. Stripe the DAT tape with SMPTE time code.

3. Play the DAT tape and note the SMPTE times when each selection starts and stops. When the CD is mastered from your tape, the mastering engineer enters the SMPTE start/stop times as PQ subcodes in the CD laser mastering machine. Then the engineer plays your DAT tape and cuts the CD.

Duplicating Your DAT Master

Once you have the DAT master tape completed, make a safety copy. Or run two DATs in parallel during the mastering session.

If you want to make a few cassette copies of your master DAT tape—for demo tapes, for instance—copy the DAT tape several times with a stereo cassette deck. For larger runs, you need an outside duplicating house. Check to see whether they can handle DAT tapes. If not, you might pay them to rent one or loan them yours.

Documenting Index Points

It's very important to document everything on your DAT tape for the duplication house. First, rewind the tape to the beginning, set the counter to 00:00, hit PLAY, and note the start and stop times of each selection or track. You might want to punch in a Start ID manually at the beginning of each track. Some CD mastering houses require this.

Tape Log

Whether you mastered to analog or digital tape, you're now ready to make a tape log describing the master tape. Be sure to include this information:

- Title of production, artist, date

- Studio, engineer, producer, their addresses, their phone numbers

- For analog tape, the tape-head format, stereo/mono, tape speed, playback equalization (usually NAB), noise reduction, tail out designation

- For DAT, the sampling rate and indexing status

- For analog tape, the location of the test tones (usually at the beginning of Reel 1), tone frequencies, level as recorded

- Counter time of the highest peak level part of the program

- Song titles and timing, total running time per side

- For DAT, the start/stop times and title for each selection

- For cassette duplication, a note about which tracks go on Side 1 and which on Side 2

- Notes on desired EQ and level changes (Some mastering houses do not perform this function, and require a ready-to-cut tape.)

Also include the packaging text, such as song lyrics, instrumentation, composers, arrangers, publishers, artwork, and so on. Stay in contact with the duplication house, especially about artwork.

Safety Copy

Be sure to make a safety copy of the master before sending the master tape, in case it is lost or damaged. When copying the master, set the calibration tone from the playback machine to read the same level on the recording machine. There's no need to reset the program levels because you already set them while recording the master tape.

Note that the master tape shouldn't leave the studio until all studio time is paid for! When this is done, insure the tape for the whole cost of the production, and send the tape to the duplication house.

It's amazing how the long hours of work with lots of complex equipment have been concentrated into that little tape—but it's been fun. You created a craftsmanlike product you can be proud of. When played, it recreates a musical experience in the ears and mind of the listener—no small achievement.

RECORDING THE SPOKEN WORD

Many studios record narration as well as music for documentary films, slide shows, educational programs, radio dramas, commercials, and books on tape. In fact, many recording engineers find work at studios recording nothing but speech. Others start with speech recording to learn the ropes and then move on to music.

In this chapter you learn ways to record the spoken word most effectively. It's not as simple as it seems.

Consistency

One of the most important qualities of a speech recording is *consistency*. The tone quality, average recording level, average pitch, and average tempo of the voice should not change noticeably throughout the recording (except for dramatic effect).

Often a complete manuscript of the narration is recorded in a single session. Then a *proof copy* of the tape is sent to the manuscript's publisher to check for errors. After corrections are received, the announcer is called back into the studio to record *inserts* or corrected sentences and paragraphs. These inserts are edited back into the original recording. If the sound of the inserts doesn't match the sound of the original, the listener hears jarring changes in the voice quality as the recording plays, so it's important to duplicate the recording setup every time the announcer is recorded.

Several factors can vary from one session to the next: recording level, microphone choice, microphone placement, text position, announcer's position, EQ, noise reduction, and even the announcer's voice itself. You need to keep all these factors constant by documenting the setup.

Take notes on the microphone used, its switch positions (if any), and its distance and position relative to the announcer. Also note any EQ or noise reduction used. To reduce the number of variables, many engineers record without any EQ. You may want to settle on a standard setup so that you can record a predictable sound.

Microphones

There are four types of microphones commonly used for voice recording:

- A top-quality lavalier condenser microphone
- A flat-response cardioid microphone (condenser or dynamic)
- A ribbon microphone
- A multiple-D dynamic microphone

A lavalier microphone is a miniature unit (such as TV newscasters use) that clips onto the announcer's tie or shirt. Most of the major microphone manufacturers have excellent models in the $200 price range. Don't skimp on this microphone, or the sound quality will suffer. Because the microphone is worn by the user, it remains a constant distance from the mouth, which aids consistency. There also is no problem with breath pops.

A cardioid condenser microphone provides a luxurious, big-budget sound—one with full lows and detailed highs. A ribbon microphone offers a warm and smooth sound. Unfortunately, the bass response of these microphones varies with the announcer's distance from the mic. The closer the talker is to the microphone, the bassier the recording. Unless the announcer can remain a constant distance away, the voice tone quality varies.

Recall that this close-up bass boost (proximity effect) occurs with a single-D unidirectional microphone. A multiple-D microphone is designed to compensate for proximity effect, with a bass response that varies only slightly with distance.

Microphone Placement

The placement of a microphone for speech recording affects the pickup of room acoustics, breath and lip noises, table thumps, and sound reflections. Each of these unwanted sounds can be prevented by proper microphone placement.

Distance

It helps to standardize on a distance between the microphone and the announcer's mouth that provides the best sound quality. A typical distance might be 8 to 12 inches. If the mic is too distant, it picks up too much room acoustics. In general, little or no room sound should be audible in a narration recording. If the mic is too close, lip and tongue noises are audible, and the voice level varies greatly when the announcer moves. Find a workable distance somewhere in the middle and stick with it. This applies to lavalier microphones as well.

An exception to this rule might be dramatic recording. In this type of session, the actors often vary miking distance for special effect.

Some studios set the miking distance with a spacer or ruler. Alternatively, announcers can set the spacing with their hands. They spread their fingers, place their thumb on their mouth, and place their little finger on the microphone grille.

Minimizing Pop

Microphones also should be placed to avoid popping. Recall that when a person says words containing the letters "p," "t," or "b," a turbulent puff of air is forced from the mouth. If this air puff hits a microphone grille, a little thump or explosion (a pop) is heard in the microphone signal. Because a pop disturbance leaves the mouth within a narrow angle, you can prevent popping by placing the microphone above, below, or to the side of the mouth. It also helps to put a foam pop filter or windscreen on the microphone. Refer to Chapter 7 for more tips on mic placement.

Minimizing Table Thumps

Suppose you're using a table to hold the manuscript, and a mic stand is on the table. Table taps—even soft ones—travel through the mic stand to the mic, and are amplified. So mount the microphone on a boom stand, and place the base of the stand on the floor. It also helps to use a shock-mounted mic-stand adapter (available from your microphone dealer). Many studios pad the announcer's table with cloth or foam to prevent noises.

Minimizing Sound Reflections

You also should place the microphone to avoid picking up sound reflections from the script or the announcer's table. When these reflections combine at the microphone with direct sound from the announcer, phase interference occurs—creating a filtered tone quality. In addition, this tone quality changes as the announcer moves.

There are a number of right and wrong ways to position microphones. In Figure 14.1, sound reflects off the script into a lavalier microphone, causing phase interference. In Figure 14.2, the script is angled back so that reflections bounce away from the microphone.

Figure 14.1 Sound reflects off the script into the microphone, causing phase interference.

In Figure 14.3, a cardioid microphone is improperly positioned because reflections off the script stand enter the microphone. In Figure 14.4, the reflections approach the "dead" back side of the cardioid microphone, and are attenuated. Paper noise is reduced as well. Figures 14.5 and 14.6 show other mic placements that prevent reflection problems. (It also helps to carpet the table or script stand.)

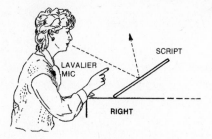

Figure 14.2 Sound reflects away from the microphone.

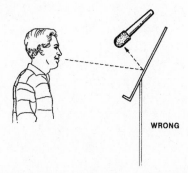

Figure 14.3 Sound reflects off the script stand into the microphone, causing phase interference.

Figure 14.4 Sound reflects into the "dead" back side of a cardioid microphone.

If you record more than one announcer at the same time, seat them at least 3 feet apart to prevent phase interference between microphones.

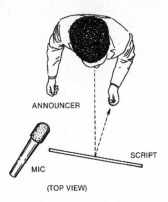

Figure 14.5 Sound reflects off the angled script, away from the microphone.

Figure 14.6 A boundary microphone on a 2-foot-square script stand.

Controlling the Announcer's Position and Voice

To promote a consistent sitting position, provide the announcer a comfortable, nonadjustable chair with a back. Advise the announcer to move as little as possible, and not to slump over the table.

An announcer's head motion can change the recorded tone quality. Low frequencies radiate from the mouth in all directions, but high frequencies radiate mostly straight out from the mouth. So, if an announcer's head moves during recording, the high frequencies ("s" sounds) may miss the microphone occasionally. This occurs with lavalier microphones as well. Caution the announcer against head movement.

Actually you're asking the announcer to become a frozen robot. A head-worn microphone allows more freedom of movement. It may be a useful alternative if you are satisfied with the sound and can position the microphone consistently.

The average pitch and speed of an announcer's voice can change from day to day. It even varies from the beginning to the end of a recording session. So, whenever you record inserts, play back some of the original tape to the announcer for voice matching. Also, let the announcer warm up by reading for a few minutes while you set the recording level.

Reducing Sibilance

Another factor to keep under control is sibilance, the emphasis of "s" and "sh" sounds. Recall from Chapter 8 that these sounds have strong high-frequency components, around 5 to 10 kHz, which can saturate the recording tape and cause distortion. You can reduce sibilance by using flat-response microphones, miking off-axis to the mouth, or cutting frequencies 5 to 10 kHz with an equalizer.

A better solution is to use a de-esser to remove excessive sibilance without affecting tone quality. If you're using a de-esser and a compressor at the same time, put the compressor after the de-esser.

Recording-Session Procedures

Now that you've taken all the precautions to assure consistent, clean sound, you're ready to record a *script* (the manuscript of the narration). The announcer is seated the proper distance from the microphone, with the script ready to read. Some announcers fold up the bottom corners of their script pages to form a handle for turning pages without noise.

The engineer, assistant engineer, or producer has an identical script on which to mark *edit points*—spots where the announcer misreads a sentence.

After a level check, you start recording. The announcer reads the script, and you or the producer follow along in your own script, marking edit points with a pen. Generally, you just leave the tape rolling when mistakes occur.

If the announcer misreads a word or makes a paper noise, go back to the beginning of the sentence where the error occurred, and have the announcer start over. There should be no attempt to correct the error in midsentence because that kind of correction is too hard to edit. Also, the speech rhythm may be off, making an edit impossible. It's much easier to make an undetectable tape splice if you're editing between sentences.

Figure 14.7 shows a typical script with edit marks. Instead of marking the words that were misread, the producer marked the beginning of the sentences containing the errors. Those marks correspond to the edit points on tape. Two marks indicate a second retake.

EDITOR'S COPY

SCRIPT FOR "COSMIC ORDER" FILM

Client: Impossible Productions, Inc.

A branch consists of two or more radiations from a common point. Its basic shape is the letter "Y."

Each branch has its own branches. For example, a tree trunk branches into large limbs. Each limb branches into smaller limbs. Each smaller limb branches into sticks. Each stick branches into twigs. Each twig branches into leaf veins. /If a tree were a symphony, you'd hear a basic melody repeated with ever-increasing refinement and complexity.

→ *remove cough*

Each small branch is a variation on the theme of branching. That is, each part resembles the whole. /For example, the veins in a leaf resemble a tree in shape; capillaries resemble veins and arteries.

→ *Noise?*

//Branches are also visible in tree roots, rivers, the circulatory system, the nervous system, the lungs, roads, audio systems, single-point grounding systems, organization of knowledge, distribution of knowledge, and more.

Let's consider that last example.///Knowledge is gathered and distributed like a tree: The research material is the ground the tree is rooted in; the roots represent research; the trunk represents the compilation of research into a new synthesis, and the branches represent the dissemination of the new knowledge to various students via publishing, broadcasting, or education in classrooms.

To digress a bit, consider this: If life seems too complicated, remember it's all happening to you here and now. "Here" is small and "now" is short. You can handle it.   *THUMP?*

/On the other hand, "here" follows you wherever you go, and "now" is continuous. Never mind!

Figure 14.7 A script with edit marks.

Editing

After the recording is done, you're ready to edit out the mistakes. Follow this procedure:

1. Play the tape and follow along in the marked-up script. When you come to an edit point, stop the tape.

2. Put the recorder in cue or edit mode.

3. Rock the tape back and forth over the playback head to find the exact beginning of the misread sentence. Mark the tape at the playback-head gap with a grease pencil.

4. Using a razor blade and splicing block, cut the tape about ½-inch to the right of the mark.

5. Put the feed-reel tape back into the tape-path slot, with the right end of the tape extending past the slot.

6. Pull the tape past the heads. You'll hear the misread sentence. The announcer stops and then restarts the sentence. Mark and cut the tape at the beginning of the corrected sentence.

7. After removing the misread section of tape, splice the two remaining tape ends together.

8. Play the edited portion to check it. You should hear no double breaths between sentences. Edit out paper noises and table thumps.

For an alternative method of editing:

1. Mark the two edit points (the beginning of the misread sentence and the beginning of the good retake) before cutting the tape.

2. Align both edit marks in your splicing block, cut both at once, and splice the ends together.

Once the tape is edited, add leader tape, label the reel and tape box, and store the tape tail out.

Proof Cassettes and Inserts

You might want to make a proof cassette copy of the tape to send to the script publisher for approval. The publisher may notice reading errors that you missed during the recording session, and send back a marked-up script showing the errors. The next time the announcer is back in your studio, rerecord the sentences or paragraphs needing corrections.

Be sure to match the recording levels, microphone position, and so on with those of the original tape. Otherwise, the inserts may sound as if another person is talking. Play some of the original tape aloud so that the announcer can duplicate the pitch and tempo. You may need to equalize the inserts to match the original take.

When the inserts are edited into place, make and send another proof tape to the publisher. If it's error-free, you can add sound effects or music as needed.

Sound Effects and Music

Many scripts require certain sound effects to accompany the narration. If you record the speech on track 1 of a 2-track tape recorder, you can record the sound effects on track 2 in the spots where the script calls for them. After the effects are recorded, mix the 2-track tape of narration and effects to mono, and record the mix on another deck. Or you can use a multitrack machine for the master recording to record music or effects in stereo.

Another technique for recording sound effects is to have dialog on one 2-track and sound effects on another 2-track. Start and stop the sound effects while recording both the dialog and the effects into a third 2-track.

Libraries of sound effects and mood music on compact disc are available from several companies, advertised in recording-industry magazines and audio-visual publications. Many require royalty payments for each use of material. Some sound-effects CDs can be ordered through record stores. You even can record the sound effects yourself in some cases.

Sound effects can also be prerecorded and sequenced on a computer hard disk. You trigger the effects to play while you record the narration.

Many productions require a musical introduction that is faded down when the announcer starts talking. These productions usually have a musical *outro* also, music that begins near the end of the narration, fading up and then out to provide a musical conclusion to the program.

Backtiming a Musical Outro

You often want the outro to end simultaneously with the narration. This can be achieved with a technique called *backtiming*. Follow these steps:

1. Find the spot in the script where you want the outro to start fading up. Play the tape starting from there, and time it to the end of the narration. For this example, it's 30 seconds from fade-up to end.

2. Put a tape recording of the outro on a tape deck. Cue up the end of the outro.

3. To make the outro recording play backwards, either reverse the reels, or thread the tape backwards around the capstan (clockwise) and counter-clockwise around the pinch roller.

4. Starting at the end of the outro, play it for 30 seconds (or whatever), and stop.

5. If you reversed the reels, turn over the tape and replace the reels. You now have a musical outro tape cued up 30 seconds from the end.

6. Put the narration tape on a 2-track machine. Narration is recorded on track 1. Set up the tape machine to rerecord the musical outro tape on track 2.

7. Start playing the narration tape several seconds before the fade-up point. Then start playing the music tape just before the fade-up point, and fade it up.

If your timing is right, the music will end just after the narration ends. This gives a tight, professional touch to the production.

There is also an easier method: use a CD for the outro music. Backtime the CD with the CD counter, and start it at the appropriate time.

Reducing Print-Through

Recall from Chapter 9 that a tape recording of narration may contain unwanted echoes or pre-echoes of speech during pauses between words. These echoes are called print-through. In the tape reel, the magnetic signal transfers or "prints" from one layer of tape to the next. This causes a repetition of the program.

Print-through is a major problem with narration recording because speech contains many silent pauses where print-through can be heard. Tips on reducing print-through are given in Chapter 9.

The spoken word should be recorded with a consistent, clean sound. Sound effects and music can enhance the production. This type of studio work should not be neglected because it is the major source of income for most studios. And it's another skill to add to your resume.

15

THE MIDI STUDIO: EQUIPMENT AND RECORDING PROCEDURES

A relatively recent development is the "tapeless" studio—the computerized world of MIDI equipment—synthesizers, sampling keyboards, drum machines, and sequencers. Because other texts explain this equipment in detail, brief definitions serve the purpose here.

MIDI stands for Musical Instrument Digital Interface. It's a standard connection between electronic musical instruments and computers that allows them to communicate with each other. Some of the things you can do with MIDI are

- Combine the sounds of two electronic musical instruments by playing them both with one keyboard.

- Create the effect of a band playing. To do this, you record keyboard performances into a computer memory, edit the recording note by note if you wish, and have the recording play through synthesizers and a drum machine in sync.

- Automate a mixdown or effects.

- Make a keyboard, electric guitar, or breath controller sound like any instrument.
- Automate the playback of sound effects and music for video productions.

The MIDI signal is a stream of digital data—not an audio signal—running at 31,250 bits per second. It sends information about the notes you play on a MIDI controller, such as a keyboard or drum pads. Up to 16 channels of information can be sent on a single MIDI cable.

MIDI is a whole subject in itself. For more information, see Appendix D.

MIDI-Studio Components

The following equipment typically is used in a MIDI studio:

- Synthesizer
- Sampler
- Drum machine
- Sequencer
- Power amplifier and speakers
- Personal computer system (optional)
- MIDI computer interface (optional)
- Recorder-mixer (optional)
- Tape synchronizer (optional)
- Mixer (optional)
- 2-track recorder
- Effects
- Audio cables
- MIDI cables
- Power outlet strip
- Equipment stand

You have learned about most of these in previous chapters, but a review might help at this point.

A synthesizer is a keyboard musical instrument that creates sounds electronically with oscillators (see Figure 15.1). Your studio might have more than one of these.

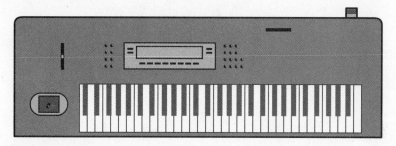

Figure 15.1 A synthesizer.

A *multitimbral synthesizer* can play two or more patches at once. A patch is a sound preset (an instrumental timbre), such as a synthesized piano, bass, snare drum, etc. A *polyphonic synthesizer* can play several notes at once (chords) with a single patch.

A sound generator or sound module is a synthesizer without a keyboard. It is triggered by a sequencer or a controller.

A sampler is a device that records sound events, or samples, into computer memory. A sample is a digital recording of one note of any sound source: a flute note, a bass pluck, an orchestra chord, a drum hit, etc. The sampling process was described in Chapter 9 in the section, "The Digital Tape Recorder."

Often a sampler is built into a sample-playing keyboard, which resembles an electronic piano. It contains samples of several different musical instruments. When you play on the keyboard, the sample notes are heard. The higher the key you press, the higher the pitch of the reproduced sample.

A drum machine is a device that plays built-in samples of all the sounds of a drum set and percussion (see Figure 15.2). It also records and plays back drum patterns that you play or program with built-in keys or drum pads. Some units can sample sounds.

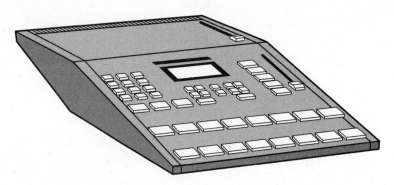

Figure 15.2 A drum machine.

A sequencer is a device that records information about the notes you play into computer memory. Unlike a tape recorder, a sequencer does not record audio. Instead, it records the key number of each note you play, note-on signals, note-off signals, and other parameters such as velocity, pitch-bend, and so on.

The sequencer can be a stand-alone unit (see Figure 15.3), a circuit built into a keyboard instrument, or a computer running a sequencer program. Like a multitrack tape recorder, a sequencer can record 8 or more tracks, with each track containing a performance of a different instrument.

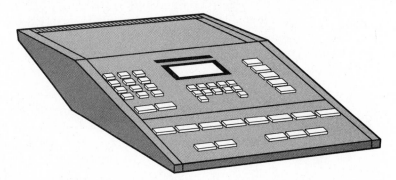

Figure 15.3 A sequencer.

Power amplifier and speakers (or powered speakers) let you hear what you're performing and recording. Usually these are small monitor speakers set up in a near-field arrangement (about 3 feet apart and 3 feet from you).

You might want a computer, disk drive, monitor, and perhaps a printer. The computer is used mainly to run a sequencer program, which replaces the sequencer. Compared to a stand-alone sequencer with an LCD screen, the computer monitor screen displays much more information at a glance, making editing easier and more intuitive (see Figure 15.4).

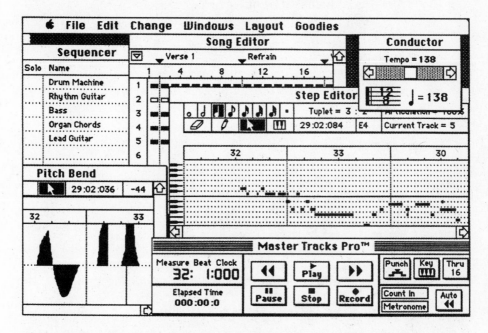

Figure 15.4 A monitor screen shot of Passport Master Tracks Pro MIDI software (Courtesy Passport Designs, Inc.).

The computer can run other useful programs. A *librarian program* manipulates patches or samples and stores them on computer disks. A *voice editor program* lets you create your own patches. A *notation program* converts your performance to standard musical notation and prints it. A *film-sound program* lets you enter a list of sound effects or music with the time each occurs, and runs through the list automatically, triggering the effects and music at the right times.

Some popular computers for music composing are the Apple Macintosh, IBM PC-compatibles, Amiga, Atari ST and Stacy, Commodore 64 or 128, and Yamaha C1 Music Computer. This last unit is an IBM-compatible portable unit with MIDI and SMPTE connectors.

A MIDI computer interface plugs into a user port in your computer, and converts MIDI signals into computer signals and vice versa. You need this only if you are using a computer in your system.

A combination mixer and recorder records vocals and acoustic instruments. A more elaborate studio might use a separate mixer and multitrack recorder, which can be open-reel or cassette.

A tape synchronizer synchronizes tape tracks with sequencer tracks, and makes the sequencer start at the same place in the song that you start the tape.

If you have two or more synthesizers, or a synth and a drum machine, you might need a mixer to mix or blend their audio outputs into a single stereo signal.

A 2-track recorder records the stereo mix of all your sound sources. The tape made on this recorder is the final product. The recorder can be open-reel, cassette, or DAT.

Effects include reverb, compression, and gating.

Audio cables carry audio signals, with connectors on each end. The connector on one end—usually a 1/4-inch phone plug—mates with synthesizers and drum machines. The connector on the other end—usually a 1/4-inch phone plug—mates with your mixer line-input connectors.

MIDI cables carry MIDI signals, and are used to connect synths, drum machines, and computers so that they can communicate with each other. MIDI cables have a 5-pin DIN plug on each end.

A power outlet strip is a row of electrical outlets to power all your equipment. It's a good idea to have surge protection in the strip.

An equipment stand is a system of tubes, rods, and platforms that supports all your equipment in a convenient arrangement. It provides user comfort, shorter cable lengths, and more floor area for other activities. Some manufacturers of MIDI studio stands include Ultimate Support Systems and Invisible Stands.

Keyboard Workstations and Digital Audio Workstations

A workstation is a system of MIDI- or computer-related equipment that works together to help you compose and record music. Usually, this system is small enough to fit on a desktop or equipment stand.

The Keyboard Workstation

A keyboard workstation includes several MIDI components in one chassis: a keyboard, a sample player, a sequencer, and perhaps a synthesizer and disk drive. That's everything you need to compose, perform, and record instrumental music. Some workstations include drum sounds so that you can get by without a separate drum machine. Some examples are the Roland W-30, Korg M-1, and Korg 01/W.

If you want to record songs with vocals, you also need a MIDI tape synchronizer plus a multitrack tape recorder or recorder-mixer. A sophisticated alternative is a computer hard-disk recording system, explained later in this chapter. If you want a permanent copy of your stereo mixes, you also need a 2-track recorder.

The Digital Audio Workstation

A *digital audio workstation (DAW)* allows you to record, edit, and mix audio programs entirely in digital form, providing the highest sound quality. The DAW can store up to several hours of digital audio or MIDI data. You can edit this data with great precision on a computer monitor screen. You also can add digital effects and perform automated mixdowns.

In Chapter 9, the section "The Digital Tape Recorder" explains how digital recording devices work. The same digital recording method is used by open-reel digital tape recorders, DAWs, DATs, and samplers.

Components in a digital workstation usually include an A/D converter, computer memory, computer monitor screen, hard-disk drive, and a set of controls—either real controls or *virtual controls* simulated on a computer monitor screen.

DAWs are available in two general forms:

- A single-chassis system

- A personal computer system, plus a special plug-in card, high-capacity hard drive, and software

The single-chassis system uses real controls—faders and/or pushbuttons. The personal computer system uses virtual controls simulated on your monitor screen. The single-chassis system costs about $30,000 and up; the multitrack personal computer workstation costs about $4,000 and up, not including the computer.

The personal computer workstation includes these components (see Figure 15.5):

- An A/D-D/A converter. Often your DAT machine can be used as the converter.

- A *direct-to-disk card* that plugs into a slot in your computer. It converts digital audio into computer data that can be stored on a hard disk.

- A *high-capacity hard-disk drive* (660M will store 1 hour of stereo audio). This could be either a computer magnetic hard disk or a magneto-optical disk.

- Software that lets you edit the audio program.

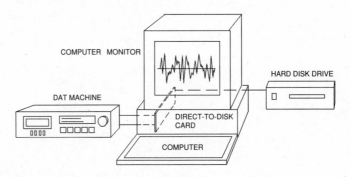

COMPUTER MONITOR

HARD DISK DRIVE

DAT MACHINE

DIRECT-TO-DISK
CARD

COMPUTER

Figure 15.5 A personal computer digital audio workstation.

Operating Procedures

With a digital workstation, you can create audio programs more rapidly and easily than in the past. Tracks can be slipped in time relative to each other, or bounced almost instantly. You can locate or edit quickly any portion of the program. To rearrange or repeat song sections, tell the computer in which order you want them played. Some systems permit *nondestructive edits*, which do not alter the original material on disk. You can listen to various edits and either delete, keep, or redo them.

One function of a 2-track DAW is for compact disc premastering. You start with your rough DAT mixdown master containing music, studio noises, and long spaces between songs. After copying it to hard disk, you edit this program with the workstation. Finally you dump the edited program onto DAT, and that is your CD premaster. Follow these steps:

1. Play your DAT mixdown master and record it onto the hard disk. This recording might be just one song or an entire album.

2. The waveform of the audio program appears on your monitor screen at any desired level of resolution (see Figure 15.6). You can *zoom out* to see the entire program, or *zoom in* to see individual samples.

3. Using a mouse, define *regions* or *zones* in the audio waveform. These are sections of the program, such as an entire song, the chorus of a song, a drum riff, or a vocal lick.

4. Edit the program by manipulating the regions, much as you do with a word processor. You can trim the start and end of each region, delete regions, move them around, copy them, insert silences, and resequence the program so that the songs progress in any desired order.

5. Once the program is edited the way you want it, copy it in real-time onto a DAT tape. During this process, the software plays the program by running down a playlist of pointers, which tell the hard-disk head where on the disk to read the data from (see Figure 15.7). That is, the playlist tells the head to jump around from point to point on the disk to play selected portions in the desired order.

6. The finished DAT is a CD premaster, which can be used to cut a compact disc (see Chapter 13). You even can record your own CDs off the workstation with a compact disc recorder (such as the Yamaha PD5 and YPDR).

Functions

Here are some of the functions found in most digital audio workstations:

Multitrack Digital Recording: From 2 tracks on up

Cut and Paste: Remove a section of a song and put it somewhere else in the song

Copy: Duplicate a section of a song (for example, a chorus) and put it somewhere else in the song

Crossfade: Fade out of one song while fading into another

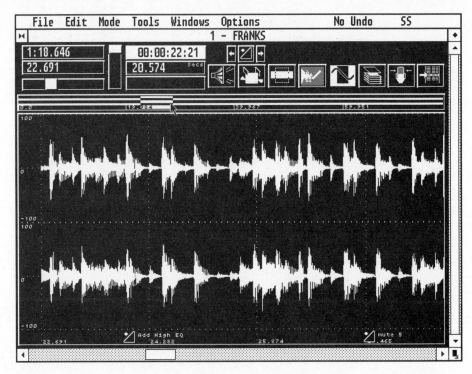

Figure 15.6 A waveform editing screen (Courtesy Turtle Beach Systems).

Slip: Move a section of a song in time, either within or across tracks, or adjust the start times of sound effects by moving them on-screen with a mouse

Scrub: Play the program slowly forward and backward (similar to rocking tape reels to move the tape back and forth across the head)

Trim: Remove or truncate unwanted portions of the waveform or program

Playlist (Edit Decision List): A list of the selections in the order you want them played (they can be reordered instantly and might be entire songs, parts of songs, or sound effects)

DSP (Digital Signal Processing): Digital control and effects, such as mixing, volume adjustments, panning, equalization, chorus, limiting, looping, compression, expansion, noise removal, and noise gating

Time Compression/Expansion: Makes a program shorter or longer without changing its pitch, useful for making radio spots fit their allotted time

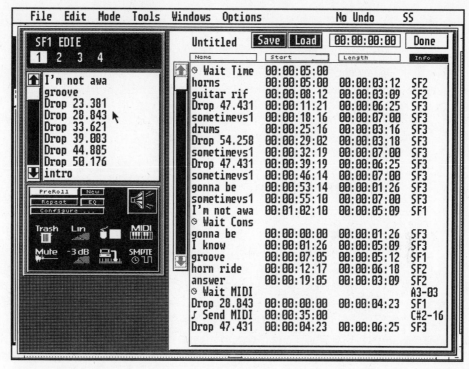

Figure 15.7 A playlist editing screen (Courtesy Turtle Beach Systems).

Automated Mixing: Computer remembers your mix moves and sets the mixer controls accordingly during the mixdown

Spectrum Analysis: A display of level versus frequency of the audio program as it progresses in time

MIDI Sequencer: Lets you import or record several tracks of MIDI performance data

Sync: Synchronization to SMPTE time code or MIDI Time Code

PQ Editing: Allows you to add song start-and-stop times and index points to create a premaster tape for compact discs

Data Storage on Disk and in RAM

When you select a hard-disk drive for a digital workstation, you choose its storage capacity based on the length of the programs you want to work with. At a sampling rate of 44.1 kHz, 1 minute of mono sound consumes about 5M, and 1 minute of stereo takes 10M. You can store a 1-hour program on a 660M drive. The disk access time must be very fast—28 milliseconds or less—so that the playlist pointers can be accessed without audible delays.

Some of the editing described earlier is done to data that is stored temporarily in RAM; some is done to data on the hard disk. Edits done in RAM, such as setting up a playlist, are much faster than edits done on disk, and are usually nondestructive.

Products

Some examples of personal computer workstations are the 56K Digital Recording System by Turtle Beach Systems, the Sonic System by Sonic Solutions, SoftSplice Digital Audio Editor by Digital Expressions, Sound Tools and Pro Tools by Digidesign, and the Digital Master by Hybrid Arts.

One example of a single-chassis workstation is the Korg Digital Audio Production System, an 8-track hard-disk unit selling for around $30,000. Another is the Yamaha DMR8 Digital Multitrack Mixer/Recorder, which includes an 8-track digital tape recorder, digital mixer, SMPTE timecode reader-generator, autolocator and automated mixing system all in one chassis. Using an 8mm tape cassette and a stationary head, the DMR8 sells for around $40,000. Some other high-end workstations are the Lexicon Opus and the Digital Audio Research Soundstation Sigma.

Stand-alone hard-disk recorders for digital audio are available, such as the Roland DM-80. Because it uses no disk space for silent portions of a track, the DM-80 can record up to 18 minutes, 4 tracks, at 44.1 kHz on its 100M hard drive. Equipped with a SCSI interface and analog/digital inputs and outputs, the DM-80 accommodates SMPTE, MIDI Time Code, and MIDI Tempo Clock. Other features include punch-in, loop-type recording, and editing functions. It also includes a mixer with EQ, pan, and gain. The 4-track model costs under $5,500, and the 8-track model is under $7,700.

Optical disk recorders are available from Akai (among others); these record data in the form of pits on a platter similar to a compact disk. Storage density is extremely high.

Integrated Sequencing/Digital Audio Recording System

This hardware/software system lets you add 2 to 4 tracks of vocals, sax, guitar, or any audio signal to your MIDI sequences. While playing MIDI tracks, you record the audio digitally to a hard disk. The system synchronizes your sequencer's MIDI data with your digitally recorded audio.

This system replaces a tape-sync setup at higher cost, but with superior sound. The sound quality is as good as that of a compact disc (16-bit quantization, 44.1 kHz sampling rate). Plus, you can edit the digital audio performances nondestructively—cut and paste, copy, rearrange, and so on. You have a tapeless studio, in which your computer can access and manipulate sequences and digital audio instantly.

The integrated MIDI/digital audio system is made of several components (see Figure 15.8). In addition to a personal computer, MIDI interface, and MIDI controller, you need:

- A direct-to-disk recording card that plugs into your computer. The card converts audio to a format that can be stored on a hard disk drive.

- An A/D-D/A converter. Units for home studios usually have two $\frac{1}{4}$-inch phone jacks. Professional units have +4 dbm XLR-type connectors. An option is a DAT recorder with digital inputs and outputs.

- MIDI/digital audio recording software, such as Opcode Studio Vision, Mark of the Unicorn Digital Performer, Passport AudioTrax, and Digidesign Deck. Deck has just a basic 32-track sequencer, but it can import MIDI files from other sequencers. Most of these programs also provide SMPTE synchronization and automated mixing. Make sure the software is compatible with your type of computer (IBM-compatible, Macintosh, etc.).

- A hard disk drive (usually external) for temporary storage of digital audio data. One track of one minute of CD-quality audio consumes about 5M, so a 600M drive could record 30 minutes of 4 tracks. Note that Opcode Studio Vision software has a feature called *strip silence* that removes data created during silent portions of tracks. In this way, one track-minute of audio might use only 1M instead of 5.

- A DAT recorder for permanent storage or for CD premastering.

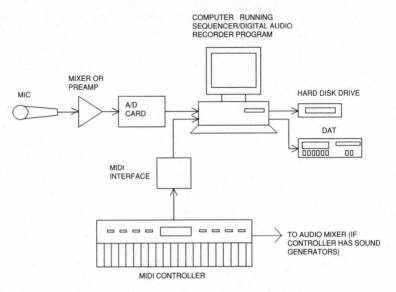

Figure 15.8 Connections for an integrated sequencing/digital audio recording system.

How much do these devices cost? The figures below are approximate list prices (note that the A/D-D/A interface might be part of a DAT recorder):

A/D-D/A interface, $1,000-$3,000

Direct-to-disk card, $1,000

Software, $350-$1,000

660M hard drive, $1,500-$4,000

DAT recorder, $800 and up

Digidesign's Sound Tools system includes various choices of an interface box, direct-to-disk card and software for about $3,000 to $6,000.

Here's how such a system might work: First use your sequencer software to record the MIDI parts—drum machine, synth, samples. Then set up a microphone to record a vocal. While listening to the MIDI tracks, record the vocal onto hard disk as digital audio. You might record a few takes of the vocal part and then cut and paste selected portions to create a perfect take. Record one good chorus and paste it in each chorus section in your song.

Your finished recording contains a hybrid of MIDI and digital audio. You add effects, mix the tracks to DAT (using automated-mixing software), and the final product is a DAT tape containing digital audio.

Introduction to MIDI Recording Procedures

The remainder of this chapter describes recording procedures for several different MIDI studio setups, from simple to complex.

Read your instruction manuals thoroughly and simplify them into step-by-step procedures for various operations. Note that each piece of MIDI gear has its own idiosyncrasies, and the instructions may have errors or omissions. If you have questions, call the technical service people at the manufacturer of your equipment.

Recording with a Polyphonic Synthesizer

Recording with a polyphonic synthesizer is the simplest method of recording (see Figure 15.9). You plug a MIDI interface into your computer, plug your synth into the interface, and run a sequencer program on the computer. You play chords and melody, record this MIDI data with your sequencer, and play back the sequence through your synthesizer. The basic steps follow:

1. Set your sequencer to record on one track.

2. Play a tune on your keyboard.

3. Play back the sequencer recording to hear it. Your performance will be duplicated by the synthesizer.

4. Quantize the track if desired.

5. Punch in/out to correct mistakes.

6. Arrange the song by combining various sequences.

7. Enter any program changes (changes in timbre).

8. Play the composition and set recording levels.

9. Start the sequencer playing, and record the synth output on a tape recorder. That recording is the final product.

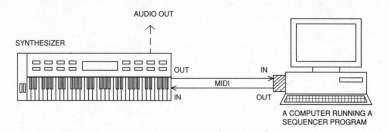

Figure 15.9 A synthesizer connected via a MIDI interface to a computer running a sequencer program.

Those are the basic procedures, but each one deserves a little more explanation. Here are the details for each step.

Setting Your Sequencer

Choose a tempo in your sequencer and choose the track you want to record on. On your computer keyboard, push the "record" key (designated in the sequencer program instructions). You'll hear a metronome ticking at the tempo you set.

Playing Music on Your Keyboard

Listen to the sequencer's metronome and play along with its beat. The sequencer keeps track of the measures, beats, and pulses. When the song is done, press the "stop" key on your computer keyboard (designated in the sequencer instructions). The sequencer stops recording, and should go to the beginning of the sequence (the top of the tune).

Another way to record your performance is in *step-time*, one note at a time. If the part is difficult to play rapidly, you also can set the sequencer tempo very slow, record while playing the synth at that tempo, and then play back the sequence at a faster tempo.

Playing Back the Sequencer Recording

On your computer keyboard, hit the "play" key (designated in the sequencer instructions). You'll hear the sequence playing through your synthesizer.

Quantizing the Track

Recall that quantizing is the process of correcting the timing of each note to the nearest note value (quarter-note, eighth-note, and so on). If you wish, press the keys to quantize the performance by the desired amount. Some sequencers don't let you alter quantization after recording, but there's a way around this:

1. Record all tracks without quantization.

2. Mute all the tracks except the one you want to quantize.

3. Plug a MIDI cable from MIDI OUT to MIDI IN on your sequencer or computer interface.

4. Set the desired amount of quantization, and record on an open track. First, enable record mode on that track.

5. To change the amount of quantization, erase the quantized track, select a new value, and rerecord.

Punching In/Out To Correct Mistakes

You can correct mistakes by punching into record mode before the mistake, recording a new performance, and then punching out of record mode. Here's one way to do it:

1. Go to a point in the song a few bars before the mistake.

2. Just before you get to the mistake, punch into record mode and play a new, correct performance.

3. As soon as you finish the correction, punch out of record mode.

Alternatively, you can use *autopunch*. With this feature, the computer punches in and out automatically at preset measures; all you have to do is play the corrected musical part. Perform an autopunch as follows:

1. Using the computer keyboard, set the punch-out point (the measure, beat, and pulse where you want to go out of record mode).

2. Set the punch-in point (just before the part you want to correct).

3. Set the cue point (where you want the track to start playing before the punch).

4. Hit the play key on your computer.

5. When the screen indicates punch-in mode, or when the appropriate measure comes up, play the corrected part.

6. The sequencer punches out automatically at the specified point in the song.

These punch-in routines were done in real-time. You also can punch-in/out in step-time:

1. Go to a point in the song just before the mistake.

2. Set the sequencer to step-time mode.

3. Step through the sequence pulse by pulse, and punch into record mode at the proper point.

4. Record the proper note in step-time.

5. Punch out of record mode.

Arranging the Song by Combining Sequences

Now your sequenced performance is perfect, so you can put together your composition. Many songs have repeated sections: the verse and chorus are each repeated several times. If you wish, you can play the verse and chorus once each and save them as a separate sequence, which you can copy for all the places each occurs in the song.

You can rearrange song sections, and append one section to another, by pressing a few keys on the computer. You also can have any section repeated. In this way, you might build a song by having the computer play sections A-A-B-A-C-A-B-B.

Entering Program Changes

To add variety to the song, you might want to have the synth play different programs (patches) at different parts of the song—for example, play a piano on the first verse, organ on the second, and marimba on the chorus. One way is to press different presets (program numbers) as you record the sequence.

Another way is to record these program changes on another track, which is called the controller track. Be sure to set the controller track to the same channel as the performance track, and turn off any patch on the controller track. Enter the appropriate program numbers at the right time on your synthesizer. Putting the program changes on a separate track makes it easy to edit them. You can punch in new program changes just as you can punch in new performances. When all the program changes are correct, you can bounce them to the performance track if you wish.

Some sequencers do not record the program *settings* on your synth. They record only program *changes*. Consequently, when you play the sequence into a synth you just turned on, you might hear the wrong sounds. To prevent this problem, insert a few blank measures at the beginning of the tune and record your initial program changes there, according to the sounds you want to hear at the beginning of the tune. Follow this procedure:

1. Insert two or four blank measures at the beginning of your composition.

2. Set each track's patch to the wrong program number. If you want patch #17, for example, set it to #16. This way, you can key in a program change later.

3. Set your sequencer to punch-in mode so that you record only on the blank measures at the beginning of the tune.

4. When the punch-in starts, key in the correct program numbers. You can perform these program changes in several passes, one track at a time.

5. When the sequence plays back, it sets the synth automatically to the correct patches at the beginning of the tune.

An alternative to this procedure is to record a *system-exclusive* or *sysex dump*—data about patch settings, and so forth—into the sequencer. This works only if your synth and sequencer implement the sysex dump.

Playing the Composition and Setting Recording Levels

Plug your synthesizer's audio output (mono or stereo) into the line inputs of your 2-track tape recorder. Hit the play key on your computer keyboard, and set the recording level for your recorder according to these guidelines:

Cassette: 0 maximum

Open-reel: +3 VU maximum

DAT: –3 db maximum

Recording the Synth Output

Once your levels are set, put your tape recorder in record mode, and start the sequencer. This produces the finished product—a stereo recording of your song.

Recording with a Multitimbral Synthesizer

When you record with a multitimbral synthesizer, you play the parts for several different instruments (patches) on the same multitimbral keyboard, and record each performance on a separate track of a sequencer. During playback, the sequencer plays the desired patches (instruments) in your synth. It sounds like a band playing. You record the synthesizer's output, and that recording is the final product.

Each track and patch are set to corresponding MIDI channels. For example, suppose both track 1 and the bass patch are set to channel 1. Then track 1's performance in the sequencer plays the bass patch in the synthesizer. Track 2 will play another patch (piano, flute, or whatever).

Some sequencers are designed so that, on power-up, track 1 goes to channel 1, track 2 goes to channel 2, and so on. You simply select a track to record on and select a patch for that track. The channel assignments are already taken care of.

Refer back to Figure 15.9 to see the connections. Here is an outline of the steps for recording:

1. Start recording on the first sequencer track.

2. Play music on your keyboard.

3. Play the recording.

4. Punch in/out to correct mistakes.

5. Record overdubs on other tracks.

6. Bounce tracks.

7. Edit the composition.

8. Mix the tracks.

9. Record the mix.

Again, these steps require a closer look. The following sections present detailed explanations for each one.

Recording on the First Sequencer Track

Adjust the metronome tempo on your sequencer as desired. Set the sequencer to record on track 1. If necessary, set sequencer track 1 to MIDI channel 1.

Select the first patch you want to hear on your synthesizer (in this case, bass guitar). You might want to adjust the timbre of the patch with the sound controls on the synthesizer in order to create unusual sounds. If necessary, set the synthesizer patch to MIDI channel 1.

Hit the record key(s) on your computer keyboard (designated in the sequencer instructions).

Playing Music on Your Keyboard

Listen to the sequencer's metronome and play along with its beat; or, record in step-time. The sequencer keeps track of the measures, beats, and pulses. When you press the stop key on your computer keyboard, the sequencer stops recording and goes to the beginning of the sequence (the top of the tune).

Playing the Recording

On your computer keyboard, hit the play key. You'll hear the sequence playing through your synthesizer.

Punching In/Out To Correct Mistakes

As described in the previous section, you can correct mistakes by punching into record mode before the mistake, recording a new performance, and then punching out of record mode. You also can quantize the track to make it correct rhythmically.

Recording Overdubs on Other Tracks

With your first track recorded and corrected, you are ready to record other tracks. Set the sequencer to record on track 2. If necessary, set sequencer track 2 to MIDI channel 2.

On your synthesizer, select the next patch (instrument timbre) you want to use (in this case, piano). If necessary, set it to MIDI channel 2.

Then hit the record key(s) on your computer keyboard. Play the piano part on the synthesizer while listening to your prerecorded bass on track 1. This track is played by the synthesizer.

Another example may help. Imagine you just recorded a drum part into the sequencer on track 1. You can go back to the start of the sequence, play the drum part, and add a bass line on track 2 in sync with the drums. Then you can go back to the top and add a piano on track 3.

In short, you record the performance of a different patch on each track in the sequencer, and play back the recording through the multitimbral synthesizer, which plays all the patches simultaneously. Or you can use several synths, one for each part, if necessary. Set each track to a different MIDI channel, and set each instrument or patch to the same channel that its track is set to.

Bouncing Tracks

What if your sequencer records eight tracks, but you want to play ten patches at once with several synths? Recall that you can make more tracks available by bouncing them. If you bounce track 5 into track 4, for instance, track 5 then can be erased so that you can record a new instrument on track 5. To do this, hit the bounce key(s) on your computer keyboard. Type in the source track and destination track (indicate to which track you want to bounce). In a few seconds, the bounce is accomplished.

You can bounce only one track at a time. You can bounce a track into a prerecorded track, however, without erasing the prerecorded track. The prerecorded track and bounced track then merge. Unlike bouncing with a tape deck, there is no generation loss (no loss of sound quality) when you bounce with a sequencer.

You can record program changes on a separate track set to the same channel as the performance track. Later, bounce the program-change track to the performance track. The performance track and program-change track merge into one. Be sure both tracks are set to the same channel, and that the program-change track has its patch turned off.

Editing the Composition

Now your sequenced performance is satisfactory, so you can put together your composition. As described in the previous section, you can rearrange song sections and append one section to another by pressing a few keys on the computer. You also can have any section replayed. Key in program changes at the beginning of the song and anywhere else you want the sounds to change.

Mixing the Tracks

Now that your song is recorded and arranged, you want to adjust the relative volumes of the tracks to achieve a pleasing balance.

If your multitimbral synthesizer doesn't have separate outputs for each patch, you have to adjust the mix at the sequencer. To do this, adjust the volume (key-velocity scaling) of each track by hitting the appropriate computer keys. This only works if your keyboard is velocity-sensitive.

After you adjust the volume of each track in this way, hit the play key on your computer keyboard to play the sequence. The desired mix of patches play on your synth. Some synths let you add internal effects to the overall mix.

If your synth has several individual outputs—one for each patch—connect them to a mixer and set up a stereo mix with panning and effects.

Recording the Mix

If your synth has a single output (mono or stereo), use your 2-track tape recorder to record the mix off that output. Plug your synthesizer's audio output into the line inputs of your 2-track recorder. Or, if your synth has several individual outputs connected to a mixer, record off the mixer stereo outputs.

Hit the play key on your computer keyboard, and set the recording level for your recorder according to these guidelines:

Cassette: 0 maximum

Open-reel: +3 VU maximum

DAT: –3 db maximum

Once your levels are set, put your tape recorder in record mode, and start the sequencer. This produces the finished product—a stereo recording of your song.

Recording with a Keyboard Workstation

To illustrate how you might record a song with a workstation's built-in sequencer, suppose you are operating a Korg M-1. Multitrack real-time recording with the M-1 is simple. The basic procedure involves seven steps:

1. Set up for recording a song.
2. Record the first musical part.
3. Do step recording (optional).
4. Overdub more parts.
5. Punch in.
6. Set effects.
7. Store the song.

The following sections present more detailed instructions for each step.

Setting Up for Recording a Song

1. Press SEQ (for SEQUENCER) on the front panel.
2. A sequencer menu appears on the LCD screen. You can move a cursor to select various parameters, and press the up or down buttons to set the value of each parameter.
3. Set the time signature (in the Initialize menu).
4. Select the song number.
5. Set the tempo (in the sequencer play/real-time record menu).
6. Select the track number (track 1 to start).
7. Select the program number for the desired sound (for example, a drum set).

Recording the First Musical Part

1. Press REC (record) and START. Listen to two measures of metronome clicks and then start playing.

2. When you finish, press STOP.

3. To hear what you just played, press START.

4. If you want to rerecord the part, press REC and START, and play the part again. You also could edit the performance, do punch-ins, and so on.

Step Recording

Instead of performing a musical part in real-time, you might prefer to enter the notes one at a time, in step-time. Here's the basic procedure:

1. Select the track number and the measure number where you want to start.

2. Press REC and START.

3. Set the length or the note value of the first note ($^1/_{32}$ to $^1/_1$).

4. If necessary, specify triplets, dotted notes, key dynamics, style of playing, and rests.

5. Press the desired note or chords on the keyboard.

6. Release all the keys; the recording proceeds to the next step.

7. After entering all the notes, press STOP.

Overdubbing More Parts

1. To record the next track, set the track number to the desired track (in this case, track 2).

2. Select the program number for the desired sound (for example, a bass).

3. Press REC and START. As you listen to track 1 playing the drum part, play a bass part on track 2.

4. Continue this procedure (steps 1-3) for up to 8 tracks, adding a new instrument each time.

Punching In

You can correct mistakes easily in each track by punching in, either manually or automatically. The procedure for an autopunch follows:

1. Play the song to find the measures needing correction.

2. Select punch-in mode.

3. Page up one page; set the punch-in measure and the punch-out measure; page down one page.

4. Set the measure number to a point a few bars before the punch-in.

5. Press REC and START. You'll hear the song playing.

6. When the punch-in measure comes up, play the corrected part.

7. Press STOP when done.

Setting Effects

You can page up to the effects menus to set overall effects: hall reverb, chorus, flanging, echo, distortion, and so on. Press 8 on the numeric keypad to get to the effects menus. (Note that these are built-in keyboard effects, not outboard studio effects.)

Storing the Song

Save the completed song in multitrack form to a plug-in RAM card or to an external sequencer and disk drive. To prevent data overload, you might have to do the external sequencer recording one track at a time with other tracks muted. If you're satisfied with the final results, record the stereo output signals of the M-1 to a 2-track recorder. In addition to these basic operations, you can

- Bounce tracks.

- Edit each note event.

- Create and copy patterns—for a drum or bass part, for example.
- Modify track and song parameters.
- Insert/delete/erase measures.
- Modify sounds and effects (in great detail).

Recording with a Drum Machine and a Synthesizer

This system combines a synthesizer with a drum machine. Figure 15.10 shows how to connect the cables. Figure 15.11 shows a preferred setup if your synth has a MIDI THRU port.

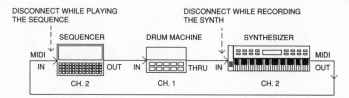

Figure 15.10 Connections to make a sequencer drive a drum machine and a synthesizer.

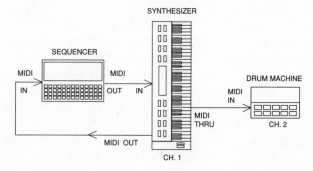

Figure 15.11 Connections to make a sequencer drive a drum machine if your synth has a MIDI THRU port.

Understanding Synchronization

The drum machine has a built-in sequencer that records what you tap on its pads. Suppose you record a drum pattern with its built-in sequencer, and you record a synthesizer melody with an external sequencer. How do you synchronize the drum patterns in the drum machine with the synthesizer melody in the sequencer? In other words, how do you get the two devices to play in sync, when both have different patterns recorded in different memories?

To synchronize the machines, use a single *MIDI clock* (timing reference) that sets a common tempo for all the equipment. The MIDI clock is a series of bytes in the MIDI data stream that conveys timing information. The clock is like a conductor's baton movements, keeping all the performers in sync at the same tempo. The clock bytes are added to the MIDI performance information in the MIDI signal. The clock signal is 24, 48, or 96 pulses per quarter-note (ppq). That is, for every quarter-note of the performance, 24 or more clock pulses (bytes) are sent in the MIDI data stream.

Decide which device you want to be your master timing reference—the sequencer or the drum machine. Set the master device to internal clock and set the slave device to external clock or MIDI clock. Then the slave follows the tempo of the master.

To make this happen, the master sends clock pulses from its MIDI OUT connector. The slave receives those clock pulses at its MIDI IN connector. The slave also passes clock pulses through its MIDI THRU connector to other slave devices down the chain.

If a slave device lacks a MIDI THRU, enable "Echo MIDI in" in the slave device. Then the incoming pulses are echoed or repeated at the MIDI OUT connector.

In the setups shown in Figures 15.10 and 15.11, the sequencer's clock drives both the drum machine and the synthesizer. In other words, the sequencer is the master tempo setter, and the drum machine and synth follow along. The drum machine's internally recorded patterns play in sync with the synthesizer's sequencer-recorded melody.

Basic Recording Procedure

Once you have addressed the synchronization problem, you are ready to begin recording with this system. There are two basic methods. The first uses the following steps:

1. Record drum patterns into the drum machine.

2. While listening to the drum patterns, record a synth part with your sequencer.

3. Sync the drums and synth by setting MIDI clocks and channels.

4. Press the play key on the sequencer.

Use these steps for the second method:

1. Record drum patterns into the drum machine.

2. Copy these patterns onto one track of your sequencer.

3. While listening to the drum track, record a synth part on another track.

4. Play both sequencer tracks.

Detailed explanations follow for recording drum patterns and synchronizing the drums with the synth.

Recording Drum Patterns

The first step in composing a song is to record a drum pattern. There are many ways to do this; the following is one suggested procedure:

1. On the drum machine, set the tempo, time signature, and pattern length in measures. For this example, the pattern is 2 bars long.

2. Start recording, and play the hi-hat key in time with the metronome beat.

3. At the end of 2 bars, the hi-hat pattern you tapped in repeats over and over (loops).

4. While this is happening, you can add a kick drum beat.

5. While the hi-hat and kick drum are looping, add a snare drum back beat, and so on.

6. Mix the recording by adjusting the faders on the drum machine for each instrument.

Next, you repeat the process for a different rhythmic pattern—say, a drum fill—and store this as Pattern 2. Then develop other patterns. Finally, you make a song by repeating patterns and chaining them together as described in the drum machine's instruction manual. A song is a list of patterns in order.

It's a good idea to add a count-off (a few measures of clicks) at the beginning so that later overdubs can start at the correct time.

Some musicians like to program a simple repeating drum groove first. While listening to this, they improvise a synth part. After recording the synth part, they redo the drum part in detail, adding hand claps, tom-tom fills, accents, and so on.

Synchronizing Drums and Synth

Now you're ready to add a synth part and synchronize it with the drum track. The following procedure refers to a sequencer; it could also be a computer running a sequencer program:

1. Record a synth part with the sequencer.

2. Set the drum machine to external clock or MIDI clock.

3. Set the sequencer to internal clock or MIDI drum.

4. Set the MIDI channels: set the drum machine to channel 1; set the sequencer synth track and the synthesizer to channel 2. In this way, the sequencer's recorded performance plays only the synthesizer. The MIDI clock still controls both devices, even though they are set to different channels.

5. Press the play key on the sequencer. As the sequencer plays its recorded synth melody, the sequencer's clock pulses drive the drum machine and synthesizer at the same tempo. The drum machine plays its internally recorded patterns while the synth plays the sequencer track.

Another way to synchronize a drum machine and a synthesizer is to record the drum patterns on one track of your sequencer. The advantage is that, whenever you rearrange parts of the music in the sequencer, you also rearrange the drum part. So you don't have to change drum patterns each time you repeat or delete a verse or a chorus. Follow this procedure to record the drum patterns into your sequencer:

1. Record a drum pattern with the drum machine's internal sequencer.

2. Enable the drum machine's clock out and MIDI data out.

3. On your sequencer, turn off the MIDI-THRU feature (if it has one).

4. Set the sequencer to external clock or MIDI clock mode, and set an open track in record mode.

5. Hit the play key on the drum machine. The sequencer records the drum pattern on the open track.

To play back the drum patterns you just recorded, follow this procedure:

1. Set the drum machine to external clock mode.

2. Set the sequencer to internal clock or MIDI drum.

3. Set the drum machine's track and the drum machine to the same MIDI channel.

4. Load an empty pattern into the drum machine so that the machine plays only the sequencer track.

5. Put the sequencer in play mode. The drum machine plays its sequencer track at the sequencer's tempo, and other synths connected to the sequencer play their tracks on their channels.

Recording with a MIDI System Plus Tape Sync

You might have a complete MIDI workstation: a synthesizer, sound generator, drum machine, sequencer, and recorder-mixer. Here is a suggested procedure for recording, overdubbing, and mixdown with this system:

1. Connect the system.

2. Record drum patterns; record synth tracks into your sequencer.

3. Record the sync tone.

4. Check the sync-tone playback.

5. Overdub acoustic parts.

6. Mix down all the tracks.

These six steps are the basic outline of the procedure. Detailed explanations follow.

Connecting the System

Figure 15.12 shows the hookup. Connect the tape-sync output connector of the sequencer (or MIDI computer interface) to your tape recorder's sync-track input connector. This is an outside track—track 4 of a 4-track recorder, or track 8 of an 8-track recorder. Connect the sync-track's output to the tape-sync input of the sequencer or interface. Plug the MIDI equipment audio outputs and the tape-track outputs into a mixer (not shown), and monitor the mixer's output. If your recorder-mixer has enough inputs, you can use it as the mixer.

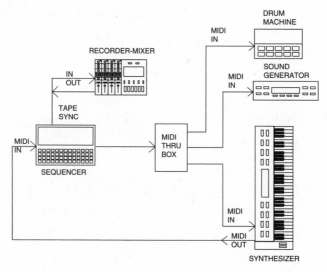

Figure 15.12 Connections for a complete MIDI workstation with tape sync.

If your sequencer lacks a tape-sync connector, you need a smart tape-sync box (converter). An example is the TascamMTS 30. Connect this system as shown in Figure 15.13.

Composing and Recording MIDI Tracks

Now that the system is set up, record drum and synth tracks. Here is a suggested procedure:

1. Set the sequencer, drum machine, and/or converter to internal sync mode.

2. Program the drum tracks into the drum machine. Be sure to set the tempo as desired, because once you record the sync tone, you can't change the tempo. Also consider programming the drum part longer than you need; the sync tone can be made shorter but not longer.

3. Develop your instrumental arrangement using the synthesizer and its sequencer, set to the same tempo as the drum machine. You can have tempo changes during the song if you enter them before recording the sync track. You might want to record the drum sequence into your sequencer so that changes in the main sequence (new arrangements, tempo changes) affect the drum track as well.

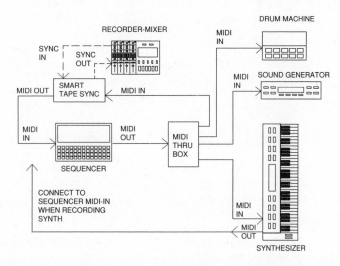

Figure 15.13 Connections for a complete MIDI workstation with smart tape sync.

Recording the Sync Tone

Either the drum machine or the sequencer can be used to generate the sync tone. In this example, use the sequencer:

1. Clean and demagnetize the tape heads.

2. Start playing the sequence. A sync tone is generated from the sync output jack.

3. Put the recorder in record-ready mode and set the recording level of the sync tone. Use a level that produces correct synchronization on playback (usually around –4 VU).

4. If you can switch off the noise reduction for the sync track, do so. Dolby is rarely a problem, but dbx can make the sync tone unreadable.

5. Stop the sequencer and reset it to the top of the tune.

6. Tape sync works best if you record the sync track before you record any other tape tracks. Start the tape recorder in record mode. A few seconds later, press play on your sequencer. You'll be recording (*striping*) the FSK or SMPTE tape-sync tone on track 4 of the recorder-mixer. This will be your master clock.

7. Let the sequencer run for the duration of the song. While striping the tone, do not record any musical material because it may not sync with material recorded later.

Checking the Sync Tone Playback

Now you play the sync tone you just recorded on tape, and it activates the drum machine and sequencer. First, reset the drum machine and sequencer to the top of the tune, and set them and the converter to external clock mode:

1. Rewind the recorder a little before the beginning of the sync tone and take the sync track out of record-ready mode.

2. Start playing the tape. (You may need to press the play key on the drum machine or sequencer first.) The sequencer should start playing when the tone starts. The tone drives the sequencer, which in turn plays the synth and drives the drum machine—all at the same tempo. They stop when the tone stops.

3. If you have sync problems, try rerecording the tone at a different level. If a tape drop-out causes loss of sync, rerecord the tone on a different section of tape, or on a new tape or track. You can rerecord the sync track before recording other tracks, but not after—you'll lose sync.

Overdubbing Acoustic Parts

Now you're ready to overdub vocals and acoustic instruments on tape:

1. Plug a mic into your recorder and assign it to an open track. If possible, don't assign percussive or bass parts to a track adjacent to the sync track because they can interfere with the sync tone.

2. Set the microphone input trim and recording level as described in Chapter 12 on recorder-mixer operation.

3. Rewind the tape to just before the beginning of the sync tone, and hit play. The drum machine and sequencer should start playing. (You may need to press the play key on the drum machine or sequencer first.)

4. While listening to the synth and drum machine playing through headphones, record any vocals and non-MIDI instruments onto tape. Because you have three tracks available, you could record, for example, lead vocal on track 1, harmony vocal on track 2, and sax on track 3.

Mixing Down All the Tracks

After all your tracks are recorded, use the mixer to set up a mix of the tape tracks and MIDI instruments. If your mixer doesn't have enough inputs for all the tape tracks, you can set a stereo mix of the tape tracks with the recorder-mixer, and combine this stereo mix with the audio signals from your MIDI instruments:

1. Adjust levels, panning, and effects. You'll have three tape tracks, probably eight tracks from the synth and sound module, plus stereo drum tracks, with stereo effects—all first generation! (Mixing procedures are described in greater detail in Chapter 12; automated mixing is covered later in this chapter.)

2. Play the song several times to perfect the mix.

3. When you're satisfied with the mix, rewind the tape to a point just before the beginning of the sync tone and hit play. Record it onto the 2-track or DAT.

4. Record the mixes for the rest of your tunes, leaving a few seconds of silence on the master tape between each song. If your 2-track mastering deck is open-reel, you can splice in leader tape before and after the program, and between each song. (This procedure is described in Chapters 9 and 13. If your 2-track deck is a DAT machine, follow the procedures in Chapter 13 to add spaces between songs.)

Congratulations! There's your finished master tape. If you plan to send it to a tape-duplication house or compact-disc manufacturer, first make a safety copy in case it is lost or damaged. Take care in setting recording levels while copying. You can make a few cassette copies by playing the master tape and copying it with a cassette deck.

Using Effects

Effects are an important part of a mix. To keep the sound lively, try to vary the effects throughout the song, or use several types of effects at once.

For example, suppose you have a multitimbral synth, and you want to add a different effect to each patch. Whether or not you can do this depends on your synth. If it has a separate output for each patch, you can use a different effect on each patch. But if your synth has only a single output (mono or stereo) and you run it through an effects device, the same effect is on all the patches.

If your song includes program changes (patch changes), you can have the effects change when the patch changes. Set up a MIDI multieffects processor so that each synth program change corresponds to the desired effect. When the synth program changes, the effect changes also.

What if you want the effect, but not the synth patch, to change during a mix? Reserve a track and channel just for effects program changes. You don't hear these program changes in your synth, but you do hear the effects change. During a mixdown, it usually is easier to change effects automatically with your sequencer, rather than manually.

If your synth is a sampling keyboard, each sample could have reverberation or some other effect already on it; in that case, each sample can have a different effect. The effect is not recorded in the sequencer; rather, the effect is part of the sampled sound. Note that the sampled reverberation cuts off every time you play a new note. Although this sounds unnatural, you can use it for special effect.

Because effects are audio signals, tape recorders can record effects but sequencers can't. If an effect is an integral part of the sound of an instrument, it's probably best to record it with the instrument on the multitrack tape. If the effect is overall ambience or reverb (to put the band in a concert hall), however, it's best to add it to almost everything during mixdown.

Automated Mixing

A multitrack mixdown is often a complicated procedure. It can be difficult to change the mixer settings correctly at all the right times, so you might want to use automated mixing—have a computer remember and set the changes for you.

During a mixdown of a song, you might adjust the mixer controls several times as the song progresses. For example, you might raise the piano's volume during a solo and then drop it back down. Or you might mute (turn off) a track to reduce noise during pauses in the performance. An automated-mixing system can remember your mix moves, and later recall and reset them.

You can even overdub mix moves, for example, do the vocal-fader moves on the first pass, drum moves on the second pass, and so on. You also can punch in fader moves to correct them. MIDI-effects changes can be automated as well.

Types of Automation Systems

Four types of automation systems are:

- Automated mixer

- Automated fader/VCA unit

- Automated-mixing software

- Moving-fader automation

Each of these is worth a closer look.

Automated Mixer

An automated mixer has built-in circuitry to perform automated mixdowns. In the mixer, volume levels and mutes are controlled either by Voltage Controlled Amplifiers (VCAs) or Digitally Controlled Amplifiers (DCAs). Control signals are FSK or SMPTE.

Automated Fader/VCA Unit

You also can automate a standard mixer by adding an external *automated fader/VCA unit*, a box with several faders that control VCAs or DCAs. The VCAs/DCAs plug into your mixer's access jacks or insert jacks (see Figure 15.14). These are in series with the signal of each channel. One VCA or DCA is needed for each channel (input, master, or return) you want to automate. Some boxes have one fader or mute button per channel; others have a single fader that you set to the desired channel. MIDI controls this type of system.

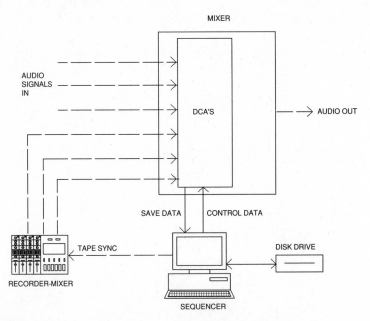

Figure 15.14 Typical connections for MIDI-automated mixing.

Examples of these insert boxes (or box/software systems) are the Niche Mix Automation Station, the Niche Audio Control Module, Mark of the Unicorn MIDI Mixer 7s, and J.L. Cooper MAGI II.

Automated-Mixing Software

Automated-mixing software is a program that runs on a personal computer. The monitor screen shows *virtual faders* that you adjust with a mouse. The mix is controlled in two ways: adjusting the gain of audio channels, and adjusting the MIDI volume or key velocity of sequencer tracks. Some programs allow cut-and-paste edits of mixes. You can append the chorus of mix 1 to the verse of mix 2, for example. Lower-cost programs let you control volume only; higher-cost programs let you control all parameters (EQ, panning, and effects). Many sequencing programs include an automated-mixing function.

Moving-Fader Automation

With this sophisticated system, SMPTE time code is used to control motorized faders. They move up and down as if controlled by a ghost. There are no VCAs to degrade the signal. In some systems, all control settings can be remembered and recalled. Examples are Neve, SSL, and GML consoles.

Storing Mix Moves

A MIDI sequencer can record your mix moves via MIDI program changes. The sequencer is either built into the automated mixer or is external (stand-alone or computer program). When you play the sequencer recording, MIDI program changes control the DCAs to mix the tracks as you did manually. Or the program changes will move motorized faders.

Snapshot versus Continuous Automation

There are two types of automation: *snapshot* and *continuous (dynamic)*. With snapshot automation, a computer memory in the mixer takes a "snapshot" of the mixer settings and stores them as MIDI program changes. To reset the mixer to any of these stored settings, punch up the appropriate number (MIDI program-change). Alternatively, your sequencer recording can reset the mixer at the correct times as a song plays. Some examples of snapshot mixers are the Akai MPX-820, Simmons 8:2, Soundtracs PC MIDI Series, AHB CMC Series, and Peavey PLM-8128.

With continuous or dynamic automation, the motion of the mixer controls is recorded. Continuous automation costs more than snapshot and consumes more memory, but permits finer resolution of mix moves. The Yamaha DMP7 digital mixer and the Euphonix mixer do both snapshot and continuous automation with their internal memory.

Some snapshot units let you program fade times so that you can fade between snapshots to simulate continuous control.

Controls

Some automated-mixing systems have several knobs and faders, one per parameter. Others have just a few "soft" controls: you assign the control one function at a time and adjust its value on a screen.

Some recorder-mixers, such as the Tascam 644 and 688, have automated muting and channel assignments, a function called MIDI-controllable scene memory.

Simulating Automatic Mixing with MIDI

If you lack an automated-mixer system, you can simulate one by recording controller data as volume changes on an open sequencer track. This lets you vary the balance among sequencer tracks, but not tape tracks. You might proceed as follows:

1. Choose a continuous controller on your master keyboard, such as a pitch-bend wheel.

2. Set the keyboard to transmit on the MIDI channel of the track you want to automate.

3. In your sound generator, assign or map the controller to affect MIDI volume for level changes.

4. Set your sequencer to record on a new track, called the controller track. Set the controller track to the same channel as your master keyboard. Be sure to turn off any patch on the controller track.

5. Start recording. While listening to the music, move the controller to adjust the volume of the track. (Later, you can edit the controller track, and perhaps bounce it to the musical track.)

6. Repeat this procedure for all the tracks you want to automate. (You can assign the controller to affect filtering or panning as well, but this takes up a lot of sequencer memory.)

MIDI studio equipment, keyboard workstations, and digital audio workstations bring new procedures into the studio with them. Typical recording procedures for MIDI setups can range from simple to complex. This relatively new technology has changed the way recordings are made.

16

ON-LOCATION RECORDING OF POPULAR MUSIC

Sooner or later you'll want to record a band—maybe your own—playing in a club or concert hall. Many bands want to be recorded in concert because they feel that's when they play best. Your job is to capture that performance on tape and bring it back alive.

There are many ways to do this, from simple two-microphone techniques to elaborate multimicrophone and multitrack setups.

Monitoring

Headphones, rather than loudspeakers, are often used for on-location monitoring because headphones are more portable and provide consistent sound in different environments. Plus, they partly block out the live sound of the band so you can better hear what's going on tape—especially if closed-cup, over-the-ear headphones are used.

If you record in the same room the band is playing in, the live sound of the band leaks through the headphones' ear seal. It's hard to hear the monitored signal clearly, especially how much bass you're putting on tape. This may be no problem if you're recording a relatively quiet acoustic group, but to clearly monitor a loud band in the same room they are playing in, you need to turn up the headphones very high. This can damage your hearing.

The preferred practice for louder groups is to set up your equipment in a room separate from the performance room. Then run some microphone extension cables (or a snake) from your mixer out to the performance area. Close the door, slip on the headphones, and monitor the sound. You can hear more clearly without the danger of blasting your ears. During intermissions, you can play back the tape to hear what you've just recorded.

Two-Track Recording with Two Microphones

A beginning recording engineer might start with just two microphones and a 2-track tape deck. This is the easiest method of recording a group. Small acoustic ensembles often can be recorded well this way, but not most musical groups. Why? We've become accustomed to the clean, tight recorded sound of musical groups picked up by multiple close-placed microphones. You can't duplicate that sound with a simple two-microphone pickup. However, such a recording is useful for musicians who want to hear how they blend in the audience area. It might even be adequate as a gig audition tape for local jobs. Recording this way is much simpler, faster, and cheaper than multimic, multitrack recording. Still, if time and budget permit, you get better sound with a more elaborate setup.

Two Crossed Cardioid Microphones

Recall from Chapter 6 that the ORTF (Office de Radiodiffusion-Television Francaise) stereo miking system is one method of recording with two microphones. First, mount two high-quality cardioid microphones on a stereo microphone-stand adapter (or improvise a holder with duct tape). Angle them 110 degrees apart (55 degrees to the right and left of center) and space their grilles 7 inches apart horizontally. You also could use a stereo microphone. Place this arrangement about 3 feet in front of a folk group or vocal quartet, or 10 to 15 feet in front of a large (or loud) musical group on stage. Use a microphone stand or hang the mics out of the reach of the audience.

Two Spaced Microphones

Many musical groups use loudspeakers at each end of the stage to reinforce the vocals and certain instruments. A centrally placed stereo pair of microphones, being far from the sound-reinforcement speakers, may not pick up the vocals adequately. To gain better control over the vocal/instrumental balance, try aiming two cardioid microphones straight ahead toward the group, spaced about 5 to 15 feet apart (see Figure 16.1).

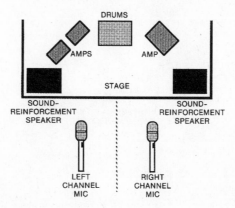

Figure 16.1 Recording a musical group with two spaced microphones.

Place the microphones far apart (that is, close to the sound-reinforcement speakers) to make the vocals louder in the recording. Do the opposite to make them quieter. The stereo imaging of this arrangement is poorer than with the ORTF system, but at least you can control the balance between instruments and vocals.

Preventing Mic-Preamp Overload

If the playback sounds distorted even though you did not exceed a normal recording level, the microphones probably overloaded the microphone preamplifiers in the tape deck. Recall that a microphone preamplifier is a circuit in the tape recorder that amplifies the level of a weak microphone signal up to a usable level. With loud sound sources such as rock groups, a microphone can put out a signal strong enough to cause distortion in the mic preamp.

Some decks include a pad or input attenuator, which reduces the microphone signal level before it reaches the preamp, thereby preventing distortion. Others have a high-impedance microphone input, which acts as an attenuator if used with a low-impedance microphone. Some condenser microphones have switchable internal pads that reduce distortion within the microphone. You or an electronics friend can build a pad with 20 db attenuation (see Figure 16.2), or buy some plug-in pads from your microphone dealer.

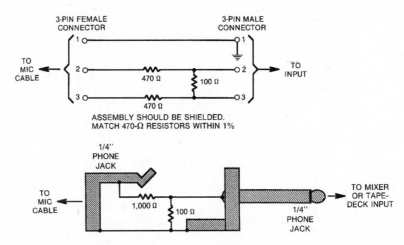

Figure 16.2 Balanced and unbalanced microphone pads.

If you have to set your record-level controls very low (less than ⅓ up) to obtain a 0 VU recording level, that's a good indication you need to use a pad.

Recording

The actual recording process is very simple. Hit the record button(s) and set the recording levels to peak around 0 maximum on your cassette-deck meters (+3 VU for an open-reel deck). Once the levels are set, leave them alone as much as possible. If you must change them, do so slowly and try to follow the dynamics of the music.

Bring enough tape for all the songs you want to record. Switch tapes during pauses or intermissions.

Recording from the Sound-Reinforcement Mixer

Sometimes you can get a good recording simply by plugging into the main output of the band's reinforcement mixer. Connect the line outputs of the mixer to the line or aux inputs of a 2-track recorder. Use the mixer output that is ahead of any graphic equalizer used to correct the speakers' frequency response (see Figure 16.3).

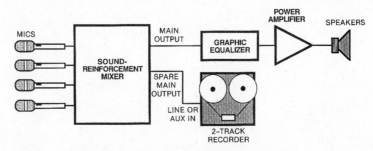

Figure 16.3 Recording from the sound-reinforcement mixer.

Mixers with balanced outputs can produce a signal that is too high in level for the recorder's line input, causing distortion. This is probably occurring if your record-level controls have to be set very low. To reduce the output level of the mixer, you could turn it down so that its signal peaks around –12 VU on the mixer meters, and turn up the P.A. power amplifier to compensate. That practice, however, degrades the mixer's S/N.

A better solution is to make a 12 db pad (see Figure 16.4). The output level of a balanced-output mixer is 12 db higher than the normal input level of a recorder with an unbalanced input.

Drawbacks

Recording from the band's mixer works best when all the instruments are miked and mixed through that mixer. The recorded mix might be bad, however—especially if the room is small-to-medium size. The operator of the band's mixer hears a combination of the band's live sound and the reinforced sound through the house system, and tries to get a good mix of both these elements. That means the signal is mixed to augment the live sound—not to sound good by itself. A recording made from the band's mixer is likely to sound too strong in the vocals and too weak in the bass. It's a compromise you have to live with unless you want to use a separate recording mixer.

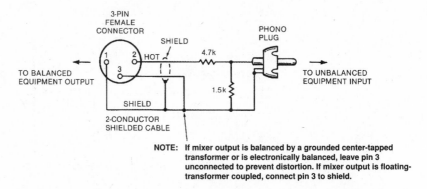

Figure 16.4 A pad for matching a balanced output to an unbalanced input.

However, if the performance is in a large hall or arena, most of the sound heard by the audience comes from the sound-reinforcement system. In this case, a recording made from the reinforcement mixer is likely to have a good mix—as good as the live mix is.

This method works best if the sound-reinforcement speakers were previously equalized to sound "hi-fi" when playing a good recording. If the frequency response of the reinforcement speakers is not wide-range and smooth, the mixer operator may equalize each instrument to compensate for the speakers. If you record this compensated mix and play it back over a good stereo system, the tonal balance is wrong because of the equalization used on the reinforcement mixer.

To record from the sound-reinforcement mixer, simply plug in, hit record, and watch your levels.

Recording Vocals with Separate Instruments

In some small systems, only the vocals are reinforced. Therefore, you can take a line-level feed from the band's mixer for vocals, and use your own microphones for the instruments. You need a separate mixer for recording. Place your microphones near each instrument, and mix their signals with the vocal signal from the band's mixer. Figure 16.5 shows the connections. Check the input-overload LEDs on the band's mixer (if any) to make sure the vocal mics aren't overloading their inputs.

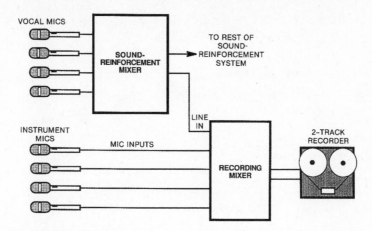

Figure 16.5 Recording from the sound-reinforcement mixer for vocals, with separate microphones for instruments.

Splitting the Microphones

As you have seen, a good house mix does not guarantee a good recording mix. It's better to make an independent recording mix by using a separate mixer and separate microphones.

The stage is cluttered if you place a recording microphone next to every reinforcement microphone. It's especially clumsy to double the vocal mics. Instead, you can plug a Y-adapter into the end of each vocalist's microphone cable (see Figure 16.6). This adapter splits the microphone signal two ways: to the reinforcement mixer and to the recording mixer.

Plug one output connector of the Y into a cable going to a reinforcement-mixer mic input. Plug the other output connector of the Y into a cable going to a recording-mixer mic input.

This arrangement might cause ground loops and hum unless both mixers are plugged into the same outlet strip. Experiment with AC-plug orientation and 3-to-2 ground-lift adapters (keeping safety in mind!) to obtain the least hum. If you use phantom powering, supply it from one console only.

A better solution is to isolate the two outputs with a transformer-isolated microphone splitter (see Figure 16.7), which is available at sound dealers and some music stores. (See Chapter 5 for more information.) You need one for every microphone you want to share with the sound-reinforcement system.

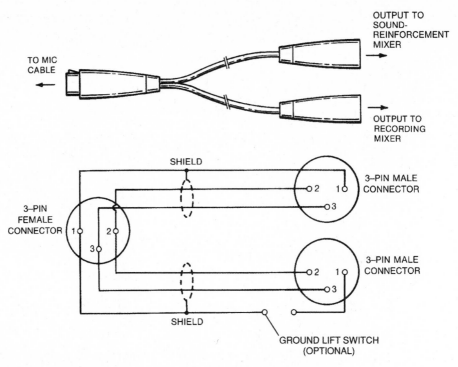

Figure 16.6 A Y-adapter for splitting microphone signals.

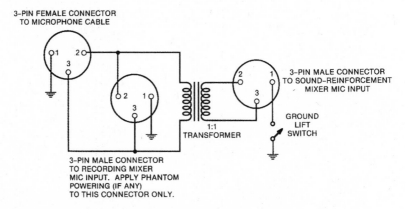

Figure 16.7 A transformer-isolated microphone splitter.

In some sound-reinforcement systems, every instrument is miked with a high-quality microphone. Then you can split all the microphones. In many other systems, only the vocals are miked for reinforcement. In that case, you split the vocal mics and use your own recording mics on the instruments.

368

For on-location work, you have to place each microphone within a few inches of its source to reject feedback, leakage, and room acoustics. (Some recommended microphone techniques are covered in Chapter 8.)

Ambience Microphones

If you have enough microphone inputs, you can add one or two ambience microphones to pick up the room acoustics and audience sounds. This helps the recording to sound live. Without ambience microphones, the recording may sound too dry, as if it were done in a studio.

One popular technique is to mount two boundary microphones on the walls or ceiling; they are said to provide a clear, realistic pickup of audience reaction. Alternatively, hang two crossed cardioids or spaced omnis over the audience.

Ambience microphones can muddy the sound if mixed in too loudly. Keep them down in level (just enough to add some atmosphere), or record them on separate tracks. Bring them up gently to emphasize crowd reactions.

Multitrack Recording

A recording mixed live to 2-track bypasses the noise and distortion added by a multitrack recorder. The mix may not be optimum, however, because you have to mix as the musicians are playing. A multitrack recorder lets you tailor the mix after the concert.

Each microphone on stage is split to feed the sound-reinforcement mixer and a separate multichannel recording mixer (see Figure 16.8). Some splitters have three outputs to feed a stage-monitor mixer as well. To prevent ground loops between the three systems, the microphone cable shields are grounded only to the recording console. The cable shields going to the house mixer and monitor mixer are floated (disconnected) at the splitter with ground-lift switches. The recording mixer supplies phantom power for any condenser mics.

Each microphone, or each instrument's group of microphones, is routed to a separate track of a multitrack recorder. After making the recording, you mix down the tracks back in the studio, spending as much time as needed to perfect the mix. You even can overdub parts that were played incorrectly during the live performance, taking care to match the overdubbed sound to the original recording.

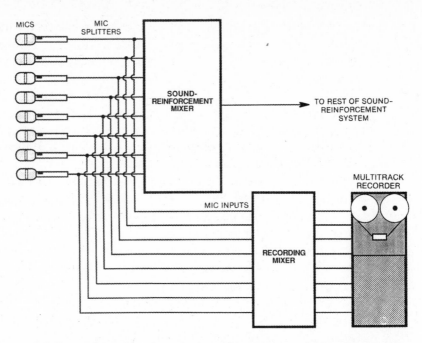

Figure 16.8 Recording with microphone splitters into a multitrack recorder.

The 4-track format is probably the most difficult to use for live recording because you have to submix several microphones onto each track, and monitor all four tracks. You must set up the 4-track monitor mix carefully because you can't change the mix within each track after recording (except slightly, with equalization).

Eight tracks are easier to work with because you do most of the mixing after the concert. You might need to mix the drum microphones to one or two tracks at the recording session, but typically each microphone feeds its own track. Most of your work during recording is level setting. Even the 2-track format is easier than 4-track. You set up only one mix while recording. There is no mixdown session.

A jazz trio might be a situation where 4-track recording is easy. You can put bass on track 1, piano on track 2, drums on track 3, and kick drum on track 4.

Twenty-Four Tracks in a Van

For the ultimate van setup, each microphone on stage is split three ways to feed the snake boxes for the recording, reinforcement, and monitor consoles. A long multiconductor snake is run to a recording truck or van parked outside the concert hall or club.

In the van, the microphone cables connect to a multichannel console, which is used to submix groups of microphones and route the signals to a multitrack tape machine. Sometimes two tape machines are run in parallel to provide a backup in case one fails, or to overlap recording during reel changes so that no music is lost. Two machines can be synchronized with SMPTE time code to increase the number of tracks available (see Appendix B).

This sophisticated setup permits total control over the sound without compromising the house mix, monitor mix, or recording mix. The engineer can set up a quick mixdown with effects to play for the musicians after the concert.

During mixdown, the recorded tracks of the ambience microphones can be faded up or down as required—up for liveness and audience reaction, down for cleanest sound.

Summary of Techniques

In general, this principle holds true for a variety of on-location recording techniques: the more sophisticated the setup, the better the sound. The methods discussed range from simple to complex:

- Place two microphones out front; use with pads into a 2-track tape deck.

- Record from the sound-reinforcement mixer into a 2-track tape deck.

- Record vocals from the sound-reinforcement mixer and mike the instruments separately. Mix together and record on a 2-track tape deck.

- Use microphone splitters. Mix all the microphones with a recording mixer live to 2-track.

- Record onto a multitrack tape machine for later mixdown.

This overview of on-location recording methods has introduced the basics. The rest of this chapter explores the details of on-location presession procedures.

Power and Grounding Practice

The following are suggestions for making AC power connections on location. You may want to review Chapter 5 on hum prevention, especially the section on connections to electric guitar amps.

Check that your AC power source is not shared with lighting dimmers or heavy machinery; these devices can cause noises or buzzes in the audio. Measure the AC line voltage. Know what your equipment can do under widely varying voltages. You may need to use a Variac, which lets you vary the line voltage. Use a 3-prong tester to check AC outlets for reversed polarity or lack of ground.

If possible, get AC power from the same place as the sound-reinforcement company. Run a long, thick (14 or 16 gauge) extension cord from that point to the control room. Plug AC outlet strips into the extension cord and then plug all your equipment into the outlet strips.

Interfacing with Telephone Lines

If you're doing a live remote for broadcast, you probably send your signal to the transmitter via rented telephone lines. The Telco (telephone company) noise level of a telephone line is specified in *dbrn*. A level of 0 dbrn is the "absolutely quiet" reference: 0 dbrn = –90 dbm. Thus, if the noise level is 30 dbrn, the S/N is 90/30 or 60 db.

Telco zero level is +8 dbm. You don't have to feed +8 dbm from your console into a phone line; +4 dbm gives 4 db more headroom. Telco test level is 0 dbm for tones above 400 Hz.

You may want to ask for lossless lines (with unity gain). Otherwise, your signal may be down about 20 db after transmission through the phone lines.

You need a 600 ohm source impedance, achieved by putting a 600 ohm resistor in series with the console output connector (300 ohms per leg of the balanced line). Have a terminated transformer on the sending end. To make a receiving line 600 ohms, put a 600 ohm resistor across pins 2 and 3.

In addition to the program lines, rent a nonequalized private line for communications. Order program lines at least two or three days in advance. Order a standard nonequalized line for communications at least a week in advance. For stereo programs, specify phase-matched lines.

Cables and Connectors

In a 3-pin connector, if you tie (connect) pin 1 to the shell grounding lug, you reduce pickup of electrostatic hum. However, with this wiring method, a ground loop is more likely to occur if the shell contacts a metallic surface on stage.

Furthermore, if pin 1 is grounded to the shell, and you plug the connector into a direct box and push the ground-lift switch, you don't lift ground! It's probably best *not* to tie pin 1 to the ground lug when you're recording on-location because a ground loop is a more likely occurrence than electrostatic hum pickup. In any case, standardize your connector wiring.

If SCR dimmer noise is a problem, insert an adapter between two mic cables to tie pin 1 to the shell.

Number the cables near their connectors. You may also want to cover these labels with clear heat-shrink tubing. Label both ends of each cable with the cable length. Put a drop of glue on each connector screw to temporarily lock it in place.

To reduce hum pickup and ground-loop problems associated with cable connectors, try to use a single mic cable between each mic and its snake-box connector.

Avoid bundling microphone cables, line-level cables, and power cables together. If you must cross mic cables and power cables, do so at right angles and space them vertically.

Don't leave a rat's nest of cables near the stage box. Coil the excess cable at each mic stand. That way, you can move the mics and reduce clutter at the stage box. Don't tape the mic cables down until the musicians are settled.

Have an extra microphone and cable offstage ready to use if a mic fails.

Preproduction Meeting

Have a preproduction meeting with the sound-reinforcement company and the production company putting on the event. Find out the date of the event, location, phone numbers of everyone involved, when the job starts, when you can get into the hall, when the second set starts, and other pertinent informaton. Decide who will provide the split, which system will be plugged in first, second, and so on. Draw block diagrams for the audio system and communications system.

If you're using a mic splitter, note that the mixer getting the direct side of the split provides phantom power for condenser mics not powered on stage. If the house system has been in use for a long time, give them the direct side of the split.

Overly loud stage monitors can ruin a recording, so work with the sound-reinforcement people toward a workable compromise. Ask them to start with the monitors quiet because the musicians always want them turned up louder.

Make copies of the meeting notes for all participants. Don't leave things unresolved. Know who is responsible for supplying what equipment.

Figure 16.9 shows a typical equipment layout worked out at a preproduction meeting. There are three systems in use: sound-reinforcement, recording, and monitor mixing. The microphone signals are split three ways to feed these systems.

Site Survey

Visit the recording site in advance and go through the following checklist:

- Listen for ambient noises—ice machines, coolers, 400 Hz generators, nearby discos, etc. If the room is noisy, you need to mike close. If not, you may want to mike at a distance to include room acoustics.

- Sketch dimensions of all rooms related to the job. Estimate distances for cable runs.

- Turn on the sound-reinforcement system to see if it functions okay by itself (no hum, for example). Turn the lighting on at various levels with the sound system on. Listen for buzzes. Try to correct any problem so that you don't document bad P.A. sound on your tape.

- Check AC power on stage with a circuit checker. Are grounded outlets actually grounded? Is there low resistance to ground? Are the outlets correct polarity? There should be a substantial voltage between hot and ground, and no voltage between neutral and ground.

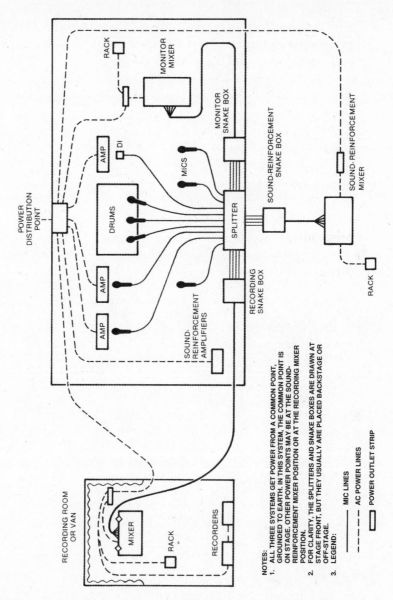

Figure 16.9 A typical layout for an on-location recording of a live concert.

- Determine locations for any audience/ambience mics. Keep them away from air-conditioning ducts and noisy machinery.
- Plan your cable runs from stage to control room.

375

- If you plan to hang mic cables, feel the supports for vibration. You may need microphone shock mounts. If there's a breeze in the room, plan on taking windscreens.

- Find a source of power for the remote truck that can handle the truck's power requirements. Find out whether you need a union electrician or stagehand to make those connections.

- Find the circuit breakers for your power source and label them. Stay away from circuits supplying heavy machinery or old cash registers. Use an assistant to see if any devices are on your circuit. Ask the custodian not to lock the circuit-breaker box the day of the recording.

- Make a file on each recording venue including the dimensions and the location of the circuit breakers.

- Determine where the control room will be. Find out what surrounds it—any noisy machinery?

- Visit the site when a crowd is there to see where there may be traffic problems.

- You might want to record the ambient noise with a portable recorder and play it back at home. This makes the ambient noise much more audible.

- If the AC power is noisy, you might need a power isolation transformer with an electrostatic shield. Use a line voltage regulator if the AC line voltage varies widely.

After doing the site survey, draw a complete system block diagram including all cables and connectors. Use this to generate an equipment list. Keep a file of system block diagrams for various recording venues.

Setting Up

The preparation is finished. It's time to get set up.

The Monitors

To optimize monitoring, first find a quiet location. Carry speakers and headphones with you. Set up the monitor speakers close to you—a near-field arrangement—to avoid hearing early reflections. Place absorbent acoustic foam (such as Sonex) on the wall behind the speakers.

While you're setting up the control room, play a familiar tape over the monitor system. This helps your ears adapt to unfamiliar surroundings.

Make a mono/stereo switch that lets you hear mono out of both speakers.

The Mixing Console

The recording system for a live recording can be set up efficiently, if time allows, by following this procedure:

1. Turn up the monitor system and verify that it is clean.

2. Plug in one mic at a time and monitor it to check for hums and buzzes. Troubleshooting is easier if you listen to each mic as you connect it, rather than plugging them all in and trying to find a hum or buzz.

3. Check and clean up one system at a time: first the sound-reinforcement system, then the stage-monitor system, then the recording system, and so on. Again, this makes troubleshooting easier because you have only one system to troubleshoot.

4. Use as many designation strips as you need for complex consoles. Label the input faders bottom and top. Also label the monitor-mix pots and the meters.

5. Monitor the reverberation returns and check for a clean signal.

6. Make a short test recording and listen to the playback.

7. Verify that left and right channels are correct, and that the pan-pot action is not reversed audibly.

8. If you're recording an orchestra with an overall stereo microphone plus spot mics, pan the images of the spot mics to coincide with those of the main stereo mic.

9. Do a preliminary pan-pot setup. Panning similar instruments to different locations helps you identify them. While panning instruments, you can create a unique stereo image, or create the performers' point of view, or create the audience's point of view. Typically, rock drums are panned for the player's perspective; jazz drums are often panned for the audience perspective.

Doing the Mix

If you're mixing live during the performance, first set the master faders and input faders to design center, then set the gain trims for a rough mix, and then fine-tune the mix with the faders. If you're recording to multitrack, first set the faders to design center and then set the gain trims for the desired record level (usually around 0 VU).

Take notes on gain-trim settings for particular mics and instruments. Then, in future sessions, you can preset the trims to these settings.

Before you start mixing, it's very important to have a preconceived notion of what you want to hear. Consider production style, stereo, sense of distance, amount of reverb, spectral balance, and so on. Hear it in your head. Compare what you hear in your head to what you monitor. Figure out what the difference is and make an adjustment.

Next, work on equalization, stereo panning, and effects. Do equalization cut as well as boost. Boosting equalization reduces headroom; cutting doesn't.

You can get a good mix by following this procedure:

1. Take your hands off the console. For some reason, you hear a lot better. It helps you relax and listen critically.

2. Listen. If you don't like something, figure out specifically what you don't like, and what you need to do to change it.

3. Make an intentional adjustment. Move the knob until you can hear a change.

4. Go back to Step 1.

Don't have "twiddle-itis." Usually the mix is untouched—you just make little finesse adjustments. You might bring out a solo and then pull the fader back down after the solo. If you make a temporary adjustment up, later make a complementary adjustment down.

Avoid drastic changes—make changes slowly and imperceptibly. Live-music mixing requires slow, elegant, fluid movements. By contrast, studio mixdowns use quick fader movements, often to premarked positions.

In a live recording, never turn off a mic completely unless you know positively that it's not going to be used. Otherwise, you invariably miss cues. This is a different procedure from studio mixdowns, where you mute silent portions of tracks to reduce noise.

While mixing, monitor frequently in mono to judge the singer/ensemble balance or soloist/ensemble balance.

To test your mix, occasionally play the monitors very quietly, and see if you can still hear everything.

Miscellaneous Tips

Here are some helpful hints for successful on-location recordings:

- Hook up and use unfamiliar equipment before going on the road. Don't experiment on the job!

- Arrive several hours ahead of time for setup. Expect failures—there's always something going wrong, something unexpected. Allow 50 percent more time for troubleshooting than you think you'll need. Have backup plans if equipment fails. Leave as little to chance as possible. Consider recording with redundant (double) systems so you have a backup if one fails.

- Learn the names of your crew members, and be friendly. These people can be your assets or your enemies. Think before you comment to them!

- Don't be caught without the little things, like spare tape reels, spare cables, hub adapters, pencil and paper, and electrical 3-to-2 adapters.

- Bring a tool kit with screwdrivers, pliers, soldering iron, connectors, adapters, cables, 9-volt batteries, guitar cords, guitar strings, AC-outlet checkers, fuses, a pocket radio to listen for interference, ferrite beads of various sizes for RFI suppression, canned air to shoot out dirt, cotton swabs and pipe cleaners, and Cramoline Red from Cague Labs to remove oxide from connectors.

- Set recording levels before the concert during the sound check. It's better to set the levels a little too low than too high because during mixdown you can reduce noise but not distortion.

- You are likely to find dbx noise reduction a great help in live recording. In addition to reducing tape hiss, it compresses the signal going on tape so that the level variations are less extreme. You're less likely to saturate the tape during loud peaks.

- If a concert will be longer than the running time of a reel of tape, switch reels at intermissions. Another method is to feed two identical tape machines the same signal in parallel. Record on one machine. As the reel of tape nears the end, start recording on the second machine so that none of the performance is lost. Edit the two tapes together back in the studio.

- Walkie-talkies are okay for preshow use, but don't use them during the performance because they can cause RF interference. Assistants can relay messages to and from the stage crew while you're mixing.

- During short set changes, use a closed-circuit TV system to show what set changes and mic-layout changes are coming up next; transmit this information to the monitor mixer and sound-reinforcement mixer.

- Don't unplug mics plugged into phantom power because this makes a popping noise in the sound-reinforcement system.

- After the gig, note equipment failures and fix broken equipment as soon as possible.

- Don't put tapes through airport X-ray machines because the transformer in these machines is not always well shielded. Ask for the tapes to be inspected by hand.

- Hand-carry your mics on airplanes. Arrange to load and unload your own freight containers, rather than trusting them to airline freight loaders. Expect delays here and at security checkpoints.

- Get a public liability insurance policy to protect yourself against lawsuits.

- In general, plan everything in advance so you can relax at the gig and have fun!

Most of the information in the second half of this chapter (starting with Power and Grounding Practice) was derived from two workshops presented at the 79th convention of the Audio Engineering Society in October, 1985. These workshops were titled "On the Repeal of Murphy's Law—Interfacing Problem Solving, Planning, and General Efficiency On-Location," given by Paul Blakemore, Neil Muncy, and Skip Pizzi; and "Popular Music Recording Techniques," given by Paul Blakemore, Dave Moulton, Neil Muncy, Skip Pizzi, and Curt Wittig.

ON-LOCATION RECORDING OF CLASSICAL MUSIC

Perhaps your civic orchestra or high school band is giving a concert, and you would like to make a professional recording. Or maybe there's an organist or string quartet playing at the local college, and they want you to record them.

This chapter explains how to make professional-quality recordings of these ensembles. It describes the necessary equipment, microphone techniques, and session procedures.

Incidentally, recording classical-music ensembles is a great way for the beginning recording engineer to gain experience. With just two microphones and a 2-track recorder, much can be learned about acoustics, microphone placement, level setting, and editing—all essential skills in the studio.

Equipment

You must have the following equipment for on-location classical-music recording:

- 2-track tape deck
- Microphones
- Cables
- Mic-stand adapters
- Mic stands
- Headphones
- Editing hardware

Optional equipment includes a noise-reduction unit and a mixer.

The Tape Deck

A good cassette recorder with metal or chromium tape can be used for live recording, but for highest quality, a 2-track open-reel tape deck or DAT recorder is preferred. Open-reel recorders have more high-frequency *headroom* than cassette decks. That is, open-reel units record high-frequency peaks with flatter response and lower distortion. Also, with open-reel machines, you can edit the tape to remove noises and pauses between musical selections. The DAT recorder offers even better sound quality, but the tape cannot be edited unless you copy from one DAT recorder to another, or edit the tape with a digital audio workstation.

A half-track open-reel tape machine is preferable to a quarter-track unit because half-track provides a better S/N and less severe drop-outs, all else being equal. Furthermore, you can record in only one direction if you plan to edit the tape later on, so half the tape width is wasted with the quarter-track format. (Tape formats are explained in Chapter 9.)

Microphones

Next on your list of equipment are quality microphones. You need two or three of the same model number. Good microphones are essential because the microphones—and their placement—determine the sound of your recording. You should spend at least $200 to $400 per microphone, or rent some good ones, for professional-quality sound.

For classical-music recording, the preferred microphones are condenser types with a wide, flat frequency response and very low self-noise (less than 21 db equivalent SPL, A-weighted). (Self-noise is explained in Chapter 6.)

These microphones are available with an omnidirectional or unidirectional pickup pattern. An omnidirectional microphone is equally sensitive to sounds arriving from any direction, so it helps to add liveness (reverberation) to a recording made in an acoustically dead hall. Omnidirectional condenser microphones have excellent low-frequency response, so they are a good choice for recording pipe organ or bass drum.

A unidirectional microphone (such as a cardioid) is most sensitive to sounds approaching the front of the microphone, and partly rejects sounds approaching the sides and rear. It helps reduce excessive reverberation in the recording. You need a pair of unidirectional mics if you want to do coincident or near coincident stereo miking (see Chapter 7).

Stands versus Hanging

You can mount the microphones on stands or hang them from the ceiling with nylon fishing line. Stands are much easier to set up, but are more visually distracting at live concerts. Stands are more suitable for recording rehearsals or sessions with no audience present. You might want to put the stands on sponges or carpet squares to reduce rumble.

The mic stands should have a tripod folding base, and should extend at least 14 feet high. You can purchase "baby booms" to extend the height of regular mic stands. Many camera stores have telescoping photographic light stands that are lightweight and compact.

A useful accessory is a *stereo bar* or *stereo microphone adapter*. This device mounts two microphones on a single stand for stereo recording.

Hiding Microphones

In some live concerts—especially those that are videotaped—the microphones must not be seen. You might be able to hang some miniature condenser microphones, or place boundary microphones on the stage floor. If the musicial ensemble is large (an orchestra, for example), and you lay the mics on the stage floor, this placement usually overemphasizes the front row of the ensemble and results in a muffled sound. If the ensemble is small (a string quartet, for example), floor placement can work very well. You also can mount boundary mics on the ceiling or on the front edge of a balcony. These placements tend to sound too distant, but they may be your only option.

Monitors

For monitoring, you can use either high-quality loudspeakers or headphones. The headphones should be closed-cup, circumaural (around the ear) types to block out the sound of the musicians. You want to hear only what's being recorded. Of course, the headphones should have a wide-range, smooth response for accurate monitoring.

You might want to set up monitor loudspeakers in a control room separate from the concert hall. Place a pair of near-field monitor speakers about 3 feet apart and 3 feet from you. An alternative is to use high-end consumer or professional loudspeakers placed several feet from the walls to weaken early reflections. You could add absorptive material such as Sonex foam to the walls behind and to the side of the speakers. For the best stereo imaging, sit exactly between the speakers, and as far from them as they are spaced apart.

Mic Extension Cables

You have to sit far from the musicians to clearly monitor what you're recording. To do that, you need a pair of 50-foot microphone extension cables. Longer extensions are needed if the mics are hung from the ceiling, or if you want to monitor in a separate room.

Recording Tape

Buy the best high-output, low-noise tape you can afford (as recommended by the recorder manufacturer). An important tape spec is thickness, which is measured in mils (thousandths of an inch). A tape thickness of 1.5 mil is preferred because it reduces print-through (the transfer of a magnetic signal from one layer of tape to the next, causing an echo or pre-echo). Don't use tape under 1 mil thick—unless needed for long programs— because the tape can stretch easily and is very prone to print-through.

You can plan how much tape you need based on the recording time and tape thickness. Use the following list as a guide for the lengths of time it takes to record on the tape in one direction at $7\frac{1}{2}$ ips:

- A 7-inch reel of 1.5 mil tape (1,200 feet) runs 30 minutes.

- A $10\frac{1}{2}$-inch reel of 1.5 mil tape (2,400 feet) runs 60 minutes.

- A 7-inch reel of 1 mil tape (1,800 feet) runs 45 minutes.

- A 10½-inch reel of 1 mil tape (3,600 feet) runs 90 minutes.

Halve all these times if the tape speed is 15 ips.

You can record at 7½ ips to conserve tape, or record at 15 ips for cleanest sound and greatest headroom. For professional-quality sound, 15 ips is recommended.

A single DAT cassette runs for 2 hours nonstop, making it an ideal medium for recording live concerts.

Noise Reduction

Noise reduction is especially important in recording classical music because it often has soft passages and silences. You may want to use a noise-reduction system—such as Dolby or dbx—to reduce analog tape hiss by 10 to 30 db. Some open-reel recorders have noise reduction built in.

Mixer

If you use a separate noise-reduction unit, you also need a small stereo microphone mixer to boost the microphones' signal level up to the line level required by the noise-reduction system. A mixer is necessary also when you want to record more than one source—an orchestra and a choir, for instance, or a band and a soloist. You might put a pair of microphones on the orchestra and another pair on the choir. The mixer blends the signals of all four mics into a composite stereo signal, and lets you control the balance (relative loudness) among microphones. You also need a mixer if you want to use *spot microphones* (*accent microphones*) placed close to each orchestra section or soloist.

Other miscellaneous equipment you might need includes a power extension cord, an outlet strip, spare mic cables, leader tape, an editing block, splicing tape, a grease pencil, a stop watch, pencil and paper, and duct tape or vinyl mats to keep cables in place.

Stereo Microphone Techniques

As a starting point, place two or three mics several feet in front of the group, raised high (see Figure 17.1). The microphone placement controls the acoustic perspective or sense of distance from the ensemble, the balance among instruments, and the stereo imaging.

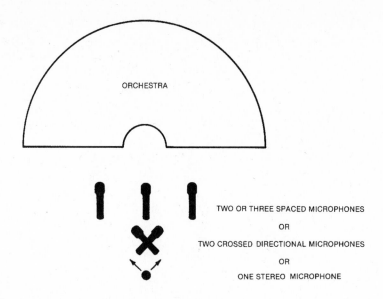

ORCHESTRA

TWO OR THREE SPACED MICROPHONES

OR

TWO CROSSED DIRECTIONAL MICROPHONES

OR

ONE STEREO MICROPHONE

(A) Top view.

(B) Side view.

Figure 17.1 Typical microphone placement for on-location recording of a classical-music ensemble.

Recall from Chapter 7 that there are three microphone techniques commonly used for stereo recording: coincident-pair, near coincident-pair, and spaced-pair.

To review, the coincident-pair technique uses two directional microphones angled apart with their grilles nearly touching and their diaphragms aligned vertically. The near coincident-pair technique uses two directional mics angled apart and spaced a few inches apart horizontally. The spaced-pair technique uses two or three matched microphones of any pattern aiming straight ahead toward the ensemble and spaced several feet apart horizontally.

Recall from Chapter 6 that boundary microphones can be mounted on clear plastic panels 2 feet square. You can space these panels apart for spaced-pair stereo, or place them with one edge touching to form a V. Aim the point of the V at the ensemble. This near coincident-pair arrangement provides excellent stereo imaging. Also available is a stereo boundary microphone that is smaller than the two panels, and provides excellent stereo imaging, extended low-frequency response, and mono-compatibilty.

Preparing for the Session

Once you have the equipment, you are ready to go on location. First, ask the musical director what groups and soloists will be playing, where they will be located, and how long the program is.

If possible, plan to record in a venue with good acoustics. There should be adequate reverberation time for the music being performed. This is very important, because it can make the difference between an amateur-sounding recording and a commercial-sounding one. Try to record in an auditorium or spacious church rather than in a band room or gymnasium. If you're forced to record in a hall that is relatively dead, you might want to add artificial reverberation.

Next, get all your equipment ready. Demagnetize the tape heads, tape guides, and capstan. Clean these components as well as the pinch roller. Check all cables and equipment for proper operation.

Keep your equipment inside your home or studio until you are ready to leave. Tape decks left outside in a cold car may become sluggish if the lubricant stiffens, and batteries may lose some voltage.

Session Setup

Allow an extra hour or so for setup and for fixing broken cables or other unforeseen irritations. There's always something unexpected in any new recording situation.

When you first arrive at the recording venue, locate some AC power outlets where you want to set up. Check that these outlets are "live." If not, ask the custodian to turn on the appropriate circuit breaker. Always check in with union technicians if the venue is a union one.

Find a table or folding chairs on which to set your equipment. Plug into the AC outlets and let your equipment warm up. Leave a few turns of AC cord near the outlet, and tape down the cord so that it isn't pulled out accidentally.

Then take out your microphones and place them in the desired stereo miking arrangement. As an example, suppose you are recording an orchestra rehearsal with two crossed cardioids on a stereo bar (the near-coincident method). Screw the stereo bar onto a mic stand, and mount two cardioid microphones on the stereo bar. For starters, angle them 110 degrees apart and space them 7 inches apart horizontally. Aim them down so that they point at the orchestra when raised.

You may want to mount the microphones in shock mounts or put the stands on sponges or carpet to isolate the mics from floor vibration.

As a starting position, place the mic stand behind the conductor's podium, about 12 feet in front of the front-row musicians. Connect mic cables and mic extension cords. Raise the microphones about 14 feet off the floor. This prevents overly loud pickup of the front row relative to the back row of the orchestra.

Leave some extra turns of mic cable at the base of each stand so you can reposition the stands. This slack also allows for people pulling on the cables accidentally. Try to route the mic cables where they won't be stepped on, or cover them with mats.

Make connections in one of the following ways:

- If you are using 2 mics, and your tape deck has high-quality mic preamps, plug the mics directly into your tape deck.

- If you are using 2 mics and a stand-alone noise-reduction unit, plug the mics into a mixer to boost the mic signals up to line level, then run that line-level signal into the noise-reduction unit connected to the recorder line inputs.

- If you're using multiple mics and a mixer without noise reduction, plug the mixer outputs into the recorder line inputs.

Now put on your headphones, turn up the recording-level controls, and monitor the signal. When the orchestra starts to play, set the recording levels to peak around 0 VU.

Microphone Placement

Nothing has more effect on the production style of a classical-music recording than microphone placement. Miking distance, stereo positioning, and spot miking all influence the recorded sound character.

Distance

The microphones must be placed closer to the musicians than a good live listening position would be. If you place the mics out in the audience where the live sound is good, the recording probably will sound muddy and distant when played over speakers. That is because the recorded reverberation is condensed into the space between the playback speakers, along with the direct sound of the orchestra. Close miking (5 to 20 feet from the front row) compensates for this effect by increasing the ratio of direct sound to reverberant sound.

The closer the mics are to the orchestra, the closer it sounds in the recording. If the instruments sound too close, too edgy, too detailed—or if the recording lacks hall ambience—the mics are too close to the ensemble. Move the mic stand 1 or 2 feet farther from the orchestra and listen again.

If the orchestra sounds too distant, muddy, or reverberant, the mics are too far from the ensemble. Move the mic stand a little closer to the musicians and listen again.

Eventually you'll find a spot where the direct sound of the orchestra is in a pleasing balance with the ambience of the concert hall. Then the reproduced orchestra will sound neither too close nor too far.

Stereo-Spread Control

Now concentrate on the stereo spread. If the spread heard over headphones is too narrow, that means the mics are angled or spaced too close together. Increase the angle or spacing between mics until localization is accurate. Increasing the angle betweeen mics makes the instruments sound farther away; increasing the spacing does not, but may make the images less focused.

If the instruments that are slightly off-center are heard far-left or far-right in your headphones, your mics are angled or spaced too far apart. Move them closer together until localization is accurate.

You localize sounds differently with headphones than with speakers. For this reason, coincident-pair recordings have less stereo spread over headphones than over loudspeakers. Take this into account when monitoring.

You can test the stereo localization accuracy of your chosen stereo miking method. If you have time, record yourself speaking from various positions on stage while announcing your position: far-left, half-left, center, half-right, and far-right. Listen to the monitor system to check whether the image of your voice is reproduced in corresponding positions. Generally, the far-left and far-right positions should be reproduced at the left and right loudspeakers, respectively.

Soloist Pickup and Spot Microphones

Sometimes a soloist plays in front of the orchestra. You have to capture a tasteful balance between the soloist and the ensemble. That is, your mics should be placed so that the relative loudness of the soloist and the accompaniment is musically appropriate. If the soloist is too loud relative to the orchestra (as monitored), raise the mics. If the soloist is too quiet, lower the mics. You may want to add a spot mic about 3 feet from the soloist and mix it with the other microphones.

Many recording companies prefer to use multiple microphones and multitrack techniques when recording classical music. Such methods provide extra control of balance and definition, and are necessary in many situations. If you use spot or accent mics on various instruments or instrumental sections, mix them at a low level relative to the main pair—just loud enough to add definition, but not loud enough to destroy depth. Operate the spot-mic faders subtly or leave them untouched. Otherwise, the close-miked instruments may "jump forward" when the fader is brought up, and then "fall back in" when the fader is brought down.

Recording

Now that the mics are positioned properly, you're ready to record. At a live concert, you might want to set your recording levels to read about –10 VU with the opening applause. This procedure should result in approximately correct recording levels when the musicians start playing. Or set the record-level controls where they were at previous sessions.

Start recording a few seconds before the music starts. Once the recording is in progress, let the recording-level meters peak at +3 VU on the loudest peaks (–3 db maximum for a DAT recorder). Leave the recording level alone as much as possible. If you must adjust the level, do so slowly and try to follow the dynamics of the music.

If there is applause at the end of a musical piece, you can fade it out over 3 to 5 seconds by carefully turning down the recording-level controls or the mixer master volume control. Or leave it alone for a later fade-out.

At the intermission, fast-forward the tape onto the take-up reel so it is stored tail out. This reduces print-through. Label the tape reel and its box.

Thread on your next reel of tape and record the second half of the concert. After the concert, pack the mics away first; otherwise, they might be stolen or damaged.

Editing

Once you have your tapes home, you may want to edit them to make a tight presentation. Using a splicing block and a single-edge razor blade, cut out the tape between musical selections and replace it with about 4 seconds of leader tape (see Chapter 9).

Instead of using leader tape, you may want to insert actual magnetic tape, recorded with "room sound," especially between movements of a symphony. To record room sound, record some silence in the concert hall before or after the session. Set the record-level controls where they were set to record the orchestra.

When editing the tape, mark and cut the tape just before the beginning of each piece, and just after the reverberant tail fades out at the end of each piece. Typically, a yellow grease pencil or china marker is used to mark edit points.

You may want to add EQ, reverb, and other effects to the recording to make the final master.

If you plan to send your tapes to a cassette-duplication company, make up two reels—one for Side 1 of the record, one for Side 2. Try to keep both sides approximately equal in length. Splice on about 30 seconds of leader at the beginning and end of each reel.

Label each reel and store the tape tail out. Time each reel with a stop watch from the start of the first song to the end of the last song, including the leader between selections. Put the timing and record-label information in the tape boxes.

Recording classical music can be as much a thrill as recording popular music, but the right equipment is essential. You need to know about stereo mic techniques and mic placement. You also need to understand session preparation and setup, recording, and editing. After following the procedures with care, you'll have your finished product—a realistic, professional recording of a classical-music ensemble.

18

JUDGING SOUND QUALITY

Seat an engineer behind a mixing console and ask him or her to do a mix. It sounds great. Then seat another engineer behind the same console and again ask for a mix. It sounds terrible. What happened?

The difference lies mainly in their ears—their critical listening ability. Some engineers have a clear idea of what they want to hear and how to get it. Some haven't acquired the essential ability to recognize good sound. By knowing what to listen for, you can improve your artistic judgments during recording and mixdown. You are able to hear errors in microphone placement, equalization, and so on, and correct them.

To train your hearing, try to analyze recorded sound into its components—frequency response, noise, reverberation—and concentrate on each one in turn. It's easier to hear sonic flaws if you focus on a single aspect of sound reproduction at a time. This chapter is a guide to help you do this.

Classical versus Popular Recording

Classical and popular music have different standards of "good sound." One goal in recording classical music (and often folk music or jazz) is to accurately reproduce the live performance. This is a worthy aim because the sound of an orchestra in a good hall can be quite beautiful. The music was composed and the instruments were designed to sound best when heard live in the concert hall. The recording engineer, out of respect for the music, should always try to translate that sound to tape with as little technical intrusion as possible.

By contrast, the accurate translation of sound to tape is not always the goal in recording popular music. Although the aim may be to reproduce the original sound, the producer or engineer may also want to play with that sound to create a new sonic experience, or to do some of both.

In fact, the artistic manipulation of sounds through studio techniques has become an end in itself. Apparently the philosophy is this: Creating an interesting new sound is as valid a goal as re-creating the original sound. There are two games to play, each with its own measures of success.

If the aim of a recording is realism or accurate reproduction, the recording is successful when it matches the live performance heard in the best seat in the concert hall. The sound of musical instruments is the standard by which such recordings are judged.

When the goal is to enhance the sound or produce special effects (as in most pop-music recordings), the desired sonic effect is less defined. The live sound of a pop group could be a reference, but pop-music recordings generally sound better than live performances. Recorded vocals are clearer and less harsh, the bass is cleaner and tighter, and so on. The sound of pop music reproduced over speakers has developed its own standards of quality apart from accurate reproduction.

Good Sound in a Pop-Music Recording

Currently, a good-sounding pop recording might be described as

- Well-mixed
- Wide-range
- Tonally balanced
- Clean
- Clear
- Smooth
- Spacious

It also has

- Presence
- Sharp transients
- Tight bass and drums
- Wide and detailed stereo imaging
- Wide but controlled dynamic range
- Interesting sounds
- Suitable production

The next sections explore each one of these qualities in detail so that you know what to listen for. Assume that the monitor system is accurate, so that any colorations heard are in the recording and not in the monitors.

A Good Mix

In a good mix, the loudness of instruments and vocals are in a pleasing balance with each other. Everything can be clearly heard, yet nothing is obtrusive. The most important instruments or voices are loudest; less important parts are in the background.

A successful mix goes unnoticed. When all the tracks are balanced correctly, nothing sticks out and nothing is hidden. Of course, there's a wide latitude for musical interpretation and personal taste in making a mix. Dance mixes, for example, can be very severe sonically.

Sometimes you don't want everything to be clearly heard. In rare occasions you may want to mix in certain tracks very subtly for a subconscious effect.

The mix must be appropriate for the style of music. For example, a mix that's right for rock music usually won't work for country music. A rock mix typically has the drums way up front and the vocals only slightly louder than the accompaniment. In contrast, a country mix might have the vocals loudest, with the drums used just as "seasoning" in the background. This distinction is lessening as country music is approaching a pop sound.

Level changes during the mix should be subtle, or should make sense. Otherwise, instruments jump out for a solo and fall back in afterwards. Move faders slowly, or set them to preset positions during pauses in the music. Nothing sounds more amateurish than a solo that starts too quietly and then comes up as it plays. You can hear the engineer working the fader.

Wide Range

Wide range means extended low-frequency and high-frequency response. Cymbals should sound crisp and distinct, but not sizzly or harsh; kick drum and bass should sound deep, but not overwhelming or muddy. Wide-range sound results from using high-quality microphones and recorders, good tape, high tape speed, and clean tape heads.

Tonal Balance

The overall tonal balance of a recording should be neither bassy nor trebley. That is, the perceived spectrum should not emphasize low frequencies or high frequencies. Low bass, midbass, midrange, upper midrange, and highs should be heard in equal proportions (see Figure 18.1). Emphasis of any one frequency band over the other eventually causes listening fatigue. Dance club mixes, however, are heavy on the bass end to get the crowd moving.

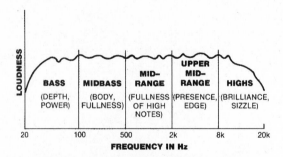

NOTE: The subjective loudness of various frequency bands should be about equal. (The frequency divisions shown here are somewhat arbitrary.

Figure 18.1 Loudness versus frequency of a good-sounding pop recording.

Recorded tonal balance is inversely related to the frequency response of the studio's monitor system. If the monitors have an extreme high-frequency roll off, the engineer compensates by boosting highs in the recording to make the monitors sound right. The result is a bright recording.

Before doing a mix, it helps to play over the monitors some records whose sound you admire. This helps you become accustomed to a commercial spectral balance. After your mix is recorded, play it back and alternately switch between your mix and a commercial record. This comparison indicates how well you matched a commercial spectral balance. Of course, you may not care to duplicate what others are doing.

In pop-music recordings, the tonal balance or timbre of individual instruments does not necessarily have to be natural. Still, many listeners want to hear a realistic timbre from acoustic instruments, such as the guitar, flute, sax, or piano. The reproduced timbre depends on microphone frequency response, microphone placement, the musical instruments themselves, and equalization.

Clean Sound

Clean means free of noise and distortion. Tape hiss, hum, and distortion are inaudible in a good recording. Distortion in this case means distortion added by the recording process, not distortion already present in the sound of electric guitar amps or Leslie speakers. Clean also means not muddy—free of low-frequency overhang and leakage.

A clean mix is one that is uncluttered, free of excess instrumentation. This is achieved by arranging the music so that similar parts don't overlap, and not too many instruments play at once in the same frequency range. Usually, the fewer the instruments, the cleaner the sound. Too many overdubs can muddy the mix.

Clarity

In a clear-sounding recording, instruments do not crowd or mask each other's sound. They are separate and distinct, and blend well. As with a clean sound, clarity arises when instrumentation is sparse, or when instruments occupy different areas of the frequency spectrum. For example, low frequencies are provided by the bass, midbass might be emphasized by the keyboards, upper midrange may be provided by lead guitar, and highs filled in by the cymbals.

In addition, a clear recording has adequate reproduction of each instrument's harmonics. That is, the high-frequency response is not rolled off.

Smoothness

Smooth means easy on the ears, not harsh, uncolored. Sibilant sounds are clear but not piercing. A smooth, effortless sound allows relaxation; a strained or irritating sound causes muscle tension in the ears or body.

Smoothness is a lack of sharp peaks or dips in the frequency response, as well as a lack of excessive boost in the midrange or upper midrange.

Presence

Presence is the apparent sense of closeness of the instruments—a feeling that they are present in the listening room. Synonyms are clarity, detail, and punch.

Presence is achieved by close miking, overdubbing, and using microphones with a presence peak or emphasis around 5 kHz. Using less reverb and effects can help. Upper-midrange boost helps too. Most instruments have a frequency range which, if boosted, makes the instrument stand out more clearly or become better defined. Presence sometimes conflicts with smoothness because presence often involves an upper-midrange boost and a smooth sound is free of such emphasis. You have to find a tasteful compromise between the two.

Spaciousness

When the sound is "spacious" or "airy," there is a sense of air around the instruments. Without air or ambience, instruments sound as if they are isolated in stuffed closets. Spaciousness is achieved by adding artificial reverberation to the recording, or by more distant miking.

Sharp Transients

The attack of cymbals and drums generally should be sharp and clear. A bass guitar and piano may or may not require sharp attacks, depending on the song.

Tight Bass and Drums

The kick drum and bass guitar should "lock" together so that they sound like a single instrument—a bass with a percussive attack. The drummer and bassist should work out their parts together so as to hit accents simultaneously, if this is desired.

To further tighten the sound, the kick drum is damped and the bass is recorded direct. They are equalized for presence and clarity. Rap music, however, has its own sound—the kick drum usually is undamped and boomy, sometimes with short reverb added.

Wide and Detailed Stereo Imaging

Stereo means more than just left and right. Usually, tracks should be panned to many points across the stereo stage between the playback loudspeakers. Some instruments should be hard-left or hard-right; some should be in the center; others should be half-left or half-right. Try to achieve a stereo stage that is well balanced between left and right (see Figure 18.2). Instruments occupying the same frequency range might be panned to opposite sides of center.

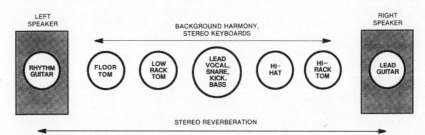

Figure 18.2 An example of image placement between speakers.

You may want some tracks to be unlocalized. Backup choruses and strings should be spread out rather than appearing as point sources. Stereo keyboard sounds can wander between speakers. A lead guitar solo can have a fat, spacious sound.

There should also be some front-to-back depth. Some instruments should sound close or up front; others should sound farther away.

If stereo imaging is intended to be realistic (for a jazz combo, for example), the reproduced ensemble should simulate the spatial layout of the live ensemble. If you're sitting in an audience listening to a jazz quartet, you might hear drums on the left, piano on the right, bass in the middle, and sax slightly right. The drums and piano are not point sources, but are somewhat spread out. If spatial realism is the goal, you should hear the same ensemble layout between your speakers. Often the piano and drums are spread all the way between speakers—an interesting effect, but unrealistic.

Pan-potted mono tracks often sound artificial because each instrument sounds isolated in its own little space. It helps if there is some stereo reverberation surrounding the instruments to "glue" them together.

Often, TV mixes are heard in mono. Sound sources are panned to 3 and 9 o'clock, not hard-right and hard-left. Hard-panned signals sound weak in mono relative to center-panned signals.

Wide but Controlled Dynamic Range

Dynamic range is the range of volume levels from softest to loudest. A recording with a wide dynamic range becomes noticeably louder and softer, adding excitement to the music. This is achieved by avoiding excessive compression (automatic volume control). An overly compressed recording sounds squashed—crescendos and quiet interludes lose their impact.

Some compression or gain-riding is needed for vocals because their dynamic range exceeds that of the instrumental backup. A vocalist may sing too loudly and blast the listener, or sing too softly and become buried in the mix. A compressor can even out these extreme level variations, keeping the vocals at a constant loudness. Bass guitar also can benefit from compression.

Interesting Sounds

The recorded sound may be too flat or neutral—lacking character or color. In contrast, a recording with creative production has unique musical instrument sounds, and typically uses special effects. Some of these are equalization, echo, reverberation, doubling, chorus, flanging, compression, and stereo effects.

Making sounds interesting or colorful can conflict with accuracy or fidelity, so effects and equalization should be used with discretion.

Suitable Production

The way a recording sounds should imply the same message as the musical style or lyrics. In other words, the sound should be appropriate for the particular tune being recorded.

For example, some rock music is rough and raw. The sound should be, too. A clean, polished production doesn't always work for high-energy rock and roll. There might even be a lot of leakage or ambience to suggest a garage studio or nightclub environment. The role of the drums is important, so they should be loud in the mix. The toms should ring, if that is what's desired.

New Age, disco, rhythm and blues, contemporary Christian, or middle-of-the-road music often is slickly produced. The sound is usually tight, smooth, and spacious. Country music is about stories or feelings, so the bass and vocals are emphasized for warmth and emotion. Acoustic guitars and drums are miked at a respectful distance, giving an airy, natural effect.

Actually, each style of music is not locked into a particular style of production. You tailor the sound to complement the music of each individual tune. Doing this may break some of the so-called rules of good sound, but that's usually okay as long as the song is enhanced by its sonic presentation.

Good Sound in a Classical-Music Recording

As with pop music, classical music should sound clean, wide-range, and tonally balanced. Because classical recordings are meant to sound realistic—like a live performance—they also require good acoustics, a natural balance, tonal accuracy, suitable perspective, and accurate stereo imaging (see Chapter 17).

Good Acoustics

The acoustics of the concert hall or recital hall should be appropriate for the style of music to be performed. Specifically, the reverberation time should be neither too short (dry) nor too long (cavernous). Too short a reverberation time results in a recording without spaciousness or grandeur. Too long a reverberation time blurs notes together, giving a muddy, washed-out effect. Ideal reverberation times are around 1.2 seconds for chamber music or soloists, 1.5 seconds for symphonic works, and 2 seconds for organ recitals. To get a rough idea of the reverb time of a room, clap your hands once, loudly, and count the seconds it takes for the reverb to fade to silence.

A Natural Balance

When a recording is well balanced, the relative loudness of instruments is similar to that heard in an ideal seat in the audience area. For example, violins are not too loud or soft compared to the rest of the orchestra; harmonizing or contrapuntal melody lines are in proportion.

Generally, the instruments are balanced acoustically by the conductor, composer, and musicians, rather than being mixed on a mixing console. There are exceptions; some recording engineers use multimiking for classical music. Certain instruments or sections may be miked individually for added definition or improved balance. Whether or not this is done, the conductor is consulted for proper balances.

Tonal Accuracy

The reproduced timbre or tone quality should match that of live instruments. Fundamentals and harmonics should be reproduced in their original proportion.

Suitable Perspective

Suitable perspective is the sense of distance of the performers from the listener—how far away the stage sounds. Do the performers sound as if they are eight rows in front of you, in your lap, or in another room?

The style of music suggests a suitable perspective. Incisive, rhythmically motivated works (such as Stravinsky's "Rite of Spring") sound best with closer miking; lush romantic pieces (a Bruckner symphony) are best served by more distant miking. The chosen perspective depends on the taste of the producer.

Closely related to perspective is the amount of recorded ambience or reverberation. A good miking distance yields a pleasing balance of direct sound from the orchestra and ambience from the concert hall.

Accurate Imaging

Reproduced instruments should appear in the same relative locations as they were in the live performance. Instruments in the center of the ensemble should be heard in the center between the speakers; instruments at the left or right side of the ensemble should be heard from the left or right speaker. Instruments halfway to one side should be heard halfway off center, and so on. A large ensemble should spread from speaker to speaker, but a quartet or soloist can have a narrower spread.

It's important that you sit equidistant from the speakers when judging stereo imaging; otherwise, the images shift toward the side on which you're sitting. Sit as far from the speakers as they are spaced apart; then the speakers appear to be 60 degrees apart, which is about the same angle an orchestra fills when viewed from the typical ideal seat in the audience (tenth row center, for example).

The reproduced size of an instrument or instrumental section should match its size in real life. Each instrument's location should be as clearly defined as it was heard from the ideal seat in the concert hall.

Reproduced reverberation (concert hall ambience) should either surround the listener, or at least it should spread evenly between the speakers. Extra speakers or add-on ambience enhancers are currently needed to make the recorded ambience surround the listener, although spaced-microphone recordings have some of this effect.

There should be a sense of stage depth, with front-row instruments sounding closer than back-row instruments. Accurate imaging is illustrated in Figure 18.3.

Training Your Hearing

The critical process is easier if you focus on one aspect of sound reproduction at a time. You might concentrate first on the tonal balance—try to pinpoint what frequency ranges are being emphasized or slighted. Next, listen to the mix, the clarity, and so on. Soon you have a lengthy description of the sound quality of your recording.

Developing an analytical ear is a continuing learning process. Train your hearing by listening carefully to recordings—both good and bad. Make a checklist of all the qualities mentioned in this chapter. Compare your own recordings to live instruments, and to commercial recordings.

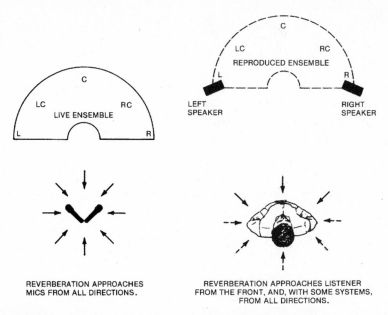

Figure 18.3 With accurate imaging, the sound source location and size are reproduced during playback, as well as the reverberant field.

A pop-music record that excels in all the attributes of good sound is "The Sheffield Track Record" (Sheffield Labs, Lab 20), engineered and produced by Bill Schnee. In effect, it's a course in state-of-the-art sound—required listening for any recording engineer or producer.

Another record with brilliant production is "The Nightfly" by Donald Fagen (Warner Brothers 23696-2), engineered by Roger Nichols, Daniel Lazerus, and Elliot Scheiner, produced by Gary Katz, and mastered by Bob Ludwig. The sound is razor sharp, elegant, and tasteful, and the music just pops out of the speakers.

The following listings are more examples of outstanding rock production, and set high standards:

"I Need Somebody"
Bryan Adams
Producer, Bob Clearmountain

"The Power of Love"
Huey Lewis & The News
Producer, Huey Lewis & The News

"Synchronicity"
The Police
Producer, Hugh Padgham and The Police

"Passion"
Peter Gabriel
Engineer, David Bottrill
Producer, Peter Gabriel

"90125"
Yes
Producer, Trevor Horn

"Dark Side of the Moon"
Pink Floyd
Producer, Alan Parsons

"Thriller"
Michael Jackson
Engineer, Bruce Swedien
Producer, Quincy Jones

"Avalon"
Roxy Music
Engineer, Bob Clearmountain
Producer, Roxy Music

Then there are the incredibly clean recordings of Tom Jung (with DMP records) and George Massenberg. You can learn a lot by emulating these superb recordings, and many others.

Once you're making recordings that are competent technically—clean, natural, and well mixed—the next stage is to produce imaginative sounds. You're in command; you can tailor the mix to sound any way that pleases you or the band you're recording. The supreme achievement is to produce a recording that is a sonic knockout—beautiful, thrilling, and/or overwhelming.

Troubleshooting Bad Sound

Now you know how to recognize good sound, but can you recognize bad sound? Suppose you're monitoring a recording in progress, or listening to a recording you've already made. Something doesn't sound right. How can you pinpoint what's wrong, and how can you fix it?

The remainder of this chapter includes step-by-step procedures to solve audio-related problems. Read down the list of "bad sound" descriptions until you find one matching what you hear. Then try the solutions until your problem disappears. Only the most common symptoms and cures are mentioned; console maintenance is not covered.

This troubleshooting guide is divided into four main sections:

- Bad sound on all recordings (including those from other studios)
- Bad sound on tape playback only (console output sounds all right)
- Bad sound in a pop-music recording
- Bad sound in a classical-music recording

Before you start, check for faulty cables and connectors. Also check all control positions; rotate knobs and flip switches to clean the contacts.

Bad Sound on All Recordings

If you have bad sound on all your recordings, including those from other studios, follow this checklist to find the problem:

- Upgrade your monitor system.
- Adjust tweeter and midrange controls on speakers.
- Adjust the relative gains of tweeter and woofer amplifiers in a biamped system.
- Relocate speakers.
- Improve room acoustics.
- Equalize the monitor system.
- Try different speakers.
- Upgrade the power amp and speaker cables.

Bad Sound on Tape Playback Only

You might have bad sound on your tape playback only, but your console output sounds okay. If your tape playback has a dull sound or drop-outs, follow these steps:

- Check that the oxide side of the tape is against the heads.
- Clean and demagnetize the tape path.
- Try another brand of tape.
- Align tape heads; calibrate the electronics.
- Do maintenance on the tape transport.
- Check and replace tape heads if necessary.

  If your tape playback is plagued with distortion, try the following:

- Reduce the recording level.
- Increase the bias level.
- Use tape that can accept higher recording levels.

  If your tape playback has tape hiss, follow these steps:

- Increase the recording level.
- Use some type of noise reduction, such as Dolby or dbx.
- Use better tape.
- Align the tape recorder.

Bad Sound in a Pop-Music Recording Session

Sometimes you have bad sound in a pop-music recording session.

Muddiness (Leakage)

If the sound is muddy from excessive leakage, try the following:

- Place the microphones closer to their sound sources.
- Spread the instruments farther apart to reduce the level of the leakage.
- Place the instruments closer together to reduce the delay of the leakage.
- Use directional microphones (such as cardioids).
- Overdub the instruments.

- Record the electric instruments direct.

- Use baffles (goboes) between instruments.

- Deaden the room acoustics (add absorptive material, flexible panels, or slot absorbers).

- Filter out frequencies above and below the spectral range of each instrument. Be careful or you'll change the sound of the instrument.

- Turn down the bass amp in the studio.

Muddiness (Excessive Reverberation)

If the sound is muddy due to excessive reverberation, try these steps:

- Reduce the effects-send levels or effects-return levels. Or don't use effects until you figure out what the real problem is.

- Place the microphones closer to their sound sources.

- Use directional microphones (such as cardioids).

- Deaden the room acoustics.

- Filter out frequencies below the fundamental frequency of each instrument.

Muddiness (Lacks Highs)

If your sound is muddy and lacks highs, or has a dull or muffled sound, try the following:

- Use microphones with better high-frequency response, or use condenser mics instead of dynamics.

- Change the microphone placement. Put the microphone in a spot where there are sufficient high frequencies. Keep the high-frequency sources (such as cymbals) on-axis to the microphones.

- Use small-diameter microphones, which generally have a flatter response off-axis.

- Boost the high-frequency equalization.

- Change musical instruments; replace guitar strings; replace drum heads. (Ask the musicians first!)

- When bouncing tracks, record bright-sounding instruments last to reduce generation loss.

- Avoid excessive recording levels with bright-sounding instruments, because the recorder's high-frequency response gradually rolls off as the recording level is increased. This is especially true of cassette recorders.

- Use an enhancer signal processor, but watch out for noise.

- Use a direct box on the electric bass. Have the bassist play percussively or use a pick if the music requires it. When compressing the bass, use a long attack time to allow the note's attack to come through. (Some songs don't require sharp bass attacks—do whatever's right for the song.)

- Damp the kick drum with a pillow or blanket, and mike it next to the center of the head near the beater. Use a wooden beater, if the song and the drummer allow it.

Muddiness (Lacks Clarity)

If your sound is muddy because it lacks clarity, try these steps:

- Consider using fewer instruments in the musical arrangement.

- Equalize instruments differently so that their spectra don't overlap.

- Try less reverberation.

- Using equalizers, boost the presence range of instruments that lack clarity.

Distortion

If you have distortion in a pop-music recording, try the following:

- Switch in the pad built into the microphone (if any).

- Increase input attenuation (reduce input gain), or plug in a pad between the microphone and mic input.

- Readjust gain-staging: set faders and pots to their design centers (shaded areas).

Tonal Imbalance

If you have bad tonal balance—the sound is boomy, dull, or shrill, for example—follow these steps:

- Change musical instruments; change guitar strings; change reeds, and so on.

- Change microphone placement. If the sound is too bassy with a directional microphone, you may be getting proximity effect. Mike farther away or roll off the excess bass.

- Use the 3:1 rule of microphone placement to avoid phase cancellations. When multiple microphones are mixed to the same channel, the distance between microphones should be at least three times the mic-to-source distance.

- Try another microphone. If a cardioid mic's proximity effect is causing a bass boost, try an omnidirectional mic instead.

- If you must place a microphone near a hard reflective surface, try a boundary microphone on the surface to prevent phase cancellations.

- Change the equalization. Avoid excessive boost.

- Use equalizers with a broad bandwidth, rather than a narrow, peaked response.

Lifelessness

If your pop-music recording has a lifeless sound and is unexciting, these steps might help you solve it:

- Work on the live sound of the instruments in the studio to come up with unique effects.

- Add special effects—reverberation, echo, doubling, equalization, etc.

- Use and combine recording equipment in unusual ways.

- Try overdubbing little vocal licks or synthesized sound effects.

  If your sound seems lifeless due to dry or dead acoustics, try these:

- If leakage is not a problem, put microphones far enough from instruments to pick up wall reflections. If you don't like the sound this produces, try the next suggestion.

- Add artificial reverberation or echo to dry tracks. (Not all tracks require reverberation. Also, some songs may need very little reverberation so that they sound intimate.)

- Use omnidirectional microphones.

- Add hard reflective surfaces in the studio, or record in a hard-walled room.

- Allow a little leakage between microphones. Put microphones far enough from instruments to pick up off-mic sounds from other instruments. Don't overdo it, though, or the sound becomes muddy and track separation becomes poor.

Noise (Hiss)

Sometimes your pop music recording has extra noise on it. If your sound has hiss, try these:

- Check for noisy guitar amps or keyboards.
- Switch out the pad built into the microphone (if any).
- Reduce console input attenuation (increase input gain).
- Use a more sensitive microphone.
- Use a quieter microphone (one with low self-noise).
- Increase the sound pressure level at the microphone by miking closer. If you're using PZMs, mount them on a large surface or in a corner.
- Apply any high-frequency boost during recording, rather than during mixdown.
- Use a lowpass filter (high-cut filter).
- As a last resort, use a noise gate.

Noise (Rumble)

If the noise is a low-frequency rumble, follow these steps:

- Reduce air-conditioning noise or shut off the air conditioning temporarily.
- Use a highpass filter (low-cut filter) that is set around 40 to 80 Hz.
- Use microphones with limited low-frequency response.
- If the cause is mechanical vibration traveling up the microphone stand, put the microphone in a shock-mount stand adapter. Or use a microphone that is less susceptible to mechanical vibration, such as an omnidirectional microphone, or a unidirectional microphone with a good internal shock mount.

Noise (Thumps)

If you have thumps in your pop-music recording, try these steps:

- Change the microphone position.
- Change the musical instrument.
- Use a highpass filter set around 40 to 80 Hz.
- If the cause is mechanical vibration traveling up the microphone stand, put the microphone in a shock-mount stand adapter. Or use a microphone that is less susceptible to mechanical vibration, such as an omnidirectional microphone, or a unidirectional microphone with a good internal shock mount.
- Use a microphone with a limited low-frequency response.

Hum

Hum is a subject in itself. See Chapter 5 for causes and cures of hum.

Pop

Pops are explosive breath sounds in a vocalist's microphone. If your pop-music recording has pops, try these solutions:

- Place the microphone above or to the side of the mouth.

- Place a foam windscreen (pop filter) on the microphone.

- Stretch a silk or nylon stocking over a darning hoop, and mount it on a mic stand a few inches from the microphone (or use an equivalent commercial product).

- Place the microphone farther from the vocalist.

- Use a microphone with a built-in pop filter (ball grille).

- Use an omnidirectional microphone, because it is likely to pop less than a directional (cardioid) microphone.

Sibilance

Recall that sibilance is an overemphasis of "s" and "sh" sounds. If you are getting sibilance on your pop-music recording, try these steps:

- Use a de-esser.

- Place the microphone farther from the vocalist.

- Place the microphone toward one side of the vocalist, rather than directly in front.

- Cut equalization in the range from 5 to 10 kHz.

- Change to a duller-sounding microphone.

Bad Mix

If you get a bad mix on your recording, some instruments or voices are too loud or too quiet. To improve a bad mix, try the following:

- Change the mix. (Maybe change the mix engineer!)

- Compress vocals or instruments that occasionally get buried.

- Change the equalization on certain instruments to help them stand out.

- During mixdown, continuously change the mix to highlight certain instruments according to the demands of the music.

Unnatural Dynamics

When your pop-music recording has unnatural dynamics, loud sounds don't get loud enough or soft sounds disappear. If this happens, try these steps:

- Check the tracking of noise-reduction units. For example, a 10 db level increase at the input of the encode unit should appear as a 10 db level increase at the output of the decode unit.

- Use the same type of noise reduction during playback that was used during recording.

- Use less compression or limiting.

- Avoid overall compression.

Isolated Sound

If some of the instruments on your recording sound too isolated, as if they are not in the same room as the others, follow these steps:

- In general, allow a little crosstalk between the left and right channels. If tracks are totally isolated, it's hard to achieve the illusion that all the instruments are playing in the same room at the same time. You need some crosstalk or correlation between channels. Some right-channel information should leak into the left channel, and vice versa.

- Place microphones farther from their sound sources to increase leakage.

- Use omnidirectional microphones to increase leakage.

- Use stereo reverberation or echo.

- Pan effects returns to the channel opposite the channel of the dry sound source.

- Pan extreme left and right tracks slightly toward center.

- Make the effects-send levels more similar for various tracks.

- To give a lead guitar solo a fat, spacious sound, use a stereo chorus. Or send its signal through a delay unit, pan the direct sound hard left, and pan the delayed sound hard right.

Lack of Depth

If the mix lacks depth, try these steps:

- Achieve depth by miking instruments at different distances.

- Use varied amounts of reverberation on each instrument. The higher the ratio of reverberant sound to direct sound, the more distant the track sounds.

Bad Sound in a Classical-Music Recording

Check the following procedures if you have problems recording classical music.

Too Dead

If the sound in your classical recording is too dead—there is not enough ambience or reverberation—try these measures to solve the problem:

- Place the microphones farther from the performers.

- Use omnidirectional microphones.

- Record in a concert hall with better acoustics (longer reverberation time).

- Add artificial reverberation.

Too Close

If the sound is too detailed, too close, or too edgy, follow these steps:

- Place the microphones farther from the performers.

- Place the microphones lower or on the floor (as with a boundary microphone).

- Roll off the high frequencies.

- Use mellow-sounding microphones (many ribbon mics have this quality).

Too Distant

If the sound is distant and there is too much reverberation, these steps might help:

- Place the microphones closer to the performers.
- Use directional microphones (such as cardioids).
- Record in a concert hall that is less live (reverberant).

Stereo Spread Imbalance

If your classical-music recording has a narrow stereo spread, try these steps:

- Angle or space the main microphone pair farther apart.
- If you're doing midside stereo recording, turn up the side output of the stereo microphone.
- Place the main microphone pair closer to the ensemble.

If the sound has excessive stereo spread (or "hole-in-the-middle"), try the following:

- Angle or space the main microphone pair closer together.
- If you're doing midside stereo recording, turn down the side output of the stereo microphone.
- In spaced-pair recording, add a microphone midway between the outer pair, and pan its signal to the center.
- Place the microphones farther from the performers.

Lack of Depth

Try the following to bring more depth into your classical-music recording:

- Use only a single pair of microphones out front. Avoid multimiking.
- If you must use spot mics, keep their level low in the mix.
- Add more artificial reverberation to the distant instruments than to the close instruments.

Bad Balance

If your classical-music recording has bad balance, try the following:

- Place the microphones higher or farther from the performers.

- Ask the conductor or performers to change the instruments' written dynamics. Be tactful!

- Add spot microphones close to instruments or sections needing reinforcement. Mix them in subtly with the main microphones' signals.

Muddy Bass

If your recording has a muddy bass sound, follow these steps:

- Aim the bass drum head at the microphones.

- Put the microphone stands and bass drum stand on resiliant isolation mounts, or place the microphones in shock-mount stand adapters.

- Roll off the low frequencies or use a highpass filter set around 40 to 80 Hz.

- Record in a concert hall with less low-frequency reverberation.

Rumble

Sometimes your classical-music recording picks up rumble from air-conditioning, trucks, and other sources. Try the following to clear this up:

- Check the hall for background rumble problems.

- Temporarily shut off the air-conditioning.

- Use a highpass filter set around 40 to 80 Hz.

- Use microphones with limited low-frequency response.

Distortion

If your classical-music recording has distortion, try the following:

- Switch in the pads built into the microphones (if any).

- Increase the console input attenuation (reduce the input level).

Bad Tonal Balance

Bad tonal balance expresses itself in a sound that is too dull, too bright, or colored. If your recording has this problem, follow these steps:

- Change the microphones. Generally, use flat-response microphones with minimal off-axis coloration.

- Follow the 3:1 rule discussed in Chapter 7.

- If a microphone must be placed near a hard reflective surface, use a boundary microphone to prevent phase cancellations between direct and relected sounds.

- Adjust equalization.

- Place the mics at a reasonable distance from the ensemble (too-close miking sounds shrill).

- Avoid microphone positions that pick up standing waves or room modes. Experiment with small changes in microphone position.

This chapter describes a set of standards for good sound quality in both popular-music and classical-music recordings. These standards are somewhat arbitrary, but the engineer and producer need guidelines to judge the effectiveness of the recording. The next time you hear something you don't like in a recording, the lists in this chapter will help you define the problem and find a solution.

19

MUSIC: WHY YOU RECORD

This book focuses on techniques for recording music, without paying much attention to the music itself. Occasionally, it's wise to remember that music is the main reason for recording!

Music can be exalting, exciting, soothing, sensuous, and fulfilling. As a recording engineer, it's to your advantage to better understand what music is all about.

Music starts as musical ideas or feelings in the mind and heart of its composer. Musical instruments are used to translate these ideas and feelings into sound waves. Somehow, the emotion contained in the music—the message—is coded in the vibrations of air molecules. Those sounds are converted to electricity, and stored magnetically. The composer's message manages to survive the trip through the mixing console and tape machines; then the signal is transfered to disc or tape. Finally, the original sound waves are reproduced in the listening room, and miraculously the original emotion is reproduced in the listener as well.

Of course, not everyone reacts to a piece of music the same way, so the listener may not perceive the composer's intent. Still, it's amazing that anything as intangible as a thought or feeling can be conveyed by tiny magnetic patterns on a cassette tape, or by pits on a compact disc.

Increasing Your Involvement in Music

Sometimes, to get involved in music, you must relax enough to lie back and listen. You have to feel unhurried, to be content to sit between your stereo speakers or wear headphones, and listen with undivided attention. Actively analyze or feel what the musicians are playing.

Music affects people much more when they are already feeling the emotion expressed in the song. For example, hearing "1999" when you're in a party mood, or hearing a composition by Debussy when you're feeling sensuous, is more moving because your feelings resonate with those in the music. When you're falling in love, any music that is meaningful to you is enhanced.

If you identify strongly with a particular song, that tells you something about yourself and your current mood, and the songs that other people identify with tells you something about them. You can understand individuals better by listening to their favorite music.

Different Ways of Listening

There are so many levels on which to listen to music—so many ways to focus attention. Try this. Play one of your favorite records several times while listening for these different aspects:

- Overall mood and rhythm

- Lyrics

- Vocal technique

- Bass line

- Drum fills

- Sound quality

- Technical proficiency of musicians

- Musical arrangement or structure

- Surprises versus predictable patterns

By listening to a piece of music carefully from several perspectives, you get much more out of it than if you just hear it as background. There's a lot going on in any song that usually goes unnoticed. Sometimes you play an old familiar record and listen to the lyrics for the first time. The whole meaning of the song changes for you.

420

Most people react to music on the basic level of mood and rhythmic motivation, but as a recording enthusiast, you hear much more detail because your focus demands sustained critical listening. The same is true of trained musicians focusing on the musical aspects of a performance.

It's all there for anyone to hear, but you must train yourself to hear selectively, to focus attention on a particular level of the multidimensional musical event. For example, instead of just feeling excited while listening to an impressive lead guitar solo, listen to what the guitarist is actually playing. You may hear some amazing things.

Here's one secret of really involving yourself in recorded music: Imagine yourself playing it! For example, if you're a bass player, listen to the bass line in a particular record, and imagine that you're playing the bass line. You'll hear the part as never before. Or respond to the music visually, see it as you do in the movie "Fantasia."

Follow the melody line and see its shape. Hear where it reaches up, strains, relaxes. Hear how one note leads into the next. How does the musical expression change from moment to moment?

There are times you can almost touch music. Some music has a prickly texture (many transients, emphasized high frequencies); some music is soft and sinuous (sine-wave synthesizer notes, soaring vocal harmonies); some music is airy and spacious (much reverberation).

Different Ways of Monitoring

Suppose you are in the control room working on a pop-music mix, and you're aiming for a realistic, natural sound. Listen to the reproduced instruments and try to make them sound as if they are really playing in front of you. That is, instead of trying to make a pleasant mix or a sonically interesting recording, try to control the sound you hear to simulate real instruments—to make them believable.

This situation is similar to that of an artist trying to draw a still life as realistically as possible. The artist compares the drawing to the real object, notes the difference between the two, and then modifies the drawing to reduce the difference.

When you're striving for a natural sound, compare the recorded instrument with your memory of the real thing. How does it sound different? Turn the appropriate knob on the console that reduces the difference.

Alternatively, when you're mixing, imagine you're creating a sonic experience between the monitor speakers, rather than just reproducing instruments. Sometimes you don't want a recording to sound too realistic. If a recording is too accurate, it sounds like musical instruments, rather than just music itself.

This approach contradicts the basic edict of high fidelity—to reproduce the original performance as it sounded in the original environment. Some songs seem to require unreal sounds. That way, you don't connect the sounds you hear with physical instruments, but with the music behind the instruments—the composer's dream or vision.

Here's one way to reproduce pure music rather than reproducing instruments playing in a room: Mike closely or record direct to avoid picking up studio ambience and then add artificial reverberation. Also add equalization, double-tracking, sampling, and special effects to make the instrument or voice slightly unreal. The idea is to make a production, rather than a documentation—a record, rather than a recording.

Try to convey the musician's intentions through the recorded sound quality. If the musician has a loving, soft message, translate that into a warm, smooth tone quality. Add a little midbass or slightly reduce the highs. If the musical composition suggests grandeur or space, add reverberation with a long decay time. Ask the musicians what they are trying to express through the music, and try to express that through the sound production as well.

Why Record?

Recording is a real service. Without it, people would be exposed to much less music, limited to the occasional live concert or to their own live music played once and forever gone.

With recordings, you can preserve a performance for thousands of listeners. You can hear an enormous variety of musical expressions whenever you want. Unlike a live concert, a recording can be played over and over for analysis. Tapes or discs are also a way to achieve a sort of immortality. The Beatles may be gone, but their music lives on.

Recordings can even reveal your evolving consciousness as you grow and change. A tape or disc stays the same physically, but you hear it differently over the years as your perception changes. Recordings are a constant against which you measure change in yourself.

Be proud that you are contributing to the recording art—it is done in the service of music.

GLOSSARY

A-B—A listening comparison between two audio programs, or between two components playing the same program, performed by switching immediately from one to the other. The levels of the two signals are matched. See also Spaced-Pair.

A WEIGHTING—See Weighted.

ACCENT MICROPHONE—See Spot Microphone.

ACCESS JACKS—Two jacks in a console input module or output module that allow access to points in the signal path, usually for connecting a compressor. Plugging into the access jacks breaks the signal flow and allows you to insert a signal processor in series with the signal.

ACTIVE COMBINING NETWORK—A combining network with gain. See Combining Network.

ALIGNMENT—The adjustment of tape-head azimuth and of tape-recorder circuitry to achieve optimum performance from the particular type of tape being used.

ALIGNMENT TAPE—A prerecorded tape with calibrated tones for alignment of a tape recorder.

AMBIENCE—Room acoustics, early reflections, and reverberation. Also, the audible sense of a room or environment surrounding a recorded instrument.

AMBIENCE MICROPHONE—A microphone placed relatively far from its sound source to pick up ambience.

AMPLITUDE, PEAK—On a graph of a sound wave, the sound pressure of the waveform peak. On a graph of an electrical signal, the voltage of the waveform peak. The amplitude of a sound wave or signal as measured on a meter is 0.707 times the peak amplitude.

ANALOG-TO-DIGITAL (A/D) CONVERTER—A circuit that converts an analog audio signal into a stream of digital data (bitstream).

ASSIGN—To route or send an audio signal to one or more selected channels.

ATTACK—The beginning of a note. The first portion of a note's envelope in which a note rises from silence to its maximum volume.

ATTACK TIME—In a compressor, the time it takes for gain reduction to occur in response to a musical attack.

ATTENUATE—To reduce the level of a signal.

ATTENUATOR—In a mixer (or mixing console) input module, an adjustable resistive network that reduces the microphone signal level to prevent overloading of the input transformer and mic preamplifier.

AUTOMATED MIXING—A system of mixing in which a computer remembers and updates console settings. With this system, a mix can be performed and refined in several stages and played back at a later date exactly as set up previously.

AUXILIARY-BUS (AUX-BUS)—See Effects Bus.

AUXILIARY-SEND (AUX-SEND)—See Effects Send.

AZIMUTH—In a tape recorder, the angular relationship between the head gap and the tape path.

AZIMUTH ALIGNMENT—The mechanical adjustment of the record or playback head to bring it into proper alignment (90 degrees) with the tape path.

BACK-TIMING—A technique of cueing up the musical background or a sound effect to a narration track so that the music or effect ends simultaneously with the narration.

BALANCE—The relative volume levels of various tracks or instruments.

BALANCED LINE—A cable with two conductors surrounded by a shield, in which each conductor is at equal impedance to ground. With respect to ground, the conductors are at equal potential but opposite polarity; the signal flows through both conductors.

BANDPASS FILTER—In a crossover, a filter that passes a band or range of frequencies but sharply attenuates or rejects frequencies outside the band.

BASIC TRACKS—Recorded tracks of rhythm instruments (bass, guitar, drums, and sometimes keyboard).

BASS TRAP—An assembly that absorbs low-frequency sound waves in the studio.

BIAMPLIFICATION (BIAMPING)—Driving a woofer and tweeter with separate power amplifiers. An active crossover is connected ahead of these power amplifiers.

BIAS—In tape-recorder electronics, an ultrasonic signal that drives the erase head. This signal is also mixed with the audio signal applied to the record head to reduce distortion.

BIDIRECTIONAL MICROPHONE—A microphone that is most sensitive to sounds arriving from two directions—in front of and behind the microphone. It rejects sounds approaching either side of the microphone. Sometimes called a cosine or figure-eight microphone because of the shape of its polar pattern.

BINAURAL RECORDING—A 2-channel recording made with an omnidirectional microphone mounted near each ear of a human or dummy head, for playback over headphones. The object is to duplicate the acoustic signal appearing at each ear.

BLUMLEIN ARRAY—A stereo microphone technique in which two coincident bidirectional microphones are angled 90 degrees apart (45 degrees to the left and right of center).

BOARD—See Mixing Console.

BOUNCING TRACKS—A process in which two or more tracks are mixed, and the mixed tracks are recorded on an unused track or tracks. Then the original tracks can be erased, which frees them up for recording more instruments.

BOUNDARY MICROPHONE—A microphone designed to be used on a boundary (a hard reflective surface). The microphone capsule is mounted very close to the boundary so that direct and reflected sounds arrive at the microphone diaphragm in phase (or nearly so) for all frequencies in the audible band.

BREATHING—The unwanted audible rise and fall of background noise that may occur with a compressor. Also called pumping.

BULK TAPE ERASER—A large electromagnet used to erase a whole reel of recording tape at once.

BUS—A common connection of many different signals. An output of a mixer or submixer. A channel that feeds a tape track, signal processor, or power amplifier.

BUS IN—An input to a program bus, usually used for effects returns.

BUS MASTER—In the output section of a mixing console, a potentiometer (fader or volume control) that controls the output level of a bus.

BUS OUT—The output connector of a bus.

BUS TRIM—A control in the output section of a mixing console that provides variable gain control of a bus, used in addition to the bus master for fine adjustment.

BUZZ—An unwanted edgy tone that sometimes accompanies audio, containing high harmonics of 60 Hz.

CALIBRATION—See Alignment.

CAPACITOR—An electronic component that stores an electric charge. It is formed of two conductive plates separated by an insulator called a dielectric. A capacitor passes AC but blocks DC.

CAPACITOR MICROPHONE—See Condenser Microphone.

CAPSTAN—In a tape-recorder transport, a rotating post that contacts the tape (along with the pinch roller) and pulls the tape past the heads at a constant speed during recording and playback.

CARDIOID MICROPHONE—A unidirectional microphone with side attenuation of 6 db and maximum rejection of sound at the rear of the microphone (180 degrees off-axis). A microphone with a heart-shaped directional pattern.

CHANNEL—A single path of an audio signal. Usually, each channel contains a different signal.

CHANNEL ASSIGN—See Assign.

CHORUS—**1.** A special effect in which a signal is delayed by 15 to 35 milliseconds, the delayed signal is combined with the original signal, and the delay is varied randomly or periodically. This creates a wavy, shimmering effect. **2.** The main portion of a song that is repeated several times throughout the song with the same lyrics.

CLEAN—Free of noise, distortion, overhang, leakage. Not muddy.

CLEAR—Easy to hear, easy to differentiate. Reproduced with sufficient high frequencies.

COINCIDENT-PAIR—A stereo microphone, or two separate microphones, placed so that the microphone diaphragms occupy approximately the same point in space. They are angled apart and mounted one directly above the other.

COMB-FILTER EFFECT—The frequency response caused by combining a sound with its delayed replica. The frequency response has a series of peaks and dips caused by phase interference. The peaks and dips resemble the teeth of a comb.

COMBINING AMPLIFIER—An amplifier at which the outputs of two or more signal paths are mixed together to feed a single track of a tape recorder.

COMBINING NETWORK—A resistive network at which the outputs of two or more signal paths are mixed together to feed a single track of a tape recorder.

COMPLEX WAVE—A wave with more than one frequency component.

COMPOSITE TRACK—The process of recording several performances of a musical part on different tracks, so that the best segments of each performance can be played in sequence during mixdown.

COMPRESSION—**1.** The portion of a sound wave in which molecules are pushed together, forming a region with higher-than-normal atmospheric pressure. **2.** In signal processing, the reduction in dynamic range or gain caused by a compressor.

COMPRESSION RATIO (SLOPE)—In a compressor, the ratio of the change in input level (in db) to the change in output level (in db). For example, a 2:1 ratio means that for every 2 db change in input level, the output level changes 1 db.

COMPRESSOR—A signal processor that reduces dynamic range or gain by means of automatic volume control. An amplifier whose gain decreases as the input signal level increases above a preset point.

CONDENSER MICROPHONE—A microphone that works on the principle of variable capacitance to generate an electrical signal. The microphone diaphragm and an adjacent metallic disk (called a backplate) are charged to form two plates of a capacitor. Incoming sound waves vibrate the diaphragm, varying its spacing to the backplate, which varies the capacitance, which in turn varies the voltage between the diaphragm and backplate.

CONNECTOR—A device that makes electrical contact between a signal-carrying cable and an electronic device, or between two cables. A device used to connect or hold together a cable and an electronic component so that a signal can flow from one to the other.

CONSOLE—See Mixing Console.

CONTACT PICKUP—A transducer that contacts a musical instrument and converts its mechanical vibrations into a corresponding electrical signal.

CONTROL ROOM—The room in which the engineer controls and monitors the recording. It houses most of the recording hardware.

CROSSOVER—An electronic network that divides an incoming signal into two or more frequency bands.

CROSSOVER, ACTIVE (ELECTRONIC CROSSOVER)—A crossover with amplifying components, used ahead of the power amplifiers in a biamped or triamped speaker system.

CROSSOVER FREQUENCY—The single frequency at which both filters of a crossover network are down 3 db.

CROSSOVER, PASSIVE—A crossover with passive (nonamplifying) components, used after the power amplifier.

CROSSTALK—The unwanted transfer of a signal from one channel to another. Crosstalk often occurs between adjacent tracks within a record or playback head in a tape recorder, or between input modules in a console.

CUE, CUE SEND—In a mixing-console input module, a control that adjusts the level of the signal feeding the cue mixer that feeds a signal to headphones in the studio.

CUE LIST—See Edit Decision List.

CUE MIXER—A submixer in a mixing console that takes signals from cue sends as inputs and mixes them into a composite signal that drives headphones in the studio.

CUE SHEET—Used during mixdown, a chronological list of mixing-console control adjustments required at various points in the recorded song. These points may be indicated by tape-counter or elapsed-time readings.

CUE SYSTEM—A monitor system that allows musicians to hear themselves and previously recorded tracks through headphones.

DAMPING FACTOR—The ability of a power amplifier to control or damp loudspeaker vibrations. The lower the amplifier's output impedance, the higher the damping factor.

DAT (R-DAT)—A digital audio tape recorder that uses a rotating head to record digital audio on tape.

db—Abbreviation for decibel.

DEAD—Having very little or no reverberation.

DECAY—The portion of the envelope of a note in which the envelope goes from maximum to some midrange level. Also, the decline in level of reverberation over time.

DECAY TIME—See Reverberation Time.

DECIBEL—The unit of measurement of audio level. Ten times the logarithm of the ratio of two power levels. Twenty times the logarithm of the ratio of two voltages.

  dbV is decibels relative to 1 volt.

  dbu is decibels relative to 0.775 volt.

  dbm is decibels relative to 1 milliwatt.

  dbA is decibels, A-weighted. (See Weighted.)

DECODED TAPE—A tape that is expanded after being compressed by a noise-reduction system. Such a tape has normal dynamic range.

DE-ESSER—A signal processor that removes excessive sibilance ("s" and "sh" sounds) by compressing high frequencies around 5 to 10 kHz.

DELAY—The time interval between a signal and its repetition. A digital delay or a delay line is a signal processor that delays a signal for a short time.

DEMAGNETIZER (DEGAUSSER)—An electromagnet with a probe tip that is touched to elements of the tape path (such as tape heads and tape guides) to remove residual magnetism.

DEPTH—The audible sense of nearness and farness of various instruments. Instruments recorded with a high ratio of direct-to-reverberant sound are perceived as being close; instruments recorded with a low ratio of direct-to-reverberant sound are perceived as being distant.

DESIGN CENTER—The portion of fader travel (usually shaded), about 10 to 15 db from the top, in which console gain is distributed for optimum headroom and signal-to-noise ratio. During normal operation, each fader in use ideally should be placed at or near design center.

DESIGNATION STRIP—A strip of paper taped near console faders to designate the instrument that each fader controls.

DESK—The British term for mixing console.

DIFFUSION—An even distribution of sound in a room.

DIGITAL AUDIO—An encoding of an analog audio signal in the form of binary digits (ones and zeros).

DIGITAL AUDIO WORKSTATION—A group of components (separate or in a single chassis) that allows you to record, edit, and mix audio programs entirely in digital form. An A/D converter converts incoming analog audio to digital and then stores it in RAM or on a computer hard disk for later editing. A D/A converter translates the edited digital program back into analog audio.

DIGITAL RECORDING—A recording system in which the audio signal is stored in the form of binary digits.

DIGITAL-TO-ANALOG CONVERTER—A circuit that converts a digital audio signal into an analog audio signal.

DIM—To reduce temporarily the monitor volume by a preset amount so that you can carry on a conversation.

DIRECT BOX—A device used for connecting an amplified instrument directly to a mixer mic input. The direct box converts a high-impedance unbalanced audio signal into a low-impedance balanced audio signal.

DIRECT INJECTION (DI)—Recording with a direct box.

DIRECT OUTPUT, DIRECT OUT—An output connector following a mic preamplifier, used to feed the signal of one instrument directly to one track of a tape recorder.

DIRECT SOUND—Sound traveling directly from the sound source to the microphone (or to the listener) without reflections.

DIRECTIONAL MICROPHONE—A microphone that has different sensitivity in different directions. A unidirectional or bidirectional microphone.

DISTORTION—An unwanted change in the audio waveform, causing a raspy or gritty sound quality. The appearance of frequencies in a device's output signal that were not in the input signal. Distortion is caused by recording at too high a level, or by components failing or vacuum tubes distorting. (Distortion can be desirable—for an electric guitar, for example.)

DOLBY TONE—A reference tone recorded at the beginning of a Dolby-encoded tape for alignment purposes.

DOUBLING—A special effect in which a signal is combined with its 15 to 35 millisecond delayed replica. This process mimics the sound of two identical voices or instruments playing in unison. In another type of doubling, two identical performances are recorded and played back to thicken the sound.

DROP-FRAME—For color video production, a mode of SMPTE time code that causes the time code to match the clock on the wall. Once every minute, frame numbers 00 and 01 are dropped, except every 10th minute.

DROP-OUT—During playback of a tape recording, a momentary loss of signal caused by separation of the tape from the playback head due to dust, tape-oxide irregularity, etc.

DRUM MACHINE—A device that plays samples of real drums, and includes a sequencer to record rhythm patterns.

DRY—Having no echo or reverberation. Referring to a close-sounding signal that is not yet processed by a reverberation or delay device.

DYNAMIC MICROPHONE—A microphone that generates electricity when sound waves cause a conductor to vibrate in a stationary magnetic field. The two types of dynamic microphone are moving coil and ribbon. A moving-coil microphone is usually called a dynamic microphone.

DYNAMIC RANGE—The range of volume levels in a program from softest to loudest.

EARTH GROUND—A connection to moist dirt (the ground we walk on). This connection is usually done via a long copper rod or an all-metal cold-water pipe.

ECHO—A delayed repetition of a signal or sound. A sound delayed 50 milliseconds or more, combined with the original sound.

ECHO CHAMBER—A hard-surfaced room containing a widely separated loudspeaker and microphone, once used for creating reverberation.

EDIT DECISION LIST (EDL)—A list of program events in order, plus their starting times.

EDITING—The cutting and rejoining of magnetic tape to delete unwanted material, to insert leader tape, or to rearrange recorded material into the desired sequence. Also, the same actions performed with a digital audio workstation, without cutting any tape.

EDITING BLOCK—A metal block that holds magnetic tape during the editing/splicing procedure.

EFFECTS—Interesting sound phenomena created by signal processors, such as reverberation, echo, flanging, doubling, compression, or chorus.

EFFECTS BUS—The bus that feeds effects devices (signal processors).

EFFECTS LOOP—A set of connectors in a mixer for connecting an external effects unit, such as a reverb or delay device. The effects loop includes a send section and a receive section. See also Effects Send, Effects Return.

EFFECTS MIXER—A submixer in a mixing console that combines signals from effects sends and feeds the mixed signal to the input of a special-effects device, such as a reverberation unit.

EFFECTS RETURN (EFFECTS RECEIVE)—In the output section of a mixing console, a control that adjusts the amount of signal received from an effects unit. Also, the connectors in a mixer to which you connect the effects-unit output signal. They might be labeled "bus in" instead. The effects-return signal is mixed with the program bus signal.

EFFECTS SEND—In an input module of a mixing console, a control that adjusts the amount of signal sent to a special-effects device, such as a reverberation or delay unit. Also, the connector in a mixer that you connect to the input of an effects unit. The effects-send control normally adjusts the amount of reverberation or echo heard on each instrument.

EFFICIENCY—In a loudspeaker, the ratio of acoustic power output to electrical power input.

EIA—Electrical Industries Association.

EIA RATING—A microphone-sensitivity specification that states the microphone output level in dbm into a matched load for a given Sound Pressure Level (SPL). SPL + db (EIA rating) = dbm output into a matched load.

ELECTRET-CONDENSER MICROPHONE—A condenser microphone in which the electrostatic field of the capacitor is generated by an electret—a material that permanently stores an electrostatic charge.

ELECTROSTATIC FIELD—The force field between two conductors charged with static electricity.

ELECTROSTATIC INTERFERENCE—The unwanted presence of an electrostatic hum field in signal conductors.

ENCODED TAPE—A tape containing a signal compressed by a noise-reduction unit.

ENVELOPE—The rise and fall in volume of one note. The envelope connects successive peaks of the waves comprising a note. Each harmonic in the note might have a different envelope.

EQUALIZATION (EQ)—The adjustment of frequency response to alter the tonal balance or to attenuate unwanted frequencies.

EQUALIZER—A circuit (usually in each input module of a mixing console, or in a separate unit) that alters the frequency spectrum of a signal passed through it.

ERASE—To remove an audio signal from magnetic tape by applying an ultrasonic varying magnetic field so as to randomize the magnetization of the magnetic particles on the tape.

ERASE HEAD—A head in a tape recorder that erases the signal on tape.

EXPANDER—**1.** A signal processor that increases the dynamic range of a signal passed through it. **2.** An amplifier whose gain decreases as its input level decreases. When used as a noise gate, an expander reduces the gain of low-level signals to reduce noise between notes.

FADE-OUT—To gradually reduce the volume of the last several seconds of a recorded song, from full level down to silence, by slowly pulling down the master fader.

FADER—A linear or sliding potentiometer (volume control), used to adjust signal level.

FEED—**1.** To send an audio signal to some device or system. **2.** An output signal sent to some device or system.

FEED REEL—The left-side reel on a tape recorder that unwinds during recording or playback.

FEEDBACK—The return of some portion of an output signal to the system's input.

FILTER—**1.** A circuit that sharply attenuates frequencies above or below a certain frequency. Used to reduce noise and leakage above or below the frequency range of an instrument or voice. **2.** A MIDI filter removes selected note parameters.

FLANGING—A special effect in which a signal is combined with its delayed replica, and the delay is varied between 0 and 20 milliseconds. A hollow, swishing, ethereal effect such as a variable-length pipe, or a jet plane passing overhead. A variable comb filter produces the flanging effect.

FLETCHER-MUNSON EFFECT—Named after the two people who discovered it, the psychoacoustical phenomenon in which the subjective frequency response of the ear changes with program level. Due to this effect, program played at a lower volume than the original level subjectively loses low- and high-frequency response.

FLOAT—To disconnect from ground.

FLUTTER—A rapid periodic variation in tape speed.

FLUTTER ECHOES—A rapid series of echoes that occurs between two parallel walls.

FLUX—Magnetic lines of force.

FLUXIVITY—The measure of the flux density of a magnetic recording tape, per unit of track width.

FLY-IN (LAY-IN)—To copy part of a recorded track onto another recorder and then rerecord that copy back onto the original multitrack tape in a different part of the song, in sync with other recorded tracks. For example, copy the vocal track from the first chorus of the song onto an external recorder or sampler. Rerecord (fly-in) that copy onto the multitrack tape at the second chorus. Then the first and second choruses have identical vocal performances.

FOLDBACK (FB)—See Cue System.

FREQUENCY—The number of cycles per second of a sound wave or an audio signal, measured in hertz (Hz). A low frequency (for example, 100 Hz) has a low pitch; a high frequency (for example, 10,000 Hz) has a high pitch.

FREQUENCY RESPONSE—**1.** The range of frequencies that an audio device reproduces at an equal level (within a tolerance, such as [±3 db). **2.** The range of frequencies that a device (microphone, human ear, etc.) can detect.

FULL TRACK—A single tape track recorded across the full width of a tape.

FUNDAMENTAL—The lowest frequency in a complex wave.

GAIN—Amplification. The ratio, expressed in decibels, between the output voltage and the input voltage, or between the output power and the input power.

GAP—In a tape-recorder head, the thin break in the electromagnet that contacts the tape.

GATE—**1.** To turn off a signal when its amplitude falls below a preset value. **2.** The signal-processing device used for this purpose. See also Noise Gate.

GATED REVERB—Reverberation with the reverberant tail cut off before it fades out.

GENERATION—A copy of a tape or a bounce of a track. A copy of the original master recording is a first generation tape. A copy made from the first generation tape is a second generation, and so on.

GENERATION LOSS—The degradation of signal quality (the increase in noise and distortion) that occurs with each successive generation of a tape recording.

GOBO—A movable partition used to prevent the sound of an instrument from reaching another instrument's microphone. Short for go-between.

GRAPHIC EQUALIZER—An equalizer with a horizontal row of faders; the fader-knob positions indicate graphically the frequency response of the equalizer. Usually used to equalize monitor speakers for the room they are in. Sometimes used for complex EQ of a track.

GROUND—The zero-signal reference point for a system of audio components.

GROUND BUS—A common connection to which equipment is grounded, usually a heavy copper plate.

GROUND LOOP—1. A loop or circuit formed of ground leads. 2. The loop formed when unbalanced components are connected together via two ground paths—the connecting-cable shield and the power ground. Ground loops cause hum and should be avoided.

GROUNDING—Connecting pieces of electronic equipment to ground. Proper grounding ensures that there is no voltage difference between equipment chassis. An electrostatic shield needs to be grounded to be effective.

GROUP—See Submix.

GUARD BAND—The spacing between tracks on a multitrack tape or tape head, used to prevent crosstalk.

HALF-TRACK—A tape track recorded across approximately half the width of a tape. A half-track recorder usually records two such tracks simultaneously in the same direction to make a stereo recording.

HARMONIC—An overtone whose frequency is a whole-number multiple of the fundamental frequency.

HARMONIZER—A signal processor that provides a wide variety of pitch-shifting and delay effects.

HEAD—An electromagnet in a tape recorder that either erases the audio signal on tape, records a signal on tape, or plays back a signal that is already on tape.

HEAD GAP—See Gap.

HEADPHONES—A head-worn transducer that covers the ears and converts electrical audio signals into sound waves. Used for monitoring the sound.

HEADROOM—The safety margin, measured in decibels, between the signal level and the maximum undistorted signal level. In a tape recorder, the db difference between standard operating level (corresponding to a 0 VU reading) and the level causing 3 percent total harmonic distortion. High-frequency headroom increases with tape speed.

HERTZ (Hz)—Cycles per second, the unit of measurement of frequency.

HIGHPASS FILTER—A filter that passes frequencies above a certain frequency and attenuates frequencies below that same frequency. A low-cut filter.

HISS—A noise signal containing all frequencies, but with greater energy at higher octaves. Hiss sounds like wind blowing through trees. It is usually caused by random signals generated by microphones, electronics, and magnetic tape.

HOT—**1.** A high recording level causing slight distortion, maybe used for special effect. **2.** A condition in which a chassis or circuit has a potentially dangerous voltage on it. **3.** Referring to the conductor in a microphone cable that has a positive voltage on it at the instant that sound pressure moves the diaphragm inward.

HUM—An unwanted low-pitched tone (60 Hz and its harmonics) heard along with the audio signal.

HYPERCARDIOID MICROPHONE—A directional microphone with a polar pattern that has 12 db attenuation at the sides, 6 db attenuation at the rear, and two nulls of maximum rejection at 110 degrees off-axis.

IMAGE—An illusory sound source located between two stereo speakers.

IMPEDANCE—The opposition of a circuit to the flow of alternating current. Impedance is the complex sum of resistance and reactance.

INPUT—The connection going into an audio device. In a mixer or mixing console, a connector for a microphone, line level device, or other signal source.

INPUT ATTENUATOR—See Attenuator.

INPUT MODULE—In a mixing console, the set of controls affecting a single input signal. An input module usually includes an attenuator, fader, equalizer, effects send, cue send, solo button, and channel-assign controls.

INPUT SECTION—The row of input modules in a mixing console.

INPUT/OUTPUT (I/O) CONSOLE (IN-LINE CONSOLE)—A mixing console arranged so that input and output sections are aligned vertically. Each module (other than the monitor section) contains one input channel and one output channel.

INSERT JACKS—See Access jacks.

JACK—A female or receptacle-type connector for audio signals into which a plug is inserted.

KEYBOARD WORKSTATION—Several MIDI components in one chassis—a keyboard, a sample player, a sequencer, and perhaps a synthesizer and disk drive.

KILO—A prefix meaning one thousand. Abbreviated k.

LAY-IN—See Fly-In.

LEADER TAPE—Plastic or paper tape without an oxide coating, used for a spacer between takes (for silence between songs).

LEADERING—The process of splicing leader tape between program selections.

LEAKAGE—The overlap of an instrument's sound into another instrument's microphone. Also called bleed or spill.

LED INDICATOR—A recording-level indicator using one or more Light Emitting Diodes.

LEDE—Abbreviation for Live-End/Dead-End, a type of control room acoustic treatment in which the front half of the control room prevents early reflections to the mixing position, and the back half of the control room reflects diffused sound to the mixing position.

LEVEL—The degree of intensity of an audio signal—the voltage, power, or sound pressure level. The original definition of level is the power in watts.

LEVEL SETTING—In a tape recorder, the process of adjusting the level of the signal sent to the record head so that the maximum tape magnetization occurs without distortion. A VU meter or other indicator shows recording level.

LIMITER—A signal processor whose output is constant above a preset input level. A compressor with a compression ratio of 10:1 or greater, with the threshold set just below the point of distortion of the following device. Used to prevent distortion of attack transients or peaks.

LINE LEVEL—In balanced professional recording equipment, a signal whose level is approximately 1.23 volts (+4 dbm). In unbalanced equipment (most home hi-fi or semipro recording equipment), a signal whose level is approximately 0.316 volt (–10 dbV).

LIVE—**1.** Having audible reverberation. **2.** Occurring in real-time, in person.

LIVE RECORDING—A recording made at a concert. Also, a recording made of a musical ensemble playing all at once, rather than overdubbing.

LOCALIZATION—The ability of the human hearing system to tell the direction of a real or illusionary sound source.

LOOP—In a sampling program, to play the sustain portion of a sound's envelope repeatedly.

LOUDSPEAKER—A transducer that converts electrical energy (the signal) into acoustical energy (sound waves).

LOWPASS FILTER—A filter that passes frequencies below a certain frequency and attenuates frequencies above that same frequency. A high-cut filter.

M—Abbreviation for megabytes.

MAGNETIC RECORDING TAPE—A recording medium made of magnetic particles (usually ferric oxide) suspended in a binder and coated on a long strip of thin plastic (usually mylar).

MASK—To hide or cover up one sound with another sound. To make a sound inaudible by playing another sound along with it.

MASTER FADER—A volume control that affects the level of all program buses simultaneously. It is the last stage of gain before the tape recorder.

MASTER TAPE—A completed tape used to generate tape copies or discs.

MEMORY—A group of integrated circuit chips, used to store digital data temporarily or permanently (such as an audio signal in digital format).

MEMORY REWIND—A tape-recorder function that rewinds the tape to a preset tape-counter position.

METER—A device that indicates voltage, resistance, current, or signal level.

MIC—An abbreviation for microphone.

MIC LEVEL—The level or voltage of a signal produced by a microphone, typically 2 millivolts.

MICROPHONE—A transducer or device that converts an acoustical signal (sound) into a corresponding electrical signal.

MICROPHONE TECHNIQUES—The selection and placement of microphones to pick up sound sources.

MIDI—Abbreviation for Musical Instrument Digital Interface, a specification for a connection between synthesizers, drum machines, and computers that allows them to communicate with and/or control each other.

MIDI CHANNEL—A route for the transmission and reception of MIDI signals. Each channel controls a separate MIDI musical instrument. Up to 16 channels can be sent on a single MIDI cable.

MIDI IN—A connector in a MIDI device that receives MIDI messages.

MIDI OUT—A connector in a MIDI device that transmits MIDI messages.

MIDI THRU—A connector in a MIDI device that duplicates the MIDI information at the MIDI-In connector. Used to connect another MIDI device in the series.

MIDSIDE—A coincident-pair stereo microphone technique using a forward-facing unidirectional, omnidirectional, or bidirectional microphone and a side-facing bidirectional microphone. The microphone signals are summed and differenced to produce right- and left-channel signals.

MIKE—To pick up with a microphone.

MILLI—A prefix meaning one thousandth, abbreviated m.

MIX—**1.** To combine two or more different signals into a common signal. **2.** A control on a delay unit that varies the ratio between the dry signal and the delayed signal.

MIXDOWN—The process of playing prerecorded tape tracks through a mixing console and mixing them to two stereo channels for recording on a 2-track tape recorder.

MIXER—A device that mixes or combines audio signals and controls the relative levels of the signals.

MIXING CONSOLE—A large mixer with additional functions such as equalization or tone control, pan pots, monitoring controls, solo functions, channel assigns, and control of signals sent to external signal processors.

MONAURAL—Referring to listening with one ear. Often incorrectly used to mean monophonic.

MONITOR—A loudspeaker or headphones, used for judging sound quality.

MONITORING—Listening to an audio signal with a monitor.

MONO, MONOPHONIC—**1.** Referring to a single channel of audio. A monophonic program can be played over one or more loudspeakers, or one or more headphones. **2.** Describing a synthesizer that plays only one note at a time (not chords).

MONO-COMPATIBLE—A characteristic of a stereo program, in which the program channels can be combined to a mono program without altering the frequency response or balance. A mono-compatible stereo program has the same frequency response in stereo or mono because there is no delay or phase shift between channels to cause phase interference.

MOVING-COIL MICROPHONE—A dynamic microphone in which the conductor is a coil of wire moving in a fixed magnetic field. The coil is attached to a diaphragm that vibrates when struck with sound waves.

M-S RECORDING—See Midside.

MUDDY—Unclear sounding; having excessive leakage, reverberation, or overhang.

MULTIEFFECTS PROCESSOR—See Multiprocessor.

MULTIPLE-D MICROPHONE—A directional microphone that has multiple sound-path lengths between its front and rear sound entries. This type of microphone has minimal proximity effect.

MULTIPROCESSOR—A signal processor that can perform several different signal-processing functions.

MULTITIMBRAL—In a synthesizer, the ability to produce two or more different patches or timbres at the same time.

MULTITRACK—Referring to a tape recorder or tape-recorder head that has more than two tape tracks.

MUTE—To turn off an input signal on a mixing console by disconnecting the input-module output from channel assign and direct out. The mute function is used to reduce tape noise during silent portions of tracks, or to turn off unused performances or microphone signals while recording.

NEAR COINCIDENT—A stereo microphone technique in which two directional microphones are angled apart symmetrically on either side of center and spaced a few inches apart horizontally.

NEAR-FIELD MONITORING—A monitor-speaker arrangement in which the speakers are placed very near the listener (usually on top of the console meter bridge) to reduce the audibility of control-room acoustics.

NOISE—Unwanted sound, such as hiss from electronics or tape. An audio signal with an irregular, nonperiodic waveform.

NOISE GATE—A gate used to reduce or eliminate noise between notes.

NOISE-REDUCTION SYSTEM—A signal processor used to reduce tape hiss (and sometimes print-through) caused by the recording process. Some of these systems compress the signal during recording and expand it in a complementary fashion during playback.

OCTAVE—The interval between any two frequencies in which the upper frequency is twice the lower frequency.

OFF-AXIS—Not directly in front of a microphone or loudspeaker.

OFF-AXIS COLORATION—In a microphone, the deviation from the on-axis frequency response that sometimes occurs at angles off the axis of the microphone. The coloration of sound (alteration of tone quality) for sounds arriving off-axis to the microphone.

OMNIDIRECTIONAL MICROPHONE—A microphone that is equally sensitive to sounds arriving from all directions.

ON-LOCATION RECORDING—A recording made outside the studio, in a room or hall where the music usually is performed or practiced.

OPEN TRACKS—On a multitrack tape recorder, tracks that have not yet been used, or have already been bounced and are available for use.

OUTBOARD EQUIPMENT—Signal processors that are external to the mixing console.

OUTPUT—A connector in an audio device from which the signal comes and feeds successive devices.

OUTTAKE—A take, or section of a take, that is to be removed or not used.

OVERDUB—To record a new musical part on an unused track in synchronization with previously recorded tracks.

OVERHANG—The continuation of a signal at the output of a device after the input signal has ceased. Sometimes called ringing.

OVERLOAD—The distortion that occurs when an applied signal exceeds a system's maximum input level.

OVERTONE—In a complex wave, a frequency component that is higher than the fundamental frequency.

PAD—See Attenuator.

PAN POT—Abbreviation for panoramic potentiometer. In each input module in a mixing console, a control that divides a signal between two channels in an adjustable ratio. By doing so, a pan pot controls the location of a sonic image between a stereo pair of loudspeakers.

PARAMETRIC EQUALIZER—An equalizer with continuously variable parameters, such as frequency, bandwidth, and amount of boost or cut.

PATCH—**1.** To connect one piece of audio equipment to another with a cable. **2.** A setting of synthesizer parameters to achieve a sound with a certain timbre.

PATCH BAY (PATCH PANEL)—An array of connectors, usually in a rack, to which equipment inputs and outputs are wired. A patch bay makes it easy to interconnect various pieces of equipment in a central, accessible location.

PATCH CORD—A short cable with a phone plug on each end, used for signal routing in a patch bay.

PEAK—On a graph of a sound wave or signal, the highest point in the waveform. The point of greatest voltage or sound pressure in a cycle.

PEAK AMPLITUDE—See Amplitude, Peak.

PEAK PROGRAM METER (PPM)—A meter that responds fast enough to follow the peak levels in a program closely.

PEAKING EQUALIZER—An equalizer that provides maximum cut or boost at one frequency, so that the resulting frequency response of a boost resembles a mountain peak.

PERIOD—The time between the peak of one wave and the peak of the next. The time between corresponding points on successive waves. Period is the inverse of frequency.

PERSONAL STUDIO—A minimal group of recording equipment set up for one's personal use, usually using a 4-track cassette recorder-mixer. Also, a simple 4-track cassette recorder-mixer for one's personal use.

PERSPECTIVE—In the reproduction of a recording, the audible sense of distance to the musical ensemble, the point of view. A close perspective has a high ratio of direct sound to reverberant sound; a distant perspective has a low ratio of direct sound to reverberant sound.

PFL—Abbreviation for Prefader Listen. See also Solo.

PHANTOM POWER—A DC voltage (usually 12 to 48 volts) on microphone signal conductors to power condenser microphones.

PHASE—The degree of progression in the cycle of a wave, where one complete cycle is 360 degrees.

PHASE CANCELLATION, PHASE INTERFERENCE—The cancellation of certain frequency components of a signal that occurs when the signal is combined with its delayed replica. At certain frequencies, the direct and delayed signals are of equal level and opposite polarity (180 degrees out of phase), and when combined, they cancel out. The result is a comb-filter frequency response having a periodic series of peaks and dips. Phase interference can occur between the signals of two microphones picking up the same source at different distances, or can occur at a microphone picking up both a direct sound and its reflection from a nearby surface.

PHASE SHIFT—The difference in degrees of phase angle between corresponding points on two waves. If one wave is delayed with respect to another, there is a phase shift between them of $2\pi FT$, where $\pi = 3.14$, F = frequency in Hz, and T = delay in seconds.

PHASING—A special effect in which a signal is combined with its phase-shifted replica to produce a variable comb-filter effect. See also Flanging.

PHONE PLUG—A cylindrical, coaxial plug (usually 1/4-inch diameter). An unbalanced phone plug has a tip for the hot signal and a sleeve for the shield or ground. A balanced phone plug has a tip for the hot signal, a ring for the return signal, and a sleeve for the shield or ground.

PHONO PLUG—A coaxial plug with a central pin for the hot signal and a ring of pressure-fit tabs for the shield or ground. Also called RCA plug.

PICKUP—A contact pickup. Also, a transducer in an electric guitar that converts string motion to a corresponding electrical signal.

PINCH ROLLER—In a tape-recorder transport, the rubber wheel that pinches or traps the tape between itself and the capstan, so that the capstan can move the tape.

PING-PONGING—See Bouncing Tracks.

PINK NOISE—A noise signal containing all frequencies (unless band-limited), with equal energy per octave. Pink noise is a test signal used for equalizing a sound system to the desired frequency response, and for testing loudspeakers.

PITCH—The subjective lowness or highness of a tone. The pitch of a tone usually correlates with the fundamental frequency.

PITCH CONTROL—A control on a tape recorder that varies the tape speed, thereby varying the pitch of the signal on tape. The pitch control can be used to match the pitch of prerecorded instruments with that of an instrument to be overdubbed. It is also used for special effects, such as "chipmunk voices," and to play prerecorded tracks slowly so that fast musical passages can be overdubbed more easily.

PITCH SHIFTER—A signal processor that changes the pitch of an instrument's sound without changing its duration.

PLAYBACK EQUALIZATION—In tape-recorder electronics, fixed equalization applied to the signal during playback to compensate for certain losses.

PLAYBACK HEAD—The head in a tape recorder that picks up a prerecorded magnetic signal from the moving tape and converts it to a corresponding electrical signal. The playback head is not the same as the sel-sync or sync head.

PLUG—A male connector that inserts into a jack.

POLAR PATTERN—The directional pickup pattern of a microphone. A plot of microphone sensitivity versus angle of sound incidence. Examples of polar patterns are omnidirectional, bidirectional, and unidirectional. Subsets of unidirectional are cardioid, supercardioid, and hypercardioid.

POLARITY—Referring to the positive or negative direction of an electrical, acoustical, or magnetic force. Two identical signals in opposite polarity are 180 degrees out-of-phase with each other at all frequencies.

POLYPHONIC—Describing a synthesizer that can play more than one note at a time (chords).

POP—1. A thump or little explosion sound heard in a vocalist's microphone signal. Pop occurs when the user says words with "p," "t," or "b" so that a turbulent puff of air is forced from the mouth and strikes the microphone diaphragm. **2.** A noise heard when a mic is plugged into a monitored channel, or a switch is flipped.

POP FILTER—A screen placed on a microphone grille that attenuates or filters out pop disturbances before they strike the microphone diaphragm. Usually made of open-cell plastic foam or silk, a pop filter reduces pop and wind noise.

PORTABLE STUDIO—A combination tape recorder and mixer in one portable chassis.

POST-ECHO—A repetition of a sound, following the original sound, caused by print-through.

POWER AMPLIFIER—An electronic device that amplifies or increases the power level fed into it to a level sufficient to drive a loudspeaker.

POWER GROUND (SAFETY GROUND)—A connection to the power company's earth ground through the U-shaped hole in a power outlet. In the power cable of an electronic component with a 3-prong plug, the U-shaped prong is wired to the component's chassis. This wire conducts electricity to power ground if the chassis becomes electrically hot, preventing shocks.

PREAMPLIFIER—In an audio system, the first stage of amplification that boosts a mic-level signal to line level.

PREDELAY—Short for prereverberation delay. The delay (about 30 to 150 milliseconds) between the arrival of the direct sound and the onset of reverberation. Usually, the longer the predelay, the greater the perceived room size.

PRE-ECHO—A repetition of a sound that occurs before the sound itself, caused by print-through.

PREFADER/POSTFADER SWITCH—A switch that selects a signal either ahead of the fader (prefader) or following the fader (postfader). The level of a prefader signal is independent of the fader position; the level of a postfader signal follows the fader position.

PREPRODUCTION—Planning in advance what you're going to do at a recording session, in terms of track assignments, overdubbing, studio layout, and microphone selection.

PRESENCE—The audible sense that a reproduced instrument is present in the listening room. Some synonyms are closeness, definition, and punch. Presence is often created by an equalization boost in the midrange or upper midrange.

PRESSURE ZONE MICROPHONE—A boundary microphone constructed with the microphone diaphragm parallel with, and facing, a reflective surface.

PREVERB—A special effect in which the reverberation of a note precedes it, rather than follows it. Preverb is achieved by playing an instrument's track backwards while adding reverberation to it, and recording the reverberation on an unused track. When the tape is reversed so that the instrument's track plays forward, preverb is heard as the reverberation plays backwards.

PRINT-THROUGH—The transfer of a magnetic signal from one layer of tape to the next on a reel, causing an echo preceding or following the program.

PRODUCTION—**1.** A recording that is enhanced by special effects. **2.** The supervision of a recording session to create a satisfactory recording. This involves getting musicians together for the session, making musical suggestions to the musicians to enhance their performance, and making suggestions to the engineer for sound balance and effects.

PROGRAM BUS—A bus or output that feeds an audio program to a tape-recorder track.

PROGRAM MIXER—In a mixing console, a mixer formed of input-module outputs, combining amplifiers, and program buses.

PROXIMITY EFFECT—The bass boost that occurs with a single-D directional microphone when it is placed a few inches from a sound source. The closer the microphone, the greater the low-frequency boost due to proximity effect.

PUNCH IN/OUT—A feature in a tape recorder that lets you insert a recording of a corrected musical part into a previously recorded track by going into and out of record mode as the tape is rolling.

PURE WAVEFORM—A waveform of a single frequency; a sine wave. A pure tone is the perceived sound of such a wave.

QUARTER-TRACK—A tape track recorded across one-quarter the width of the tape. A quarter-track recorder usually records two stereo programs (one in each direction).

447

RACK—A 19-inch-wide metal or wooden cabinet used to hold audio equipment.

RADIO FREQUENCY INTERFERENCE (RFI)—Radio frequency electromagnetic waves induced in audio cables or equipment, causing various noises in the audio signal.

RAREFACTION—The portion of a sound wave in which molecules are spread apart, forming a region with lower-than-normal atmospheric pressure. The opposite of compression.

R-DAT—See DAT.

REAL-TIME RECORDING—**1.** Recording notes into a sequencer in the correct tempo, for later playback at the same tempo as recorded. **2.** A recording made direct to lacquer disc or direct to 2-track without any overdubs or mixdown.

RECIRCULATION (REGENERATION)—Feeding the output of a delay device back into its input to create multiple echoes. Also, the control on a delay device that affects how much delayed signal is recycled to the input.

RECORD—To store an event in permanent form. Usually, to store an audio signal in magnetic form on magnetic tape. Recording is also possible on hard disk, on magneto-optical disk, and in RAM.

RECORD EQUALIZATION—In tape-recorder electronics, equalization applied to the signal during recording to compensate for certain losses.

RECORD HEAD—The head in a tape recorder that puts the audio signal on tape by magnetizing the tape particles in a pattern corresponding to the audio signal.

RECORDER-MIXER—A combination tape recorder and mixer in one chassis.

RECORDING/REPRODUCTION CHAIN—The series of events and equipment that are involved in sound recording and playback.

REFLECTED SOUND—Sound waves that reach the listener after being reflected from one or more surfaces.

REGENERATION—See Recirculation.

RELEASE—The final portion of a note's envelope in which the note falls from its sustain level back to silence.

RELEASE TIME (RECOVERY TIME)—In a compressor, the time it takes for the gain to return to normal after the end of a loud passage.

REMIX—To mix again; to do another mixdown with different console settings or different editing.

REMOTE RECORDING—See On-Location Recording.

RESISTANCE—The opposition of a circuit to a flow of direct current. Resistance is measured in ohms, abbreviated Ω, and may be calculated by dividing voltage by current.

RESISTOR—An electronic component that opposes current flow.

RETURN-TO-ZERO—See Memory Rewind.

REVERBERATION—The persistence of sound in a room after the original sound has ceased, caused by multiple sound reflections (echoes), decreasing in intensity with time, so closely spaced in time as to merge into a single continuous sound, eventually being completely absorbed by the inner surfaces of the room. The timing of the echoes is random, and the echoes increase in number as they decay. An example of reverberation is the sound you hear just after you shout in an empty gymnasium. Artificial reverberation is reverberation in an audio signal created mechanically or electronically rather than acoustically. An echo is a discrete repetition of a sound; reverberation is a continuous fade-out of sound.

REVERBERATION TIME (RT60)—The time it takes for reverberation to decay to 60 db below the original steady-state level.

REVERSE ECHO—A multiple echo that precedes the sound that caused it, building up from silence into the original sound. This special effect is created in a manner similar to preverb.

REVERSE REVERB—A reverb that builds up and then abruptly decays, often used for rhythmic effect.

RFI—See Radio Frequency Interference.

RHYTHM TRACKS—The recorded tracks of the rhythm instruments (guitar, bass, drums, and sometimes keyboards).

RIBBON MICROPHONE—A dynamic microphone in which the conductor is a long metallic diaphragm (ribbon) suspended in a magnetic field.

RIDE GAIN—To turn down the volume of a microphone when the source gets louder, and turn up the volume when the source gets quieter, in an attempt to reduce dynamic range.

RINGING—See Overhang.

ROOM MODES—See Standing Wave.

RT60—See Reverberation Time.

SAFETY COPY—A copy of the master tape, to be used if the master tape is lost or damaged.

SAFETY GROUND—See Power Ground.

SAMPLE—**1.** To record a short sound event, such as a single note, into computer memory. **2.** A recording of such an event.

SAMPLING—Recording a short sound event into computer memory. The audio signal is converted into digital data representing the signal waveform, and the data is stored in memory chips for later playback.

SATURATION—Overload of magnetic tape. The point at which a further increase in magnetizing force does not cause an increase in magnetization of the tape oxide particles. Distortion is the result.

SCRATCH VOCAL—A vocal performance that is done simultaneously with the rhythm instruments so that the musicians can keep their place in the song and get a feel for the song. Because it contains leakage, the scratch-vocal recording is usually erased. Then the singer overdubs the vocal part that is to be used in the final recording.

SENSITIVITY—**1.** The output of a microphone in volts for a given input in sound pressure level. **2.** The sound pressure level a loudspeaker produces at one meter when driven with one watt of pink noise. See also Sound Pressure Level.

SEQUENCER—A device that records a series of synthesizer note parameters (performance gestures) into computer memory chips for later playback. A computer can act as a sequencer when it runs a sequencer program. During playback, the sequencer activates the synthesizer sound generators.

SHELVING EQUALIZER—An equalizer that applies a constant boost or cut above or below a certain frequency, so that the shape of the frequency response resembles a shelf.

SHIELD—A conductive enclosure (usually metallic) around one or more signal conductors, used to keep out electrostatic fields that cause hum or buzz.

SHOCK MOUNT—A suspension system that isolates a microphone mechanically from its stand or boom, preventing the transfer of mechanical vibrations.

SIBILANCE—In a speech recording, excessive frequency components in the 5 to 10 kHz range, which are heard as an overemphasis of "s" and "sh" sounds.

SIGNAL—A varying electrical voltage that represents information, such as a sound.

SIGNAL PATH—The path a signal travels from input to output in a piece of audio equipment.

SIGNAL PROCESSOR—A device that is used to alter a signal intentionally in a controlled way.

SIGNAL-TO-NOISE RATIO (S/N)—The ratio in decibels between signal voltage and noise voltage. An audio component with a high S/N has little background noise accompanying the signal; a component with a low S/N is noisy.

SINE WAVE—A wave that follows the equation $y = \sin x$, where x is degrees and y is voltage or sound pressure level. The waveform of a single frequency. The waveform of a pure tone without harmonics.

SINGLE-D MICROPHONE—A directional microphone having a single distance between its front and rear sound entries. Such a microphone has proximity effect.

SINGLE-ENDED—**1.** An unbalanced line. **2.** A single-ended noise reduction system is one that works only during tape playback (unlike Dolby or dbx, which work both during recording and playback).

SLAP, SLAPBACK—An echo following the original sound by about 50 to 200 milliseconds, sometimes with multiple repetitions.

SLATE—At the beginning of a recording, a recorded announcement of the name of the tune and its take number. The term is derived from the slate used in the motion-picture industry to identify the production and take number being filmed.

SMPTE TIME CODE—A modulated 1,200 Hz square-wave signal used to synchronize two or more tape transports. An abbreviation for the Society of Motion Picture and Television Engineers, who developed the time code.

SNAKE—A multipair or multichannel microphone cable. Also, a multipair microphone cable attached to a connector junction box.

SOLO—On an input module in a mixing console, a switch that lets you monitor that particular input signal by itself. The switch routes only that input signal to the monitor power amplifier.

SOUND—Longitudinal vibrations in a medium (such as air) in the frequency range 20 Hz to 20,000 Hz.

SOUND GENERATOR—**1.** A synthesizer without a keyboard, containing several different timbres and voices, which are triggered or played by certain MIDI signals from a computer sequencer program, or by an external keyboard. **2.** An oscillator.

SOUND PRESSURE LEVEL (SPL)—The acoustic pressure of a sound wave, measured in decibels above the threshold of hearing. The higher the SPL of a sound, the louder it is. db SPL = 20 log (P/P_{ref}), where P = the measured acoustic pressure and P_{ref} = 0.0002 dyne/cm^2.

SOUND WAVE—The periodic variations in sound pressure radiating from a sound source.

SPACED-PAIR—A stereo microphone technique using two identical microphones spaced several feet apart horizontally, usually aiming straight ahead toward the sound source.

SPEAKER—See Loudspeaker.

SPECIAL EFFECTS—See Effects.

SPECTRUM—The output versus frequency of a sound source, including the fundamental frequency and overtones.

SPL—See Sound Pressure Level.

SPLICE—To join the ends of two lengths of magnetic tape or leader tape with tape. Also, a splice is the taped joint between two lengths of magnetic tape or leader tape.

SPLICING BLOCK—See Editing Block.

SPLITTER—A transformer or circuit used to divide a microphone signal into two or more identical signals to feed different sound systems.

SPOT MICROPHONE—In classical-music recording, a close-placed microphone that is mixed with more-distant microphones to add presence or to improve the balance.

STANDING WAVE—An apparently stationary waveform, created by multiple reflections between opposite room surfaces. At certain points along the standing wave, the direct and reflected waves cancel, and at other points the waves add together or reinforce each other.

STEP-TIME RECORDING—Recording notes into a sequencer one at a time without regard to tempo, for later playback at a normal tempo.

STEREO, STEREOPHONIC—An audio recording and reproduction system with correlated information between two channels (usually discrete channels), and meant to be heard over two or more loudspeakers to give the illusion of sound-source localization and depth.

STEREO BAR, STEREO MICROPHONE ADAPTER—A microphone stand adapter that mounts two microphones on a single stand for convenient stereo miking.

STEREO IMAGING—The ability of a stereo recording or reproduction system to form clearly defined audio images at various locations between a stereo pair of loudspeakers.

STEREO MICROPHONE—A microphone containing two microphone capsules in a single housing for convenient stereo recording. The capsules usually are coincident.

STUDIO—A room used or designed for sound recording.

SUBMASTER—**1.** A master volume control for an output bus. **2.** A recorded tape that is used to form a master tape.

SUBMIX—A small preset mix within a larger mix, such as a drum mix, keyboard mix, or vocal mix. Also a cue mix, monitor mix, or effects mix.

SUBMIXER—A smaller mixer within a mixing console (or stand-alone) that is used to set up a submix, a cue mix, an effects mix, or a monitor mix.

SUPERCARDIOID MICROPHONE—A unidirectional microphone that attenuates side-arriving sounds by 8.7 db, attenuates rear-arriving sounds by 11.4 db, and has two nulls of maximum sound rejection at 125 degrees off-axis.

SUPPLY REEL—See Feed Reel.

SUSTAIN—The portion of the envelope of a note in which the level is constant. Also, the ability of a note to continue without noticeably decaying, often aided by compression.

SWEETENING—The addition of strings, brass, chorus, etc., to a previously recorded tape of the basic rhythm tracks.

SYNC, SYNCHRONOUS RECORDING—Using a record head temporarily as a playback head during an overdub session, to keep the overdubbed parts in synchronization with the prerecorded tracks.

SYNC TONE—See Tape Sync.

SYNC TRACK—A track of a multitrack tape recorder that is reserved for recording an FSK sync tone or SMPTE time code. This allows tape tracks to synchronize with virtual tracks recorded with a sequencer. A sync track also can synchronize two audio tape machines, or an audio recorder and a video recorder, and can be used for console automation.

SYNTHESIZER—A musical instrument (usually with a piano-style keyboard) that creates sounds electronically, and allows control of the sound parameters to simulate a variety of conventional or unique instruments.

TAIL OUT—Referring to a reel of tape wound with the end of the program toward the outside of the reel. Tapes stored tail out are less likely to have audible print-through.

TAKE—A recorded performance of a song. Usually, several takes are done of the same song, and the best one—or the best parts of several—become the final product.

TAKE SHEET—A list of take numbers for each song, plus comments on each take.

TAKE-UP REEL—The right-side reel on a tape recorder that winds up the tape as it is playing or recording.

TALKBACK—An intercom in the mixing console used by the engineer and producer to talk to the musicians in the studio.

TAPE—See Magnetic Recording Tape.

TAPE LOOP—An endless loop formed from a length of recording tape spliced end-to-end, used for continuous repetition of several seconds of recorded signal.

TAPE RECORDER—A device that converts an electrical audio signal into a magnetic audio signal on magnetic tape, and vice versa. A tape recorder includes electronics, heads, and a transport to move the tape.

TAPE SYNC—A special signal recorded on a tape track, used to synchronize a tape recorder to a sequencer, or to synchronize two tape machines. Tape sync also permits the synchronized transfer of sequences to tape. See also Sync Track.

3-PIN CONNECTOR—A 3-pin professional audio connector used for balanced signals. Pin 1 is connected to the cable shield, pin 2 is usually connected to the signal hot lead, and pin 3 usually connects to the signal return lead. See also XLR-Type Connector.

THREE-TO-ONE RULE—A rule in audio applications which states that when multiple microphones are mixed to the same channel, the distance between microphones should be at least three times the distance from each microphone to its sound source to prevent audible phase interference.

THRESHOLD—In a compressor or limiter, the input level above which compression or limiting takes place. In an expander, the input level below which expansion takes place.

TIE—To connect electrically, for example, by soldering a wire between two points in a circuit.

TIGHT—**1.** Having very little leakage or room reflections in the sound pickup. **2.** Referring to well-synchronized playing of musical instruments. **3.** Having a well-damped, rapid decay.

TIMBRE—The subjective impression of spectrum and envelope. The quality of a sound that allows us to differentiate it from other sounds. For example, if you hear a trumpet, piano, and a drum, each has a different timbre or tone quality that identifies it as a particular instrument.

TIME CODE—A modulated 1,200 Hz square-wave signal used to synchronize two or more tape transports. See also Tape Sync, Sync Track, SMPTE.

TONAL BALANCE—The balance or volume relationships among different regions of the frequency spectrum, such as bass, midbass, midrange, upper midrange, and highs.

TRACK—A path on magnetic tape containing a single channel of audio.

TRANSDUCER—A device that converts energy from one form to another, such as a microphone or loudspeaker.

TRANSFORMER—An electronic component containing two magnetically coupled coils of wire. The input signal is transferred magnetically to the output, without a direct connection between input and output.

TRANSIENT—A relatively high-amplitude, rapidly decaying, peak signal level.

TRANSIENT RESPONSE—The ability of an audio component (usually a microphone or loudspeaker) to follow a transient accurately.

TRANSPORT—The mechanical system in a tape recorder that moves tape past the heads. A transport controls tape motion during recording, playback, fast forward, and rewind.

TRIM—1. A control for fine adjustment of level, as in a Bus Trim control. **2.** A control that adjusts the gain of a microphone preamplifier to accommodate various signal levels.

TWEETER—A high-frequency loudspeaker.

UNBALANCED LINE—An audio cable having one conductor surrounded by a shield that carries the return signal. The shield is at ground potential.

UNIDIRECTIONAL MICROPHONE—A microphone that is most sensitive to sounds arriving from one direction—in front of the microphone. Examples are cardioid, supercardioid, and hypercardioid.

VIRTUAL CONTROLS—Audio-equipment controls that are simulated on a computer monitor screen. You adjust them with a mouse.

VIRTUAL TRACK—A sequencer recording of a single musical line, recorded as data in computer memory. A virtual track is the computer's equivalent of a tape track on a multitrack tape recorder.

VU METER—A voltmeter with a specified transient response, calibrated in VU or volume units, used to show the relative volume of various audio signals and to set recording level.

WAVEFORM—A graph of a signal's sound pressure or voltage versus time. The waveform of a pure tone is a sine wave.

WAVELENGTH—The physical length between corresponding points of successive waves. Low frequencies have long wavelengths; high frequencies have short wavelengths.

WEBER—A unit of magnetic flux.

WEIGHTED—Referring to a measurement made through a filter with a certain specified frequency response. An A-weighted measurement is taken through a filter that simulates the frequency response of the human ear.

WINDSCREEN—See Pop Filter.

WOOFER—A low-frequency loudspeaker.

WORKSTATION—A system of MIDI- or computer-related equipment that works together to help you compose and record music. Usually, this system is small enough to fit on a desktop or equipment stand. See also Keyboard Workstation and Digital Audio Workstation.

WOW—A slow periodic variation in tape speed.

XLR-TYPE CONNECTOR—An ITT Cannon part number that has become the popular definition for a 3-pin professional audio connector. See also Three-Pin Connector.

X-Y—See Coincident-Pair.

Y-ADAPTER—A cable that divides into two cables in parallel to feed one signal to two destinations.

DB OR NOT DB

In the studio, you must know how to set and measure signal levels, and match equipment levels. You also need to evaluate microphones by their sensitivity specs. To learn these skills, you must understand the decibel, the unit of measurement of audio level.

Definitions

In a recording studio, *level* originally meant power, and amplitude referred to voltage. Nowadays, many audio people also define level in terms of voltage or sound pressure, even though this terminology is not strictly correct. You should know both definitions in order to communicate.

Audio level is measured in decibels (db). One db is the smallest change in level that most people can hear—the just-noticeable difference. Actually, this change varies from 0.1 db to about 5 db, depending on bandwidth, frequency, program material, and the individual. However, 1 db is generally accepted as the smallest change in level that most people can detect, and subjectively, a 6 to 10 db increase in level is considered by most listeners to be "twice as loud."

Sound pressure level, signal level, and change in signal level all are measured in db.

Sound Pressure Level

Sound pressure level (SPL) is the pressure of sound vibration measured at a point. It's usually measured with a sound level meter in db SPL (decibels of sound pressure level).

The higher the sound pressure level, the louder the sound (see Figure A.1). The quietest sound you can hear, the threshold of hearing, is 0 db SPL. Average conversation at one foot is 70 db SPL. Average home-stereo listening level is around 85 db SPL. The threshold of pain—so loud that the ears hurt and can be damaged—is 125 to 130 db SPL.

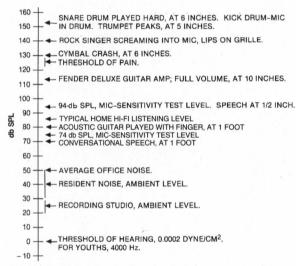

Figure A.1 A chart of sound pressure levels.

Sound pressure level in decibels is 20 times the logarithm of the ratio of two sound pressures:

$$\text{db SPL} = 20 \log \frac{P}{P_{ref}}$$

where P is the measured sound pressure in dynes/cm^2, and P_{ref} is a reference sound pressure: 0.0002 dyne/cm^2 (the threshold of hearing).

Signal Level

Signal level also is measured in db. The level in decibels is 10 times the logarithm of the ratio of two power levels:

$$db = 10 \log \frac{P}{P_{ref}}$$

where P is the measured power in watts, and P_{ref} is a reference power in watts.

Recently it's become common to use the decibel to refer to voltage ratios as well:

$$db = 20 \log \frac{V}{V_{ref}}$$

where V is the measured voltage, and V_{ref} is a reference voltage.

This expression is equivalent mathematically to the previous one because power equals the square of the voltage divided by the circuit resistance:

$$db = 10 \log \frac{P_1}{P_2}$$

$$= 10 \log \frac{V_1^2/R}{V_2^2/R}$$

$$= 10 \log \frac{V_1^2}{V_2^2}$$

$$= 20 \log \frac{V_1}{V_2}$$

The resistance R (or impedance) in this equation is assumed to be the same for both measurements, and thus divides out.

Signal level in decibels can be expressed in several ways, using various units of measurement:

- dbm: decibels referenced to 1 milliwatt

- dbu or dbv: decibels referenced to 0.775 volt (dbu is preferred)

- dbV: decibels referenced to 1 volt

dbm

If you're measuring *signal power*, the decibel unit to use is dbm, expressed in the equation

$$dbm = 10 \log \frac{P}{P_{ref}}$$

where P is the measured power, and P_{ref} is the reference power (1 milliwatt).

For an example of signal power, use this equation to convert 0.01 watt to dbm:

$$dbm = 10 \log \frac{P}{P_{ref}}$$

$$= 10 \log \frac{0.01}{0.001}$$

$$= 10$$

So, 0.01 watt equals 10 dbm (10 decibels above 1 milliwatt).

Now convert 0.001 watt (1 milliwatt) into dbm:

$$dbm = 10 \log \frac{P}{P_{ref}}$$

$$= 10 \log \frac{0.001}{0.001}$$

$$= 0$$

So, 0 dbm equals 1 milliwatt. This has a bearing on voltage measurement as well.

Any voltage across any resistance that results in 1 milliwatt is 0 dbm. This relationship can be expressed in the equation

$$0 \; dbm = \frac{V^2}{R} = 1 \; milliwatt$$

where V is the voltage in volts, and R is the circuit resistance in ohms.

For example, 0.775 volt across 600 ohms is 0 dbm. One volt across 1000 ohms is 0 dbm. Each results in 1 milliwatt.

Some voltmeters are calibrated in dbm. The meter reading in dbm is accurate only when you're measuring across 600 ohms. For an accurate dbm measurement, measure the voltage and circuit resistance, then calculate:

$$dbm = 10 \log \frac{(V^2/R)}{0.001}$$

dbv or dbu

Another unit of measurement for expressing the relationship of decibels to voltage is dbv or dbu. This means decibels referenced to 0.775 volt. This figure comes from 0 dbm, which equals 0.775 volt across 600 ohms (because 600 ohms used to be a standard impedance for audio connections):

$$dbu = 20 \log \frac{V}{V_{ref}}$$

where V_{ref} is 0.775 volt.

dbV

Signal level also is measured in another unit—dbV (with a capital V), or decibels referenced to 1 volt:

$$dbV = 20 \log \frac{V}{V_{ref}}$$

where V_{ref} is 1 volt.

For example, use this equation to convert 1 millivolt (0.001 volt) to dbV:

$$dbv = 20 \log \frac{V}{V_{ref}}$$

$$= 20 \log \frac{0.001}{1}$$

$$= -60$$

So, 1 millivolt equals –60 dbV (60 decibels below 1 volt).
Now convert 1 volt to dbV:

$$dbV = 20 \log \frac{1}{1}$$

$$= 0$$

So, 1 volt equals 0 dbV.
To convert dbV to voltage, use the formula

$$Volts = 10^{(dbV/20)}$$

Change in Signal Level

Decibels also are used to measure the change in power or voltage across a fixed resistance. The formula is

$$db = 10 \log \frac{P_1}{P_2}$$

or

$$db = 20 \log \frac{V_1}{V_2}$$

where P_1 is the new power level, P_2 is the old power level, V_1 is the new voltage level, and V_2 is the old voltage level.

For example, if the voltage across a resistor is 0.01 volt, and it changes to 1 volt, the change in db is

$$db = 20 \log \frac{V_1}{V_2}$$

$$= 20 \log \frac{1}{0.01}$$

$$= 40 \ db$$

Doubling the *power* results in an increase of 3 db; doubling the *voltage* results in an increase of 6 db.

The VU Meter, Zero VU, and Peak Indicators

A VU meter is a voltmeter of specified transient response, calibrated in volume units or VU. It shows approximately the relative volume or loudness of the measured audio signal.

The VU-meter scale is divided into volume units, which are not necessarily the same as db. The volume unit corresponds to the decibel only when measuring a steady-state sine wave tone. In other words, a change of 1 VU is the same as a change of 1 db *only* when a steady tone is applied.

Most recording engineers use 0 VU to define a convenient "zero reference level" on the VU meter. When the meter on your mixer or recorder reads 0 on a steady tone, your equipment is producing a certain level at its output. Different types of equipment produce different levels when the meter reads 0 (see Figure A.2). 0 VU corresponds to

- +8 dbm in older broadcast and telephone equipment

- +4 dbm in balanced or professional recording equipment

- –10 dbV in unbalanced (nonprofessional) recording equipment

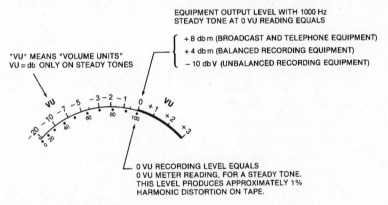

Figure A.2 A VU meter scale.

When a tape operator says to a mixing engineer, "Send me a 0 VU tone," it means, "Send me a tone that reads 0 on your VU meter." The signal level itself isn't too important because the tape operator receiving the tone just wants to match the tape-deck meters to those on the console.

A *0 VU recording level* (0 on the record level meter) is the normal operating level of a recorder; it produces the desired recorded flux on tape. A "0 VU recording level" does not mean a "0 VU signal level."

With a VU meter, 0 VU corresponds to a recording level 8 db below the level that produces 3 percent third-harmonic distortion on tape at 400 Hz. Distortion at 0 VU typically is below 1 percent.

The response of a VU meter is not fast enough to track rapid transients accurately. In addition, when a complex waveform is applied to a VU meter, the meter reads less than the peak voltage of the waveform. (This means you must allow for undisplayed peaks above 0 VU that use up headroom.)

By contrast, a peak indicator responds quickly to peak program levels, making it a more accurate indicator of recording levels. One type of peak indicator is an LED that flashes on peak overloads. Another is the LED bargraph meter commonly seen on cassette decks. Yet another is the PPM (peak program meter). It is calibrated in db, rather than VU. Unlike the VU meter reading, the PPM reading does not correlate with perceived volume.

Balanced versus Unbalanced Equipment Levels

Generally, audio equipment with balanced (3-pin) connectors works at a higher nominal line level than equipment with unbalanced (phono) connectors. There's nothing inherent in balanced or unbalanced connections that makes them operate at different levels; they're just standardized at different levels.

These are the nominal (normal) input and output levels for the two types of equipment:

- Balanced: +4 dbm (1.23 volts)

- Unbalanced: –10 dbV (0.316 volt)

In other words, when a balanced-output recorder reads 0 VU on its meter with a steady tone, it is usually producing 1.23 volts at its output connector. This voltage is called +4 dbm when referenced to 1 milliwatt. When an unbalanced-output recorder reads 0 on its meter with a steady tone, it is usually producing 0.316 volt at its output connector. This voltage is called –10 dbV when referenced to 1 volt.

Interfacing Balanced and Unbalanced Equipment

There's a difference of 11.8 db between +4 dbm and –10 dbV. To find this, convert both levels to voltages:

$$db = 20 \log \frac{1.23}{0.316}$$

$$= 11.8$$

So, +4 dbm is 11.8 db higher in voltage than –10 dbV (assuming the resistances are the same).

A cable carrying a nominal +4 dbm signal has a signal-to-noise ratio (S/N) of 11.8 db better than the same cable carrying a –10 dbV signal. This is an advantage in environments with strong radio frequency or hum fields, but in most studios with short cables, the difference is negligible.

Connecting a +4 dbm output to a –10 dbV input might cause distortion if the signal peaks of the +4 equipment exceed the headroom of the –10 equipment. If this happens, use a pad to attenuate the level 12 db (see Figure A.3). The pad converts from balanced to unbalanced, and reduces the level 12 db. You may have to substitute a stereo phone plug for the 3-pin connector.

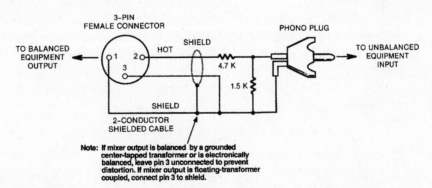

Figure A.3 Use a pad of 12 db to match a balanced +4 dbm output to an unbalanced –10 dbV input.

You don't always need that pad. Many pieces of equipment have a *+4/–10 level switch*. Set the switch to the nominal level of the connected equipment.

Microphone Sensitivity

Decibels are an important concern in another area: microphone sensitivity. A high-sensitivity microphone puts out a stronger signal (higher voltage) than a low-sensitivity microphone when both are exposed to the same sound pressure level. A *microphone-sensitivity specification* tells how much output (in volts) a microphone produces for a certain input (in SPL). There are several ways to express this specification:

- dbV per microbar
- millivolts per pascal
- dbm per 10 dynes/cm^2
- dbm, EIA rating

Each of these expressions has its use and its explanation. First note that

10 dynes/cm^2 = 10 microbars = 1 pascal = 94 db SPL
1 dyne/cm^2 = 1 microbar = 74 db SPL

A typical sensitivity spec is –65 dbV/microbar for a condenser microphone and –75 dbV/microbar for a dynamic microphone. Here is a microphone-sensitivity specification expressed in dbV per microbar:

open-circuit voltage: –60 db re 1 volt per microbar

This expression means that when the mic is *unloaded* (not connected to a load), and the mic is exposed to a sound pressure level of 1 microbar (74 db SPL), it produces –60 dbV. You put 74 db SPL in; you get –60 dbV out.

Another way to express a microphone sensitivity that measures –60 dbV/microbar is

open-circuit voltage: 10 millivolts per pascal

That means that the mic produces 10 millivolts, unloaded, when exposed to a sound pressure level of 1 pascal (94 db SPL). You put 94 db SPL in; you get 10 millivolts out.

Here's another, less common way to specify the same sensitivity:

power level: –38 dbm per 10 dynes/cm^2

In other words, the mic produces –38 dbm into a *matched load*, when exposed to an SPL of 10 dynes/cm^2 (94 db SPL). Matched load means that the load impedance equals the microphone impedance. If the mic impedance is 150 ohms, the load impedance of the mic preamp input is also 150 ohms. This is unlikely to occur in practice; usually the load impedance is at least 7 to 10 times the mic impedance, so that the microphone is effectively unloaded.

The EIA (Electronics Industries Association) rating is useful for calculating the microphone output into a matched load for a given SPL:

SPL + db (EIA) = dbm output into a matched load

To compare the sensitivities of two microphones specified in different ways, convert them to the same reference using these formulas:

Millivolts per pascal = $10^{(4 + dbV/20)}$
dbV/microbar = 20 log (mV per pascal/1000) – 20 db
dbm/10 dynes/cm^2 = dbV/microbar +22.2 db (if mic impedance = 150 ohms)
db (EIA) = dbm/10 dynes/cm^2 – 94 db

If you put a microphone in a 20 db louder sound field, it produces 20 db more signal voltage. For example, if 74 db SPL in gives you –75 dbV out, then 94 db SPL in gives you –55 dbV out. 150 db SPL in gives you +1 dbV out, which is approximately line level! That's why you need so much input padding when you record a kick drum or other loud source.

INTRODUCTION TO SMPTE TIME CODE

Have you ever wished you had more tracks? Suppose you've filled up all the tracks of a 16-track recorder, the band you're recording wants to overdub several more instruments, and you don't have a 24-track machine.

There is a solution: Synchronize the 16-track machine with an 8-track machine by using SMPTE time code. This is a special signal recorded on tape that can sync together two tape recorders so that they operate as one. Time code also can synchronize an audio recorder with a video recorder, or even an automated mixing system to a multitrack recorder.

SMPTE stands for the Society of Motion Picture and Television Engineers. The SMPTE standardized the time code signal for use in video production, and you can use it in audio recording as well. SMPTE time code is something like a digital tape counter, where the counter time is recorded as a signal on tape.

How the Time Code Works

A *time code generator* creates the time code signal (a 1200 Hz modulated square wave). You record—or *stripe*—this signal onto one track of both recorders. A *time code reader* reads the code off the two tapes. Then a *time code synchronizer* compares the codes from the two transports and locks them together in time by varying the motor speed of one of the transports.

The counter time is recorded as a signal on tape. Pictures on a video screen are updated approximately 30 frames per second, where a frame is a still picture made of 525 lines on the screen. SMPTE time code assigns a unique number (address) to each video frame—8 digits that specify HOURS:MINUTES:SECONDS:FRAMES.

Each video frame is identified with its own time code address; for example, **01:26:13:07** means "1 hour, 26 minutes, 13 seconds, and 7 frames." These addresses are recorded sequentially; for each successive video frame, the time code number increases by one frame count. There are approximately 30 frames per second in the American TV system, so the time code counts frames from 0 to 29 each second.

Time Code Signal Details

The SMPTE time code is a data stream that is divided into *code words*. Each code word includes 80 binary digits (or *bits*) that identify each video frame (see Figure B.1).

The 80-bit time code word is synchronized to the start of each video frame. The code uses binary 1s and 0s. During each half-cycle of the square wave, the voltage may be constant (signifying a 0) or changing (signifying a 1). That is, a voltage transition in the middle of a half-cycle of the square wave equals a 1. No transition signifies a 0. This is called *biphase modulation* (see Figure B.2). It can be read forward or reverse, at almost any tape speed. A time code reader detects the binary 1s and 0s, and converts them to decimal numbers to form the time code addresses.

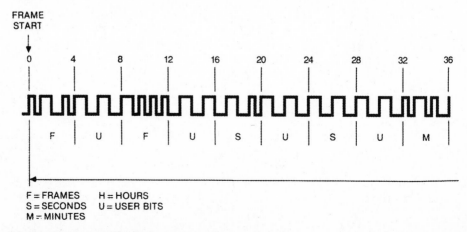

F = FRAMES   H = HOURS
S = SECONDS   U = USER BITS
M = MINUTES

Figure B.1 An 80-bit time code word.

SMPTE words also can include user information. There are 32 multi-purpose bits (8 digits or 4 characters) reserved for the user's data, for example, the take number.

The last 16 bits in the word are a fixed number of 1s and 0s called *sync bits*. These bits indicate the end of the time code word so that the time code reader can tell whether the code is being read forward or in reverse.

Drop-Frame Mode

SMPTE code can run in various modes depending on the application. One of these, Drop-Frame mode, is needed for specific reasons.

Black-and-white video runs at 30 frames/sec. A time code signal also running at 30 frames/sec will agree with the clock on the wall. Color video, on the other hand, runs at 29.97 frames/sec. If a color program is clocked at 30 frames/sec for one hour, the actual show length will run 3.6 seconds (108 frames) longer than an hour.

The *Drop-Frame mode* causes the time code to count at a rate to match the clock on the wall. Each minute, frame numbers 00 and 01 are dropped, except every 10th minute. (Instead of seeing frames ...27, 28, 29, 00 on the counter, you see frames ...27, 28, 29, 02.) This speeds up the time code counter to match the rate of the video frames.

The video frames still progress at 29.97 frames/sec, and the time code progresses at 30 frames/sec, but it drops every few frames—so the effective time code frame rate is 29.97 frames/sec.

You program the time code generator to operate in Drop (Drop-Frame) or *Non-Drop* (Non-Drop-Frame) mode. Non-Drop can be used for audio-only synchronizing, but Drop mode should be used if the audio will be synched to a video tape later on.

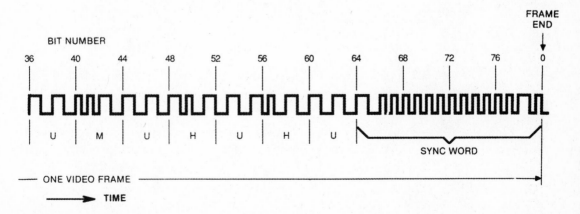

Figure B.1 Continued.

473

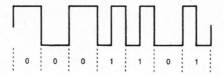

Figure B.2 Biphase modulation used in SMPTE time code.

Setting Up a Time Code System

To use the SMPTE time code, you need a time code generator, reader, and synchronizer. These may be all-in-one or separate units. Three typical synchronizers are the Fostex 4030, Fostex 4050, and Adam-Smith Zeta III. Figure B.3 shows a typical system hook-up, in which the generator, reader, and synchronizer are combined in one unit.

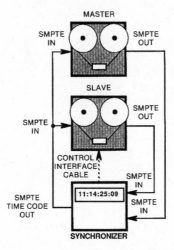

Figure B.3 Typical hookup for synchronizing two tape transports with SMPTE time code.

Set the generator to Time-of-Day code, or any other convenient starting time. If you are synching to video, feed the generator a sync signal from the video source being recorded. This locks the generator together in time with the video source. For audio-only applications, use the internal crystal sync.

Select Drop-Frame or Non-Drop-Frame mode, and stay with it for the entire production. Use Drop-Frame mode if you anticipate synching audio to video in the future.

Next, set the frame rate: 29.97, 30, 24, or 25 frames/second, using the following guidelines:

- Color video productions require 29.97 frames/sec.

- Black-and-white TV or audio-only productions use 30 frames/sec.

- Film usually runs at 24 frames/sec.

- European TV—using EBU (European Broadcast Union) time code—requires 25 frames/sec.

The time code signal appears at the generator output, which is a standard 3-pin audio connector. Signal level is +4 dbm. The signal is fed through a standard 2-conductor shielded audio cable. To avoid crosstalk of time code into audio channels, separate the time code cables from audio cables. Patch the time code signal into an outside track of the recorders you want to lock together. Then patch the outputs of those time code tracks to the inputs of the time code reader.

The reader decodes the information recorded on tape and, in some models, displays the time code data in HOURS:MINUTES:SECONDS:FRAMES format. Some readers have an *error bypass* feature that corrects for missing data.

The time code synchronizer matches bits between two time code signals to synchronize them. The synchronizer compares tape direction, address, and phase to synchronize two SMPTE tracks via servo control of the transport motors. The two tape machines to be synched are called "master" and "slave." The synchronizer controls the slave by making its tape position and speed follow that of the master.

Connect the shielded multipin interface cable between the synchronizer and slave machine to control the slave's tape transport and motors. This interface cable has channels for controlling the capstan motor, tape direction, shuttle modes, and tachometer (more on the tach later).

Because the time code signal becomes very high in frequency when the tape is shuttled rapidly, special playback amplifier cards with extended high-frequency response may be needed to reproduce the SMPTE signal accurately. These cards are available from the recorder manufacturer.

Unfortunately, when the tape is in shuttle mode (fast forward or rewind), the tape usually is lifted from the heads—losing the SMPTE signal. In this case, the recorders are synchronized using tach pulses from the recorders as a replacement for the SMPTE time code. Some synchronizers are fed tach pulses from the slave only.

If *chase mode* is available, the slave follows the shuttle motions of the master. If the master is put in fast-forward, the slave goes into fast-forward, and so on. Without chase mode, the synchronizer notes the address of the master tape when it is stopped and cues the slave to match that location. Chase mode is useful for repetitive overdubs.

How To Use the SMPTE Time Code

Suppose you want to synchronize two multitrack recorders. Follow this procedure:

1. Clean the heads and the tape path.

2. Record the SMPTE time code on an outside track of both recorders at –5 to –10 VU, leaving the adjacent track blank, if possible, to avoid time code cross talk. Don't put high-transient sounds (such as drums) on that adjacent track; they can cause sync problems.

3. Start recording, or striping, the code about 20 seconds before the music starts, and continue nonstop with no breaks in the signal. Stripe the two tapes simultaneously. If that is not possible, you need a *time code editor* to correct or insert an offset.

4. During playback, manually cue the slave to approximately the same point as the master tape, using time code address information as a reference.

5. Engage the synchronizer in Lock and Chase mode, and enable it.

6. Put both recorders in Play mode.

7. Adjust the slave's tape speed to gradually reduce the error between transports to less than one time code frame.

With some synchronizers, this operation is automatic. You set the slave tape to approximately the same point as the master tape. Then put the master in play. When the synchronizer detects master time code, it sets the slave machine in play mode and, in a few seconds, adjusts the slave's speed to synchronize the two recorders. This condition is called *locked up*.

When you're recording on two synchronized transports, try not to split stereo pairs between two tapes. The slight time differences between machines can degrade stereo imaging. Keep all stereo pairs on the same tape, copying them if necessary onto the other tape.

Restriping Defective Code

You may encounter degraded or erased sections on a time code track. This lost code must be replaced with good code in proper sequence. If you need to rerecord (restripe) a defective SMPTE track, use the *Jam Sync* mode on the time code generator. This feature produces new code that matches the original addresses and frame count.

For example, suppose the slave tape needs to be restriped. Follow this procedure:

1. Patch the slave's time code track into the generator set to Jam Sync mode.

2. Patch the generator output into the time code track input on the slave machine (or into another track).

3. Play the tape. The time code reader built into the generator detects a section of good code and initializes the generator with that information.

4. Start recording the new, regenerated code over the bad data (or on a new track).

Jam Sync also should be used when you copy a tape containing time code. With Jam Sync in operation, the code is regenerated to create a clean copy. This procedure is preferable to copying the time code track directly because each generation can distort the code signal.

Audio-for-Video SMPTE Applications

With the advent of music videos and other audio/video combinations, there's a widespread need to sync audio to video. Studios doing sound track work for film or video can use SMPTE time code to synchronize sound and picture for overdubbing narration, dialog, lip-sync, music, environmental sounds, or sound effects.

Synchronizing to Video

Running audio and video tapes in synchronization for TV audio editing is a typical postproduction method. You can edit the audio and video portions of a program independently even though they are locked together in time.

When you sync audio and video, select *Longitudinal Time Code (LTC)* or *Vertical Interval Time Code (VITC)*. Longitudinal code records along the length of an audio track on the video tape. Vertical Interval code is combined with the video signal and is placed in the vertical blanking interval—the black bar seen over the TV picture when it is rolling vertically. VITC frees up an audio track for other purposes.

If you record the time code signal on an audio or cue track of the videotape, do not use automatic level control because it may distort the SMPTE waveform. Instead, adjust the time code signal level manually.

When you play an audio tape synched to video, the time code track on the audio tape is delayed with respect to the video's code due to the spacing between the record and playback heads in the audio recorder. This delay (about 5 frames) can be corrected by the *offset* function in the synchronizer.

Some time code systems include a *character inserter* that displays the address on the video monitor. If desired, these addresses can be recorded with (*burned into*) the picture, a feature called *window dub*.

The Audio-Tape Synchronization Procedure

At a typical on-location video shoot, the video from the camera(s) is recorded on a video-cassette recorder, and the audio from the microphones is recorded on a separate high-quality tape recorder or a portable DAT with SMPTE time code capability. Both video and audio tapes are prestriped with SMPTE time code so that they can be synchronized later in postproduction.

Back at the studio, you connect the audio and video decks for SMPTE sync as described earlier. When you play the video tape, the SMPTE time code locks the picture and sound together. You can equalize the audio tape or change levels and then lay it back (copy it) to the video cassette.

If you sync video to a multitrack tape recorder, you can run the video over and over as you refine the mix. Update your mix moves with an automated mixer or automated mixing program. Finally, when the mix is satisfactory, record the mixer output signal onto the video tape.

This procedure eliminates the dubbing step when transferring the audio soundtrack to video tape. That is, you can mix the multitrack tape master directly to the video tape (keeping sync), rather than mixing down to 2-track and dubbing that to video tape.

The Film/Video Soundtrack Program

SMPTE can be used with a film/video soundtrack program you run on a computer (see Figure B.4). This software package automates the playback of music and sound-effects cues for motion-picture and video postproductions. Using SMPTE time code, you can synchronize audio events, such as sound effects, to film or video tape. You create a *cue list* (also known as an *Edit Decision List* or *EDL*) of audio events, each with its own time code address. These events are played by MIDI instruments, or are played from recordings on a computer hard disk.

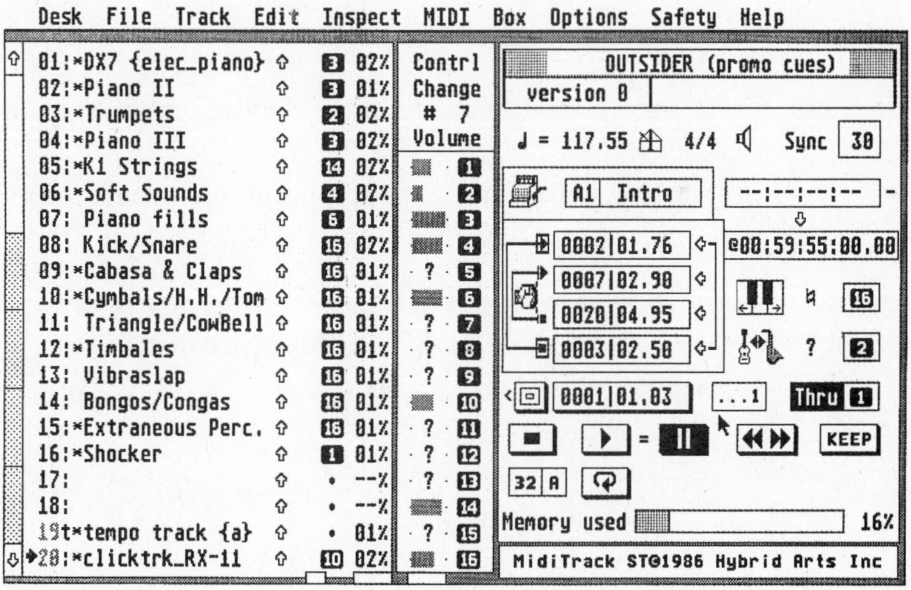

Figure B.4 A film soundtrack program screen (courtesy Hybrid Arts Inc.).

Some examples of this program are the Auricle Control Systems Auricle III, Opcode Systems Cue, Digidesign Q-Sheet A/V, Fostex F.A.M.E., Hybrid Arts SMPTE Tracks, Dr. T's The Phantom and CLiX, and Passport Designs Clicktracks. The typical cost is around $1,000.

Soundtrack Program Features

The following are some of the many tasks that are offered in a soundtrack program.

- Spot and layback sound effects (turn them on at the proper times and record them onto the video tape).

- Do automated mix.

- Backtime events.

- Repeat events.

- Name events.

- Print cue lists, libraries, and recording logs.

- Map keyboards (show each effect's location on a piano-style keyboard).

- Show soundtrack visually (for exact cueing).

- Cut/copy/paste, insert, and delete events.

- Enter cue locations by tapping on the space bar as the program progresses.

- Display sound-effect cues graphically along with the music.

- Convert sequencer files to a cue sheet (hit list).

- Indicate both SMPTE time code and bar/beat for each event.

- Expand or compress the duration of a soundtrack.

- Enter subtle tempo variations, or introduce time offsets, to make cues fall exactly on the beat.

- Write standard MIDI files with meter, beat, tempo, and event data for use in a sequencer.

- Lock to MIDI Time Code and SMPTE.

You also can perform various other tasks found in sequencer programs, such as quantization, tap-in tempo, and so on.

Digital Audio Editing

It's becoming common to record the elements of a soundtrack—dialog, ambience, music, and sound effects—into a digital audio workstation and then edit the soundtrack with that. Either SMPTE or MIDI time code keeps the soundtrack and video in sync. With MIDI time code, you can cue MIDI devices to play music and effects at various SMPTE times relative to the video program. This process can go through various steps:

1. First, you're handed a *work tape*, which is a video tape of the program you're working on. It has SMPTE time code already striped on tape, and the SMPTE time code appears in a window on-screen called a window dub.

2. Watch the picture. Using a MIDI keyboard workstation, compose musical parts related to the video scenes and their SMPTE start/ stop times. These times indicate how long the music needs to be for each musical segment. This music can be recorded with a MIDI sequencer or tape recorder synched to the video recorder.

3. Dialog and wild sound are often recorded on a portable 2-track recorder with a center track for time code. (Wild sound is ambient noise recorded on the set while shooting, not synched with the video.) Sync the dialog tape to the video tape.

4. Missing or poorly recorded dialog is replaced during a process called *looping* or *ADR (Automatic Dialog Replacement)*. Have actors watch the work tape and lip-sync their lines onto a synched multitrack audio recorder.

5. Record sound effects so that they line up with corresponding events in the video. Audition several sound effects from CD libraries, pick the ones you like, and sample them into the digital audio workstation.

6. Using slow motion or freeze frame, go through the video and note the SMPTE times where each sound effect should occur.

7. Using a sequencer program, enter the cue point (SMPTE time) for each sound effect. This creates the EDL.

8. Play the video. The sequencer runs down the cue list. Each cue point (SMPTE time code address) triggers the computer to play a corresponding sound effect or music at the correct time.

9. If you wish, redo the SMPTE time cues or change the effects independently.

Other Time Code Applications

SMPTE time code allows video editing under computer control. In editing a video program, you copy program segments from two or more video tapes onto a third recorder. On a computer you specify the *edit points* (time code addresses) where you want to switch from one video source to another. You can rehearse edits as often as required.

Time code is used also as an index for locating cue points on tape. During a mixdown, you can use these cue points to indicate where to make changes in the mix.

Time code also can be used as a timing reference for console automation and MIDI instruments. With this latter application, MIDI synthesizers can be cued to any point within a sequence, rather than having to start at the beginning.

By using SMPTE time code to lock together multiple audio or video transports, you can greatly expand your operating flexibility.

CONTROLLING ROOM RESONANCE

Room resonances or room modes can cause certain bass notes to boom out. In addition, room modes can change the amount of bass you hear from a monitor speaker, depending on where you sit. For these reasons, it is important to control room modes when you build a studio or when you modify an existing room for recording.

Room modes occur in physical patterns called *standing waves*. Standing waves are uneven sound-level distributions in a room caused by sound waves reinforcing themselves continuously as they reflect between opposing surfaces. Opposite walls (or the ceiling and floor) can support standing waves between them (see Figure C.1). Weaker modes can occur between other surfaces.

The frequencies at which the room resonates depend on the dimensions of the room—its length, width, and height. The formula for the most basic room-mode resonance frequencies is

$$f = \frac{N \times 565}{D}$$

where f is resonance frequency (in Hz), N is 1,2,3..., and D is room dimension (in feet).

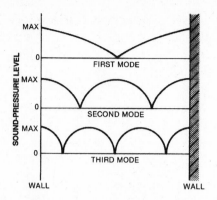

(A) Pressure distribution between two opposing walls, for the first three room modes.

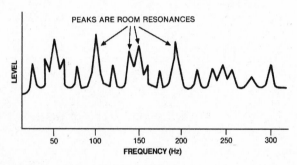

(B) An example of frequency response of a room with standing waves.

Figure C.1 Standing-wave phenomena.

For example, a room 12 feet long has room modes at 47 Hz, 94 Hz, and so on. Those frequencies or notes are overemphasized in the music unless there is sufficient bass-trapping in the room to dissipate them.

Other frequencies are reinforced by other room dimensions. If the height, width, and length of the room are identical, the same modal frequencies are reinforced in all three dimensions, greatly emphasizing certain low frequencies. On the other hand, if the dimensions are not multiples of each other, the modes are different for each dimension. Then each room mode is reinforced in only one dimension, and there is a more even distribution of resonance frequencies.

Several ratios of room dimensions appear in Table C.1. They represent the optimum ratios of width vs. length that will minimize standing waves. Notice that a constant height is assumed for all the ratios.

Table C.1 Ratios of room dimensions.

Height	Width	Length
1	1.14	1.39
1	1.17	1.47
1	1.26	1.41
1	1.28	1.54
1	1.45	2.10
1	1.47	1.70
1	1.60	2.33
1	1.62	2.62

Taking the first ratio in the table as an example, if the ceiling height is 10 feet, the room width should be 11.4 feet and the length should be 13.9 feet for the best distribution of modes.

By choosing certain ratios of room dimensions, you minimize the effect of room modes and prevent their boomy coloration of the acoustics.

FURTHER EDUCATION

The following books and magazines were valuable resources for this book, and are recommended to anyone desiring further education in recording technology.

Books and Magazines

These books are available from *The Mix Bookshelf Catalog*, 6400 Hollis St. #12, Emeryville, CA 94608:

Anderton, Craig. *Home Recording for Musicians*. New York: GPI Publications, Music Sales Corp., 1978.

Anderton, Craig. *MIDI for Musicians*. New York: GPI Publications, Music Sales Corp., 1986.

Bartlett, Bruce. *Stereo Microphone Techniques*. Stoneham, Massachusetts: Focal Press, 1991.

Bartlett, Bruce. *Your MIDI Recording Studio*. Commack, New York: Elar Publishing, 1992.

Borwick, John. *Sound Recording Practice*. Second Edition. London: Oxford University Press, 1980.

Clifford, Martin. *Microphones*. Second Edition. Blue Ridge Summit, Pennsylvania: Tab Books, 1977.

Cooper, Jeff. *Building a Recording Studio*. Revised Edition. Calabasas, California: Synergy Group, 1984.

Davis, Don and Davis, Carolyn. *Sound System Engineering*. Second Edition. Indianapolis: Howard W. Sams & Co., Inc., 1986.

Eargle, John. *Handbook of Recording Engineering*. New York: Van Nostrand Reinhold Co., 1987.

Eargle, John. *The Microphone Handbook*. Plainview, New York: Elar Publishing, 1981.

Everard, Chris. *The Home Recording Handbook*. New York: Amsco Publications, 1986.

Everest, F. Alton. *How to Build a Small Budget Recording Studio from Scratch*. Blue Ridge Summit, Pennsylvania: Tab Books, 1979.

Horn, Delton. *Creative Sound Recording on a Budget*. Blue Ridge Summit, Pennsylvania: Tab Books, 1987.

Huber, David. *Microphone Manual*. Indianapolis: Howard W. Sams & Co., Inc., 1988.

Huber, David. *The MIDI Manual*. Indianapolis: Howard W. Sams & Co., Inc., 1991.

Keene, Sherman. *Practical Techniques for the Recording Engineer*. Hollywood: Sherman Keene Publications, 1981.

Nisbett, Alec. *The Use of Microphones*. Second Edition. New York: Hastings House, 1977.

Pohlmann, Ken. *Principles of Digital Audio*. Second Edition. Indianapolis: Howard W. Sams & Co., Inc., 1989.

Rona, Jeff. *MIDI—In's, Out's, and Thru's*. Milwaukee: Hal Leonard Publishing Co., 1987.

Runstein, Robert and Huber, David. *Modern Recording Techniques*. Third Edition. Indianapolis: Howard W. Sams & Co., Inc., 1989.

Williams, George. *The Songwriter's Demo Manual and Success Guide*. Riverside, California: Music Business Books, 1984.

Woram, John. *Sound Recording Handbook*. Indianapolis: Howard W. Sams & Co., Inc., 1989.

Woram, John and Keefauver, Alan. *The Recording Studio Handbook*. Second Edition. Commack, New York: Elar Publishing, 1982.

The following books are not in the *Mix Bookshelf Catalog,* but are useful references:

Connelly, Will. *The Musician's Guide to Independent Record Production.* Chicago: Contemporary Books, Inc.

Everest, F. Alton. *Handbook of Multichannel Recording.* Blue Ridge Summit, Pennsylvania: Tab Books, 1975.

Hickman, Walter A. *Time Code Handbook* (Cipher Digital, Inc., P.O. Box 170, Frederick, MD 21701, 1987).

Martin, George. *All You Need Is Ears.* New York: St. Martin's Press, 1979.

Rapaport, Diane Sward. *How to Make and Sell Your Own Record.* Tiburon, California: Headland Press, 1984.

Rosmini, Dick. *Teac Multitrack Primer.* Montebello, California: Teac Corporation, 1978.

Shemel and Krasilovsky. *This Business of Music.* New York: Billboard Books, 1990.

Teac Corporation. *Are You Ready for Multitrack?* Montebello, California: Teac Corporation, 1977.

Much information was gained from the following recording industry magazines:

db
203 Commack Rd.
Suite 1010
Commack, NY 11725

EQ
939 Port Washington Blvd.
Port Washington, NY 11050

Home & Studio Recording
Music Maker Publications, Inc.
22024 Lassen St., Suite 118
Chatsworth, CA 91311

Mix
6400 Hollis St., #12
Emeryville, CA 94608

R-E-P *(Recording-Engineering-Production)*
9221 Quivira Rd.
Overland Park, KS 66215

Studio Sound and Broadcast Engineering
(formerly *Studio Sound*)
Link House Magazines, Ltd.
Link House
Dingwall Avenue
Croydon CR9 2TA
England

Guides, Brochures, and Other Literature

For those who wish other reading material, the *Mix Bookshelf Catalog* mentioned earlier describes many excellent books on recording techniques, audio, studio construction, microphones, MIDI, and the music business:

- *Careers in Audio Engineering* and the *Journal of the Audio Engineering Society* are available from the Audio Engineering Society, 60 E. 42nd St., New York, NY 10165. AES conventions are held in October in New York (and often in Los Angeles), and they are wonderful sources of information. You can try equipment hands-on. Anyone may attend.

- Microphone application guides are available from:

AKG Acoustics Inc.
77 Selleck Street
Stamford, CT 06902

Audio-Technica U.S. Inc.
1221 Commerce Drive
Stow, OH 44224

Countryman Associates Inc.
417 Stanford Ave.
Redwood City, CA 94063

Crown International
1718 W. Mishawaka Rd.
Elkhart, IN 46517

Sennheiser Electronic Corporation
6 Vista Drive, P.O. Box 987
Old Lyme, CT 06371

Shure Brothers Inc.
222 Hartrey Ave.
Evanston, IL 60202

- Much valuable information also can be found in operation manuals and free descriptive literature provided by manufacturers of recording equipment.

- The International MIDI Association has MIDI technical information for sale (such as the MIDI specification, and a detailed 50-page explanation of MIDI). International MIDI Association, 5316 W. 57th St., Los Angeles, CA 90056, (213) 649-MIDI.

- Musicians' magazines (such as *Electronic Musician*, *Guitar Player*, and *Keyboard*) are often excellent sources of recording advice.

Guides to Recording Schools

Each July issue of *Mix* magazine contains a comprehensive directory of recording schools, seminars, and programs. Universities and colleges in most major cities have recording engineering courses. Investigate them thoroughly, however, before making a decision. No job is guaranteed.

The book *New Ears: A Guide to Education in Audio and the Recording Sciences* (Second Edition, edited by Mark Drews, and published by New Ear Productions, 1992) is a complete reference guide to audio education. It has it all: course descriptions of all the known recording schools; directories of industry-related magazines, journals, and textbooks; professional audio, music, and broadcasting associations; audio research facilities, nonprofit studios, and other helpful resources. The book is available from New Ear Productions, 1033 Euclid Ave., Syracuse, NY 13210.

INDEX

I

J-K

You're On The Cutting Edge
with Sams' Audio & Video Books